Virtue Ethics and Conf

M000213746

This volume presents the fruits of an extended dialogue among American and Chinese philosophers concerning the relations between virtue ethics and the Confucian tradition. Based on recent advances in English-language scholarship on and translation of Confucian philosophy, the book demonstrates that cross-tradition stimulus, challenge, and learning are now eminently possible. Anyone interested in the role of virtue in contemporary moral philosophy, in Chinese thought, or in the future possibilities for cross-tradition philosophizing will find much to engage with in the twenty essays collected here.

Stephen Angle is Professor of Philosophy at Wesleyan University.

Michael Slote is Michael Slote is UST Professor of Ethics at the University of Miami.

Virtue Ethics and Confucianism

Edited by
Stephen C. Angle and
Michael Slote

Routledge
Taylor & Francis Group

NEW YORK AND LONDON

First published 2013
by Routledge
711 Third Avenue, New York, NY 10017

Simultaneously published in the UK
by Routledge
2 Park Square, Milton Park, Abingdon, Oxfordshire OX14 4RN

First issued in paperback 2015

Routledge is an imprint of the Taylor & Francis Group, an informa business

Library of Congress Cataloging in Publication Data
Virtue ethics and Confucianism / edited by Stephen C. Angle and Michael Slote. — First [edition].
    pages cm
    Includes bibliographical references (pages) and index.
    1. Ethics. 2. Virtue. 3. Confucianism. I. Angle, Stephen C., 1964– II. Slote, Michael A.
    III. Chen, Lai, 1952– Virtue ethics and Confucian ethics.
    BJ1521.V5655 2013
    170.951—dc23
    2012042592

ISBN13: 978-1-138-93360-6 (pbk)
ISBN13: 978-0-415-81548-2 (hbk)

Typeset in Sabon
by Swales & Willis Ltd, Exeter, Devon

For Debbie and Jane

Contents

Contributors

Stephen C. Angle received his B.A. from Yale University in East Asian Studies and his Ph.D. in Philosophy from the University of Michigan. Since 1994 he has taught at Wesleyan University, where he is now Professor of Philosophy. Angle is the author of *Human Rights and Chinese Thought: A Cross-Cultural Inquiry* (Cambridge, 2002), *Sagehood: The Contemporary Significance of Neo-Confucian Philosophy* (Oxford, 2009), and *Contemporary Confucian Political Philosophy: Toward Progressive Confucianism* (Polity, 2012), as well as numerous articles on Chinese ethical and political thought and on topics in comparative philosophy.

CHEN Lai, born in 1952 in Beijing, read geology at the now Central South University and graduated in 1976. He received his master's and doctoral degrees at Peking University in 1981 and 1985, respectively. Among his teachers were Zhang Dainian and Feng Youlan. Before assuming his current position at Tsinghua University, he taught at Peking University for twenty-eight years. Chen is currently the dean of the Tsinghua Academy of Chinese Learning and professor at the Department of Philosophy of Tsinghua University. Chen has held visiting positions in various institutions, including Harvard University (1986–88, 1997, 2006–07), University of Tokyo (1995–96), Kansai University (1999), the Chinese University of Hong Kong (1999–2000), the Hong Kong University of Science and Technology (2002), the City University of Hong Kong (2003), Academia Sinica, Taiwan (2004), and National Central University, Taiwan (2008–09). He has published many academic monographs (all in Chinese), including *A Study of Zhuxi's Philosophy* (1987 and 2000); *The Realm of Existence and Nonexistence: The Spirit of Wang Yangming's Philosophy* (1991); *Ancient Religion and Ethics: The Roots of Confucianism* (1996); *The World of Ancient Thoughts and Culture* (2002); *Interpretation and Reconstruction: The Spirit of Wang Chuanshan's Philosophy* (2004); and *Studies on Bamboo and Silk Versions of Wuxing and Other Newly Unearthed Confucian Texts* (2009).

Marion Hourdequin is an Associate Professor of Philosophy at Colorado College. She holds an undergraduate degree from Princeton University, and she earned her Ph.D. in Philosophy from Duke University. Hourdequin specializes in ethics, comparative philosophy, and environmental philosophy. She has published articles in a variety of journals, including *Philosophy East and West, Journal of*

Chinese Philosophy, Ethical Theory and Moral Practice, and *Environmental Ethics*, and she is currently working on a textbook in environmental ethics.

HUANG Yong, Ph.D in Philosophy (Fudan University) and Th.D in Religious Studies (Harvard University), is a professor of philosophy at the Chinese University of Hong Kong. The editor-in-chief of *Dao: A Journal of Comparative Philosophy* and *Dao Companions to Chinese Philosophy* (both published by Springer), Huang also edited *Rorty, Pragmatism, and Confucianism: With Richard Rorty's Responses*. Author of *Religious Goodness and Political Rightness: Beyond the Liberal-Communitarian Debate* (Harvard Theological Studies series 49), *Confucius: A Guide for the Perplexed* (Continuum), and three books in Chinese, *Religion in a Global Age*, *Ethics in a Global Age*, and *Politics in Global Age* (all by National Taiwan University Press), Huang has also completed a new book manuscript: *Why Be Moral: Learning from the Neo-Confucian Cheng Brothers*, and is completing another book manuscript, *Ethics of Difference: Learning from the Zhuangzi*. In addition, he has published nearly 50 journal articles and book chapters each in Chinese and English.

Benjamin I. Huff is Associate Professor of Philosophy at Randolph-Macon College. He completed a B.A./B.S. in Philosophy and Mathematics at Brigham Young University in 1996 and a Ph.D. in Philosophy at the University of Notre Dame in 2006. His research and teaching interests include ethics (especially virtue ethics), philosophy of religion, and philosophy of education. His current research is focused on developing a contemporary eudaimonist ethical theory, drawing on classical Greek and Confucian thought.

Philip J. Ivanhoe (Ph.D. Stanford University) is Chair Professor of East Asian and Comparative Philosophy and Religion at City University of Hong Kong. He specializes in the history of East Asian philosophy and religion and its potential for contemporary ethics. Among his publications are: *Confucian Moral Self Cultivation* (Hackett Publishing Company, 2000), *The Daodejing of Laozi* (Hackett Publishing Company, 2003), *Readings in the Lu-Wang School of Neo-Confucianism* (Hackett Publishing Company, 2009), *The Essays and Letters of Zhang Xuecheng* (Stanford University Press, 2009), and, with Rebecca Walker, *Working Virtue: Virtue Ethics and Contemporary Moral Problems* (Oxford University Press, 2007).

LEE **Ming-huei**, born in Taipei, Taiwan, Ph.D., University of Bonn, is Research Fellow at the Institute of Chinese Literature and Philosophy, Academia Sinica, Taipei, as well as Professor of the Graduate Institute of National Development, National Taiwan University, Taipei. He is now also Changjiang Scholar Chair Professor of Philosophy at Sun Yat-sen University, Guangzhou. His main works include *Das Problem des moralischen Gefühls in der Entwicklung der kantischen Ethik*, *Konfuzianismus im modernen China*, *Confucianism and Kant* (in Chinese), *Confucianism and Modern Consciousness* (in Chinese), *Kant's Ethics and the Reconstruction of Mencius' Moral Thinking* (in Chinese), *The Self-transformation of Contemporary Confucianism* (in Chinese), *The Four Buddings and the Seven Feelings* (in Chinese), and *Political Thought from a Confucian*

Perspective (in Chinese), as well as numerous articles on Confucianism and Kant's philosophy.

Lɪᴜ **Liangjian** (Sky Liu) received his Ph.D. in Philosophy from East China Normal University (ECNU) in Shanghai. Since 2006 he has worked for Department of Philosophy and Institute of Modern Chinese Thought and Culture at ECNU, where he is now Associate Professor of Philosophy. Liu is the author of *Heaven, Humans, and the Fluctuating Boundary: A Metaphysical Exposition of Wang Chuanshan* (Shanghai, 2007), as well as many Chinese and English articles concerning ethics, linguistic philosophy, history of Chinese philosophy and comparative philosophy. He is also the Chinese translator of Barry Allen's *Knowledge and Civilization* (Hangzhou, 2010) and Karyn L. Lai's *An Introduction to Chinese Philosophy* (Beijing, 2013).

Lᴏ **Ping-cheung** received his B.A. in Philosophy from National Taiwan University, Ph.D. in Philosophy from State University of New York at Buffalo, Ph.D. in Religious Studies at Yale University. He has been teaching at Hong Kong Baptist University since 1990, and is now Professor in the Department of Religion and Philosophy and Director of the Centre for Applied Ethics. His research areas include Chinese–Western comparative bioethics and Chinese–Western comparative ethics of war and peace; his current book project is entitled "Chinese Just War Ethics: Ancient Thought, Contemporary Explications, and Comparative Analysis".

Kai Marchal holds a Ph.D. in Sinology and Philosophy from the University of Munich and is Associate Professor in the Department of Philosophy at Soochow University (Taipei). He has published a book on the twelfth-century Neo-Confucian political thinker Lü Zuqian (*Die Aufhebung des Politischen*, Wiesbaden: Harrassowitz, 2011), as well as numerous articles on Chinese intellectual history and cross-cultural philosophy in English, Chinese, and German. He is about to publish a book-length essay in German on Zhu Xi (1130–1200) and his relevance for contemporary philosophy.

Sara Rushing is an Assistant Professor of Political Science at Montana State University in Bozeman. She received her B.A. from Mount Holyoke College and her Ph.D. from University of California, Berkeley. She co-edited, with Mark Bevir and Jill Hargis, the volume *Histories of Postmodernism* (Routledge, 2007), and her current scholarship brings together contemporary political theory, virtue ethics, feminist theory and comparative philosophy to examine humility as a distinctly political virtue.

Michael Slote has taught at several universities, including Columbia, Swarthmore, Trinity College Dublin, and the University of Maryland. He is now UST Professor of Ethics at the University of Miami. A member of the Royal Irish Academy and former Tanner lecturer, he is the author of many books and articles in ethics, political philosophy, and moral psychology. His most recent books include *Moral Sentimentalism* (Oxford University Press, 2010), *Education and Human Values* (Routledge, 2012), and *From Enlightenment to Receptivity: Rethinking*

Our Values (Oxford University Press, 2013); and his current work focuses on the role of sentiment in epistemology and the philosophy of mind and, separately, on the role that motives that are neither egoistic nor altruistic centrally play in all human lives.

Andrew Terjesen received his B.A. in Philosophy from the State University of New York – College at Geneseo and his Ph.D. in Philosophy from Duke University. He is currently pursuing a J.D. at the University of Virginia School of Law. After receiving his Ph.D. he held visiting Assistant Professor of Philosophy positions at Austin College, Washington and Lee University, and Rhodes College. He has published contributions in *Applying Care Ethics to Business* (Springer, 2011) and *Civility in Politics and Education* (Routledge, 2011), as well as several articles on empathy, moral psychology, and Adam Smith.

Bryan W. Van Norden received his B.A. from the University of Pennsylvania and his Ph.D. from Stanford University (both in philosophy). Since 1995 he has taught at Vassar College, where he is now Professor of Philosophy. Van Norden is the author, editor, or translator of several books, including *Introduction to Classical Chinese Philosophy* (Hackett, 2011), *The Essential Mengzi* (Hackett, 2009), *Mengzi: With Selections from Traditional Commentaries* (Hackett, 2008), *Virtue Ethics and Consequentialism in Early Chinese Philosophy* (Cambridge, 2007), and *Confucius and the Analects* (Oxford, 2001), among others.

Matthew D. Walker is Assistant Professor of Humanities (Philosophy) at Yale-NUS College. He works primarily in ancient Greek philosophy (especially Aristotle) and ethics. His recent papers have appeared, or are forthcoming, in *Archiv für Geschichte der Philosophie, British Journal for the History of Philosophy, Journal of Moral Philosophy, Apeiron, Rhizai,* and *Ancient Philosophy*.

Sean Drysdale Walsh received his B.A. in Philosophy from the University of North Carolina at Chapel Hill and his Ph.D. in Philosophy from the University of Notre Dame. He is an Assistant Professor of Philosophy at the University of Minnesota Duluth, and is currently in residence as a visiting scholar at the Institute for Advanced Study of the University of Minnesota. Walsh is the author of articles on metaphysics, ethics, comparative philosophy, and the history of philosophy. His work may be found in journals such as *Philosophical Studies* and *Ratio*.

Wong Wai-ying is an associate professor in the Department of Philosophy, Lingnan University, Hong Kong. She has published four books in philosophy (in Chinese): *Confucian Ethics: Its Substance and Function* (2005), *Lao Sze-kwang's An Annotation to Daxue and Zhongyong* (ed.) (2000), *Caring About Morality* (1995), *The Fundamental Problems of Meta-ethics* (1988). She has also translated R.M. Hare's *Moral Thinking: Its Levels, Method and Point* (1991) into Chinese. Some of her articles written in English are: "*Ren*, Empathy and the Agent-Relative Approach in Confucian Ethics" (2012); "The Moral and Non-Moral Virtues in Confucian Ethics" (2011); "The Thesis of 'Single-Rootedness' in the Thought of Cheng Hao" (2010); "The Morally Bad in the Philosophy of Cheng

Brothers" (2009); "Can the Two-level Moral Thinking Reconcile the Rivalry of Contextualism and Principled Ethics?" (2006); and "Virtues in Aristotelian and Confucian Ethics" (2006).

XIAO **Yang** is Associate Professor of Philosophy at Kenyon College. He received his Ph.D. from the New School for Social Research, and was a Postdoctoral Fellow at UC Berkeley and Harvard University. His research interests include ethics, political philosophy, Chinese philosophy, and philosophy of language. He is the co-editor of *Moral Relativism and Chinese Philosophy: David Wong and His Critics* (The State University of New York Press, 2013).

YU **Jiyuan** is Professor of Philosophy at the State University of New York at Buffalo and the President of the International Society for Chinese Philosophy (ISCP). He is also Chiangjiang Professor at Shandong University. His recent books include *The Structure of Being in Aristotle's Metaphysics* (2003), *The Blackwell Dictionary of Western Philosophy* (with Nick Bunnin, 2005), *Rationality and Happiness: From the Ancients to the Early Medievals* (co-ed. with Jorge Gracia, 2005), *Ethics of Confucius and Aristotle* (2007), and *Plato's Republic* (2009, 2011).

Acknowledgments

Grateful acknowledgment is made to the following publishers for the permission to reprint the following previously published articles.

Springer. *Dao*, Volume 9, Number 3 (September 2010). 275–287. "Virtue Ethics and Confucian Ethics," Lai Chen, with kind permission from Springer Science and Business Media.

Springer. *Dao*, Volume 9, Number 3 (September 2010), p. 289–302. "The Practicality of Ancient Virtue Ethics: Greece and China," Jiyuan Yu, with kind permission from Springer Science and Business Media.

1 Introduction

Stephen C. Angle and Michael Slote

This volume presents the fruits of an extended dialogue among American and Chinese philosophers concerning the relations between virtue ethics and the Confucian tradition. Based on recent advances in English-language scholarship on and translation of Confucian philosophy, as well as on corresponding advances in the familiarity of Chinese scholars of Confucianism with current Western philosophical trends, the book demonstrates that cross-tradition stimulus, challenge, and learning are now eminently possible. This Introduction will speak of some major themes that lie behind and are exemplified in the present volume, and of the potential pitfalls, but also the likely intellectual promise, of the present sort of cross-traditional enterprise.

Context

Virtue ethics dominated the ethical landscape of Western "classical antiquity," that is, of ancient Greece and Rome; but during much of the period of "modern philosophy" in the West, virtue ethics has been dead or dormant, and it is only in the last half-century that interest in virtue ethics began to revive. The original impetus to that revival was G. E. M. Anscombe's "Modern Moral Philosophy," an article that appeared in the journal *Philosophy* in 1958 and that expressed dismay about and even contempt for the utilitarian and Kantian moral philosophies that were then dominating the scene in theoretical ethics. Anscombe called for a return to Aristotelian moral psychology and Aristotelianism more generally, and that call did not go unheeded. It helped to crystallize discontent with the reigning Kantian and utilitarian approaches to ethics and led, not surprisingly, to a new interest in trying to develop contemporary ethics along Aristotelian lines.

Initially, that interest was anti-theoretical—as the theoretical character of utilitarianism and Kantian ethics were blamed for the deficiencies of those approaches. But Aristotle himself was a theorist rather than an anti-theorist, and eventually forms of contemporary virtue ethics appeared that viewed themselves as *theoretical alternatives* to utilitarianism and Kantianism. In this process the emphasis shifted from an exclusive focus on Aristotelian ideas and methods to include other figures in the history of virtue ethics: Plato, the Stoics, Nietzsche, and, especially, Hume. This was part of the general emphasis on history and historical figures that one finds in almost all recent moral philosophy, but in the case of virtue ethics, what developed in particular was two incipient traditions of contemporary virtue-ethical thinking: the older and more dominant one stressing the insights we can gain from working with Aristotle, the other and recently strengthening one emphasizing what can be done with ideas originating with Hume and the other British moral sentimentalists.

Equally important for the dialogue that this volume represents are important developments in the study of Confucianism in the West that now enable U.S.-trained philosophers to engage seriously with Confucianism. Two issues are particularly significant. First, over the last several decades, a few pioneering scholars have been able to teach Confucian texts and ideas within the framework of U.S. philosophy departments. They and their students have explored various aspects of the Confucian tradition while at the same time being cognizant of styles of reasoning and salient theoretical concerns within contemporary Western philosophy. The result has been a developing body of English-language literature that shows the fruits of viewing Confucian texts through some of the lenses of contemporary philosophy. A second and related trend has been the production, by many of these same scholars and their students, of translations that are scholarly and philosophically informed. For many of the key early Confucian texts, we now have multiple translations whose different strengths complement one another. The combination of a burgeoning secondary literature and quality translations seems to have passed a critical threshold, such that philosophers without Chinese-language background can now access the Confucian tradition in a serious way.

In 2008, the two of us directed an NEH Summer Seminar at Wesleyan University called "Traditions Into Dialogue: Confucianism and Contemporary Virtue Ethics." We placed primary emphasis on the development of Aristotelian and Humean virtue-ethical theorizing in relation to Confucian philosophy. There are important resemblances between Aristotle's virtue-ethical views and views to be found in Confucianism, but the same can also be said about Humean virtue ethics and *other* views that can be found within the Confucian tradition. (There are reasons to think that comparative work with Stoic, Platonic, or Nietzschean thought may be fruitful as well, but so far this has been less-well explored.) The idea for a seminar on the relation between Confucian thought and Western virtue ethics originated with Stephen Angle, and on the recommendation of Roger Ames, he contacted Michael Slote about the possibility of applying to the NEH to do a joint Summer Seminar for American academics. We agreed about approaching the NEH, and the NEH in turn rewarded our efforts by agreeing to fund the seminar and offering additional money for a conference, involving both Chinese and American philosophers, to be held subsequently in Beijing.

The seminar took place during the summer of 2008 with fifteen participants from American colleges and universities. Some of the time was spent getting ourselves on the same page in regard to the nature and variety and traditions of virtue ethics; but the largest part of our efforts was devoted to reading classics of Confucian and neo-Confucian ethics and attempting to understand them both for their own sake and in relation to ideas that have been developed, either historically or more recently, in Western virtue ethics. Seminar participants began thinking about possible topics on which to write papers for the conference in Beijing that was being planned for a later date—and that would also involve participation from the Chinese end.

To set the stage for the conference, let us take a step back and look both at "Confucianism" and at philosophy in China today. The tradition of thought and practice stemming from Confucius (551–479 BCE) is rich and complex. It can plausibly be divided into at least five phases of development, including the classical era (from Confucius's lifetime until the Qin unification in 221 BCE); Han Dynasty and thereafter (two highlights are a focus on institutions and on a broad cosmological vision; 200 BCE–1000 CE); the "Neo-Confucian" revival that is centered on the Song and Ming dynasties (including significant exchange with Buddhism, resulting in a more complex metaphysics and epistemology; 1000 CE–1648 CE); the Qing dynasty reaction to Neo-Confucianism and early encounters with Western thought (1648–1911); and the modern/contemporary period of "New Confucianism," which is ongoing. Our seminar focused on the classical and Neo-Confucian periods, both because these have been the most influential and because they have been the most studied (and translated) in the West. Clearly, though, the broader Confucian tradition offers many other opportunities for lines of comparison and engagement.

In contrast to the Confucian tradition, explicit concern in China with something categorized as "philosophy" (or with "*zhexue*," the neologism coined to translate "philosophy") has been much briefer. Chinese intellectuals began to talk about "Chinese philosophy" around the turn of the twentieth century; this concept took on a more concrete meaning with the publication of the first histories of "Chinese philosophy" by Hu Shi in 1919 and by Feng Youlan in 1934. In a sense, then, we can see the work of these pathbreaking Chinese scholars as helping to lay the groundwork for our comparative endeavor. Today, specialists in Confucianism (and other Chinese traditions) can be found on the staffs of philosophy departments throughout China, Taiwan, Hong Kong, and Korea, alongside colleagues who teach Plato, phenomenology, Marx, analytic philosophy of language, and so on. However, things are not quite so simple as this picture makes it appear. The category of "Chinese philosophy" is actually quite controversial in China today, and at the present time, Chinese scholars trained in Chinese traditions rarely engage in significant comparative endeavors. This latter fact is partly a reflection of the kind of (historically and philologically focused) training that these scholars have received, but underlying both this and the controversy surrounding the category of "Chinese philosophy" are some important concerns that we believe must be taken seriously if an endeavor like ours is to have a constructive result outside the somewhat parochial limits of the U.S. philosophical scene.

The concerns have two complementary aspects. On the one hand, viewing Confucianism as "philosophy"—and viewing Confucian ethics as "virtue ethics"—can seem to privilege a historically contingent Western way of categorizing the world. Indeed, it might seem to make Confucian moral teachings in all their complexity into one sub-type of Western morality—and a relatively minor one (until recently) at that. The other side of this concern is that when one construes Confucianism as "philosophy," one loses out on many other important aspects of the tradition, and one may also misunderstand even those aspects on which one focuses. Some examples of what may be lost are the "practical" character of Confucianism (including both concrete moral education and broader policy objectives) and its spiritual dimension. Critics of the "Chinese philosophy" category charge that by shoehorning Confucianism into categories like "ethics," "metaphysics," "epistemology," and so on, one turns it into something unrecognizable and of little relevance to Chinese culture.[1]

We offer three distinct responses to these challenges. First, nothing in our approach nor in those of the authors collected in this volume suggests that Confucianism must or should be understood solely as "philosophy." The exact configuration of practice and theory that has made up "Confucianism" has varied over the centuries; its future today is very much contested. Our contention is that in all these phases it is both interpretively valuable and philosophically rewarding to view at least some of the relevant theorizing as "philosophy," and to think about it in connection with other traditions of philosophy.[2] Second, while some of the contributors to this volume are primarily engaged in an interpretive exercise, for others the goal of creative, constructive philosophizing is at least as important. No matter whether one is American or Chinese, as philosophers we must be cognizant of new realities, and critical of limitations in past philosophical efforts. To some degree, then, viewing Confucianism as philosophy (and as virtue ethics) can be seen as an effort to make philosophical progress. Finally, we share with some of the critics of "Chinese philosophy" a sense that professional philosophy as it is currently practiced may be narrower than is wise, and narrower than philosophy has been in the past. In Pierre Hadot's memorable phrase, Hellenistic Western philosophy was "a way of life"(Hadot 1995). Contemporary Western philosophy is certainly not. One strength of virtue ethics, though, is the connections that it encourages to serious work in the human sciences (like psychology) and to practical efforts of school teachers and educational policy makers concerning moral education. This response suggests that even with regard to critics of our enterprise, there is ample room for us to learn from one another—a theme to which we shall return below.

The conference occurred in May of 2010, and on the American side involved papers given by ten of the original fifteen attendees of the Summer Seminar and by a number of other scholars from the United States. As a result of earlier planning and a Chinese-language Workshop on contemporary Virtue Ethics at Tsinghua University in Beijing that we both organized and attended, many philosophers from China (including Taiwan and Hong Kong) also gave papers during the conference, and the American organizers—Angle and Slote—then sought out papers that had been given at the conference for inclusion in an English-language volume of such papers. (Those helping to organize things from the Chinese end are also hoping to put together a Chinese-language volume of original and translated papers from the 2010 conference.) The results of that process are visible in the present book.

Mutual Learning

The presupposition of our 2008 Summer Seminar was that Western, and in particular American, virtue ethicists would be able to learn something interesting from studying Confucianism: that ideas gleaned from studying some of the classics of Confucian philosophy would be useful or helpful to Western virtue ethicists in the(ir) doing of virtue ethics. This hope and belief was partly encouraged by the fact that so much Confucian thinking seems virtue-ethical or close to virtue-ethical in character, but in studying the Confucian classics one also finds many particular instances of ideas that can be helpful to the Western virtue ethicist. Let us mention one example.

The Confucians stressed moral humility in a way that traditional Aristotelianism never did. If someone harms you, retaliation or punishment shouldn't be the first thing one thinks of, and various Confucian texts tell us to consider, rather, whether we ourselves may not be (somewhat) at fault for what is being done to us. Perhaps we have hurt or insulted the person who hurts us in ways we have previously ignored and perhaps we ought to immediately consider or worry about what we have done to the person who has decided to harm us.[3] Such advice exemplifies a kind of moral humility that Aristotelianism never encouraged. Aristotelianism treats proper pride as a virtue and leaves no room for the just-mentioned form of Confucian humility (which differs from the Christian kind in ways we needn't enter into here). But, as Jerome Schneewind has noted in his paper "The Misfortunes of Virtue," the fact that the virtuous Aristotelian individual was supposed to have no reason to defer or even listen to other people's (putatively mistaken) moral views meant that Aristotelianism wasn't well suited to dealing with the kinds of mutual concession and tolerance that are essential to the functioning of modern-day (religiously or ethnically) pluralistic societies (Schneewind 1990). Schneewind argues that this helps to explain why Aristotelianism went into eclipse in modern circumstances, but if that is so, then contemporary Aristotelian virtue ethics needs to find a way of dealing with this issue without giving up on its own essential Aristotelianism.

Humility in the Confucian manner may well be helpful toward that end, so it would seem that contemporary Aristotelianism has reason to learn or even borrow from Confucian thought. But, interestingly, contemporary Humean virtue ethics may have less of a problem here because of the emphasis that Hume placed and it places on empathy. Empathy means seeing things from the other's point of view, and when the Confucian asks us to consider whether we have harmed or insulted the person who has harmed or hurt us, they are in effect asking us to consider things from that other person's point of view. So Confucian moral humility has much in common with the empathy that Humean or, more generally, sentimentalist virtue ethics recommends to us, and this alliance, as it were, may be useful both to the Humean virtue ethicist who rejects Aristotelianism and to the contemporary or new Confucian thinker who seeks a more universal support for ideas that have their historically original place in Confucian thought.

And this, in turn, indicates a way in which contemporary Chinese/Confucian philosophers can learn from Western thought. Chinese thinkers seem to have latched on to the notion or phenomenon of empathy long before this happened in the West: arguably, Cheng Hao, Wang Yangming, and even perhaps Mengzi had the notion long before Hume first described empathy in fairly modern terms. But we in the West have subsequently *worked on* empathy. Our psychologists of moral learning stress its importance in the development of altruism and have studied how empathy varies in strength with various degrees and kinds of relationship to or with those in need of our empathy. In addition, some Western ethicists have stressed the importance of empathy to understanding basic moral distinctions and to motivating morally good or acceptable behavior. But the Chinese, who originated the study of empathy, haven't yet taken much advantage of what ethical argument and psychological studies in the West have shown or suggested about the moral importance of empathy, and doing so might very well enrich the possibilities for ongoing Confucian ethical thought.

So far, the kind of learning from one another that we have described is in keeping with what Angle has called "rooted global philosophy," which means to work within a particular live philosophical tradition, but to do so in a way that is open to stimulus and insights from other philosophical traditions (Angle 2009a, 6). For example, the "roots" of some of our contributors lie primarily within contemporary Aristotelianism and contemporary moral philosophy and extend ultimately to Aristotle himself. Others are clearly rooted in the Confucian tradition and are exploring ways that the language and argument of contemporary virtue ethics might be productive from their Confucian vantage point. We should note, though, that the question of rootedness and of distinct traditions of inquiry is not always so clear. For example, Jiyuan Yu is Chinese, educated in both China and the U.S., and much of his scholarship has focused on ancient Greek philosophy. Yet he also explores and reflects on Confucianism, and in his article here relates both Greek and Chinese philosophy to current trends in Western moral philosophy. A complementary example is Bryan Van Norden, educated in the U.S. but a specialist in ancient Confucianism, who here offers us thoughts on how Confucianism and Aristotelianism might contribute to one another in a contemporary context. Are these (and other) projects best understood as rooted in a particular tradition?

Our suggestion is to consider that in addition to the possibilities of enrichment that exist both for Confucianism and for Western virtue ethics on the basis of what each individually can borrow or assimilate from the other, there is also the possibility—in the light of what we know about these similar but historically separate traditions—of occupying a theoretical position that remains uncommitted to either one, but that, on the basis of good arguments and evidence, seeks to construct or articulate a viable ethical perspective borrowing from each of them and from other sources as well. We do not mean to suggest that there exist uncontroversial, standpoint-independent criteria for "good argument" and "good evidence"; the possibility that we are exploring is not a "view from nowhere." Rather, as communication, travel, and translation all become easier, there may be emerging not just rooted global philosophy, but actually a transnational philosophical community that can itself be a source of criteria and evaluation. As those of us involved in organizing the 2010 conference are acutely aware, there remain many barriers and limitations to the fluid development of such a transnational philosophical community. In fact, some of these challenges are in their own way good things, since we are certainly not calling for abandoning the study and development of distinctly rooted traditions of inquiry. We believe that the conference and this volume demonstrate that whether one envisions oneself as working within a single tradition, or as working within a transnational framework, we can still successfully communicate with and learn from one another.

Applicability

Debate over the meaning and applicability to Confucianism of "virtue" and "virtue ethics" constitutes one of the core themes that one finds in the essays of this volume. Even those papers that do not take up these questions explicitly, but instead proceed directly to work on particular issues by drawing on resources and concepts from both Confucianism and Western virtue ethics, can still be seen as addressing the issue of "applicability" indirectly. After all, if the approach of such papers tends to produce fruitful results, this offers some confirmation for their implicit premise that Confucianism and virtue ethics do have things to say to one another. Admittedly, judging fruitfulness itself can be a contested matter, so it is well that many of our papers address the question of applicability head on.

One important piece of context is the prominent role of Kantian categories in the thought of Mou Zongsan (1909–95), the most important twentieth-century Confucian philosopher. In part to combat the common view among his modernizing contemporaries that Confucianism was a rigid morality of adherence to conventional hierarchies, Mou insisted that at the core of Confucianism lay the autonomous moral heartmind (*xin*), which he explicitly compared to Kant's notion of the free, good will. (We translate "*xin*," sometimes rendered as simply "mind" or "heart," as "heartmind" in order to express the fact that for all Confucians, including Mou, the *xin* is understood as the seat of both cognition and conation.) Mou parts company with Kant in several crucial ways, though, not least of which is his insistence that the human heartmind is capable of accessing or even partly constituting moral reality. Mou borrows Kant's term "intellectual intuition" to label this phenomenon, in full knowledge that Kant denied the possibility of human intellectual intuition. It is not our purpose here to fully introduce Mou's complex philosophy, nor to assess its relation to virtue ethics.[4] For our purposes, the key issue is whether Confucian ethics is correctly understood as centered on the autonomous moral heartmind, and if so, whether this means that Confucianism entails a variety of deontological ethics, rather than virtue ethics.

Several issues are tangled together here. First, it is now common practice to distinguish between "virtue theory" and "virtue ethics." "Virtue theory" refers to that aspect of a given ethical theory dealing with the ideas of virtue and character; Kant and Confucians—and even, on some accounts, consequentialists—clearly have virtue theories. The question, though, is how central these aspects are to the overall theory. Only when virtues are understood to be appropriately central or fundamental to an ethical theory can we speak of a "virtue ethic" as opposed to a "deontological ethic" or a "consequentialist ethic."[5] Second, "deontology" is also subject to multiple interpretations, and a virtue ethics seems to be able to account for at least some understandings of deontology. For example, Slote has argued that the idea of deontological restrictions—that is, that certain sorts of positive acts like killing are *prima facie* wrong—can be explained within a broadly virtue-ethical framework.[6] Third, some ways of developing the distinction between deontological and consequentialist theories rest on whether value is understood to be strongly "heterogeneous": deontologists deny and consequentialists accept that "moral" value is ultimately reducible or dependent upon "non-moral value." So, for example, Lee argues in this volume that since Confucians insist upon an autonomous moral heartmind, distinct from considerations of "profit (*li*)," they are best seen as deontologists; a related view is defended in Wong's essay. At least two lines of response may be open to those favoring a virtue-ethical reading of Confucianism: (1) one can argue that virtue ethicists, too, can make a distinction between what is moral and what is prudentially rational, or (2) one can deny that Confucians make such a hard distinction between moral and non-moral value.[7] Fourth, there is the issue of "principles." It is common to associate both deontological and consequentialist ethics with principles for action, and virtue ethics with standards of character or types of agents, but we should grant both that a virtue ethics often says quite a lot about principles and that its rivals—and particularly deontology—may have quite a bit to say about the nature of agents and agency.[8]

Our goal here is not to prejudge the debate that takes place in the volume, but simply to clarify some of the issues at stake. With this in mind, it is worth dwelling briefly on a further question that may seem prior to any argument about "virtue ethics": is there actually an idea of "virtue" present in Confucianism? There has been some considerable discussion of this matter in both the Chinese and English secondary literatures, but our authors appear convinced that Chinese term *de* and words like *arête* and virtue are closely enough related that there is no barrier here to comparative investigation. Both Liu's and Chen's essays discuss some of the dimensions of *de*'s meaning. Liu rightly emphasizes the vexed nature of translated terms and neologisms, and proposes a distinctive translation for "virtue ethics" into Chinese. For his part, Chen explores some of the different aspects of *de* as he seeks to spell out certain crucial, but lesser-appreciated dimensions of virtue within early Confucianism. Among other things, Chen argues that we can see a "dualism of meaning" in Confucius's *de*, simultaneously covering internal character and the "practical application and development of the requirements of the social system of that time," by which he means ritual practices. To be sure, *de* is not rigidly encoded in any particular practice, but the "understanding" and "love" of the rites—and thus its expression in public practices—is a vital part of *de*. The importance of ritual practices to Confucian ethics is also emphasized in our volume by Hourdequin, who sees rituals as crucially (albeit somewhat problematically) involved in giving Confucian ethics an adequately determinative content. Angle's essay also discusses the role that external ritual standards play, though his emphasis is on the ways in which conscientious behavior—that is, consciously forcing oneself to follow norms like rituals—is seen by early Confucians as falling short of virtue. Each of these essays contributes to a growing body of literature that recognizes the distinctiveness and importance to theories of virtue of Confucian ideas about ritual.[9]

Symmetry

As mentioned above, the majority of the volume's essays do not explicitly raise questions about the overall relationship between Confucianism and virtue ethics, but rather engage in more piecemeal argumentation concerning particular points of contact. Before turning to some discussion of the themes we observe running through these essays, let us first pause to consider an important methodological issue. In a recent essay, Kwong-loi Shun has observed that studies in comparative ethics, no matter whether Anglophone or Sinophone, have tended to exhibit a troubling asymmetry:

> [T]here is a trend in comparative studies to approach Chinese thought from a Western philosophical perspective, by reference to frameworks, concepts, or issues found in Western philosophical discussions. ... Conversely, in the contemporary literature, we rarely find attempts to approach Western philosophical thought by reference to frameworks, concepts, or issues found in Chinese philosophical discussions.
>
> (Shun 2009, 470)

We agree with Shun that there has been such an asymmetry, and find much of his analysis to be compelling: among other things, we agree that Western philosophical categories are not more universal than Chinese ones, nor are Chinese traditions somehow more historically limited. However, we believe that the present volume represents a step toward a more symmetrical kind of philosophical practice. These essays do not simply attempt to fit Confucian texts or ideas into pre-existing Western categories, but in many cases use Confucian concepts and insights in order to challenge Western views or to provide creative solutions to Western conundrums. Huang's essay argues that the Cheng brothers' "one *li* of differences" framework is more persuasive than either the generalist or radical particularist ideas seen in Western writings. In somewhat similar ways, Walker and Huff maintain, respectively, that Mengzi and Wang Yangming show us how to conceive the structure of human flourishing or happiness. Liu repeatedly uses ideas from Confucianism to rebut criticisms against virtue ethics, despite the fact that the criticisms were initially launched in a purely Western and Anglophone context. Rushing draws on early Confucians in order to articulate a notion of humility with an important political dimension; she submits that this understanding of humility would be extremely valuable in communities around the globe. Hourdequin argues—explicitly engaging with recent work by Slote—that Mengzi shows us both why empathy has a vital role in morality, and why it should not be our sole moral guide. One aspect of Van Norden's essay is the argument that a contemporary virtue ethics of flourishing (to borrow Ivanhoe's term from this volume) should be more Mengzian. In all these cases (and there are more) we see Western thought being interpreted via, or challenged by, Chinese and Confucian categories.

Even when essays in this volume "approach Chinese thought from a Western philosophical perspective," as when Terjesen uses Western research to interrogate the possible meanings of *shu* in relation to the idea of empathy, or when Angle asks whether we can find the idea of conscientiousness in early Confucian writings, we submit that this is not a simple privileging of Western perspectives. Angle's motivation, after all, is the lack of clarity about conscientiousness in recent Western writing, and he argues that there is a satisfying consistency and cogency about conscientiousness in the Confucian texts that may be useful not just in understanding Confucianism, but also in settling some of the confusion in Western debates. For his part, Terjesen is drawing on a recent body of philosophical and psychological work concerning (various senses of) empathy that seems to have no parallel in China, although Terjesen does acknowledge and refer to the relevant insights of Dai Zhen. Slote's essay on the impossibility of perfection, finally, both takes its point of departure from a Western philosopher (Aristotle) and serves as a challenge to Confucian ideas of perfection. Since the gauntlet that Slote throws down is equally aimed at Western perfectionisms, though, it is hard to see this as in any way troubling.

Still, it might still be maintained that our whole framing of the Summer Seminar, Conference, and volume reflects an asymmetry: "virtue ethics" is stripped of its Western origin and becomes putatively universal, while "Confucianism" remains a kind of local knowledge. Our response is to return to some of the themes from earlier in this Introduction. First, as "virtue ethics" has emerged as a name for a family of ethical theories, it has emerged as something potentially universal. Virtue ethics is not simply another name for the thought of Aristotle. Still, its universality exists in relation to the growing variety of particular texts and textual traditions that provide it with specificity, and some of this clearly comes out of China. Second, though Confucianism was understood by most of its practitioners over its long history to be universal in scope, that idea came under radical challenge in the twentieth century and is only now being reborn. We believe that it is clear that the contributors to the present volume treat Confucianism not just as a historically specific set of texts and terms, but also as a source of universal categories and knowledge.

Acknowledgements

Finally, it remains for us to acknowledge all those without whom the Summer Seminar, Conference, and volume would have been impossible. Barbara Ashbrook of the NEH offered her support throughout the application process, and her advice as we turned our vision into reality, for which she has our thanks; we are also grateful to the NEH more generally for its support of the Seminar and Conference. Migdalia Pinkney and Jeremy Finch assisted us and all the seminar participants in many ways, large and small. Thanks in part to the timely intervention of Peng Guoxiang (now of Peking University), Xu Xiangdong, Director of Peking University's Institute for Foreign Philosophy, provided us with invaluable aid at a crucial moment, and we would also like to acknowledge the important support we received from Lo Ping-cheung and Hong Kong Baptist University's Centre for Applied Ethics. Other crucial help came from Baoli Yang and Alan Baubonis, who translated the Chinese essays prepared for the conference into English, and whose translations form the basis of three of the chapters included here. Of course, all of the participants in the seminar and all of the speakers at the conference—whether or not their essays are included in the present volume—have contributed to the success of the whole enterprise, and have our thanks. Two of the essays included here—those by Chen Lai and

Jiyuan Yu—have been published separately (in *Dao: A Journal of Comparative Philosophy* 9:3), and we thank Springer Science and Businiess Media for permission to reprint them here. Our thanks, also, to Hilda Vargas for her assistance in compiling the bibliography, and especially to Andy Beck and his team at Routledge, with whom it has been a pleasure to work. We dedicate the volume to our wives, Debbie and Jane, with affection and gratitude for the balance that they bring to our lives.

Part I

Debating the Scope and Applicability of "Virtue" and "Virtue Ethics"

2 Virtue Ethics and Confucian Ethics

Chen Lai

There has been a significant development in the study of virtue ethics in recent decades. The following discussion first considers the possible light that virtue ethics might shed on the study of ancient Confucian ethics and examines the Confucian theory of virtue from the perspective of virtue ethics; second, it will make a limited comparison between Confucius's *Lunyu* (*Analects*) and Aristotle's *Nicomachean Ethics*, with the former as representative of the Confucian theory of virtue and the latter as representative of the Greek philosophy.

Virtuous Conduct (*Dexing*)

Confucius said, "Supreme indeed is the mean as a moral virtue. It has been rare among the common people for quite a long time" (*Analects* 6.29). The word *de* can be defined here as both virtuous conduct and virtuous character. *Dexing* 德行 (virtuous conduct) is the perfection of moral standards of behavior, while *dexing* 德性 (virtuous character or, simply, virtue) refers to the quality and character behind the behavior. However, within traditional ancient Chinese culture, the word *de* incorporates both meanings. Its actual meaning can be determined only in the context of the actual text. Generally speaking, during the time of the Western Zhou Dynasty, within the texts of the Spring and Autumn Period, *de* refers to virtuous conduct and behavior. Here, the *Analects* presents a direct example:

> The Master said, "None of those who were with me in Chen and Cai ever got as far as my door." Virtuous conduct: Yan Yuan, Min Ziqian, Ran Boniu, and Zhonggong; speech: Zaiwo and Zigong; government: Ran You and Jilu; culture and learning: Ziyou and Zixia.
>
> (*Analects* 11.2; 11.3)

Here the *Analects* clearly presents the concept of "virtuous conduct." The first appearance of these two words as a phrase (*dexing*) is in the *Book of Odes* (*Shijing*) during the Spring and Autumn Period, wherein it broadly refers to behaviors and attitudes, both good and bad. When used in a narrower sense, it refers to moral conduct and the attitude behind such conduct.

In any case, the ancient reference of *dexing* 德行 is to the conduct and not only the traits of character. For example, the *Zuo Zhuan* (the *Zuo Commentary on the*

Spring and Autumn Annals) states that "Therefore when the superior man, occupying a high position, inspires awe; and by his beneficence produces love; and his advancing and retiring are according to rule; and all his intercourse with others affords a pattern; and his countenance and steps excite the gaze of admiration; and the affairs he conducts serve as laws; and his virtuous actions lead to imitation; and his voice and air diffuse joy; and his movements and doings are elegant; and his words have distinctness and brilliance; when thus he brings himself near to those below him, he is said to have a dignified manner" (Legge 1895: 5. 567). The virtuous conduct refers to bodily expressions and movement that can be seen and, therefore, symbolized or manifested (*kexiang*). The *Xiao Jing* (the *Book of Filial Piety*) states that "other than the virtuous conduct of the previous kings, no other forms of conduct are allowed" (SSJZS 1997: 2547). Here again virtuous conduct refers to the manifestations in behaviors and events.[1] Overall, the term *dexing* was a concept that was often cited in ancient times, while the term *dexing* 德性 (virtue) surfaces only much later (during the period of the Warring States) in the text of the *Zhongyong*. In fact, though the term virtue originated during that period, specific virtues, or items of virtue (*demu*) as applications of virtue were already in place before the time of Confucius. Nonetheless, the representative theory of ethics from the period between Spring and Autumn and the time of Confucius is "virtuous conduct" and not "virtuous character." This is something that deserves particular attention.

Understanding Rites (*zhili*)

> Meng Yizi asked about being filial. The Master answered, "Never turn away." Fan Chi was driving. The Master told him about the interview, saying, "Meng Sun asked me about being filial. I answered, never turn away." Fan Chi asked, "What does that mean?" The Master said, "When your parents are alive, comply with the rites in serving them; when they die, comply with the rites in burying them and comply with the rites in sacrificing to them."
>
> (*Analects* 2.5)

Rites (*li*) do not reach the common people, and Meng Yizi is from a noble clan; when Confucius replied to Meng Yizi about being filial, in fact, he was emphasizing *li*. By not "turning away" (*wuwei*), what he had in mind was "not to turn away from the rites": when parents are alive, follow the ritual rules to care for them; when they die, follow the ritual rules to bury them; after they die, follow the ritual rules to honor them. These practices are derived from the culture of the time, which is a culture of rituals and music. It is apparent that in the answers to the various questions within the *Analects*, Confucius often pinpointed the situations for specific items of virtue. For example, Meng Yizi's behavior took place when the culture of rituals and music deteriorated during the last part of the Spring and Autumn Period. That is the reason why Confucius answered the questions from his disciples in this way. He emphasized that although rites are about external ritual behaviors, they must be respected, followed, and acted upon according to the prescribed parameters. When the parents die, if their mourning and burial ceremonies are not proper, criticism will be forthcoming, resulting in those unfilial people being shamed by the entire clan.

The way in which Confucius gave this answer seems to be different from many of his other discussions in regard to the issue of being filial (*xiao*), where the emphasis is on the internal virtuous character rather than the external ritual practices. This demonstrates that, although he emphasized the importance of virtuous conduct, at the same time this conduct must be related to common social practices. Further, the practice of *xiao* must be in accordance with the ritual precepts and social constraints that originate in the social structure and cultural precepts of rites (*li*) from the period of the Western Zhou Dynasty to the Spring and Autumn era. At the same time, this view of Confucius's can be explained from a political point of view. He was trying to uphold the practices of propriety and music of the Zhou Dynasty and to remedy the situation where such practices were deteriorating towards the end of the Spring and Autumn Period. This kind of political position elucidates the significance and importance of *xiao* and other forms of virtuous conduct, which must not turn away from the principles of political stratification.

From this, we can see that the *de* that Confucius expounded has two emphases. On the one hand, it is the foundational or universal aspect of virtue; on the other hand, it is the practical application and development of the requirements of the social system of that time. The former has primarily an ethical meaning, while the latter includes political and social meanings. This dualism of meaning was particularly apparent during the time of Confucius and slowly decreased during the time of Mencius. This was especially obvious in regard to the issue of the rites.

Alasdair MacIntyre has explained that the virtue of the heroic society and the structure of the society are actually one and the same.[2] He emphasizes the virtue of a period in connection with the social structure of that time, allowing the virtues to be completely a by-product of that period and to completely lose their universality for basic human nature. Fortunately, upon analysis of classical Athenian society, he confirms that "the conception of a virtue has now become strikingly detached from that of any *particular* social role" (MacIntyre 1981: 124). He acknowledges that the relationship between the leading roles in Greek tragedy and the community is not the same as that either in heroic society or in contemporary society. He said that a hero "both belongs to a place in the social order and transcends it" (MacIntyre 1981: 124). This is a position that we should support, although MacIntyre later appears to abandon it when he rejects the distinction in Aristotle's ethics between that which is "permanently valuable" and that which "merely reflect[s] the ideological and cultural biases of Aristotle and his milieu" (MacIntyre 1991: 104). It is exactly this kind of perspective that allows the view that "there is no way to possess the virtues except as part of a tradition in which we inherit them" (MacIntyre 1981: 119).

Most of the uses of "understanding of the rites" in the *Analects* are as ethical judgments; this is similar to the frequent use, in the *Spring and Autumn Annals* (*Zuo Commentaries and Gongyang Commentaries*), of value judgments like "ritually proper," "ritually improper," "conforming to ritual," and "understanding ritual" (see Lin 2003). For example, Confucius says, "If even Guan Zhong understood the rites, who does not understand them?" (*Analects* 3.22). Here the understanding of rites does not point to knowing the rites but, rather, to paying attention to the operational behavioral aspect of the rites. This "understanding of the rites" is an ethical category; the notion of the rites must experience the practical aspect where the action is congruent with the principle and precepts of the rites. As such, what is said here is that "the understanding of the rites" is not a cognitive judgment but, rather, a judgment based on actual virtuous conduct. Therefore, we believe that, for Confucius, "the rite" is neither virtuous conduct nor virtue itself. The virtuous conduct related to the rites is the understanding of *li*, while the related virtue is love for the rites (*haoli*).

In the *Analects*, besides loyalty and trustworthiness, it is rather obvious that Confucius placed particular importance on *gong* (courtesy) and *jing* (respect). What, then, is the relationship of courtesy and respect in regard to the rites, and does it belong to the category of the rites? The Master said, "unless a man has the spirit of the rites, in being respectful he will wear himself out, in being careful he will become timid, in having courage he will become unruly, and in being forthright he will become intolerant. When the gentleman feels profound affection for his parents, the common people will be stirred to benevolence. When he does not forget friends of long standing, the common people will not shirk their obligations to other people" (*Analects* 8.2). Based on this, the rites are the supplement, pattern of guidance, and parameter for various forms of virtuous conduct: being respectful, careful, courageous, and forthright. In characterizing being filial as not "turning away" from the rites, this "turning away" from the rites is slightly different from being "without (*wu*)" the rites. The ordinary meaning of the rites is very broad, but here the meaning is directed to the foundation of social norms from which we cannot turn away, and this is the meaning of "turning away from the rites (*weili*)." On the other hand, "without the rites (*wuli*)" is referring to the lack of control in regard to the rites, rather than to the lack of behavior in accordance with the rites, since it is not possible for courtesy and respect to exist at the same time as ritually improper behavior. In any event, in this case, courtesy and respect are not the rites; on the contrary, they need to utilize the rites as a form of standardization. This is different from the later views of Zisi and Mencius.

The position that Confucius held relating the social standards with regard to virtuous conduct and virtue is understandable. However, could the practice of virtues turn away from the rites? Which virtues can turn away from the rites? From what Confucius has said, in practice this seems a valid question. That is, if the mourning and burial rites do not follow the standards set by ritual procedures, then it is considered to be non-filial. If bravery damages the standard ritual procedures, this would not be considered courage. On this topic Aristotle takes a middle way to solve the problem. For example, courage is the middle way between anxious fear and reckless toughness. On a theoretical level, this is completely workable. However, because the rites function as the controlling factor to establish internal constraint within a society with comprehensive standardization, established criteria are needed to guide behavior in a specific manner. Therefore, people can easily actualize the concepts in their everyday practices. That is the reason for the saying that "the rites are the controlling factor within."[3]

Finally, let us discuss the relationship between the rites and justice. Alasdair MacIntyre believes that the rites are virtues unique to Confucianism. The ancient tradition of the West did not place emphasis upon the ethics of deployment of consensual harmony (conducting oneself in a manner conducive to harmonious alignment of desires for the self as in regard to others); therefore, examples of the rites as examples of virtue are not found. However, although no specific content of the rites was found within the specific item of virtue of ancient Greek ethics, some of the content of the rites from the Spring and Autumn Period was apparent during the time of ancient Greece. From the perspective of these two concepts, each having its own status within its own civilization, I have previously pointed out that if we are to use the emphasis on politics from ancient Greece as a comparison, we could say that the special characteristics of political thought existed during the Spring and Autumn Period, where special prominence was given to the position of the rites. The Spring and Autumn Period utilized *li* and non-*li* as the fundamental principle in political judgment. The goal of political pursuit is to be congruous with the rites, while the understanding of the rites is the primary political ethic. The status of the rites can be compared to the status of justice in ancient Greece. The Greek idea of justice is not necessarily a single meaning. It has undergone a process of mutation from the time before Aristotle, when the early Greek mode of thought included the meaning of cosmic order, where events and matters could reach equilibrium. It was only at a later date that it became virtue. The concept of the rites is certainly not that of justice, but it contains a spirit and quality that is similar to the pre-Aristotelian, early classical Greek mentality. At the same time, both the rites and justice underwent the process of change from the sense of order to that of virtue.

However, Alasdair MacIntyre misunderstood some related matters. He has said that, from the point of view of Confucianism, if a person does not go through training in rituals in the Confucian manner, then one cannot become a gentleman. In fact, the meaning of the rites surpasses training in rituals and the deployment of consensual harmony. A gentleman must appeal to the refined knowledge and practice of rites and music, but the rites include various social norms. Courage without the rites will lead to chaos. This shows the need not to turn away from social norms, which is not to say that all virtuous conduct must be aligned with the training in rituals. From these discussions, we can see that Confucius respected and was committed to the social and cultural norms of the time. Here, we are faced with an important fact, that is, when Confucius espouses virtuous conduct, he is often doing so in relation to the virtuous conduct of the gentleman, which is more demanding than the virtuous conduct of ethics in the broad sense. This is the reason why the congruity of virtuous conduct and fundamental social norms is a universal theoretical topic within ethics of virtuous conduct. In actuality, Aristotle also recognized the fact that it is necessary to supplement virtue ethics with a distinctive discussion related to having complete control of the different types of specific conduct.

The Love of Learning

Similar to the Greek "love of wisdom," Confucius advocated the "love of learning." The "love of learning" is definitely not just an ordinary concept for

Confucius; we can say that it is a fundamental idea central to his thought. Not only does it have educational aspects, but it also takes up an especially important position within his entire system of thought.

The Master said, "In a hamlet of ten households, there are bound to be those who are my equal in doing their best for others and in being trustworthy in what they say, but they are unlikely to be as eager to learn as I am" (*Analects* 5.28). That is to say, those with "the virtues of loyalty and trustworthiness" are not rare, but those with "love of learning" are rarely seen. Loyalty and trustworthiness are the fundamental virtues of the Spring and Autumn Period, yet, from this phrase, we can see that Confucius has placed greater importance on the "love of learning" than on "loyalty and trustworthiness," as a much more precious quality which is hard to find. Although I cannot say that "the love of learning" is higher than benevolence (*ren*) and loyalty (*zhong*) in the virtue ethics of Confucius, as far as Confucius is concerned, the quality of "the love of learning" certainly has a unique dimension of importance in practical application.

Now we need to ask, is "the love of learning" a virtue? On the surface, it seems that the love of learning and the virtues that Confucius broadly expounded on, such as benevolence, wisdom, and courage, are different, and that the love of learning is not virtue. However, how do we explain the fact that Confucius named Yan Hui as the one and only person with "the love of learning," and at the same time also put Yan Hui in the category of those with "virtuous conducts" amongst the different types of his disciples (*Analects* 11.3)? In classical Greece, intellectual virtues are separated from practical virtues; comparatively speaking, could we say that benevolence, wisdom, and courage are practical virtues, while the love of learning is an intellectual virtue? I think that this is absolutely the case. In fact, the *Zhongyong* clearly states that "to be fond of learning is to be near the knowledge" (Legge 1895: 1.407). Aristotle said in the *Nicomachean Ethics*:

> Excellence, then, being of two kinds, intellectual and moral, intellectual excellence in the main owes both its birth and its growth to teaching for which reason it requires experience and time, while moral excellence comes about as a result of habits, whence also its name is one that is formed by a slight variation from the word for "habit."
>
> (Aristotle 1984: 1103a 14–18)

From this perspective, the nurturing of intellectual virtue is related to education. The Confucian love of learning should belong to the category of education, and therefore the love of learning can be named as an educational virtue. In relation to education, love of learning and intellectual virtue have similarities. Certainly, intellectual reason is related to the virtues involved in contemplation, which is different from the love of learning, which is viewed as an outstanding capacity. At the same time, Confucius does not consider that ethical virtue is not related to education. In any event, Confucius understood the love of learning as having a different kind of quality and activity from ethical virtue.

The importance of the love of learning in Confucius's thought was prominently expressed through his discussion of the "six qualities and the six faults":

The Master said, "You, have you heard about the six qualities and the six attendant faults?" "No." "Be seated and I shall tell you. To love benevolence without loving learning is liable to lead to foolishness. To love cleverness without loving learning is liable to lead to deviation from the right path. To love trustworthiness in word without loving learning is liable to lead to harmful behavior. To love forthrightness without loving learning is liable to lead to intolerance. To love courage without loving learning is liable to lead to insubordination. To love unbending strength without loving learning is liable to lead to indiscipline."

(Analects 17.8)

This passage is very important. The fondness toward being benevolent, clever, trustworthy, forthright, courageous, and unbending refers to virtues as well as virtuous conduct. Generally, as virtuous conduct, they express the meaning of individual virtue for human existence. However, these virtues are not independent of each other. They are mutually dependent, supported, and cultivated. Proper character of the gentleman and the sage is formed based on non-deviation (*bupian*) from the path through mutual support and mutual cultivation of these virtues. At the same time, within the structure of this mutual support and mutual cultivation, unknowingly, the love of learning takes up a prominent position. The love of learning is not only a distinguishing capacity and special strength but also a kind of tendency for intrinsic wisdom. This kind of capacity and tendency clearly points toward the knowledge of learning and the educational process.[4]

Foundational Virtue

The six virtues—benevolence, wisdom, trustworthiness, forthrightness, courage, and unbending strength (*gang*)—are ethical virtues, but Confucius emphasized that the pursuit of ethical virtues cannot be without the love of learning. All the ethical virtues must be integrated so as to develop their accumulated functions and cannot depart from the virtue of the love of learning or the practice of the love of learning. If there is a departure away from the love of learning, these ethical virtues will deviate from the path and will not be upright. In this case, the ethical virtues and educational virtues (intellectual virtues) are combined. This is very similar to the emphasis that Aristotle placed on wisdom or the emphasis that Augustine placed on the truth. For all of them, each virtue must be mutually integrating, constraining, and supporting, as each single virtue by itself will have its own flaw at the time of practical application. If this touches upon the question of the unity of the various forms of virtuous conduct, then it could be said that Confucius believes that virtues are not always united: there are those who are fond of benevolence, courage, or trustworthiness but not the love of learning, and so on. This is different from Aristotle. Confucius emphasized that when virtue is not united, the experience of the people will have deficiencies and flaws and therefore cannot reach the ultimate wholeness of practical virtuous conduct.

The above discussion is a broad explanation of development in regard to the mutual dependency and inter-relatedness of virtues based on the Confucian point of view. Confucius himself has never actually mentioned that each virtue has the function of mutual constraint. He emphasizes the love of learning in the passage on the six qualities and six faults. In another passage, he emphasized the special importance of the rites not as a virtue: "Unless a man has the spirit of the rites, in being respectful he will wear himself out, in being careful he will become timid, in having courage he will become unruly, and in being forthright he will become intolerant" (*Analects* 8.2).[5] Amongst other virtues, any two virtues can have the mutual support of each other; however, the foundational virtue is only "the love of learning." This is worth noting, though this is obviously not to say that "the love of learning" and "understanding of the rites" are the most important Confucian virtues. Still, it can be said that these two virtues contain foundational meaning within the system. The love of learning is the foundation of nurturing the body or self-cultivation (*xiushen*), and the "understanding of the rites" is the foundation of conduct. This kind of "foundational virtue" and the "core virtue" of benevolence (*ren*) possess different kinds of status within the entire system of virtues.[6]

Benevolence as Virtue and Principle

Confucius was the integrator and synthesizer of ethical theories of the Spring and Autumn Period and was also the creator of the system of virtuous conduct for the Confucian tradition. The Confucian system of virtuous conduct inherited as well as continued and further developed the virtue concepts of the Western Zhou Dynasty to the Spring and Autumn Period. Confucius added a new ethical element to the system of virtuous conduct of the ceremonial and musical culture, which allowed the inheritance and continuation as well as the development of the Confucian school of virtuous conduct from the school of virtuous conduct of the Western Zhou to the Spring and Autumn Period.

The *Analects* records the thoughts of Confucius. Other than two citations of benevolence, wisdom, and courage, rarely is there any list of items of virtue in the *Analects*. That means that Confucius was not interested in lists of virtues that might be very different from those of the past. As far as virtuous conduct is concerned, within the *Analects*, the most apparent distinction from what was established during the Period of Spring and Autumn and those before him is the prominent place that Confucius attributed to the virtue of *ren* (benevolence). *Ren* occupies an outstanding and dominant place in the entire Confucian school of ethical thought. Confucius's discussion of *ren* is unique in comparison with the discussion of *ren* before the Spring and Autumn Period: (1) the repetitive discussion of *ren* as a virtue (*ren* has more than 100 appearances in the *Analects*); (2) division of the virtue of *ren* into different levels of application, where the highest level transcends all individual and particular virtues; and (3) those before the Spring and Autumn Period placed *li* and lack of *li* (*wuli*) as the highest form of principle for the assessment of behavior, while in the thought of Confucius clearly *ren* is higher than *li*.

Equal attention should be paid to the fact that *ren* is not only a virtue (*de*) but is also a *dao* (way). *Ren* is not only a virtue but also a principle. For example:

> The Master said, "Wealth and high station are what men desire but unless I got them in the right way I would not remain in them. Poverty and low station

are what men dislike, but even if I did not get them in the right way I would not try to escape from them. If the gentleman forsakes benevolence, in what way can he make a name for himself? The gentleman never deserts benevolence, not even for as long as it takes to eat a meal. If he hurries and stumbles one may be sure that it is in benevolence that he does so."

(Analects 4.5)

Here, this way (*qidao*) is the way of *ren* (*rendao*). When the gentleman is troubled he does not turn away from this way, which is *ren*. This way of *ren* contains ethical principles. *Ren* is not only the principle in regard to wealth and poverty; it is also the basic principle of ethical conduct. The disciple Zhonggong asked Confucius regarding *ren*, "Do not impose on others what you yourself do not desire" (*Analects* 12.2). In this case, *ren* is a fundamental concept in relations between the self and others. This is also what the contemporary advocates of global ethics are promoting for the global community of different religious orders so as to mutually confirm their basic ethical principle: the golden rule.

The Gentleman

Since Sidgwick, especially in contemporary ethics, the unique feature of a particular ethical theory is often identified by examining whether good or right is prior. If we examine the thought of Confucius within this framework, certainly Confucius started from the "good." In order to elucidate the thought of Confucius, it is possible to say that Confucius is concerned with the enterprise of a holistic human existence. Confucius is not so much concerned with any particular behavior as with the excellence of a person. What is ideal in human personality? How to reach this excellent personality? How can the perfect goodness be manifested? What is ideal existence? What is the norm and ideal realm of human existence? These concerns are aligned with virtue ethics.

At the same time, if we examine in detail the recording of discussions with Confucius within the *Analects*, we will discover that it is mostly deliberating virtuous conduct of individual people, rather than making expositions on specific virtues. Comparing this to the Spring and Autumn Period, we see comparatively little use by Confucius of items of virtue as a form of exposition. Even more notably, unlike texts from the Spring and Autumn Period, Confucius used the "gentleman" to discuss the topic of virtuous conduct in a multitude of ways, expounding on the relevant personality, behavior, obligations, and ideals. This, finally, is the fundamental feature within the ethical thought of Confucius. These expositions are not in the form of specific virtues as expressions but, rather, use the form of guiding human existence, where the gentleman represents the concept of a holistic persona. Through this, the clarification of what are good behaviors, good boundaries, good ideals, and good personality is expressed. In this sense, though Confucian ethics inherited from earlier tradition the concern with virtuous conduct, it can at the very least be said to have transcended a narrowly specified form of virtue ethics.

The above discussion of the gentleman clearly manifested a difference from the character of typical ethical lessons. What I mean is that it mainly concerns the virtuous conducts of sages and gentlemen, which transcends the normal ethics of virtuous conduct and virtue itself and points higher, toward a standard of behavior and virtue outside of ethical duties. Therefore, what Confucius was concerned with is not just the minimal standards of virtues and ethical duties. For example, the phrase "learning and its becoming habit, is this not a joy?" (*Analects* 1.1) is not a descriptive phrase; it shows that Confucius used "learning and its becoming habit" as a form of excellent human activity, which is worth using as a model in forming human attitude. However, "learning and not becoming habit" is definitely not an unethical behavior. Furthermore, if human behavior can be separated into ethical, unethical, non-ethical, and trans-ethical, then it follows that a large number of phrases of the *Analects* embody a higher human ideal than is required by basic ethics, and contain a trans-ethical (trans-duty) character. Trans-ethical language is affirmative and promotional, yet it has already transcended the boundaries of basic ethical demands. This fully manifests the difference between good and right. Contemporary ethics is generally seen as ensuring the minimal demands of social life (see O'Neill and Williams 2008: 12), which would naturally entail abandonment of the ancient concept of the trans-duty life ideals of the gentleman.

The *Analects* discusses the way of the gentleman and the virtues of the gentleman as the most prominent topic. Based on this, Confucius does not emphasize any individual virtue so as to point out which conduct is good and which conduct is not good, but discusses the integrative nature of the forms of virtuous conduct that belong to the gentleman. The discussion of particular virtuous conduct is based on the holistic framework of the gentleman. Therefore, Confucius surpassed the discussion of individual types of virtuous conduct and entered into the discussion of a holistic persona, which is related to the exposition of the gentleman and cannot be encompassed within virtue theory. For example: "The gentleman devotes his mind to attaining the Way and not to securing food. ... The gentleman worries about the Way, not about poverty" (*Analects* 15.32); "There is no point in seeking the views of a gentleman who, though he sets his heart on the Way, is ashamed of poor food and poor clothes" (*Analects* 4.9). A "gentleman sets on the Way" clearly expresses that the gentleman is of the highest ideal; the gentleman "considers the Way" and "worries about the Way" as the ultimate transcendent ideal. A gentleman's will does not focus on the pursuit of materialistic life but, rather, on the pursuit of social and virtuous ideals. This kind of gentleman is already outside the scope of narrowly defined virtue ethics. More importantly, the Confucian notion of gentleman is discussed as virtuous conduct and virtue of "the highest esteem" and not as correct or wrong basic behavior. The gentleman does not have any particular individual characteristic; the gentleman represents the totality of human characteristics.

The Reflection (*si*) of Benevolence and Wisdom: Virtuous Conduct and Moral Psychology

After Confucius, the theory of virtuous conduct underwent a process of internalization. This begins with the *Wu Xing Pian* of Zisi, wherein benevolence has been internalized and becomes manifested in external virtuous conduct, presenting a way in which internal benevolence is manifested in the form of benevolent reflection:

Benevolence is reflection at an essential level. Essence leads to observance; Observance leads to peace; Peace leads to mildness; Mildness leads to happiness; Happiness leads to intimacy; Intimacy leads to endearment; Endearment leads to love; Love expresses the quality of jade; The quality of Jade is manifest; Manifestation results in Benevolence.

(In Li 2007: 101)

Wisdom is reflection at the deepest level. Depth facilitates gain; Gain will eliminate loss; Loss eliminated will reach clarity; Clarity is the way of the Worthies; The way of the worthies expresses the quality of jade; The quality of Jade is manifest; Manifestation results in wisdom.

(In Li 2007: 101)

Sages will have thoughts of the lightest level; Lightness expressed eliminates loss; Loss eliminated will reach brilliance; Brilliance will guide the noble way; Noble ways are the quality (sound) of the jade; The quality of Jade is manifest; Manifestation results in sagehood.

(In Li 2007: 101)

Here the character, *xing*, translated as manifestation, actually refers to the external expressions of the relevant qualities rather than to the intrinsic content. It seems to me that benevolence, wisdom, and sagehood are different ways of internal reflection. This is not simply thinking but also includes different kinds of attitudes and features for internal activities. Yet each type of reflection, if we use the *Zhongyong*'s framework of moving from the not-yet-expressed (*weifa*) to the expressed (*yifa*), includes experiences at various stages of development: one experiences the process of opening up and externalization of internal psychology as one moves from virtue to conduct.

For example, the reflection of benevolence is the subtle consciousness related to other people, indicating a kind of micro observation (analysis) in regard to the intuitive activities of the other party. This most original form of internal examination, during the process of "development," will have the experience of a series of different stages such as: peace, mildness, happiness, intimacy, endearment, and love. In this process, happiness is most important.[7] Finally, when the intuitive attitude of love is reached, benevolence gets its most complete manifestation. Love, breaking through from emotional intuition, will at the same time appear on the external facial colors, manifesting the color of jade. That "the quality of Jade is manifest, and Manifestation results in benevolence" expresses the "reflection of benevolence," allowing the appearance of a benevolent expression. From "benevolence is reflection at an essential level" to "manifestation results in benevolence," there is the entire process of internal virtue moving to external expression. It must be emphasized here that the achievement of the color of jade can come only from moving the internal virtue to externally manifested conduct, thus placing great importance on the internal elements of the process. If we develop the argument from the last section, "manifestation results in benevolence," forward, it can then be said that "benevolence is thought at an essential level" is the first step in cultivation of benevolence as a virtuous conduct within the innermost part of the heart/mind. This type of development is not reached via an emotional sense; it is reached via the mentality of thoughts. This is the difference between the bamboo slips of the *Wu Xing* text and Mencius. On the other hand, however, the former also influenced the latter.

What we have discussed above is a system which we will refer to as the "Three Reflections and Three Manifestations." Within it, the emphasis is on the process of psychological actualization of virtuous character toward its external appearance. What is important is the fundamentality and originality of the initial, internal appearance of the ethical consciousness to the actualization of virtuous conducts, establishing a complete moral psychology. This indicates the correlation between virtue and virtuous conduct, on the one hand, and both external conduct and external coloration/manifestation, on the other. This shows that a stress on countenance and apparent disposition was an important tendency in ancient virtuous conduct theory.

Goodness: The Foundation of Virtuous Conduct in a Theory of Human Nature

Mencius makes a contribution by laying down the foundation for a systematic theory of goodness for Confucian theory of virtuous conduct. Mencius's idea of benevolence, dutifulness, observance of rites, and wisdom is already different from the previous theory of the five virtues, as it is developed as a virtue theory. When Mencius discussed the goodness of human nature, he said:

> As far as what is genuinely in him is concerned, a man is capable of becoming good. That is what I mean by good. As for his becoming bad, that is not the fault of his native endowment. The heart of compassion is possessed by all men alike; likewise the heart of shame, the heart of respect, and the heart of right and wrong. The heart of compassion pertains to benevolence, the heart of shame to dutifulness, the heart of respect to the observance of the rites, and the heart of right and wrong to wisdom. Benevolence, dutifulness, observance of the rites, and wisdom are not welded on to me from the outside, they are in me originally.
>
> (*Mencius* 6A: 6)

This shows that conducts are good because they originate from the nature of goodness. Benevolence, rightness, observance of the rites, and wisdom are internal, not influenced by external factors. This means that they are virtues; the theory of their internalization expresses the idea that they are the actual content of human nature, whilst ethical intuitions are the manifestation of virtue and human nature: "The heart of compassion is the germ of benevolence; the heart of shame, of dutifulness; the heart of courtesy and modesty, of observance of the rites; the heart of right and wrong, of wisdom" (*Mencius* 2A: 6). The germ is the manifestation; and sympathy and other feelings are the ethical intuitions which are all the representation and manifestation of the benevolence, righteousness, propriety, and wisdom of human nature. Therefore he also said, "that which a gentleman follows as his nature, that is to say, benevolence, rightness, the rites, and wisdom, is rooted in his heart" (*Mencius* 7A: 21).

From the perspective of virtue ethics, Mencius brought forth the question of virtuous conduct as it relates to human nature. First, from the position of Mencius, theories of virtuous conduct have their foundation and origin in theories of human nature. The pre-Mencian Confucian list of virtues (as interpreted by Confucius) clearly is not only virtues but also human nature. In another sense, Mencius's thought relates the nature of virtues and humans. Virtuous nature is quality and human nature is essence; how these elements are structured within the heart/mind is a question that we can explore. Mencius said:

> An extensive territory and a vast population are things a gentleman desires, but what he delights in lies elsewhere. To stand in the centre of the Empire and bring peace to the people within the Four Seas is what a gentleman delights in, but that which he follows as his nature lies elsewhere. That which a gentleman follows as his nature is not added to when he holds sway over the Empire, nor is it detracted from when he is reduced to straitened circumstances. This is because he knows his allotted station. That which a gentleman follows as his nature, that is to say, benevolence, rightness, the rites and wisdom, is rooted in his heart, and manifests itself in his face, giving it a sleek appearance. It also shows in his back and extends to his limbs, rendering their message intelligible without words.
>
> (*Mencius* 7A: 21)

Based on this passage, human nature with the content of benevolence, righteousness, propriety, and wisdom is basically good. This type of human nature is not created externally by the outside environment but is innate and immediate. This type of ethical human nature would not follow behavior and change, nor would it increase or decrease the existence of virtuous conduct. Virtuous conduct will not influence the basic nature of the human being. Obviously, this is not to say that virtuous conduct is absolutely not important. Mencius is in fact placing great importance on the expansion of the basic foundation of human nature so as to further develop the virtue ethics of humankind.

Acknowledgement

This article is translated by Elizabeth Woo Li.

3 Virtue Ethics and the Chinese Confucian Tradition

Philip J. Ivanhoe

Introduction[1]

My primary aim is to introduce two representative examples of thinkers from different periods within the Chinese Confucian tradition who advocated forms of virtue ethics: Mengzi ("Mencius," 391–308 BCE) and Wang Yangming (1472–1529). I choose these particular figures for a variety of reasons. They are among the most famous and influential Confucian philosophers in the Chinese tradition, their philosophies are complex, rich, and powerful, and they represent different and important aspects of virtue-ethical theory. Mengzi seems to advocate the kind of theory that one finds in thinkers like Aristotle, whose conception of virtue is connected to a theory about human nature and a related view of human flourishing described in terms of an ideal agent.[2] I will refer to this type of theory as VEF (virtue ethics of *flourishing*). On the other hand, parts of Mengzi's view, particularly his emphasis on the role of the emotions and empathy, reveal significant similarities with thinkers like Hume and other sentimentalists, who describe the virtues primarily in terms of certain broadly construed emotions, and especially the degree of empathy that a disposition exhibits. I will refer to this type of theory as VES (virtue ethics of *sentiments*) and will describe both VES and VEF in more detail in the first part of the following section. Wang Yangming appears to be even closer to Hume and other sentimentalists; nevertheless, Wang's form of virtue ethics is more like Aristotle's in relying upon a theory about human nature and a conception of human flourishing described in terms of an ideal agent. In light of these similarities and differences, and others I shall describe below, it is clear that neither Mengzi nor Wang fits neatly or completely within either of these two forms of virtue ethics, at least as they are represented in the Western tradition. What I hope to show is that in coming to understand the views of these two Chinese thinkers against the background of some current debates about the nature and variety of Western forms of virtue ethics we are led to understand more not only about them but also about virtue ethics as a distinctive type of theory.

A Genus and Not a Species

Christine Swanton (Swanton 2003, 1) makes the important point that, as a type of ethical theory, virtue ethics is a genus and not a species. In other words, virtue ethics is a class of ethical theories that share a common emphasis on virtues as central features of their account of morality. Different species of virtue ethics disagree not only about what the proper list of virtues is, but also about the nature of the virtues, how they relate to one another, and how they do or do not fit or hang together to define a good life. In order to prepare the way for our discussion of Chinese forms of virtue ethics, it will help to have a general description of two of the main types of virtue ethics found in the Western tradition.[3] While my description of these types is rough and incomplete, it does succeed in capturing two versions of virtue-ethical theory that are particularly important for understanding not only contemporary accounts of Chinese ethics but also some of the most important features of the works of the Chinese philosophers we shall discuss below.

The most familiar and widely analyzed form of virtue ethics in the Western tradition finds its source and model in the writings of Aristotle; Aristotle describes a distinctive version of VEF. For our purposes, two related features of his theory are most significant: (1) it is grounded in a comprehensive and detailed conception of human nature that seeks to describe the content, structure, and overall shape of human nature; (2) it is developed in terms of a teleological view about the flourishing of human nature expressed in an ideal or paradigmatic model of what it is to be human. Both of these features are familiar and widely studied aspects of Aristotle's philosophy, and, as we shall see, they also are prominent features of most Chinese Confucian forms of virtue ethics. We shall, though, discover significant differences between Aristotle and Confucians when we move from the general down to the particular level of description. For example, Confucians hold very different beliefs about the content, structure, and shape of human nature. Aristotle's view is intimately connected with his claim that the most characteristic function or *ergon* of human beings is rational activity and, consequently, the good life for human beings will have such activity not only at its core but as its acme: the most valuable type of activity that human beings can engage in is contemplation.[4] The Chinese Confucians, whose thought we will explore, share a belief in the critical contribution that reflection and attentiveness make to the process of self-cultivation, but they do not share Aristotle's views on the nature, role, and value of reason. The second feature of Aristotle's view also is an important feature of Chinese Confucian forms of virtue ethics. In this case too, there are critically important differences, which do not lie in the general features of their respective ethical philosophies but in the particular ideals and paradigms they recommend.

VES describes a second very influential form of virtue ethics in the Western tradition. Sentimentalist virtue ethics finds its most distinguished representatives in thinkers such as Shaftesbury (1671–1713), Hutcheson (1694–1746), Hume (1711–76), and Smith (1723–90). Contemporary proponents of an ethics of care, such as Nel Noddings (Noddings 2003 (1986)) and Virginia Held (Held 2006), offer views that share important features of such an approach. The most sophisticated and comprehensive attempt to defend a modern version of VES is found in the work of Michael Slote (Slote 2007, 2010a), who emphasizes the critical role of empathy or, more precisely, empathic caring as the basis of moral value. As in our discussion of VEF, we will focus on two features of VES as most significant: (1) it is grounded in a general conception of human nature that focuses on aspects of human psychology; (2) it describes the virtues in terms of dispositions conducive to smooth, agreeable, and beneficial interactions between individuals within and between different societies.

In regard to the first feature, VES resembles VEF, but while VEF seeks to provide a comprehensive and detailed account of human nature that describes its content, structure, and shape, VES focuses more exclusively upon general emotional resources, tendencies, and capacities. As for the second feature, unlike VEF, the set of virtues that VES describes does not fit together to yield a single ideal of human flourishing expressed in a related paradigmatic model. Instead the virtues hang together only loosely to form a conception of what kind of life is most agreeable and beneficial under certain circumstances.[5] In contrast to those who promote versions of VEF, advocates of VES are more concerned with ideal traits and their benefits than with ideal persons and their character. One consequence of this difference is that for VES the virtues are more expressions of features of human psychology within the confines of particular social conditions than they are direct manifestations of human nature in its authentic, full, or proper form.[6] For example, instead of describing and holding up the man of practical wisdom as the ideal standard for the good and the aim of every human life, Hume describes what people must be like in order to form and maintain a humane and cooperative society and interact with other societies around the world in an agreeable and beneficial manner. He distinguishes what people in *his age* need for successful and harmonious living from what was needed in past ages, when life was simpler and people lived in more intimate arrangements. In other words, for Hume, the virtues are practical expressions of what is needed to live well in particular social conditions; human nature serves as a resource for crafting the best kind of life, but the virtuous life is not in any direct way the expression of human nature's flourishing. VES has a firm but general psychological foundation, not a specific trajectory or goal. Modern advocates of VES regularly appeal to the findings of contemporary psychology in order to support their views, and contemporary psychologists tend to focus on psychological capacities, tendencies, and mechanisms and eschew the kind of comprehensive, normative accounts of human nature that are characteristic of VEF. Overall, the approach is more empirical than what one finds in VEF and more oriented toward discovering what is agreeable and beneficial than toward revealing the most authentic form of human flourishing.

Mengzi

Mengzi's ethical philosophy exhibits both of the characteristic features of VEF discussed above. He relies explicitly and directly on a comprehensive and detailed theory of human nature that seeks to describe its content, structure, and shape; he presents a program of moral self-cultivation that leads to a distinctive conception of human flourishing, which he describes in terms of the paradigmatic models of the "gentleman" (*junzi*) and "sage" (*sheng ren*). Let us explore the particular form that these features take in various passages from the *Mengzi* and how together they describe his distinctive expression of VEF.

Mengzi is famous for his theory that human nature is good, by which he means not that people are innately perfectly good but that they are born with moral sensibilities, which incline them toward becoming virtuous. Specifically, Mengzi argues that human beings possess four "sprouts" (*duan*) of virtue.[7]

> From this we see that the heart and mind of compassion, the heart and mind of shame, the heart and mind of complaisance, the heart and mind of judging right and wrong are essential to human beings. The heart and mind of compassion is the sprout of benevolence, the heart and mind of shame is the sprout of righteousness, the heart and mind of complaisance is the sprout of propriety, the heart and mind of judging right and wrong is the sprout of wisdom. Human beings have these four sprouts just as they have four limbs.
>
> (*Mengzi* 2A6)

Mengzi's use of the agricultural metaphor of "sprouts" to describe our nascent moral sensibilities or tendencies is not an isolated or unimportant feature of his view. Such metaphors are found throughout his descriptions of the content, structure, and proper course of human development.[8] For example, he likens the growth or failure of the moral sprouts to the natural but still contingent development of barley plants.

> In years of plenty, many young people are reliable, but in years of want many cannot control themselves. It is not because of their Heavenly conferred endowments that such differences exist. It is because [some] allow their hearts and minds to become mired.
>
> Now take the case of barley. Sow it and cover it up. If the soil is the same and the time of planting is also the same, it will sprout and grow. And when its proper time has come, it all will be ripe. Though there are differences [in the yield of the barley], these are because the soil was rich or poor, there was unequal nourishment by rain and dew, or unequal application of human effort.
>
> (*Mengzi* 6A7)

Mengzi makes a number of points in this passage: that all humans have an equal capacity for moral development; that such development, while natural, requires human attention and effort, and that barring differences in environment, influence, attention, and effort people all will tend toward a common moral end. Self-cultivation is very much like agriculture; it consists of reflective endeavor aimed at realizing a natural end, and that end is an ideal of flourishing thought to apply to all human beings. In fact, Mengzi offers one of the clearest examples of an ethic of human flourishing, as his agricultural metaphors consistently invoke or imply the notion that moral self-cultivation seeks to facilitate the blossoming or "flourishing" (Latin *florere*) of human nature.

Mengzi's use of agricultural metaphors is not just a literary embellishment; his repertoire of agrarian images not only expresses his fundamental claims about moral self-cultivation but also informs and conveys subtle and distinctive features of his ethical view. For example, in the parable of the Farmer of Song, he uses another agricultural metaphor to warn against trying to force the process of moral cultivation.

Do not be like the man of Song! There was a man of Song who pulled at his shoots of grain, because he was anxious for them to grow. Having finished, he went home, not realizing what he had done. He said to his family, "I am worn out today; I have been helping the grain to grow." His son rushed out of the house to look at their plants and found that they all had withered.

(*Mengzi* 2A2)

Leaving aside a full analysis and evaluation of this teaching of Mengzi's, his central point is that one can try too hard to be moral and such effort not only will not improve one's character but will in fact harm and perhaps even doom one to failure. Self-cultivation is like farming, and we must learn to be dedicated but patient farmers.

Mengzi was wise to develop his philosophical views around the ideas, images, processes, and rhythms of agricultural production. On the one hand, agricultural metaphors are part of every person's way of thinking because of the critical role that agrarian endeavors have played and continue to play in human life. Agriculture was the key to settled human life and the distinctive type of cultures that developed around such communities; it is natural and fitting to see a strong analogy between cultivating domesticated plants and cultivating civilized people. This is why Mengzi's imagery and arguments still resonate so well with people from any part of the modern world. On the other hand, agricultural activity played a particularly important and dramatic role in the Chinese society of Mengzi's time. Not only did most of the people of his time engage in agricultural production, which still is true of China today, but, more importantly, agriculture was an integral part of Chinese society and culture at every level. The health of states depended on the success of agriculture; among the most important political goals of rulers of his time was to attract farmers to their states, to expand their territory and thereby the amount of cultivated land under their control. Major state projects, such as irrigation and flood control and the development and maintenance of an accurate calendar, and crucial religious practices, such as the annual sacrifices at the Altar to the Land and Grain and the emperor ritually plowing in spring to initiate the New Year, attest to the vital importance that agricultural endeavors played in traditional Chinese life.

There remains but one final feature of Mengzi's ethical philosophy to complete the case that he was an advocate of VEF; we need to show that his account of the virtues and the flourishing of human nature is expressed in an ideal or paradigmatic model of what it is to be human. The evidence is easy to find and unambiguous. Mengzi relies directly and explicitly upon numerous examples of actual sages and worthies in order to craft his account of the moral ideal.[9] In this regard, it is important to recognize that he used "the Way of Yao and Shun" (*Yao Shun zhi dao*) as a more complete expression of the Confucian Way. This exemplifies an important feature of most versions of virtue ethics: they rely upon thick descriptions of the virtues, and this often leads virtue ethicists to invoke the lives of actual historical individuals as part of their explanation of what the virtues are. This practice is characteristic of Confucian thinkers. Many scholars have noted that Chinese thinkers tend to see a very close relationship between history and ethics; when we interpret these thinkers as advocates of VEF, we understand the reason for this close association.[10]

The appeal to sages and other worthies plays numerous roles in Mengzi's ethical philosophy. One point that he was careful to emphasize and repeat is that these paragons of morality are not different in kind from the rest of humanity; they represent the best in all of us and offer a goal which we should take as both a standard and an inspiration. For example, "Yao and Shun were the same as any other human being" (*Mengzi* 4B32, 6B2).[11] Mengzi also notes that sages from different places and widely diverse backgrounds all develop toward the same moral ideal.

> Shun was born in Zhu Feng, moved to Fu Xia, and passed away in Ming Tiao. He was an Eastern barbarian. King Wen was born in Qi Zhou and passed away in Bi Ying. He was a Western barbarian. The distance separating them was more than a thousand *li*[12] and the time between them more than a thousand years. And yet the ways in which they ruled over China fit together like the two halves of a seal. The former sage and the later sage had a single standard.
>
> (*Mengzi* 4B1)

Such passages make clear that these moral paragons are models of a shared conception of flourishing that is within the reach of all normally endowed human beings. This is made even more explicit in the following passage, which claims that proper standards of taste in cuisine, music, and aesthetics, as well as morality, display an informed and cultivated consensus that reflects the refined expression of human nature. The sages are simply the first to discover what all human beings will approve and delight in, when given proper knowledge, experience, and time to reflect.

> All palates agree in savoring the same flavors, all ears agree in appreciating the same sounds, and all eyes agree in enjoying the same beauties. Is it only in the case of our hearts and minds that there is nothing shared in common? What is it about which our hearts and minds agree? I say it is concerning what is right and proper. The sages were the first to grasp what my heart and mind shares in common with other human beings. That is why what is right and proper pleases my heart and mind just as grain-and-grass-fed meat please my palate.
>
> (*Mengzi* 6A7)

As shown in the passage cited above, Mengzi's use of the sage or gentleman as moral exemplar is not limited to actual historical figures. He deploys a general concept of such exemplars throughout his work. For example, Mengzi quotes with approval a disciple who extols Kongzi ("Confucius") as the greatest sage ever to have lived, but lest we be led to think that the standard he sets is somehow beyond us, in the same passage, the disciple reminds us, "The sages are the same in kind as other human beings" (*Mengzi* 2A2, 6A7). Mengzi also invokes the idea of future sages and insists that they will share the same moral sense and reach the same moral judgments as cultivated people in his own place and time, "Were a sage to arise once more, surely he would agree with what I have said" (*Mengzi* 2A2, 3B9).

From all that has been shown above, it is clear that Mengzi made extensive use of an ideal or paradigmatic model of what it is to be human in order to express his conception of human flourishing. These paragons of humanity offer examples of how the virtues function and hang together to constitute a good life.

Mengzi has a carefully worked out account of human flourishing. His panoply of agricultural metaphors relies upon a teleological view of human nature that offers an analogy between the growth of plants—from nascent sprouts to fully flowering, mature specimens—and the development of the moral sense—from "sprouts" to virtues. His ethical philosophy expresses the successful completion of the process of moral self-cultivation in terms of actual and hypothetical ideal agents. Such paragons of virtue are presented as the healthy specimens of the species and offer a normative standard for measuring a person's moral progress and level of achievement. Mengzi uses agricultural metaphors to describe not only human nature and moral self-cultivation but also his account of moral failure. This makes him one of the clearest exponents of VEF one ever could hope to find.

A number of contemporary philosophers (Yearley 1990, Van Norden 2007) have argued that Mengzi is productively and even best thought of as an exponent of VEF. Others (Liu 2002, 2003) have noted similarities between his views and those of David Hume, and on this basis argued that he should be understood as a proponent of VES. Opinions on this matter will turn for the most part on the particular conceptions of VEF and VES that one embraces, and so it is essential to begin with clear and workable definitions of these types. Those who hold that Mengzi is an advocate of VEF tend to point to his discussion of virtues and claim that he described an ideal of flourishing; those who hold that Mengzi is an advocate of VES focus on his discussions of the four sprouts and highlight how each of these describes an emotional response that enables us to empathize with others. There is truth in all these claims, but in addition to making clear what one means by VEF and VES, one also needs to offer a careful account of things like: (1) what one means by flourishing and how the virtues relate to this ideal, and (2) the nature of empathic caring and what role it plays not only in understanding but also in justifying moral claims.[13] I have provided two ideal types, VEF and VES, and used these to argue that Mengzi is an advocate of VEF.[14] In the concluding section of this paper I shall explore some additional and distinctive features of Mengzi's form of VEF.[15]

Wang Yangming

One of the most dramatic and distinctive features of Wang Yangming's ethical philosophy is the emphasis that he places on achieving and living in the light of a sense of oneness between self and world; this ideal is captured in his teaching about how we should regard Heaven, earth, and the myriad creatures as one body (*tian di wan wu wei yi ti*). Along with other aspects of Wang's philosophy, this ideal of *feeling one with* all the people, creatures, and things of the world gives the very strong impression that empathic care is an important part of Wang's ethics, and such an impression is not incorrect. As will be clear from the following discussion, Wang's conception of empathic care and the role it plays in moral life are critical features of his ethical philosophy; we shall devote considerable attention to these issues in our analysis of Wang's teachings and return to them in our conclusion. Nevertheless, as in the case of Mengzi, the importance of empathy *per se* is not our central concern. The question that we are seeking to answer is whether Wang is a virtue ethicist and, if so, what kind of virtue ethicist he is.

Until recently, modern scholars who write about Wang have tended to focus on the more religious aspects of his philosophy and not simply on his ethical theory (Tu 1976, Ching 1976, Tien 2004). This is because they recognized the degree to which all of Wang's views depend upon an underlying comprehensive metaphysical scheme that is more characteristic of religion than of contemporary analytic ethics. While there surely is no impediment to analyzing Wang's metaphysical views as an integral part of his ethics, modern philosophers interested in ethics, as a whole, have tended to avoid philosophers whose ethical systems depend upon strong metaphysical commitments. In this respect, Wang's ethical philosophy is more like many forms of Buddhism or the ethical philosophy of Thomas Aquinas, which are more often discussed in departments of religious studies than in departments of philosophy. I have argued (Ivanhoe 2000, 2002a) that Wang's views cannot be understood accurately or adequately without appreciating the degree to which they were influenced by Buddhism and, to a lesser but not insignificant extent, Daoism, and I will build upon this work in arguing that Wang is best thought of as an advocate of VEF.

The core of my case for understanding Wang as a proponent of VEF is, that his ethical philosophy exhibits both the characteristic features of VEF that we described earlier and found in Mengzi's philosophy. Wang relies explicitly and directly on a comprehensive and detailed theory of human nature that purports to describe its content, structure, and shape. His theory of human nature shares certain similarities with Mengzi's, but the influence of Buddhism and Daoism alters the fundamental basis of his conception of human nature. Instead of grounding his account of human nature in a philosophical anthropology, as Mengzi does, he relies on a comprehensive metaphysical theory. As we shall see, this shift transforms not only the nature but also the range of his ethical sensibilities. Wang presents a program of moral self-cultivation that leads to a distinctive conception of human flourishing, which he describes in terms of an ethical and spiritual ideal of the "sage" (*sheng ren*).[16] Here too we see continuities with the philosophy of Mengzi, but also quite profound differences as well. For example, under the influence of Buddhism, and especially Chan (Japanese: Zen), Wang and his contemporaries were preoccupied with a Confucian form of "enlightenment" (*wu*) resulting in the attainment of sagehood. This emphasis, and the possibility of this occurring "suddenly," were not part of Mengzi's way of thinking.[17] Let us explore more of the similarities and differences between Mengzi and Wang as we describe Wang's ethical philosophy and present the case for understanding him as an advocate of VEF.

It is important to keep in mind that Wang saw himself as a follower and defender of Mengzi's philosophy not only against rivals outside the Confucian tradition, such as Daoism and Buddhism, but also against alternative interpretations of Confucianism and, in particular, what was known as the Cheng-Zhu School.[18] In particular, Wang thought that only *his* interpretation of the Confucian tradition preserved Mengzi's most important contributions about the goodness of human nature and the role that our innate moral sensibilities play in self-cultivation. However one understands this aspect of Wang's self-conception, his belief that he merely shared Mengzi's views about human nature and our innate moral sensibilities is untenable. Wang looked to Mengzi for inspiration and borrowed ideas and terminology from the *Mengzi*, but he filled these old wineskins with new wine that catered to the tastes and responded to the challenges of his age.

Wang embraced a constellation of related beliefs that were common among neo-Confucian thinkers, many of which would be viewed as highly untenable today. I have referred to such beliefs as the "heroic metaphysical" aspects of Wang's view, and here seek only to describe and not to defend them. In the conclusion, I shall discuss some of the ways in which versions of Wang's views remain important resources for contemporary virtue ethics. Wang accepted the view that all human beings are endowed at birth with a pure and perfect moral heart-mind (*xin*).[19] In its original and unadulterated state, this heart-mind consists of the set of "principles" (*li*) that determine the underlying, normative patterns and processes of the world. The pure form of the human mind is the active and knowing mode of the principles of the universe. This happy correspondence offered Wang a way to account for a wide range of phenomena and to resolve several vexing philosophical problems. For example, it offered him a way to explain how it is that we can come to understand the world around us. Since our heart-mind is principle, we understand the world whenever the principles of our heart-mind properly match up with the principles of things and events.

This correspondence played a critical role in another of Wang's signature teachings: the idea that we and the world "form a single body" (*yiti*). The basic metaphysical belief behind this teaching is that we and the world share the same principles, or, expressed in other ways that Wang often invoked, we share a common "original heart-mind" (*ben xin*) or "nature" (*ben xing*). The practical effect of this shared principle, heart-mind, or nature is that we *feel* connected to every single thing in the world, in a way analogous to the way in which we feel connected to every part of our physical bodies.[20] The only thing that prevents us from realizing—in the sense both of understanding and of feeling the full force of—this fact is that our heart-minds are embodied in physical forms that separate us from and tend to generate misleading impressions of the true state of affairs. Our embodied physical form subjects our pure heart-minds to the influence of a kind of ether (*qi*), which obscures our true nature and underlying relationship with the rest of the world.[21] This separation leads to the mistaken view that we exist as unconnected and independent creatures and leads us to an excessive concern with satisfying our individual needs and desires. This is why most people tend to be self-centered and fail to see the world for what it is: a unified and interconnected whole.[22] Such a perspective works only to deepen our alienation, frustration, and delusion, generating ever more numerous and intense "self-centered desires" (*si yu*), which, in turn, further muddies our *qi* and distorts our perception of both ourselves and the world around us.

Following earlier neo-Confucian thinkers, Wang described a lack of feeling for the welfare of people, creatures, and things as being "numb" (*buren*) to the world. This expression fits well into his overall picture, within which we and the world are "one body," for in the language of Wang's day, the term *buren* not only meant to be "unfeeling" toward suffering or distress; it was a medical term describing paralysis in some part of the body. Neo-Confucians were quick to point out that someone who is unfeeling (i.e. lacking in benevolence) toward the world is like someone with a paralyzed limb. He might deny connection with his arm and even pay no attention when it is injured, but still he is "one body" with both the world and his afflicted limb.[23] As this picture suggests, Wang insists that no matter how deluded people become, at some deep level, they still possess a pure and perfect moral heart-mind; even though one's moral heart-mind may be blocked and has disappeared behind "clouds" of self-centered desires, above these clouds, the sun still shines (Ivanhoe 2002a, 50). The only way out of this sad state of affairs is an active program of self-cultivation focused on the removal of self-centered desires and the consequent refinement of one's *qi*. All of the beliefs that I have described above are presented together in the following long passage.

Great people regard Heaven, earth, and the myriad creatures as their own bodies. They look upon the world as one family and China as one person within it. Those who, because of the space between their own bodies and other physical forms, regard themselves as separate from [Heaven, earth, and the myriad creatures] are petty persons. The ability great people have to form one body with Heaven, earth, and the myriad creatures is not something they intentionally strive to do; the benevolence of their heart-minds is originally like this. How could it be that only the heart-minds of great people are one with Heaven, earth, and the myriad creatures? Even the heart-minds of petty people are like this. It is only the way in which such people look at things that makes them petty. This is why, when they see a child [about to] fall into a well, they cannot avoid having a sense of alarm and concern for the child.[24] This is because their benevolence forms one body with the child. Someone might object that this response is because the child belongs to the same species. But when they hear the anguished cries or see the frightened appearance of birds or beasts, they cannot avoid a sense of being unable to bear it.[25] This is because their benevolence forms one body with birds and beasts. Someone might object that this response is because birds and beasts are sentient creatures. But when they see grass or trees uprooted and torn apart, they cannot avoid feeling a sense of sympathy and distress. This is because their benevolence forms one body with grass and trees. Someone might object that this response is because grass and trees have life and vitality. But when they see tiles and stones broken and destroyed, they cannot avoid feeling a sense of concern and regret. This is because their benevolence forms one body with tiles and stones.

This shows that the benevolence that forms one body [with Heaven, earth, and the myriad creatures] is something that even the heart-minds of petty people possess. Such a heart-mind is rooted in the nature endowed by Heaven and is naturally luminous, shining, and not beclouded. This is why it is called "bright virtue." The heart-minds of petty people have become cut-off and constricted, and yet the benevolence that forms one body [with Heaven, earth, and the myriad creatures] is able to be as unbeclouded as what Heaven originally endowed. This occurs in those times when they have not yet been moved by desires or obscured by self-centeredness. Once they have been moved by desires or obscured by self-centeredness, beset by thoughts of benefit and harm and stirred by feelings of indignation and anger, they will then attack other creatures, injure their own kind, and stop at nothing. At the extreme, they even will murder their own kin and wholly lose the benevolence that forms one body [with Heaven, earth, and the myriad creatures]. And so, if only they are without the obscuration of self-centered desires, even the heart-minds of petty people will have the same benevolence that forms one body [with Heaven, earth, and the myriad creatures] that great people possess. As soon as there is obscuration by self-centered desires, then even the heart-minds of great people will become cut off and constricted, just like those of petty people. This is why the learning of the great person indeed lies only in getting rid of the obscuration of self-centered desires, thereby making bright one's bright virtue and restoring the original condition of forming one body [with Heaven, earth, and the myriad creatures]. It is not that anything can be added to this original state.

(Ivanhoe, 2009c, 160–162)

Wang used a special term of art, "pure knowing" (*liang zhi*), which he picked up from Mengzi, to describe the original heart-mind's response to moral situations.[26] For Wang, pure knowing is a faculty of moral sapience; if unobstructed by self-centered desires or obscuring *qi*, it spontaneously responds to any moral situation in a seamless process of perceiving, understanding, judging, willing, and action (Ivanhoe 2002a, 99–100). Wang likened the responsiveness of pure knowing to the reflective quality of a mirror, or the ways in which we are spontaneously drawn to beauty or repelled by a bad odor. These and other metaphors describe pure knowing as an innate, fully formed, complex, and spontaneously functioning faculty. Wang was adamant and eminently clear about how such *moral vision* functioned in a properly ordered life and how it alone was sufficient to ensure complete and unerring moral understanding and action. The real risk was not any inherent *lack* on the part of the pure knowing of our heart-mind but a lack of confidence or faith in its power and ability. We must trust in pure knowing thoroughly and completely, not interfere with its spontaneous operation, and not make even the slightest effort to help it along. Any attempt to improve upon our pure knowing adds something alien to the heart-mind, some less-than-pure element, which can only "stick to" and interfere with our naturally clear moral vision.

> The Master once said to his disciples, "No thought should stick to the heart-mind in itself, just as not the least bit of dirt should stick to the eye. It requires very little dirt to cover the eye and blot out Heaven and earth."

He also said,

> The thought need not be a self-centered thought. Even good thoughts should not become stuck in any way. It is like putting gold or jade dust in the eye; just the same, the eye cannot open.

(Ivanhoe 2002a, 73 (slightly modified))

As a result of these very different views about human nature, our moral faculty, and the source of moral failure, Wang presented a different account of self-cultivation. While Mengzi described an agriculturally inspired *development model* of self-cultivation, Wang advocated an individually focused, therapeutic, *discovery model* (Ivanhoe 2002a, 88–108). The latter model relies upon a variety of very different metaphors, such as the mind as a clean mirror hidden beneath dust, the sun obscured but ever shining behind clouds, or, as in the passage above, the mind is described in terms of its innate ability to see; its "pure knowing" presented as a kind of moral sapience. Mengzi counseled a gradual, steady course of care, nurture, and attention; Wang sought to inspire his students to maintain an intense attentiveness, a Confucian form of Buddhist mindfulness, to the movements and responses of their own heart-minds. The goal was to be ever alert and vigilant, to search out and eradicate any taint of self-centeredness in order to purify one's *qi* and allow the myriad principles of the original heart-mind to shine forth and illuminate the Way.

> This effort must be carried out continuously. Like eradicating robbers and thieves, one must resolve to wipe them out completely. In idle moments, one must search out and discover each and every self-centered thought for sex, wealth, fame and the rest. One must resolve to pluck out and cast away the root of the sickness, so that it can never arise again. Only then may one begin to feel at ease. One must, at all times, be like a cat catching mice—with eyes intently watching and ears intently listening. As soon as a single [self-centered] thought begins to stir, one must conquer it and cast it out. Act as if you were cutting a nail in two or slicing through iron. Do not indulge or accommodate it in any way. Do not harbor it, and do not allow it to escape.
>
> (Ivanhoe 2002a, 102, slightly modified)

Wang's ultimate aim was to engage and bring into complete play the power of pure knowing.

Once we begin to cultivate the required awareness and attentiveness, our pure knowing will start to inform and guide us. Pure knowing has the power to melt away and loosen the grip of self-centered desires and light our path along the Way. This process will move us from what Wang called ordinary knowledge (*chang zhi*) to real knowledge (*zhen zhi*) (Ivanhoe 2002a, 78–80). Roughly speaking, we will move from *knowing about* ethics to committed ethical understanding, which is analogous to moving from acting in accordance with what virtue requires to acting out of genuine virtue. The latter is substantially constituted by a strong disposition to attend and respond affectively to ethical situations and act properly, without hesitation. This is the crux of one of Wang's most famous teachings: the "unity of knowing and acting."[27] There is no *real* moral knowledge that does not lead one to act; one cannot *really* possess moral knowledge if one has not properly engaged in moral activity.[28]

Throughout this process, the underlying unity between the self and all things in the world both guides and motivates us to continue the process of self-cultivation. As we succeed in freeing pure knowing from the grip of self-centeredness and interfering *qi*, we feel a more extensive and profound sense of oneness with all things.[29] For Wang, empathic concern is not simply a feature of human psychology; it is the practical result of appreciating the true nature of the self and its relationship to the world. Wang's conception of empathic concern was not the source of or justification for regard for other people, creatures, and things or an expression of altruism; both the causal and justificatory relationship were very much the other way around: it is *because* of and as a function of our sense of oneness that we experience empathic concern and act in the interests of other people, creatures, and things.[30] Wang was not exploring the possibility of altruism; he was describing the implications of oneness. While it is true that feelings of oneness help to guide and motivate the practice of self-cultivation, this must not obscure where these feelings come from or what they tell us about ourselves and our relationship to the world.

We find in Wang a distinctive variation on the set of themes that Mengzi first set forth. Like Mengzi, Wang offers a comprehensive and detailed conception of human nature that seeks to describe the content, structure, and overall shape of human nature. All that remains to complete the case that Wang is an advocate of VEF is to show that his teachings about moral self-cultivation are developed in terms of a view about the flourishing of human nature that is expressed in an ideal or paradigmatic model of what it is to be human. This is easy to demonstrate; like Mengzi, Wang made extensive and critical use of the concepts of the "gentleman" (*junzi*) and "sage" (*sheng ren*) in describing his moral ideal. While there is complete agreement between Mengzi and Wang in regard to employing both historical figures and general conceptions of such ideal individuals, Wang focused much more upon the ideal of sagehood.[31] Moreover, unlike Mengzi, Wang was regarded by his followers and thought of himself as a living example of his ideal.[32] This claim may seem less startling in light of the fact that Wang insisted that "the streets are full of sages" (Wang 1963, 240). This, in turn, is something that we could infer from the parts of his philosophy that we already have introduced. Since everyone is endowed with a pure and perfect original heart-mind and thereby possesses all the principles of the world, each and every person is a hidden sage; all that one needs to do is to discover or uncover what lies within.

While Wang relied extensively on a conception of sagehood to describe his moral ideal and upheld the realization of sagehood as the goal of spiritual practice, his notion of what makes a sage a sage was different from what one finds in Mengzi. Mengzi recognized that the ultimate source for moral judgment was the wise sensibilities of virtuous individuals, and so he made clear that one cannot rely upon any set of fixed rules or principles as inviolable guides to moral action. Like most virtue ethicists, Mengzi was a particularist. Nevertheless, he thought that the moral judgments of virtuous individuals show an impressive level of regularity and consensus; as a result, the actions of past sages serve as reliable precedents for emulation. For Mengzi, studying the actions of past sages was an important and substantial component of moral education; an important part of what we seek to understand is the *moral content* of their actions. The aim is to act in ways that resemble, in significant and fairly direct ways, the deeds that they performed. Wang appealed to historical sages and to an ideal of sagehood, but not so much in order to convey a substantial model to emulate. His appeals to historical sages are aimed at exhibiting a *mode or style* of action rather than precedents for particular acts. Roughly put, we are not to do what the sages did, but to act as they acted, and in Wang's view they acted without regard to precedent or tradition; they simply followed pure knowing.[33]

> As for Shun taking a wife without first notifying his parents, was there some-one before him who took a wife without notifying *his* parents who served as an example? Did Shun first have to consult some text or ask some per-son before he could act? Or did he search within his own mind and, in an instant of thought, pure knowing weighed all factors and determined what was proper, after which he could not have turned from acting as he did? And as for King Wu launching a military expedition before burying his father, was there someone before him who launched a military expedition without bury-ing *his* father who served as an example? Did King Wu first have to consult some text or ask some person before he could act? Or did he search within his own mind and, in an instant of thought, pure knowing weighed all the factors and determined what was proper, after which he could not have turned from acting as he did?
>
> (Ivanhoe 2002a, 125)

Wang's distinctive conception of sagehood and his views about how sages figure into the process of moral self-cultivation led him to develop a much more ambigu-ous attitude toward historical sages and tradition in general.

> In learning, the important thing is to "get it with the heart-mind." Even words from the mouth of Kongzi, if one seeks in one's heart-mind and finds them to be wrong, they dare not be accepted as true.
>
> (Ivanhoe 2002a, 130)[34]

This, though, did not mean that Wang failed to accord to the standard of the sage the respect and authority characteristic of Confucianism. He still regarded sages as ideals and moral standards, but in Wang's scheme, everyone possessed this ideal and standard within his or her own breast.

> Kongzi lies within the heart-mind of each and every person,
>   But he is hidden and lost by the suffering caused by sights and sounds.
> In this very moment, he points to your true face.
> It is none other than pure knowing doubt no more!
>
> (Ivanhoe 2009c, 181)

While Wang insisted that he was a true follower of Mengzi, our discussion of his teachings shows that this cannot be granted, if understood as the claim that he was a *faithful adherent* to Mengzi's core beliefs. Wang did share with Mengzi the view that human nature is good, but as we have seen, he meant by this something radi-cally different from what Mengzi had claimed. Like Mengzi's ethical philosophy,

Wang's view was grounded in a comprehensive and detailed conception of human nature that seeks to describe the content, structure, and overall shape of human nature, and Wang developed his ethical philosophy in terms of a view about the flourishing of human nature, expressed in an ideal or paradigmatic model of what it is to be human. These and other similarities attest to the fact that Wang surely was inspired by Mengzi's philosophy; the last features also show that Wang's ethical philosophy exhibits the two primary characteristics of VEF. Nevertheless, as noted, Wang also talked a great deal about empathic care, not only for other people, but for other creatures, plants, and even inanimate objects. The extent of his care for the world went far beyond anything that we find in Mengzi and is a direct consequence of the comprehensive metaphysical foundation of his philosophical system. This same metaphysical foundation makes clear that one cannot make any quick and simple comparison between Wang's views about empathic concern and well-known Western conceptions, much less say that on the basis of this shared interest in empathy he is an advocate of VES. Wang's conception of oneness with the rest of world challenges the dominant Western understanding of empathic concern. In the conclusion, I will suggest ways in which a version of Wang's view can avoid the liabilities of his metaphysical commitments while preserving his core idea that we are indeed one with the world and that it is the recognition and appreciation of this oneness that serves as the source and justification for empathic concern.

Conclusion

In conclusion, I would like to highlight some of the strengths of Mengzi's and Wang's ethical views and explore ways in which we might modify or reinterpret some of their core teachings in order to avoid weaknesses in certain of their assumptions. I hope that it will be clear not only how and to what extent the latter suggestions depart from the historical views of Mengzi and Wang, at least as I understand and have presented them, but also the ways in which these contemporary versions of their views are inspired and connected to their original teachings.

If we look to Mengzi as a source for contemporary ethical philosophy, two aspects of his thought are of particular interest and importance. The first is a feature not only of Mengzi's ethics but, arguably, of all Confucian thought: his notion of flourishing is explicitly linked to the good of larger social units, and not just to the good of individuals.[35] Mengzi's discussion of historical sages and his more general account of the virtues make clear that what makes a Confucian life good is inextricably connected with what makes families thrive and society orderly and humane. While Mengzi believes that a morally good life is good for the person who lives it and that such a life constitutes that person's proper state of flourishing, such flourishing has at its core the good of families and society at large. Families and society in general are not simply the context or enabling conditions for human flourishing; they set constraints upon our behavior and offer core elements of what makes life good. These features of Confucian virtue ethics explain a number of qualities that distinguish it from most if not all its Western cousins. Confucianism is well known for its emphasis on the family and virtues such as filial piety;[36] many scholars have noted that Confucianism espouses a more communal conception of the good and that the Confucian notion of the self is more relational than individualistic.[37] And so, while Mengzi does link his account of the virtues to a fairly clear and detailed conception of human flourishing, which he illustrates with a corresponding notion of sagehood, we must keep in mind that his notion of what makes a life good is intimately linked in complex ways to a wide range of people beyond the individual in question. This is one reason why it is correct to see his view as sharing important similarities with certain versions of VES, and especially with contemporary feminist advocates of VES who emphasize the centrality of relationships both to a good life and to the individuation of the self.[38]

The second aspect of Mengzi's ethical philosophy that I would like to explore concerns the specificity and detail of his notions of human nature and flourishing; these features of his teachings are examples of a general weakness in traditional forms of VEF and are aspects of his thought that require reinterpretation and modification. This weakness is not avoided and is made even more severe by the fact, noted above, that he links his views on human nature and flourishing to normative accounts of larger social units. No one should want to defend Mengzi's historical views on these issues, since they present too restricted and implausible an account of what human beings are, can become, and enjoy and the kinds of societies that they can fashion and be proud of.[39] It is not clear, though, that one cannot argue for a looser and more plausible version of Mengzi's vision; one that leaves open the question of how human needs, desires, and capacities can be developed and brought into harmony within larger familial and social orders. This would require a pluralistic form of Confucianism and might even allow for a version of what I call ethical promiscuity.[40] Adopting a general, flexible, and open-ended theory of human nature and its flourishing would lead such a version of Confucianism to abandon important features of traditional versions of VEF. Such changes would include the need to allow for and perhaps even celebrate a broader variety of larger social units in the Confucian conception of the good.

If we bracket parts of Wang's teachings, we can retain valuable insights about the nature of certain moral problems and the practical business of overcoming them. For example, if we set aside his views about an innate moral faculty and simply assume that we are talking about the sensibilities possessed by mature moral agents, Wang's way of describing the interference of self-centered desires often makes a good deal of sense and captures important features of moral epistemology and the phenomenology of moral perception. In at least a wide range of situations, when we fail to act morally our problem is not a lack of knowledge but an excessive concern with our own, self-centered desires (Tien 2010). Desires often operate in a quite subtle and convoluted manner that leads us to "see" things in ways that make improper action look pretty good and make it difficult to perceive or pay attention to ethically preferable alternatives. Self-centered desires can enlist reason in the service of excessive self-concern and lend further force to its cause, reinforcing such a view of the world. This often is roughly what we mean when we talk about "rationalizing" self-serving actions, decisions, or beliefs.[41] Breaking free of the grip of such errant perceptions requires us to become aware of and focus attention upon our excessive self-centeredness and turn to concentrate on more other-directed desires, already present within us.[42] It often requires us to recognize that other people, creatures, and things, while clearly not part of our physical bodies, are parts of our lives and our conception of who we are. In Wang's terms, we must come to recognize and appreciate that we are "one" with at least many parts of the world. In such a view, moral perception is more about one's fundamental conception of the self and one's related view about personal welfare than it is about the proper use of reason.[43] Altering or shifting from one self-conception to another can greatly affect one's perception of events; one can experience a kind of gestalt-shift that results in seeing the same thing in a dramatically different way.[44]

Wang's views about moral self-cultivation have many other things to offer. Among these is the idea that moral learning occurs most often and effectively when it is grounded in and engages the actual events of one's own life.[45] Wang roundly criticized many of his contemporaries for detaching moral learning from the actual actions and affairs of daily life and instead casting it excessively or even exclusively in terms of the study of overly abstract speculative theories, staid historical accounts, or hollow displays of ritual (Ivanhoe 2002a, 130). In contrast, he insisted that we learn to be better, if at all, when we work on engaging pure knowing as it operates in the actual actions and affairs of our own lives. Wang would urge us to concentrate on cultivating a heightened awareness and attentiveness to how we think, feel, and behave as we live out our lives, rather than to dedicate ourselves to the *study of morality* in its various forms. We should reflect on whether we have been living up to the standard that we already possess within, our pure knowing, and whether we are being the kind of father, mother, husband, wife, child, sister, brother, teacher, truck driver, judge, cashier, etc. that we know we should be, or whether we are allowing excessively self-centered desires to block and misdirect us.

Wang's claims about the role that a sense of oneness between the self and the rest of the world plays in our moral lives are also remarkably revealing and important (Tien 2012). In order to see and appreciate the value of these claims we need to separate them from Wang's heroic metaphysical assumptions, but this is much easier than it might at first appear to be. We need not think of ourselves as linked to the rest of the world directly, through the sharing of "principles" or some other metaphysically obscure entity, but still can defend a robust sense of being inextricably connected with the world in ways that reveal aspects of it that we fail to see and that can and should guide our understanding and move us to action. In fact, several contemporary psychologists have argued that a sense of oneness, and *not* empathic concern, is what motivates people to help others (Cialdini, Brown, Lewis, Luce, and Neuberg 1997). Such research relies upon the idea that most often people feel *and act* in a benevolent manner not because they experience more *empathic concern* for another, but "because they feel more *at one* with the other— that is because they perceive more of themselves in the other" (Cialdini, et al. 1997, 483).[46] In such a view, our concern for others is not purely selfless or altruistic, because it is grounded in an expanded view of the self. In addition to a growing number of experimental results, this view is supported by notions like "inclusive fitness" in evolutionary theory. Here, the sense of oneness is more palpable and related to shared genetic inheritance. A sense of oneness, though, is not limited to or even primarily related to genes; we can feel one with others in many different ways; for example, we can identify just as strongly with ideas, beliefs, images, symbols, and practices transmitted and inherited across generations. In both cases, a non-metaphysical interpretation of Wang's idea of shared "principles" readily lends itself as a general way to explain what we share.

Wang's way of looking at the phenomenon of oneness takes us considerably beyond the work of contemporary psychologists who tend to focus exclusively on the possibility of genuine concern for other *human beings*. Recall that Wang thought that we were one not only with other people, but also with other animals, plants, and even inanimate objects. There is every reason to think that we in fact can and to some extent already do feel a sense of oneness with many of these, and that such a sense is essential for getting us to act on behalf of these other creatures and things. For example, it is quite plausible to maintain that it is not possible to sustain anything resembling an adequate commitment to protecting Nature without believing and feeling that we are one with Nature, and such a belief and sensibility need not in any way conflict with science or be irrational or mystical. Quite the contrary, a *denial* of—or, in Wang's terms, being "numb" to—our intimate connection to the natural world, properly understood, and our linked common future is clearly contrary to our best scientific understanding, irrational, and a dire threat to human welfare as well as to many other forms of life on earth.[47] Wang's view suggests that one of the most powerful bases of our concern for other people, creatures, plants, and things is an enlarged sense of self; at least in a number of cases, for example in the cases of inclusive fitness and our general, evolutionary interrelationship with Nature, this is more than just a stance on the world: it reflects important facts about how we are related to things in the world that we hold dear.

One challenge to this kind of view is that is seems to deny the possibility of altruism, for it appears to say that when we act in the interest of other people, creatures, plants, and things we really are simply helping ourselves.[48] Altruism requires that our acts be *selfless*, but to some extent oneness includes the other within the self. This is a complex and subtle issue, which I will not attempt to settle here. I do, though, want to suggest that some have sought to settle it too quickly. For example, Cialdini et al. claim that "When the distinction between self and other is undermined, the traditional dichotomy between selfishness and selflessness loses meaning" (Cialdini, et al. 1997, 491). I am not so sure about this. If we could not *in any way* distinguish between self and other, the notions of excessive self-centeredness and selflessness would indeed lose meaning. That, though, is not what modern psychologists, like Cialdini, or neo-Confucians, like Wang Yangming, have argued for. They have described an expanded sense of self and identified varying types and degrees of "interpersonal unity" (Cialdini, et al. 1997, 490). For example, while Wang insists that underneath it all there are shared principles, he does not dissolve the self into the world; *qi* preserves the world of physical things and a hierarchy of concern even for the sage. What the proposed, modern conception of oneness brings with it is a need to *rethink* the meaning of notions like selfishness and selflessness, but that is nothing particularly new. What is new is to do this from a global perspective on what philosophical resources are available, and in light of recent findings in psychology.

Wang's ethical philosophy offers a startlingly different version of VEF from anything that we find in the Western philosophical tradition. His metaphysical beliefs entail that each and every person already possesses complete and perfect knowledge and only needs to work at uncovering, unfolding, and fully implementing the pure knowing that lies within. This leads him to adopt distinctive views about moral self-cultivation, the nature and extent of our feelings for other people, creatures, and things, and the character of the sage. As different as his beliefs are in regard to these and other issues, his philosophy retains the core features of VEF that have guided our analysis and discussion. We can and should take away from our study of Mengzi and Wang a greater appreciation of the fascinating variations among the known species of virtue ethics and the recognition that careful analysis and reflection upon these can enrich our understanding of virtue ethics and our ethical lives more generally.

4 Confucianism, Kant, and Virtue Ethics

LEE Ming-huei

In recent years, a trend of adopting the Western concept of "virtue ethics" to interpret Confucian ethics has emerged and gained popularity in the English-speaking world. Bryan W. Van Norden's *Virtue Ethics and Consequentialism in Early Chinese Philosophy* (Van Norden 2007), Jiyuan Yu's *The Ethics of Confucius and Aristotle* (Yu 2007), and May Sim's *Remastering Morals with Aristotle and Confucius* (Sim 2007), for example, are representative of this popular trend. Recently, Michael Slote, an advocate of virtue ethics, has also begun to concern himself with this theme. A series of lectures focusing on "virtue ethics," entitled "Humanistic Value Lectures," that he delivered at National Chengchi University, Taiwan in October 2008 represents this effort. What he promotes, however, is not Aristotelian "virtue ethics" but what is called "sentimentalist virtue ethics," of which David Hume is the major representative. Taking this as a reference point, he also made some comments on Van Norden's aforementioned book (Slote 2009).

There is no doubt that behind the emergence of this trend is the revival of contemporary Western virtue ethics. As is generally known, it was G. E. M. Anscombe's 1958 essay entitled "Modern Moral Philosophy" that triggered the resurrection of the intellectual trend of virtue ethics (Anscombe 1958). In this essay, Anscombe makes a sharp contrast between "ancient moral philosophy" as represented by Aristotelian ethics and "modern moral philosophy" as represented by Kantian ethics and consequentialist ethics (mainly utilitarianism). This theme has been further developed in Alasdair MacIntyre's masterpiece *After Virtue*. Thereafter, "virtue ethics" seemingly became the third type of ethics, beside "deontological ethics" and "teleological ethics."

Before engaging in further discussion of the concept of "virtue ethics," I would like first to introduce two aspects of its intellectual background which have been neglected recently in the discussion of virtue ethics and Confucianism in the English-speaking world. The first aspect is an intellectual trend in modern German philosophy; that is, the so-called "rehabilitation of practical philosophy" (*Rehabilitierung der praktischen Philosophie*). This trend obtains its dynamic directly from studies of Hegel after the Second World War. Hegel distinguishes between "*Moralität*" and "*Sittlichkeit.*" Based on this distinction, he criticizes Kantian ethics, assuming that Kantian ethics is still at the stage of "*Moralität*," and has not yet entered into the stage of "*Sittlichkeit.*" In this sense, some German scholars trace "practical philosophy"—or "the second philosophy" as it is called by

Manfred Riedel (Riedel 1988)—back to Aristotle, regarding Hegel as the modern inheritor of "practical philosophy." In 1960, Joachim Ritter published his essay "On the Foundation of Practical Philosophy in Aristotle" (Ritter 1960), which triggered discussion of the "rehabilitation of practical philosophy." Afterwards, Manfred Riedel collected essays of different views on the subject and compiled a two-volume book entitled *The Rehabilitation of Practical Philosophy* (Riedel 1972, 1974). Among the authors of the essays were such well-known scholars as Leo Strauss, Hermann Lübbe, Hans-Georg Gadamer, Karl-Otto Apel, Karl-Heinz Ilting, Otto Pöggeler, and Hans Lenk among others. Although the intellectual trend in the German-speaking world and the intellectual trend of virtue ethics in the English-speaking world emerge along different intellectual lines, they both confront the same question of "Kant or Aristotle?" In this sense, they can be said to reach the same goal through different approaches. Unfortunately, this German intellectual trend has seldom been included in the discussion of virtue ethics in the English-speaking world.

Another neglected aspect is the approach by which contemporary New Confucianism interprets Confucianism by means of Kantian philosophy and its contrast with virtue ethics. Even people with basic knowledge about contemporary New Confucianism cannot fail to know that Mou Zongsan borrows concepts and frameworks from Kantian philosophy to classify and evaluate Confucianism from the pre-Qin period (before 221 BCE) to the Song (960–1279) and Ming (1368–1644) dynasties. As far as pre-Qin Confucianism is concerned, adopting Kant's concepts of "autonomy versus heteronomy" as the criterion, he classifies the ethics of Confucius, Mencius, *Zhongyong* (Doctrine of the Mean), and the commentaries to *Yijing* (Book of Changes) as the pattern of autonomy, and that of Xunzi (298–238 BCE) as the pattern of heteronomy. In his three-volume masterpiece *Xinti yu xingti* (The Heart/Mind as Reality and Human Nature as Reality) (Mou 1968, 1969), he still adopts this criterion to classify and evaluate the philosophical systems within Song-Ming Confucianism: The line from the three Confucian masters Zhou Dunyi (1017–1073), Zhang Zai (1020–1077), and Cheng Hao (1032–1085) in the Northern Song, the line from Lu Xiangshan (1139–1192) to Wang Yangming (1472–1529) in latter times, and the line from Hu Hong (1105?–1161) to Liu Zongzhou (1578–1645) inherit the philosophical orientation of Confucius, Mencius, *Zhongyong*, and the commentaries to *Yijing*, representing the ethics of autonomy. The line from Cheng Yi (1033–1107) to Zhu Xi (1130–1200) is a deviation from it, representing the ethics of heteronomy. Therefore, he defines Zhu Xi as the establisher of another philosophical line. In the first half of his book *Yuanshan lun* (On the Highest Good), Mou adopts Kant's principle of autonomy to interpret most chapters of the first half of Book 6 of *Mencius* and several chapters of Book 7. In the second half of the book, he follows Kant's question of the "highest good" to explain the patterns of "perfect teaching" (*yuanjiao*) in Confucianism, Buddhism, and Daoism, so as to answer the question of "how to unify virtue and happiness" raised by Kant in his *Critique of Practical Reason*.

If we admit that Kant's ethics is a system of deontological ethics, then, in light of Mou Zongsan's interpretation, Confucian ethics is basically also a system of "deontological ethics," despite the fact that he never used this term. I have published a series of essays following Mou's way of thinking, collected in my book

Confucianism and Kant (Lee 1990). Due to the traditional affinity between scholasticism and Aristotelian philosophy, some Taiwanese scholars with Catholic
backgrounds, however, attempt to interpret Confucian ethics as "virtue ethics" so
as to counterbalance the interpretive approach of New Confucians, especially Mou
Zongsan. For example, Shen Qingsong (Vincent Shen), Huang Huo, Pan Xiaohui,
and some others are representative of this type of scholarship (Shen 1992, 1992a,
1995, 1998; Huang, H. 1996, 1999; Pan 1992, 2006). I once took Shen Qingsong's
arguments as a target to clarify his misunderstanding of Kantian ethics and Confucian ethics (Lee 2005a).

However, all the authors of the three books mentioned at the beginning of this
essay completely ignored this intellectual background. This not only made them
miss an opportunity to dialogue with the Chinese academic community, but also
led them to some misunderstandings. Yu Jiyuan, for instance, in the beginning of
his book *Confucius and Aristotelian Ethics*, mentions that the contemporary New
Confucians' "Manifesto Regarding Chinese Culture to People all over the World"
was published in the same year as Anscombe's "Modern Moral Philosophy," using
them as signals to mark the "revival of Confucianism" and the "revival of Aristotelian ethics" respectively. Moreover, he emphasizes, "Indeed, the philosophical
orientation of these two rivals is the same, that is, a virtue approach to ethics" (Yu
2007, 2).[1] As a matter of fact, however, the respective philosophical directions that
these two represent are diametrically opposite.

After explaining these two neglected philosophical backgrounds, we will now
return to the question of the relationship between Western ethics and Confucian
ethics. In Western ethics, the distinction of "deontological ethics" and "teleological ethics" is a typological distinction based on dichotomy, which is to a large
extent equivalent to the distinction between "*Gesinnungsethik*" and "*Erfolgsethik*"
in the German-speaking world. In brief, teleological ethics insists that the ultimate criterion for moral duty or moral value is the non-moral values that it brings
about—the good in a non-moral sense—such as joy, happiness, utility, and so
on. In other words, this type of ethics reduces the good in a moral sense to the
good in a non-moral sense. Or, in Kant's words, it reduces the "moral good" (*das
moralische Gut*) to the "physical good" (*das physische Gut*) (Kant, *Anthropologie in
pragmatischer Hinsicht*. In *Kants Gesammelte Schriften* [hereinafter referred to as
KGS, Vol. 7]: 277). On the contrary, deontological ethics is opposed to reducing
the good in a moral sense to the good in a non-moral sense, insisting that the ultimate criterion for evaluating the moral significance of an act or a rule of action is
not the non-moral value that it brings about, but its own character or the motive
of the agent. In John R. Silber's terminology, while deontological ethics affirms the
heterogeneity of the good (Silber 1967), teleological ethics regards all the good as
homogeneous. Furthermore, for deontological ethics, since the moral value of an
act does not depend on the non-moral value that it produces or may produce, its
moral value lies in its "moral character or morality" (*Moralität*), not in its "legal-
ity" (*Legalität*). In other words, it must be done "out of duty" (*aus Pflicht*), rather
than merely "conforming to duty" (*pflichtmäßig*).

As we all know, the first chapter of *Mencius* already raises the issue of the distinction between righteousness and utility. As a matter of fact, the distinction

between righteousness and utility is by nature a distinction between the "moral good" and the "natural good," and it implies the heterogeneity of the good. Actually, Confucius had already made such a statement: "Superior persons understand what is righteous whereas mean persons understand wherein their own utility lies" (*Analects* 4:16). Moreover, when discussing with Zaiwo about the preservation or possible abolishment of the three-year mourning period for parents (*Analects* 17: 21), Confucius explicitly expresses his deontological viewpoint. I published an essay focusing especially on this topic, in which I discussed in detail the respective ethical viewpoints that Confucius and Zaiwo held in the discussion, and the philosophical issues concerned (Lee 1999). Zaiwo has two reasons for his suggestion to curtail the three-year mourning period for parents. His first reason is, "If a noble man abstains for three years from performing the rituals, then the rituals will definitely be lost. If for three years he abstains from playing the music, then the music will definitely be ruined." The second is, "When old grain is exhausted, the new grain will be on the ground; in making fire by friction, we must choose the proper wood for every season within one year; therefore, after one year, the mourning should stop." Among these two reasons, while the former is a viewpoint of consequentialism or a teleological stance, the latter proves "ought to be" (moral laws) by "is" (natural laws), and also presupposes a teleological standpoint. Confucius, on the contrary, asks Zaiwo whether or not he feels at ease in his heart, which means that Confucius establishes the meaning of "three-year mourning period" on the basis of the agent's motivation. This is a viewpoint of "*Gesinnungsethik*," and therefore it implies a deontological viewpoint.

Since the distinction between deontological ethics and teleological ethics is based on dichotomy, as a result, the relationship between the two is both exhausting and excluding each other. Here I would like to especially emphasize that there is an asymmetrical relationship between these two ethical viewpoints. Because, if the moral value of an act is evaluated from the viewpoint of teleological ethics, the motivation of the agent does not matter at all unless it can give rise to the expected result. Deontological ethics, on the contrary, is opposed to weighing the moral value of an act by the results or the possible results that it may bring about, but it still admits that these kinds of results have non-moral value. Let us take the principle of utility as an example. Though deontological ethics is opposed to using it to evaluate moral value, it probably still would accept it as a derivative moral principle. For example, even though Kant insists that the moral value of an act has nothing to do with the possible happiness that it may bring to either oneself or others, he still regards "to improve other people's happiness," along with "to perfect oneself," as a "duty of virtue" (*Tugendpflicht*) (Kant, "Metaphysik der Sitten." [Hereinafter referred to as *KGS*, Vol.6]: 391ff.). He takes a step toward deriving an indirect duty of improving one's own happiness from the duty of "increasing one's own perfection. (Kant *KGS*, Vol. 6: 388; cf. Lee 1990a). No matter whether it is one's own happiness or others' happiness, it can be ascribed to the principle of utility. Therefore, this means to accept the principle of utility as a derivative moral principle.

On the contrary, if a teleological ethicist accepts, more or less, the fundamental principles of deontological ethics, it actually means to retreat from the standpoint of teleological ethics. For example, suppose someone faces a moral choice and must choose between two different actions. He follows the principle of utility to assess these two actions, only to find that the possible consequences that these two may bring about are either too complicated to weigh, or even if measurable, too close to distinguish. Under such circumstances, if he takes the purity of his motivation (duty for the sake of duty) into consideration when making a choice, this means that he retreats from the utilitarian standpoint, and abandons the unity of his viewpoint. He may defend himself by saying that the reason why he takes the purity of his motivation into consideration is precisely because this motivation could bring about positive results, and this is why he still maintains a utilitarian stance. But this is just playing with concepts, because the so-called "purity of motivation" precisely means "completely ignoring the result of an act." Therefore, as long as the distinction between teleological ethics and deontological ethics theoretically remains strict, there is an asymmetrical relationship between the two. In this sense, I would argue that William K. Frankena's so-called "mixed deontological theory" is a misleading concept (Frankena 1973).

Now we can start to discuss the concept of "virtue ethics." Because the distinction between teleological ethics and deontological ethics is exhaustive and mutually exclusive, logically it is not possible that there exists a third type of ethics. The only possibility is that there are sub-types subject to these two types of ethics. Virtue ethics, for example, can be viewed as a sub-type of teleological ethics. When advocates of virtue ethics regard it as a third type of ethics besides teleological ethics and deontological ethics, they must explain what the criterion for this trichotomous typology is. Though many ethicists try to define the concept of "virtue ethics," it remains confusing throughout. If such different ethical views as Aristotle's and Hume's can be put in this one single concept, then how could this concept not be confusing?

Let us put aside Slote's "sentimentalist virtue ethics" for the time being, and take Aristotle's ethics as the major representative of virtue ethics and Kant's ethics as the major representative of deontological ethics, to see the fundamental distinction between the two. We can summarize the popular views of the distinction in three points: (1) deontological ethics emphasizes "duty," while virtue ethics emphasizes "virtue"; (2) the former stresses "principle" or "rule," while the latter stresses "character"; and (3) the former attaches importance to "action," while the latter gives importance to "agent."

As far as the first point is concerned, first of all, "duty" is undoubtedly an important concept in Kant's ethics, but isn't the concept of "virtue"? In recent years, a lot of scholars have explored Kant's concept of "virtue" to illustrate the important position of this concept in Kant's ethical system. Robert R. Louden (1986), Onora S. O'Neill (1983, 1996), Robert N. Johnson (1997), Nancy Sherman (1997, 1997a), Andrea Marlen Esser (2004) are among these scholars. Lately, Monika Betzler edited a book entitled *Kant's Ethics of Virtue* (Betzler 2008), which includes a group of essays related to this topic and which is an important reference. Here the editor carries special implications in using the term "ethics of virtue" rather than "virtue ethics." She states in the introduction to this anthology, "The essays here suggest that Kant's ethics, to be sure, are not to be assimilated into virtue ethics [...] But Kant's later writings help us to see that virtue is a core element in his ethics, precisely because it helps us to do our duty" (Betzler 2008, 27).

As is well known, Kant published his book *Metaphysical First Principles of the Doctrine of Virtue* (*Metaphysische Anfangsgründe der Tugendlehre*) in 1797.[2] In this book, Kant not only provides a detailed explanation of the concept of "virtue," but also regards "to increase one's own perfection" as a "duty of virtue." According to his explanation, this duty includes: (1) to cultivate our natural perfection, that is, to cultivate our ability for cultural creation; and (2) to cultivate our inner morality, that is, to cultivate our moral feelings (Kant *KGS*, Vol. 6, S. 386f. and 391f). I completely agree with Betzler's view that Kant's ethics does not pertain to "virtue ethics" as represented by Aristotle, but it contains an "ethics of virtue." In this sense, it is meaningless to distinguish between deontological ethics and virtue ethics by means of contrast between duty and virtue.

As far as the second point is concerned, in Kant's ethics, the moral principle refers to categorical imperative, and moral rules are concrete norms derived from the categorical imperative. The categorical imperative is undoubtedly the core concept of Kant's ethics, but we should not forget that in Kant's ethics of autonomy, the categorical imperative comes from the self-lawgiving of the moral subject. In this sense, the moral subject is a more fundamental factor. In *Critique of Pure Reason*, Kant discusses the dual "character" of human beings, that is, the "intelligible character" and the "empirical character" (Kant, *Kritik der reinen Vernunft* [hereinafter referred to as *KrV*], A444–452/B472–480). While the "intelligible character" is the moral subject, the "empirical character" is composed of qualities that are to be cultivated, including our natural instincts, social habits, and moral feelings. Therefore, it is hard to say that Kant's ethics emphasizes only principles and rules but disregards "character." After clarifying the first two points, then naturally it is not difficult to explain the third point. Because, in Kant's ethics, a moral act is the act of the moral subject (agent), therefore it is not possible that it emphasizes only "act" but disregards "agent."

In terms of interpretive strategies, the purpose of interpretation is to make the object of interpretation emerge from ambiguity to clarity. Given that "virtue ethics" is so ambiguous a concept, the strategy to interpret Confucianism with it can only make things go from bad to worse. For example, many years ago, a Taiwanese scholar, Cai Xin'an, published an essay entitled "On Mencius' Moral Choice," asserting that Mencius' theory of act-choice is a sort of "act-utilitarianism," but it appears in the guise of "rule-deontological ethics" (Cai 1987, 139). Afterward however, he published another essay entitled "Mencius: Virtue and Principle," assuming that Mencius is a "virtue ethicist" (Cai 2002, 55). This makes the image of Mencius more ambiguous. Pan Xiaohui, to give another example, acknowledges that Confucian ethics as represented by Confucius, Mencius, and Xunzi pertains to the "deontological type rather than the teleological type," on the one hand, but she also stresses that it isn't a "pure deontological type," on the other. She concludes:

> Looking at Confucian moral philosophy represented by Confucius, Mencius, and Xunzi from this perspective, we find that it is basically a synthesized type

attaching importance to both virtue and principle. If we must distinguish the relative superiority or inferiority of each one, I would argue that it should be construed as a synthesized type giving top priority to virtue while simultaneously borrowing from deontological ethics.

(Pan 1992, 81and 85)

If, as advocates of virtue ethics point out, the "deontological ethics" represented by Kant and the "virtue ethics" represented by Aristotle are so diametrically opposed to one another, then how can she find a synthesized type of these two ethics in Confucianism?

Western scholars encounter a similar problem when they borrow the term of "virtue ethics" to interpret Confucianism. Van Norden, for example, in his book *Virtue Ethics and Consequentialism in Early Chinese Philosophy*, attempts to define "virtue ethics." According to him, a virtue ethics has at least four components: (1) an account of what a "flourishing human life" is like; (2) an account of what virtues contribute to leading such a life; (3) an account of how one acquires those virtues; and (4) a philosophical anthropology that explains what humans are like (Van Norden 2007, 33–34). After that, he mentions different forms of "virtue ethics":

In its most moderate form, virtue ethics can be seen as a complement to consequentialist or rule-deontological versions of ethics, filling out one of the latter by adding on to it accounts of human virtues, flourishing, cultivation, and philosophical anthropology that are consistent with it. However, in the more moderate versions of virtue ethics, the four components above are logically dependent on consequentialist or deontological aspects of the ethical view. Kant, for example, has a conception of the four items above, but they appear primarily in his seldom-read *The Doctrine of Virtue*, and he thinks of virtues as helping one to follow the deontological strictures of the categorical imperative. In its most radical formulations, virtue ethics attempts to serve as a foundation for all of ethics and to completely supplant consequentialist and rule-deontological foundations.

(Van Norden 2007, 34)

According to what is said there, the concept of "virtue ethics" is so broadly defined that it almost loses its function as a marker. Because in its most extreme form, virtue ethics is in diametrical opposition to the deontological ethics that Kant's ethics represents; in its moderate form however, even Kant's ethics can be viewed as a form of "virtue ethics"! Since the connotations of "virtue ethics" are so divergent, no wonder that Guido Rappe in an essay calls "the mainstream of ancient ethics," including Confucian and Aristotle's ethics, "deontological virtue ethics" (Rappe 2010, 318)!

Though Kant in his formal publications never tries to define the position of Aristotle's ethics directly, he levels harsh criticism at the "eudaemonist" in the preface to "Metaphysical First Foundations of the Doctrine of Virtue": "if *eudaimonism* (the principle of happiness) is set up as the basic principle instead of *eleutheronomy* (the principle of the freedom of internal law giving), the result of this is the *euthanasia* (easy death) of all morals" (Kant, *KGS*, Vol. 6, S. 378). This is undoubtedly a criticism of Aristotle's ethics. In recent years, studies of Kant fully display that, contrary to the understanding of many advocates of virtue ethics, Kant's ethics is not in diametrical opposition to Aristotle's ethics, nor without any overlap with the latter, because it contains an "ethics of virtue" in itself. Nevertheless, it can by no means be equated to "virtue ethics" as represented by Aristotle. I would argue that scholars who have attempted to interpret Confucian ethics by means of "virtue ethics" in recent years at best reveal that we can find the concept of "virtue" and other relevant traits in Confucian ethics, but this in no way proves that Confucian ethics is in the same family as Aristotelian "virtue ethics."

Finally, I would like to take this opportunity to discuss the relationship between what Slote calls "sentimentalist virtue ethics" and Confucian ethics. It is true that what Mencius calls "the four buddings" (*siduan*) readily remind us of the Scottish ethics of "moral sense" in the 18th century. A Taiwanese scholar, Huang Jinxing, for instance, once construed Mencius' "four buddings" as a kind of "'moral sense' with empirical meaning" (Huang, J. 1994, 12), and he consequently asserted, "Instead of saying that Confucian moral philosophy has something in common with Kant's philosophy, it is better to say that Confucian moral philosophy has more similarities with Hutcheson's and Hume's theories to which Kant is opposed. Both persons insist that human beings have an innate 'moral sense' as the criterion for moral judgment" (Huang, J. 1994, 14–15). Because Kant in his late works classifies what Hutcheson called "moral sense" as "principle of heteronomy," Huang Jinxing relies on this to question Mou Zongsan's interpretive strategy of using Kantian philosophy to interpret Confucianism.

In response to Huang Jinxing's question, I published a series of essays (Lee 1990), which were eventually enough to develop into a book entitled *The Four Buddings and the Seven Feelings: A Comparative Philosophical Investigation of Moral Feelings* (Lee 2005b). Since the problems concerned are too complicated, it is impossible to discuss them in every detail here. The reason why Kant in his late works is opposed to regarding "moral sense" as the basis for moral judgment, as the Scottish ethics of "moral sense" does, is because he views all feelings (including moral feelings) as sensible, and thus excludes them from the structure of the moral subject as a rational agent. Nevertheless, in the latter stage of Kant's ethics, moral feelings still have two important functions; that is, both as a moral incentive (the driving force for moral conduct) and as an anthropological basis for moral cultivation. These two functions are directly related to his concept of "virtue." "The four buddings" mentioned by Mencius, however, is not, contrary to what Huang Jinxing asserted, a kind of "'moral sense' with empirical meaning"; rather, it is a kind of *a priori* feeling, belonging to what some phenomenological ethicists like Max Scheler and Nicolai Hartmann call *a priori* "*Wertfühlen.*" Therefore for Mencius, the moral subject (the original heart/mind) is not merely a rational subject as construed by Kant; rather, it possesses explicit emotionality, expressing itself as "the four buddings": the dispositions of compassion, of shame and dislike, of yielding and deference, and of discriminating between right and wrong. Here reason and emotion are unified.

Confucius also affirms the moral subject which unifies reason and emotion. As mentioned earlier, Confucius and Zaiwo once discussed the issue of preservation and possible abolishment of the three-year mourning period for one's parent. In the dialogue, Confucius, on the one hand, bases the meaning of the three-year mourning on whether one's conscience feels at ease or not ("If your heart/mind feels at ease, then do it"); on the other hand, he adopts the "principle of gratitude" to refute Zaiwo's reason for shortening the three-year mourning period, "It is not until three years old that one is able to leave one's parents' arms. This is why the three-year mourning is a universally observed rite under Heaven. Didn't Zaiwo also receive three years of love of the sort from his parents?" (*Analects* 17: 21) It is made quite clear here that Confucius, unlike Kant, does not regard the moral subject merely as the rational subject, nor consequently deprive it of all its emotionality. Therefore, the assertion of David L. Hall and Roger T. Ames that pre-Qin Confucians build moral judgment on aesthetic intuition rather than on the reflection and application of moral principles is absolutely not true (Hall and Ames 1987, 267). Though Confucius and Mencius have a different understanding of the structure of the moral subject from Kant's, this does not prevent both ethics from belonging to deontological ethics. It is true that pre-Qin Confucian ethics contains plenty of discussions of virtue and abundant relevant intellectual resources, but this at most can prove that pre-Qin Confucianism also has an "ethics of virtue." This, however, cannot prove itself to be a "virtue ethics" because it cannot belong to both Kantian deontological ethics and Aristotelian virtue ethics at the same time.

5 Toward a Synthesis of Confucianism and Aristotelianism[1]

Bryan W. Van Norden

Western scholars such as Lee H. Yearley (1990) and Chinese scholars such as Wan Junren (2004) have shown how we can attain a deeper understanding of the varieties of Confucianism by applying the concepts of virtue ethics, and tracing out the similarities and differences between the Confucian and Western species of the virtue ethics genus. In more recent scholarship, Steve Angle (2009a), Philip J. Ivanhoe (2000), May Sim (2007), Jiyuan Yu (2007) and I have argued in detail for similar theses. Of course, virtue ethics is an extremely complex and diverse movement, even if we limit ourselves to discussing its Western forms. However, in *Virtue Ethics and Consequentialism in Early Chinese Philosophy* (2007) I identify four areas that are a focus of interest for virtue ethics: first, a conception of what a flourishing human life is like; second, a view of which virtues contribute to leading such a life; third, an account of what human nature is like, such that humans can have those virtues and flourish in that kind of life; and fourth, a theory of how, given what human nature is like, humans can cultivate the virtues so as to lead a flourishing life. Virtue ethics can take either moderate or radical forms. (1) In its moderate formulation, virtue ethics is simply a supplement to a rule-deontological or consequentialist normative theory. Kant, for example, presents a theory of the virtues in Part II of his *Metaphysics of Morals*. However, for a rule-deontologist like Kant, the nature and significance of the virtues is ultimately derived from deontological constraints: "Hence virtue is the moral strength of the will of a human being in obeying his duty ..." (Kant, 1994, 64, Ak. 405). (2) In its more radical formulation, virtue ethics is an alternative to both consequentialist and rule-deontological moralities. In my book, I argue for three theses regarding early Confucians like Kongzi (Confucius) and Mengzi (Mencius). First, human flourishing, the virtues, human nature and ethical cultivation were central topics in their philosophies. Second, they held that the Way cannot be achieved simply by maximizing good consequences, nor can it be captured by rules that would be exceptionless, substantive and useful for human agents. Third, they believed that, while all normal humans are responsive to Virtue to some extent, there are ethical distinctions that only the highly cultivated can grasp and appropriately respond to. For these reasons, Confucianism can be understood as a radical form of virtue ethics.

Lee Ming-huei has questioned whether virtue ethics can be a distinctive third normative theory (Lee, this volume). His objection turns on the assumption that consequentialism and deontology are jointly exhaustive and mutually exclusive. If we use the most broad characterization of deontology – as the view that sometimes the right action to perform is not the one that will produce the best non-moral consequences – then consequentialism and deontology are our only options. However, I think it is crucial to distinguish between rule deontology and its other forms.[2] A rule deontologist will identify the right actions by their adherence to (or at least consistency with) a moral rule. In contrast, a radical virtue ethicist will claim that a good person is responsive to aspects of situations that are more complex than could be captured by any inviolable, informative and practically tractable set of rules. The virtues are the dispositions that allow one to identify and properly respond to these rule-transcending characteristics of situations.[3] Furthermore, there is much more to living well than simply following the ethical rules that we could expect any normal human to understand and comply with. A person might avoid committing murder, theft or assault his whole life, and even provide a "reasonable" amount of charity and assistance to others, while still leading a life that was desultory, crass and shallow. Virtue ethics draws attention to the aspiration to be a better person, who holds herself to a higher ethical standard than others, and to the value of taste, grace and style in human life.[4]

If Confucianism is a form of virtue ethics, then the concepts, issues and insights from Western virtue ethics may help us to understand it better. But do the benefits flow in the other direction as well? Can Confucianism contribute something of value to contemporary virtue ethics, or is it of purely historical interest? The present volume is a testament to just some of the ways in which Confucianism can improve our understanding in each of the four areas of virtue ethics that I identified: flourishing, the virtues, human nature and ethical cultivation.[5] In addition, I am at work on a long-term project of developing a contemporary form of virtue ethics that synthesizes Aristotelianism with elements of other systems of thought, including Confucianism, Daoism and Buddhism. In this paper, I would like to sketch a part of this project: what Confucianism (and to some extent Daoism) has to contribute to contemporary discussions of human flourishing.[6]

Let me begin with a few caveats lector. Confucianism has a history going back 2,500 years. It is a common misconception that Confucianism is a monolithic movement. In reality, Confucianism (like every great philosophical tradition) is extremely diverse and has evolved considerably during its history. "Daoism" is even more problematic. For the purposes of this paper I am particularly interested in the views of Zhuangzi. But the term "Daoism" was unknown to him; this was a retrospective classification by Chinese historians who grouped him together with other thinkers for their own purposes. Finally, we can quibble about when, precisely, Western virtue ethics started, but it is surely well over two millennia old itself. Even if we limit our discussion to virtue ethicians influenced by Aristotle, we find considerable diversity in the views of, say, Aquinas, Alasdair MacIntyre and Martha Nussbaum. (Furthermore, Michael Slote (2010a) has drawn our attention to the value of the sentimentalist approach to the virtues, which stems from figures like Hume.) In a brief paper like this, I have to oversimplify and gloss over many complexities. So I am aware, and I ask you to bear in mind, that I am giving just a sketch of how certain Confucian and Daoist elements can contribute to our understanding of human flourishing.

"Flourishing" is a technical term in virtue ethics. The fact reflects, I think, the poverty of contemporary English as a language for discussing virtue ethics. As Stuart Hampshire laments, in English, "[e]ven the word 'virtue' itself now has an archaic and unnatural ring, sounding like a translation from Greek or Latin" (Hampshire 1983, 41). But it is important to see that, while the term "flourishing" does not come easily to us in ordinary language, there is nothing particularly esoteric or parochial about the general notion. To flourish is to "live well." Most of us at least understand the topic when someone talks about "living the good life." And, whatever philosophical position we pay lip-service to, we sometimes act as if we think some ways of life are worth living, while others are not. For instance, running is the exercise of a human capacity. But we agree that, if someone is unable to run, due to birth defect, illness or injury, she can still lead a "full" or "worthwhile" life. This can be seen as reflecting the assumption that the human capacities exercised in running, while important parts of being a human, are not the most important aspects of being a human. There are other activities (such as engaging in caring relationships with other people) that are of a much higher order.

The classic Western virtue ethicians identified flourishing lives in terms of the goods that they attempted to achieve. Several candidates for flourishing lives were rejected on the grounds that what they aimed at either were not genuine intrinsic goods, or were good, but not high-enough orders of good to be the focus of a flourishing life. For example, Aristotle rejects as a candidate for flourishing a life dedicated solely to the pursuit of wealth, on the grounds that wealth is useful as a means to obtaining other goods, but has no intrinsic value. As Aquinas explains in more detail (1981, I–II, Q. 2, Art. 1), wealth consists of either financial instruments for purchasing things or physical goods such as food, clothing, etc. Both kinds of wealth are valuable only as instruments to obtain goods distinct from them. We value food because the body needs it for subsistence (or for the pleasure of taste). We value financial instruments because of the things we can buy with them. Intrinsically, neither kind of wealth is valuable. Admittedly, some humans do act as if accumulating wealth is the goal of their lives. However, Aquinas's argument shows that those who act in such a way are guilty of an error in practical reasoning, because it is simply unintelligible to suggest that wealth, by itself, could be a "final end," or ultimate goal of action. (Notice that this illustrates the substantive practical implications of a virtue-ethics analysis.)

Bodily health is a somewhat different case. Aquinas acknowledges that health is a genuine good in itself. We are embodied creatures, after all, so having a healthy body is a very plausible candidate for an intrinsic good. However, Aquinas argues that there are much greater goods than having a healthy body (Aquinas 1981, I–II, Q. 2, Art. 5). To illustrate Aquinas's point, suppose that you were offered a drug that would give you perfect health throughout your life, and a longer lifespan to boot. The only side-effect of the drug is that it causes brain damage that would effectively cost you 20 IQ points. Since you – *mon semblable, mon frère* – were motivated to peruse the present volume, you probably could lose at least 20 IQ points and still be of at least average intelligence. However, I imagine that few, if any, of my readers would take the drug. If I am right about this, it supports the Thomistic intuition that bodily health (which is the "virtue" of our physical body), while good, is not as high an order of good as exercising the intellectual virtues.[7] Similar lines of argument to those used regarding wealth and bodily health are used by Aristotle and Aquinas to reject fame, social prestige, power and physical pleasure as candidates for the primary goods achieved in flourishing lives. Confucians show remarkable agreement with Aristotelians in evaluating these goods. So, for example, Confucius stated,

> Wealth and social eminence are things that all people desire, and yet unless they are acquired in the proper way I will not abide them. Poverty and disgrace are things that all people hate, and yet unless they are avoided in the proper way I will not despise them.
>
> (*Analects* 4.5; Confucius 2003)

But even if we know what a flourishing life is *not*, we still want to know what it *is*. Participation in political activity seems to be suggested as the highest good by Aristotle in Book I of the *Nicomachean Ethics* and by Cicero in *The Dream of Scipio*. Plato suggests that theoretical contemplation is the highest good, as does Aristotle in Book X, Chapter 7 of the *Nicomachean Ethics*. In his *Summa Theologiae*, Thomas Aquinas argues that the highest good is contemplating God (Aquinas 1981, I–II, Q. 3, Art. 8).

It is perhaps worth reminding you here of my earlier caveat. I am aware that there are interpretations of Plato that make his views closer to those of Aristotle, and there are ways of reading Aristotle that attempt to reconcile the theoretical and practical strands in the *Nicomachean Ethics*.[8] But here I am just trying to survey some candidates for flourishing that have been advanced in the Western tradition. So among the major classic Western candidates for human flourishing are the life of political activity aimed at the good of the community, the life of accumulating theoretical knowledge and the life of contemplating God. Incidentally, I find an interesting parallelism here with the three major spiritual disciplines of the *Bhagavad Gita*: the discipline of action (*karma yoga*), the discipline of knowledge (*jnana yoga*) and the discipline of devotion (*bhakti yoga*).

There are at least three significant limitations of the accounts of flourishing lives that we have inherited. First, there are ways of life that many of us today would regard as fully flourishing that do not appear on the traditional list. Part of the project of this paper will be an effort to propose additional categories of flourishing lives. However, even after we have expanded the list, we may have the following concern: how do we know that we have an exhaustive list of the plausible candidates for human flourishing? I think that determining what the flourishing lives are is something that we cannot do either a priori or onceand for all. Recognizing what has intrinsic value requires individual experience, cultural growth and sympathetic imagination. This is why Aquinas has a more developed and nuanced list of goods than did Aristotle, and why we can have a more developed and nuanced list than did Aquinas. So, developing a rich conception of human flourishing is to a great extent an a posteriori task. This is one of the reasons why studying other traditions of the virtues, such as that found in Confucianism, can enrich our understanding of flourishing. A third limitation of the traditional lists of flourishing lives is that each is monistic. By this I mean that each (at least on a standard interpretation of the relevant philosophers) argues for one particular way of life as the best or most flourishing. For example, Aquinas regards the lives of theoretical contemplation and political activity aimed at the good of the community as second best to that of contemplation of God. What I shall propose here, in contrast, is a pluralistic conception of human flourishing. I submit that there are multiple ways for humans to flourish, and that each is, at least potentially, of equal value.[9]

Let us now turn to the question of what is missing from Aristotle's and Aquinas's lists. Consider the following individuals. (i) Bobby is a grandmaster at chess. He was a child prodigy who, at the age of 14, became the top player in the US. As a young adult, he is poised to be the next world chess champion. Bobby's skill at chess awes those capable of appreciating it. (ii) While Bobby is skilled at chess, Miles is a talented jazz musician. Through a combination of innate talent and training, Miles has reached a stage at which he can improvise complex and beautiful music. (iii) Whereas Miles is an artist, G.E. is a connoisseur of art. Through his own experience and the guidance of others, G.E. has developed a superb taste in judging painting and sculpture. He enjoys not only viewing art, but also discussing art. In these discussions, G.E. seeks to refine his own sensibility through comparing his opinions with those of others. (iv) Ozzie is a dedicated family man. He is very active in his children's lives in a way that is loving but not indulgent, and nurturing but not overweening. He enjoys spending time with and engaging in recreational activities with his spouse and children. (v) Ozzie found satisfaction in his family, but James rebelled against the lifestyle of his family of origin, including their religious and political beliefs. James has forged his own individual style, which is evident in his clothes, his opinions, his career choice and many other aspects of his life.

We would, I think, be chary of making an overall evaluation of Bobby, Miles, G.E., Ozzie and James as people, or even an evaluation of their ways of life. We don't know enough about them, yet. However, I think we have the intuition that there is something admirable and "choice worthy" about their ways of life, at least given what we know. Bobby's life manifests skill at a challenging activity. Miles has a life that includes the good of skillful artistic performance. G.E.'s life has the good of artistic appreciation. Ozzie's life has loving relationships with other humans. James has freely created his own life. But in each case, it is not immediately obvious how Aristotle or Aquinas (at least) could do justice to our intuition that this life has something admirable and choice worthy in it.

What I think these examples illustrate is that classic Aristotelians have failed to fully appreciate engaging in skillful activities, artistic creation and appreciation, being in loving relationships with other humans and freely creating one's own life. I want to stress that I am only claiming that those who follow Aristotle have "failed to *fully* appreciate" these goods. Aristotelians do have something to say about each of these activities. In addition, more recent philosophers (some virtue ethicians and some not) have had helpful things to say about each of the kinds of activities that I want to identify as flourishing. For example, the "ethics of care" of Nel Noddings (2003), Carol Gilligan (1993) and others has emphasized the ethical importance of loving human relationships.[10] However, I want to suggest that the goods of artistic creation and appreciation, being in loving relationships, engaging in skillful activities and freely choosing one's own life have, at the least, been underemphasized in the Aristotelian tradition. Furthermore, we are in need of, and can supply, more nuanced accounts of each of these goods. Classical Confucians and Daoists offer rich resources for starting to supply what is missing in several of these areas. I'll say a little bit about each.

Skill

Aristotle has a nuanced discussion of skill in relation to virtue. To put it in its most stark terms, skill must be distinguished from virtue, since a skill may be used in the service of evil as well as good, whereas a genuine virtue can be used only for good. This leaves skill as something that has merely instrumental value (*Nicomachean Ethics* 6.4–5). In contrast, one of the most famous stories in the "Daoist" classic, the *Zhuangzi*, is about a butcher whose skillful dismembering of an ox carcass amazes a ruler. When questioned, the butcher explains, "What your servant values is the Way, which goes beyond technique" (Zhuangzi 2005, 225). In other words, the butcher does not merely have a rote knack for cutting up oxen. Rather, through years of intensive practice, the butcher has learned to follow the "Heavenly patterns" of the ligaments, tendons and joints of the ox's carcass. This kind of practice is remarkably effective, which occasioned the ruler's initial praise. But Zhuangzi holds up the butcher's skill as an activity which is not just efficacious, but also valuable in itself. How so? Zen Buddhism, deeply influenced by Zhuangzian Daoism, endorsed skillful activity as a way of overcoming the dichotomy between oneself and the rest of the world. To the extent that we focus on being responsive to something external to ourselves, we overcome self-centeredness. In addition, there is an underlying intuition that bringing one's actions into alignment with the complex and ever-changing "patterns" of the world manifests intrinsic beauty and nobility. Hence, archery, calligraphy, the martial arts, painting, swordsmanship and flower arrangement all came to be seen as activities that could be stimuli to and manifestations of virtue.

Our contemporary Western attitudes toward skillful activities are complex. When we are outside the classroom and the conference hall, many of us admire the grace of a well-executed slam-dunk in basketball, or the powerful elegance of a triple axle in figure skating. And skill can also be manifested in more cerebral practices. A professional poker player has an impressive skill, as does a top rocket scientist. It is tempting to try to categorize these last two examples as instances of theoretical contemplation. But something like engineering a rocket is far too banausic a task to count as theoretical contemplation for Aristotle or Aquinas. Whether skill is primarily physical or mental, popular culture (to a greater or lesser degree) acknowledges its value. However, we intellectuals generally seem unwilling to grant that such skillful activities could be a significant component of a flourishing life.

But why? One concern is that, as Aristotle observes, a skill may be used for good or evil. Werner von Braun, perhaps the greatest rocket scientist ever, worked on the US Apollo program in the 1960s, and on the German V-2 program in the 1940s. (As comedian Mort Sahl mordantly joked, "He aimed at the moon, but often hit London.") Contrary to NASA propaganda, von Braun was happy to work for the Nazis, and even helped to orchestrate the transfer of slave labor to his underground rocket factories, where the infernal working conditions led to the deaths of approximately twenty workers a day.[11] In addition, even if a skill is not itself in the service of evil, we are painfully aware that those who are skillful in one area may still be quite bad people. Bobby Fisher, undoubtedly one of the greatest chess players who ever lived, ended his life as a ranting anti-Semitic conspiracy theorist. So perhaps we reject skillful activity as a component of flourishing because it does not have a necessary connection with living ethically.

However, the same could arguably be said of any one aspect of a flourishing life. Since I am a professor of philosophy, I obviously think that theoretical inquiry and contemplation can be part of a worthwhile life. However, we all know from personal experience of very good philosophers who are poor people overall. In general, thinking that a person has manifested some genuine good in their life does not commit us to thinking that their life is good overall. This raises a serious challenge to virtue ethics in general, though. For part of the appeal of the virtue ethics approach is that it typically attempts to show that "living well," in the sense of living a life that is worthwhile for the agent because of the goods that it realizes, is co-extensive with "living ethically." Von Braun did not live ethically, but didn't he live well? I think the Confucian and Buddhist traditions have something insightful to say on this topic too, but I shall have to reserve that for another occasion.[12]

So, if the Aristotelian tradition is correct, an astronomer or philosopher, a senator or dean, a monk or nun – all could be living flourishing lives (of theoretical contemplation, political activity or religious devotion). But if the Daoists are right, we can broaden our vision of flourishing to include lives of skillful activity, such as those of a chessmaster, basketball player, engineer, actor or poker player.

Art

Considering the value of skill leads naturally into a discussion of skill at artistic performance and production. Indeed, the exercise of artistic skill is arguably just a special case of skillfulness in general. However, it is common in the West, and to a lesser extent in China, to treat artistic production as a special category, so I shall do that here. Painting, sculpting, composing music and writing works of imaginative literature are all very valuable activities, and living well could consist, at least in large part, of engaging in these or other sorts of artistic production. Aristotle, of course, would regard each of these as a kind of *poiêsis*, "production." In *Nicomachean Ethics* 6.4, Aristotle distinguishes *poiêsis* from *praxis*, "production" from "action." "Production" is an activity that is instrumental to something distinct from itself, while "action" is a constitutive means. So manufacturing a wrench or sculpting a statue is mere "production," since it is valuable only as a means to *producing* some distinct good, while moving a piece on the chessboard is partially constitutive of the *action* of playing chess. Consequently, in Aristotle's view it follows almost by definition that producing works of art cannot be part of living well. This fails to capture, though, the intuition that we, at least, have that activities like painting and writing poetry are valuable.

Confucians have had great respect for artistic production and appreciation, particularly in calligraphy, painting, music and poetic composition. In later Confucianism, appreciation of art often merges with a "Daoist" reverence for the ethical value of skillful activity. The character Lin Daiyu, in the classic novel *Dream of the Red Chamber*, expresses a very common Chinese view about playing the *Qin* (a sort of zither). She says, "I realized that playing the Qin is a form of meditation and spiritual discipline handed down to us from the ancients. ... The essence of the Qin is restraint. It was created in ancient times to help man purify himself and lead a gentle and sober life, to quell all wayward passions and to curb every riotous impulse. ... [When you play, your] Soul may now commune with the Divine, and enter into that mysterious Union with the Way" (Cao 1982, 152, 154). We see here a view similar to the one that we found in Zhuangzi's story of the skillful butcher. These activities are valuable both for the virtues that they express and reinforce (such as selfless restraint) and also because of how they bring the individual into alignment with something greater than herself. (We do not have the space here to discuss the value of the artistic product itself, except to note that it adds another dimension to the value of the productive activity.) If we find something plausible in this view of artistic activity, we can explain why we are inclined to feel that an artistic life – like that of Miles, our hypothetical jazz musician – can be a life worth living.

Appreciation

From skill in general we moved to consider artistic skill, and from skill in artistic production and performance we move naturally to a consideration of artistic appreciation. Confucians have been artistic connoisseurs from the beginning. Kongzi, commenting on a particular performance of a piece of classical music, sighed, "I never imagined that music could be so sublime" (*Analects* 7.14; Confucius 2003). Confucians believe that artistic appreciation has a morally edifying effect, because fine works of art "teach" our emotions. Thus, Kongzi observed of a particular ode that it "expresses joy without becoming licentious, and expresses sorrow without falling into excessive pathos" (3.20; Confucius 2003). Of course, the notion that appreciating works of art has ethical value is not unheard of in the West. Aristotle connects tragedy to the training of the emotions through the concept of catharsis. And in *Principia Ethica* G.E. Moore singles out a person appreciating a work of beauty as one of the "organic wholes" that has significant intrinsic goodness. The Confucian aesthetic is distinctive, though, in that it combines a view of art as edifying with an appreciation for a wide range of artistic products, including poetry, painting, calligraphy, music, sculpture and ceramics.

Love

What about Ozzie, our hypothetical family man? Clearly, both Aristotle and Aquinas have places in their systems for friendship and love. Books 8 and 9 of the

Nicomachean Ethics are devoted to friendship, and love is, for Aquinas, the fundamental motive force of the universe, at the ethical, biological and cosmological levels. However, consider the following list of personal relationships, adopted and adapted from an ancient Confucian list: the relationship between parents and children, between siblings, between supervisors and subordinates, between romantic partners and between social equals who are friends. The Confucian view is that participating in each of these relationships is partially constitutive of living well. It is not clear that Aristotle and Aquinas fully do justice to these relationships. For example, Aquinas attributes a significant value to celibacy. It is important to keep in mind that this does not make familial life or sexuality "bad"; celibacy is a "calling" and not an ethical requirement. However, it has for Thomists an ethical value that would be unintelligible to Confucians. (Indeed, Confucians were harsh critics of Buddhists who advocated celibacy, charging that this practice was both unnatural and ultimately selfish, since it broke one of the bonds that tied the individual to the larger human community.)

Aristotle does not share Aquinas's view on celibacy. However, for Aristotle the household (including wife, children and servants) is simply a means to producing and supporting individuals who can pursue genuine goods such as communal political activity and theoretical contemplation. Confucians see an intrinsic value in the familial relationships that Aristotle would relegate to the instrumentally valuable. This is not, I think, a trivial point. I have often asked colleagues, including ones who were friendly to virtue ethics, to tell me what aspects of their lives they thought made their lives worth living. They typically mention their research, the distinctive satisfaction of writing books and articles and the joy of an intelligent philosophical discussion. A few will add, "Oh yes, and teaching students too." I follow up by asking something like, "What role do your partner and children have in your life?" They are often taken off-guard by this question. Because we have been raised to think in Aristotelian terms, the life of the mind has assumed an almost hegemonic role in our conception of human flourishing. I think that we should at least take seriously the possibility that a person with limited intellectual interests but a healthy and happy family life might just be living as well as a lonely but successful academic.

Freedom

So far I have focused on differences between the Aristotelian and Confucian conceptions of flourishing. But they share a common blindness. Stuart Hampshire remarked that, despite the immense power of Aristotle's moral view, "the barrier of modernity" has "the effect of making Aristotle's reconstruction of moral, and particularly of political, thought seem incorrigibly incomplete. The succinct phrase for the barrier, and for the missing element, is the concept of freedom." (1983, 43) Hampshire might have made the same observation regarding Confucian morality, for neither in Confucianism nor in Aristotelianism is freedom, in the distinctively modern sense, a key notion. Of course, it is not at all clear what "the distinctively modern sense" of freedom is. However, we typically have the intuition that it is good for people to be able to make significant choices about things ranging from the style of their hair to their job and their religion. In addition, while we frequently disagree over what it is to make a free or an "authentic" choice, we approve of people's doing so.[13] So the challenge of incorporating freedom into their conceptions of flourishing is something that both Confucians and Aristotelians have to face. But I think that there is nothing in principle that prevents them from answering this challenge.

In summary, there are at least four areas in which the Aristotelian conception of human flourishing could helpfully be expanded: to include (i) the life of skillful activity; (ii) the life of artistic performance and creation; (iii) the life of aesthetic appreciation; (iv) the life of loving interpersonal relationships; and (v) the life of free self-creation. On the first four of these, Confucians and Daoists offer deep insights that we have yet to learn from.

6 Virtue Ethics and Confucianism

A Methodological Reflection[1]

Liu Liangjian

Introduction

Nowadays in both the Chinese- and English-speaking worlds, it is not strange at all to put virtue ethics and Confucianism together. As a matter of fact, *Virtue Ethics and Confucianism* is the title of volume in which this chapter is included. But how does the particle word "and" function here? Does it indicate a parallel, equal and static relationship between virtue ethics and Confucianism, or something else? The question is not so trivial as it seems at first glance, since it really leads to a methodological reflection.

Following the revival of virtue ethics in the West, more and more scholars with a background in Chinese philosophy have started to focus on the relationship between Confucianism and virtue ethics. Representatives of this trend include scholars born and raised in the West, like May Sim and Bryan W. Van Norden (see Sim 2007, Van Norden 2007), and those born and raised in China, like Yu Jiyuan (see Yu Jiyuan 2007). In the complex development of Western thought, the ethics of Aristotle could stand as the paragon of virtue ethics. The Confucian ethical doctrine presents some similar tendencies of thought to the ethics of Aristotle. In the Wittgenstinnian sense of family resemblance (*Familienähnlichkeiten*), there is no harm in saying that we have a Confucian virtue ethics which is similar to Aristotelian virtue ethics. Because of this, the comparative study of Confucianism and Western (specifically Aristotelian) virtue ethics is of course meaningful work.

In making the comparison, scholars usually adopt the approach of studying Confucianism from the perspective of virtue ethics. Their intention is to use the new perspective of virtue ethics to reevaluate Confucian ethics or, rather, "to discover" the implied meaning of virtue ethics in Confucianism, and the construction of Confucian virtue ethics comes only subsequently. However, in this way Confucian virtue ethics remains nothing more than a negative image of Confucianism in the mirror of virtue ethics. "Negative" here means: it doesn't obstruct the mirror from being a mirror, even though there is no image, and the mirror remains absolutely as itself, without any change, when some image comes into being. This is an unfortunate truth. The misfortune here lies both in the misfortune that has been allotted to Confucianism in the dependent position that it has been forced to occupy in the East–West conversation; and also in the unfortunate lot of virtue ethics, which it has allotted to itself by throwing away the opportunity to seek its own reflection in the other, while upholding the haughty air that it has cultivated during several centuries of intercultural communication dominated by the West. "Comparison" as a methodology is by no means satisfying, since it easily leads to a so-called objective and detached observation of objects compared—for instance, virtue ethics and Confucianism—so as to discover their similarities and/or differences. Once there is an announced or tacit ranking between objects compared, a comparative study will be too enthusiastic to subordinate the lower-ranked object to the higher. In a glocal age, it is necessary for us to move from comparison to dialogue. In the remaining sections, I shall carry out two case studies to demonstrate how fruitful the interaction-dialogue of Eastern and Western thought could be in Confucian virtue ethics: first, the relationship between "virtue" and "*meide*"; second, the use of Confucianism to respond to Peter Singer's Critique of Aristotelian virtue ethics (Singer 2010), especially focusing on the Is-Ought issue concerning human nature. To finish, I will return to the particle "and" connecting virtue ethics and Confucianism.

Virtue and *Meide*: Comparison and Dialogue

Firstly, let's just take "virtue" and its usual Chinese counterpart "*meide*" as an example.[2] "Virtue" is doubtless a key word for thought concerning virtue ethics. In 1958, Anscombe presented her thesis "Modern Moral Philosophy," in which she stated: "Eventually it might be possible to advance to considering the concept 'virtue;' with which, I suppose, we should be beginning some sort of a study of ethics"(Anscombe 1958: 15). That "study of ethics" which she advocated was pushed even further by scholars like MacIntyre, who catalyzed the revitalization of contemporary virtue ethics. Following this development back to what Anscombe originally meant, we see that the conceptual analysis of "virtue" in the end provides the true starting-point of virtue ethics. If this is indeed the case, then Confucian virtue ethics must begin not only with a conceptual analysis of "virtue," but also with that of "*meide*." We cannot but undertake a conceptual investigation that crosses linguistic and cultural boundaries, and such a conceptual investigation itself is a study of both comparison and dialogue.

In Western languages, "virtue" is roughly equivalent to the ancient Greek word "ἀρετή," In Aristotle, "ἀρετη" is used in the narrow sense in the domain of morals, but in the broad sense it is not so limited. For instance, when Aristotle discusses "ἀρετη" in *Nicomachean Ethics*, he speaks of the "ἀρετη" of horses, the "ἀρετη" of eyes, and of course the "ἀρετη" of human beings; but aside from the moral domain, the "ἀρετη" of human beings also concerns the domain of skills that includes running and wrestling (See Aristotle 1926: 1106 a15–20). In ancient Chinese, "*de*" (德) is also used in similar ways. Broadly speaking, "(*de* 德) means to acquire (*de* 得)"(*Guanzi*, Chapter 36; in Li Xiangfeng 2004: 770). *De* (德) is any one of those things which is acquired from nature. For human beings, *de* is not limited to moral qualities. In general, even one's physical shape and physiognomy fall under the scope of *de*. For example, *Zhuangzi* states, "I am tall and large, elegant and handsome, and all those who see me are pleased with me—this is a *de* acquired from my parents" (*Zhuangzi*, Chapter 29; in Guo Qingfan 2004: 994). Even with regard to moral qualities, *de* is a neutral concept, that is, it doesn't necessarily contain positive value: *The Book of History* considers harmony and compliance as good *de*, and resentment and revulsion as ominous *de* (see *The Book of History*, Chapter 20; in Kong Anguo and Kong Yingda 1999: 455–466). This certainly differs from Aristotle's conception of virtue. In Aristotle, "ἀρετη" is almost always used in combination with "ἀγαθός" (good), "κάλος" (excellent), "καλῶς" (excellently) and other such entirely positive terms. For example, Aristotle claims that the good of man (τὸ ἀνθρώπινον ἀγαθόν) means that the soul has excellently (καλῶς) completed its actualization and activities in accordance with logos or its actualization in accordance with virtue (κατ' ἀρετήν) (Aristotle 1926: 1098a 15–20). There is nothing to stop us from saying, then, that what the ancient Greeks meant by *virtue* (ἀρετη) is what ancient Chinese designated as good-*de* (*shande*) or what modern Chinese call beautiful-*de* (*meide*). In this sense, "virtue" could be translated into modern Chinese as "*meide*," and hence there may be such a thing as "Confucian *virtue* ethics," which shows that there are some good grounds for comparison and, further, dialogue between virtue ethics and Confucianism.

There is something interesting in the evolution of the Chinese language from ancient "*shande*" to modern "*meide*." In modern Chinese, when "*de*" is used as a semantic particle to compose compound words, it generally connotes appraisal. For example, "*niangao-deshao*" is a compound meaning "of venerable age and exemplary virtue"; the compound word "*quede*" ("lacking de") is depreciatory and is used to reprimand; "*dexing*" (德性) ("virtuous character") and "*dexing*" (德行)(virtuous conduct) are sarcastic rhetorical devises ("Just look at how virtuous your conduct is!" "Oh, what a virtuous character you have!"). Thus, the modern Chinese compound word *meide* and the ancient Chinese word *shande* are not completely identical in terms of the way they are constructed: the *shan* in *shande* is used to modify and qualify a neutral *de*, whereas the *mei* in *meide* is used to accentuate and emphasize an already praiseworthy *de*.

Besides the difference between *shande* and *meide*, what is particularly worth attention is the following: from the perspective of Confucianism, virtue (*de* or *meide*) is always the unity of the internal nature of character and external behavior, that is, the unity of *dexing* (virtuous character) and *dexing* (virtuous conduct). "Virtuous conduct" emphasizes behaving (*xing* 行), while virtuous character emphasizes the nature of the human being (*xing*). Just as Chen Lai notes, within traditional ancient Chinese culture, the word *de* incorporates both meanings.[3] Etymologically speaking, it seems that *de* by itself already contains both meanings, insofar as the character *de* is constructed out of the radical *xin*, which adds the meaning of "the heart or the sensitive mind" and the radical *xing*, which adds the meaning of "to act/to carry out/action oriented." Normative ethics in the history of Western philosophy (including utilitarianism and Kantian ethics) is act based, and hence mainly theorizes on the action-oriented *de* (*dexing* 德行), while Aristotle's virtue ethics is agent based, and hence mainly theorizes on the virtue of human character (*dexing* 德性). Comparatively speaking, although the ultimate concern of Confucian virtue ethics is likewise happiness, together with the achievement of virtuous nature, it also explores to great depth the action-oriented *de* (德行), and so it could be said to surpass Aristotle in richness.[4] On the question of the behavioral dimension of *de*, Confucians have tended to focus on the motive of behavior and the intrinsic value of rules (rules in the form of ritual (*li*) or Principle (*li*)): Pre-Qin Confucianism stresses ritual, Neo-Confucianism stresses Principle, while Qing Dynasty thinkers such as Ling Tingkan, Ruan Yuan and Sun Xingyan advocated replacing Principle with ritual.[5] Moreover, the distinction between the virtue of human nature (德性) and the virtue of human behavior (德行) is one of the most important components of Confucian virtue ethics; the themes surrounding this distinction include: the cultivation of virtuous behavior and a virtuous human nature; the verification of virtuous behavior and a virtuous human nature; the controlling of virtuous behavior by the moral sensitivity of human nature; virtuous character, virtuous behavior, and rules and so forth (Yang Guorong 2009a: 146–181; Yang Guorong 2009b: Appendix II "Confucianism and Virtue Ethics"). These themes may conceal within Confucian virtue ethics the possibility of a reverse impact upon virtue ethics. In the following, we will examine another possible reverse impact through discussing whether it is possible to ground virtue ethics in a Confucian theory of human nature.

Peter Singer's Critique of Virtue Ethics and A Confucian Response

Peter Singer's Critique of Aristotle's Virtue Ethics

The entry for "ethics," written by Peter Singer in *Encyclopedia Britannica*, summarizes Aristotle's virtue ethics as follows:

> Aristotle conceived of the universe as a hierarchy in which everything has a function. The highest form of existence is the life of the rational being, and the function of lower beings is to serve this form of life. … From this perspective also came a view of human nature and an ethical theory derived from it. All living things, Aristotle held, have inherent potentialities, which it is their nature to develop. This is the form of life properly suited to them and constitutes their goal. What, however, is the potentiality of human beings? For Aristotle this question turns out to be equivalent to asking what is distinctive about human beings; and this, of course, is the capacity to reason. The ultimate goal of humans, therefore, is to develop their reasoning powers. When they do this, they are living well, in accordance with their true nature, and they will find this the most rewarding existence possible.
>
> (Singer 2010)

Peter Singer then points out some fallacies in Aristotle. This is one of the most serious ones:

> A broader and still more pervasive fallacy underlies Aristotle's ethics. It is the idea that an investigation of human nature can reveal what one ought to do. For Aristotle, an examination of a knife would reveal that its distinctive capacity is to cut, and from this one could conclude that a good knife is a knife that

cuts well. In the same way, an examination of human nature should reveal the distinctive capacity of human beings, and from this one should be able to infer what it is to be a good human being. This line of thought makes sense if one thinks, as Aristotle did, that the universe as a whole has a purpose and that human beings exist as part of such a goal-directed scheme of things, but its error becomes glaring if this view is rejected and human existence is seen as the result of a blind process of evolution. Whereas the distinctive capacity of a knife is a result of the fact that knives are made for a specific purpose—and a good knife is thus one that fulfills this purpose well—human beings, according to modern biology, were not made with any particular purpose in mind. Their nature is the result of random forces of natural selection. Thus, human nature cannot, without further moral premises, determine how human beings ought to live.

(Singer 2010)

According to Singer, since human nature is the result of random forces and natural selection, it is a fallacy to infer what human beings ought to be from what human nature is, whereas Aristotle does ground his ethics upon what human nature is. This touches upon a fundamental problem: can a theory of human nature lay the foundation for Aristotle's ethics or any virtue ethics in general? Singer's reply is distinctly negative.

The Is-Ought Problem Concerning Human Nature

However, Singer's argument is debatable. First, while the blindness of evolution and the randomness of natural selection may serve as proof of the purposelessness of human nature in its origin, it still cannot show us what human nature is, which is precisely the problem. Discerning where human nature comes from constitutes one problem, while discerning what human nature is constitutes another. If we were to replace the question concerning what human nature is with the question concerning the origins of human nature, we would commit the "genetic fallacy." Furthermore, to infer how humans ought to be from what human nature is would involve a particular form of inference from Is to Ought. Could such an inference hold validity? Let us take a closer look at this Is-Ought problem concerning human nature.

The Is-Ought problem can certainly be traced back to David Hume. From the perspective of Confucianism, to distinguish between "Is" and "Ought" corresponds to separating "knowing" from "acting." In his *Treatise of Human Nature*, Hume distinguishes "Is" and "Ought" based on the principle that reason has no impact upon morality and, moreover, that knowledge cannot engender action: we come to know "what is" through reasoning, but reason alone cannot influence action, which in actuality does not correspond to "what is" but, rather, to "what ought to be"; thus, directly deducing "Ought" from "Is" involves an illogical leap. In other words, "it is necessary that it should be observed and explained" if we were to make such a deduction (Hume 1978: 469). Although Hume reminds us of the gap between "Is" and "Ought," he certainly doesn't hold it to be an absolute abyss, since he claims that it is emotion that connects "Is" to "Ought", knowing to action (Hume 1978: 457).

However, the important question here is not whether or not the gap between "Is" and "Ought" can be bridged. Rather, it is the following questions which matter: Does this gap really exist? If so, in which cases does it exist? Does it exist everywhere and always? Anscombe's discussion of the transition from "is" to "need" in "Modern Moral Philosophy" may shed some light on these questions. She claims that, in most cases, *that* such-and-such "ought to be" or "is needed" has no direct influence upon actions. "In the case of a *plant*, let us say, the inference from 'is' to 'needs' is certainly not in the least dubious." "Certainly in the case of what the plant needs, the thought of a need will only affect action if you want the plant to flourish." In other words, "needs" here still works on the level of knowing, and thus does not bear directly upon action without the intervention of the middle term "wanting." Let us proceed: "But there is some sort of necessary connection between what you think you need, and what you want." In other words, knowing what you need is a special kind of knowing, since it inevitably induces wanting and consequently leads to action (see Anscombe 1958: 6–8; emphasis added).

The Direct Connection between "Is" and "Ought" Concerning Human Nature: A Confucian Perspective

We can easily find in Confucianism many cases wherein the growing of a plant is used as a metaphor for human nature.[6] Mencius is wellknown for his doctrine of the FourSprouts (*siduan*).[7] The Chinese character 端 (*duan*) was originally written as 耑. According to Xu Shen, "'耑' describes the sprout of plants, the upper part [of the character] resembles the shape of something growing and the nether part the shape of the roots." Duan Yucai then explains further: "'耑' is an ancient character, which expresses the meaning of 'sprout.' Nowadays '端' is prevalent while '耑' has been abandoned" (see Duan Yucai 1997). Thus, for Confucianism, what human nature is is simultaneously what human nature needs and there is no gap between them. Furthermore, what human nature needs is what a person himself fundamentally needs, and thus knowing what one needs will inevitably engender wanting and, consequently, action. Human nature is, therefore, what human beings are in accordance with their nature; it is "that which is needed" or "what ought to be" according to their nature, and thus it is also the "ought to do" according to their nature. In this sense, nothing can bridge the gap in human nature between "Is" and "Ought" because there is no such gap.

Here, the kind of "knowing" which involves knowing "human nature" would not, properly speaking, be that of some representational object. As far as human nature is concerned, it would better to speak of "becoming aware of human nature [in his or her own]" (*mingxing*) rather than of "knowing human nature [as an object]" (*zhixing*). Chapter 21 of the *Zhongyong* states: "Given becoming sincere, there will be aware" (*cheng ze ming*). In his interpretation of this sentence, Wang Chuanshan, a great Confucian scholar in the 17th century, argues that becoming aware in this case involves not only knowing but also acting (Wang Chuanshan 1988b: 571); so it must be distinguished from the knowledge of representational objects. To become aware of human nature is to become self-aware, to understand "the being of the human being," i.e. that which the human being is. This kind of self-aware grasp of "that which the human being is" functions as a formal index according to which one can project one's existence into the world. "The being of the human being" becomes "that which the human being ought to be" and, consequently, influences how one conducts oneself in the world (see Chen Yun 2003). Because of this, to become aware of human nature is precisely to obtain consciousness of one's own being, to grasp the active forces of one's own being, and hence even to initiate the process of one's own being. In other words, becoming aware of human nature becomes the way in which human nature unfolds.

The continuity between Is and Ought on the level of human nature is based on the following ontological fact: human nature becoming aware of itself impacts on human nature to such a degree that human nature can no longer be understood as something ready made. Here, we must take notice of the complicated relationship between virtue as human behavior and virtue as human nature, which we have discussed above. Virtuous deeds are the external verification of virtuous character, but, at the same time, virtuous deeds have a reverse impact upon the character or nature of the human being (that which the human being is). The Is–Ought relationship could then be restated thus: "Is" engenders "Ought," and "Ought" correspondingly reacts back upon "Is." Because of this, the communication between Is and Ought is no longer characterized by one dimension—the flow from "Is" to "Ought"; rather, it has two dimensions in reciprocal interaction. On this basis, human nature unfolds as a continuous process of becoming. In Wang Chuanshan's words: "Human nature is in growth; [it] grows daily and is daily achieving something" (Wang Chuanshan 1988a: 300; also see Liu Liangjian 2007).

In modern Chinese, "*xing*" usually serves as a translation term for "nature" and "essence" and is understood to express the meaning of these terms, because it is supposed to translate them. It is thus understood to be the unchanging substance which lies behind phenomena and causes phenomena to appear. The English-speaking world thus usually understands *xing* in traditional Chinese writings to express the sense of "nature" or "essence." "Nature" derives from the Latin word "nascor," which means "I am born." Because of this, English speakers usually understand "nature" as something innate and given by birth. However, as A. C. Graham has already observed, when early Chinese thinkers spoke of "*xing*," they very rarely thought of some intrinsic, unchanging nature that things gain at the very moment of their birth, unless they were thinking of non-living things like water; it was precisely the opposite case for them. That which they were concerned with was the unfolding development of things: things naturally are the way they are, and they adequately actualize their potentials solely in conditions where they are not suffering injury and are sufficiently nourished. This is especially so for Mencius, who seems to have never even cast his sight back upon the moment of birth; he was always looking ahead at the mature state that continuous growth brings about (see Graham 1990: 8). A. C. Graham noticed the processual and generative meaning which *xing* had during the pre-Qin period (also see Fu Sinian 2006). In some sense, Wang Chuanshan's concept of *xing* as human nature growing daily and maturing daily is precisely a return to this pre-Qin tradition.

Human nature is growing daily and maturing daily, and thus human nature is neither readymade nor determined at the moment of birth; it is not "fully formed at the moment it is received and unchanging up to the moment of death" (Wang Chuanshan 1998b: 750–751). On the contrary, it has not yet become something, but it is becoming and pending completion. Human nature is not complete, it is to complete itself; it depends upon the human being himself to go out and complete it. In the affair of achieving one's own nature, a human's nature is always completing itself and incomplete; it is in an imperfect process of perfecting itself at every moment, intensely cautious, as though walking along the edge of an abyss or treading on thin ice; it can be spoken of as finished only after death. Recorded in *The Book of Rites* there is a situation that became the canonical case of Confucian *meide* ethics: on the brink of death, Zengzi rose to his feet and changed beds out of the desire to die in perfect observation of ritual propriety (see Zheng Xuan and Kong Yingda 1999: 186–187). A human being facing death at the final hour still doesn't dare to slack off from upholding and cultivating human nature! So it is that kind of responsibility!? Confucian ethics expresses its own fundamental position via Zengzi: to perfect the human being or to refine virtue is the intrinsic demand of human nature. Because of this, we should say that, at least on the level of a formal index, human nature can determine how the human being ought to live. In this way, we also reply to the question inspired by Singer's critique of Aristotle's virtue ethics in the affirmative: A theory of human nature can lay the foundation of virtue ethics.

Concluding Remarks

At the beginning of this chapter we asked: what does the particle "and" imply when we say "virtue ethics and Confucianism?" From the perspective of a glocal philosophy, "and" here indicates a relationship which could be well expressed with a category explored by Wang Chuanshan, that is, *ji*. For Wang, a relationship of *ji* is dialectically characterized by, at the same time, identity or similarity (*xiangji*), difference (*fenji*) and interactivity (*jiaoji*) (see Liu Liangjian 2007, especially ch. 1). Through *ji* of virtue ethics and Confucianism, *Confucian virtue ethics*, according to its ideal form, it might make Confucianism and virtue ethics inspire one another, strengthen one another, and push both of these ethics of heterogeneous origin into a new development, and thereby benefit the becoming of a glocal philosophy.[8]

7 Confucian Ethics and Virtue Ethics Revisited

Wong Wai-ying

Preface

In 2001 I published "Confucian Ethics and Virtue Ethics,"[1] which, as its title implies, discusses the relevance of Confucian ethics to virtue ethics. The aim of that article is primarily to explain the characteristics and core concepts of Confucian ethics, rather than to define and categorize the Confucian ethical system.[2] Since then, discussions on virtue ethics as well as on the relationship between Chinese philosophy and virtue ethics have made considerable progress; however, to my disappointment, the understanding and interpretation of Confucian ethics expressed in these discussions have often been off the mark. This article is an attempt to explain and clarify further some of the biased and inaccurate interpretations. It shares the focus of the previous article, namely, that it is not to compare the system of Confucian ethics with the ethical systems of Kant, Aristotle, and Hume and then to discuss the appropriateness of categorizing Confucian ethics as Humean, Aristotelian or Kantian virtue ethics;[3] instead, it will concentrate on examining the position of Confucian ethics with regard to the features of virtue ethics, so as to reveal its character and significance. What I would like to emphasize is that Confucian ethics should not be limited by (certain types of) "virtue ethics," thereby depriving it of its richer connotation. In "The Moral and Non-Moral Virtues in Confucian Ethics,"[4] I argued that in Confucian ethics, non-moral virtue is independent of moral virtue, so the system of Confucian ethics is not confined to a narrow sense of moral system.[5] As will be shown below, this discovery is significant to the current issue.

Bryan W. Van Norden joined the debate on whether Confucianism is a kind of virtue ethics in his monograph on the early Chinese philosophy and virtue ethics.[6] Unlike other Western philosophers, he is aware that Confucianism is "different in many respects from the forms of virtue ethics that have been dominant in the West," even though he thinks that it counts as a form of virtue ethics.[7] In this article I will take Van Norden's discussion as an example to illustrate the central problems of the whole issue. In the present discussion I will restrict the scope of Confucian ethics to the thoughts of Confucius and of Mencius.

Flourishing Life

Virtue ethics as understood by Van Norden is an ethical system focusing on "what sort of person one should be, and what way of life one should live."[8] He lists four components of virtue ethics: first, an account of what a "flourishing" human life is like; second, an account of what virtues contribute to the leading of such a life; third, an account of how one acquires those virtues; and fourth, a philosophical anthropology that explains what humans are like, such that they can acquire those virtues so as to flourish in that kind of life.[9] Due to the constraint of length, in this article I will focus on the first two elements and touch on the others only when this is deemed necessary.

"Flourishing," as conceived by Van Norden, is a technical term in virtue ethics. It corresponds to Aristotle's "*eudaimonia*" in Greek and Aquinas' "*beatitudo*" in Latin. "To flourish is to live a certain kind of life: a life characterized by the ordered exercise of one's capacities as a human."[10] The term "ordered" indicates that some activities are considered to be more valuable, as compared with some others. In Confucianism, a human's various capacities can definitely be regarded as having different levels of importance in relation to the ultimate goal of cultivation, i.e. to become a sage (*chengsheng*). This view is manifested in Mencius' discussion on the distinction between the greater body (*da ti*) and the lesser body (*xiao ti*) (*Mencius*, 6A1), which highlights the slight difference between humans and beasts (*Mencius*, 4B28). A great person (*daren*) is one who always acts from his/her greater body and therefore lives a flourishing life. The greater body that Mencius refers to is the original heart-mind (*ben xin*), also known as the heart-mind of *ren* and *yi* (*ren yi zhi xin*). At this point, a problem arises: if *ren* and *yi* are understood merely as moral virtues and hence the original heart-mind denotes a moral capacity that enables one to observe these virtues, then flourishing life, which embodies the goal of Confucianism, is but a synonym of moral life, and a great person would merely be a moral person. If that were the case, then flourishing life as the core component of virtue ethics would not have taken up such centrality as it does in the system of Confucianism.

For Confucius, a "gentleman" (*junzi*, a person of noble character), striving to achieve the ultimate goal, has a significant status just less than that of a great person. A person is regarded as a gentleman only if he lives up to *ren* and *yi* (*Analects* 15.18; 17.24; 4.10; 4.16; 4.5; 12.4). In many chapters of the *Analects*, *ren* and *yi* have a moral connotation (such as *Analects* 6.28; 12.1; 12.2). Moreover, in the *Analects*, the notion of gentleman is not only explained in terms of *ren* and *yi*, but also involves a moral meaning (such as *Analects* 14.42; 13.25). Therefore it is natural to think that a gentleman is one who has great accomplishment in the moral realm. As discussed above, if *ren* and *yi* are nothing but moral virtues, then flourishing life is just the same as moral life. If that be the case, these are not what *ren* and *yi* are referred to in Confucianism, and hence Confucianism does not possess the core component of virtue ethics, and thus it is dubious to classify it as virtue ethics.

It is absolutely true that one of the multi-faceted meanings of *ren* and *yi* refers to moral virtues. Van Norden discerns that, for Confucius, the broad sense of *ren* refers to "the summation of human virtues," whereas its narrow sense refers to a specific virtue, namely, "loving others." Apparently *ren* is a virtue in any senses. He translates *ren* as "benevolence" with the following connotation: "to be benevolent is to be pained by the suffering of others and to take joy in the happiness of others," which is close to empathy.[11] Van Norden points out that this meaning of benevolence applies to Mencius.[12] In an article entitled "*Ren*, Empathy and the Agent-Relative Approach in Confucian Ethics,"[13] I argued at length that neither "loving others" nor empathy is the primary meaning of *ren*, rather, the capacity of "transference (with others)" (*gantong*) (which differs from empathy) is.[14] I also argued that only with the capacity of transference, which implies impartial evaluation (*yi*), is moral judgment of the good and the bad possible.

The problem of "what sort of person one should be, and what way of life one should live" is indeed a central issue for Confucianism; that is why there have been so many discussions on the "sage," the "great man," the "gentleman" and the "*cheng ren*," etc. Nevertheless, if the ideal personality is merely moral oriented, then flourishing life understood in terms of the ideal person would have to be very narrow. We have argued that *ren* and *yi*, which play a significant role in characterizing the ideal person, do not merely refer to moral virtues, as Van Norden sees it. Still, this cannot disprove the conclusion that flourishing life in Confucianism is limited to moral life, since, in our discussion so far, *ren* and *yi* in their primary meanings are wedded to morality.

Li as a Virtue Leading to the Flourishing Life

Van Norden views *li* as an important virtue, at least for Confucius, that contributes to leading the flourishing life. Although he is aware of the broad coverage of activities where *li* is involved, Van Norden believes that it is useful to think of *li* as "ritual."[15] Ritual, as Van Norden rightly sees it, is learned human activity that is regarded as sacred. He also explains that to regard something as sacred is to think that the proper attitude toward it is awe or reverence (*jing*).[16] In this regard, we can consider reverence as the spirit of the activity. For Confucius, the importance of ritual does not rest on the form of its performance but, rather, on the spirit that the ritual manifests. Apart from reverence, which is the common spirit of ritual, specific rituals manifest specific spirits. For example, mourning should manifest the feeling of grief, while making an offering should manifest respectfulness (to a certain object) (*Analects*, 3.4; 19.1). However, no matter what kind of spirit it manifests, a ritual should be presented from the heart-mind of *ren*. Thus Confucius said: "If a man is without *ren*, then of what use are the rites!" (*Analects* 3.3) He criticized Zaiwo's objection to the three-year period of mourning as opposed to *ren*, since the latter failed to consider the issue from the original heart-mind (*Analects* 17.21). Therefore, *li* has a deeper meaning than rituals: the former is grounded on the heart-mind of *ren* and *yi*, whereas the latter is not necessarily so. Only when the connection of rituals and the heart-mind is revealed can the value of *li* which goes beyond the form of rituals be discovered. *Ren* also provides *li* with a moral meaning. In this regard, the heart-mind of *ren* and *yi* is the criterion for the adjustment of rituals, and their forms will not be arbitrary (*Analects* 9.3). Now we can conclude that the difference between ritual and *li* lies in the awareness of *ren* as the latter's ground. *Li* in this sense can be regarded as an expression of the heart-mind of *ren* and *yi*, and since the urge of being expressed is rooted in the heart-mind, therefore *li* is also rooted in the heart-mind. Hence, *li* is considered by Mencius as one of the four elements of human nature.

Mencius also says that "the great man does not perform acts of *li* which are not truly in accord with *li*, nor acts of *yi* which are not truly in accord with *yi*" (*Mencius* 4B6). In the phrase "acts of *li* which are not truly in accord with *li*," the former "*li*" should be read as social norms or rituals in general and the latter "*li*" as the underlying spirits. If those spirits are essentially moral in sense, then it seems that all rituals are moral laden. Furthermore, if, in the passage quoted above (*Analects* 3.3), *ren* merely refers to a moral attribute, then flourishing life (of which *li* is a significant way of expression) is not only inseparable from morality, but is even stipulated by morality. If this is the case, then can Confucian ethics still be classified as virtue ethics?

Non-Moral Virtues for Good Life

In "The Moral and Non-Moral Virtue in Confucian Ethics," I argue that in Confucian ethics there is a domain of non-moral values which is independent of morality and is a constituent of good life. The character traits that can help one to accomplish non-moral values, which are called "admirable character traits" by Slote,[17] are non-moral virtues. In the *Analects* 14.13, Confucius thinks that "wisdom," "lacking desire," "bravery," and "(mastery of) the arts" are quintessential virtues for the all-rounded person (*cheng ren*). It is remarkable that none of these virtues is embedded with moral meaning, and they may be considered as non-moral virtues. Confucius goes on, mentioning that on top of these non-moral virtues, one should be "cultivated by means of rites and music." The rites and music mentioned here are not necessarily moral laden. In this passage, subsequent to the above discussion, it is added that "perhaps today we need not ask all this of the all-rounded person. One who, when he sees a chance of gain, stops to think whether to pursue it would be acting in accordance with *yi*; when he sees that one is in danger, is ready to lay down his life; when the fulfillment of an old promise is exacted, stands by what he said long ago." This second set of qualifications differs from the first set, in that the former is more moral oriented. Therefore we may boldly infer from this passage that non-moral virtues are more important than moral virtues, in order to be an all-rounded person.

There is no doubt that the virtues that Confucianism advocates include both moral and non-moral virtues. The question is: if the non-moral domain is defined by morality (for example, a non-moral act is, judged from a moral point of view, an act or choice that is neither morally right nor wrong), then the non-moral domain is only "a supplementary set" of the moral domain. Since the non-moral domain is determined by the moral point of view, therefore it loses its independence. We can query whether certain acts or choices should be guided by the moral mind (or moral principles) and are not able to be guided by non-moral principles. Another question emerges: what (principles) do we adopt when we decide that we "should" take the moral point of view, rather than the non-moral point of view, and vice versa? (This is related to the priority of moral values and non-moral values.) Here, "should" is not used in a moral sense, otherwise it would be question begging. Therefore, "should" must go beyond both the moral and the non-moral sense. From the text of the *Analects* and *Mencius*, it makes perfect sense to interpret "should" as referring to the appropriateness, "all things, including both the moral and non-moral points of view, considered."[18] This meaning of "should" is signified also by the notion of ren (e.g. Mencius, 7A46) and yi (e.g. Analects, 4.10 and Mencius 4B11). Remarkably, the ability to make judgment of appropriateness is not an ability separate from making moral judgment, but the former is exactly the same as the latter, namely, the heart-mind of ren and yi. The judgment of appropriateness, in which moral and non-moral values are considered and weighed against each other, is called ethical judgment.[19] Therefore, the heart-mind of ren and yi, understood as the ability to make ethical judgment, already includes the recognition of non-moral values, and the judgment sprung from it is not limited to the narrow sense of "moral ought." Thus we may call the mentioned prescription aiming at appropriateness "the ethical ought."

The distinction between moral and non-moral virtues is made merely for the sake of discussion. In an actual situation, when one makes an ethical judgment, he or she has already taken both the moral and non-moral values into consideration, and a Confucian would make an ethical judgment by the heart-mind of ren and yi. Both moral and non-moral virtues can assist one in accomplishing (moral and non-moral) values. In some extraordinary circumstances, realizing moral values or observing moral principles may result in something contrary to the ethical judgment, and in some other circumstances it may be the case that two different moral values cannot simultaneously be realized (or two different moral principles cannot simultaneously be observed). Then the heart-mind of ren and yi can also serve to guide one to choose the value that should be realized or to amend the original moral principle(s) in question. In addition, choices between a moral value and a non-moral one, or between two non-moral values, can also be guided by the heart-mind of ren and yi.[20] What should be emphasized is that the heart-mind of ren and yi is not some ready-made virtues or principles but, rather, an ability to make ethical judgment that is more fundamental than virtues. In this regard, to categorize Confucian ethics as virtue ethics may have resulted from confusion about the different meanings and functions of ren and yi.

Flourishing Life Within a Community

Some people may think that in a Confucian ethical world every particular act or the way of living in general cannot deviate from morality, so the whole life of humans must be dominated by morality. However, although Confucianism endeavors to actualize an ethical perfect state, morality is only one aspect of it. Non-moral values, such as harmonious and ordered interpersonal relationships, a warm and consonant family life, aesthetic satisfaction, a free and unfettered quality of life, broad and sagacious wisdom, and courage in facing confusion and obstacles, all play an important role and can be attained by the cultivation of non-moral virtues.

"A flourishing life" in Confucian thought must not be an isolated life (Analects 18.6), and therefore, on the one hand, a person should contribute to his/her community in one way or another and people should support each other; on the other hand, a perfect community is also an important factor for the realization of a flourishing life. For Confucius, an ideal society is a World of Great Harmony (cf. "The Conveyance of Rites," in *Book of Rites*). A World of Great Harmony is a selfless world in which everyone contributes his/her best to the community and takes what he or she needs, and in which everyone does not merely love his/her own parents and children, but also loves others' parents and children. Because people display this kind of loving care for each other, "the old are properly cared for, the able are suitably employed, and the young can decently grow up." Even the lonely and helpless are taken good care of. Because there is no personal property, theft does not exist. It is noteworthy that in such a world the virtues of *li* and *yi* are not necessary for maintaining social order, as everyone voluntarily treats each other selflessly. *Li* and *yi* are only required in a "Society of Small Tranquility" (fairly well-off society) controlled by a single family (with the same family name). A society in which individual or family interest is the paramount focus needs virtues such as *li* and *yi* in order to secure personal interest and to solidify the ruler's power. Since a distinction is made between self and others, as well as the intimate and the distant, consequently, people require laws so as to keep social order, and *li* and *yi* can help in this respect. Moreover, Confucian thought holds that duplicity and wars emerge because of the emphasis on "self" and "distinction." It is thus clear that *li* and *yi* can be viewed as rules enforced upon and especially made for a specific society.

From the above description, we can see that for Confucianism, the most accomplished flourishing life is embodied in a selfless society. The ultimate goal of practicing moral virtue (such as *ren*) is to achieve selflessness. When everyone is selfless there is no need for virtue. From another perspective, the heart-mind of *ren* is a selfless mind, so activating the heart-mind of *ren* is more effective than blindly following virtue step by step towards the realization of a flourishing life. In the "Society of Small Tranquility," even though virtue plays a role in correcting the misfortune and harm brought about by the pursuit of self-interest, a heart-mind of *ren* should be employed to revise the abuse and limitation of virtue (and adjust it accordingly) at all times.

Conclusion

This paper has discussed what a flourishing human life is like in Confucianism and what virtues may contribute to the leading of such a life. We can see that the flourishing life that Confucianism constructs is one in which moral and non-moral values are realized. However, virtues that contribute to this realization are not of the greatest significance because their (moral and non-moral) meanings are attributed by the original heart-mind (of *ren* and *yi*). Because of this, it is doubtful that Confucian ethics can be classified as virtue ethics.

As stated in my preface, the aim of this article is not to classify Confucian ethics as any one of the types of Western ethical systems. On the contrary, I have attempted to demonstrate that criteria abstracted from Western philosophy are not necessarily applicable to Chinese thought. I have also tried to characterize the features and meaning of Confucian ethics. I hope that this article has succeeded in its aim.

Part II
Happiness, Luck, and Ultimate Goals

8 The Impossibility of Perfection[1]

Michael Slote

Everyone knows—at least everyone here knows—that Western virtue ethics and Confucian thought have a great deal in common. But, of course, there are some important differences too. Aristotle, for example, believed in a strong doctrine of the unity of the virtues—to have one virtue, one must have them all—and there is reason to think that Confucius, at least, didn't subscribe to such a doctrine. At any rate, that is how *Analects* 14.4 has often been interpreted. Other Confucians seem to have held to something like the unity doctrine, but, interestingly enough, some Western Aristotelians, notably Peter Geach (1977, 160–68), have *denied* the unity doctrine.

However, whether or not they subscribe to the unity thesis (or some very specific theses like the Aristotelian doctrine of the mean), all the Confucians and Aristotelians do seem to agree on one thing. Perfect virtue is possible in principle, and such virtue occurs through a harmonization and unification of all the virtues within the perfectly virtuous person—or sage.[2] But there are people who take a quite opposite view. I'm thinking not only of Nietzsche, whose ideas are often hard to interpret, but also of Isaiah Berlin (1997), whose views, however impressionistically he defended them, are very clear. And what Berlin in particular says is that perfection either of the virtues or of human happiness is, in principle (he says "conceptually"), impossible.

Today I am going to talk about why I think Berlin may have been right. But what will be pushing me in that direction is largely different from the examples and thinking that led Berlin to his conclusions. What has moved me into agreement with Berlin is some facts about the recent social and cultural history of the West, facts revealed by but also to a large extent brought about by what in America is known as "the women's movement." I believe that feminist thinking and its impact (at least) on Western society offer us more powerful reasons for accepting Berlin's views than anything Berlin himself gave or offered, but those more powerful reasons also seem to me to strengthen the case that can be made for Berlin's thesis using the kinds of (non-feminist) examples that were familiar to Berlin.

Ethics in the largest sense not only asks about moral right and wrong and moral good and evil, but also considers questions about the good life (what kind of life is good for us) and questions about various virtues that lie partly or wholly outside morality proper. Thus, when we praise resourcefulness and strength of purpose as individual virtues, we don't necessarily think of these qualities of character as specifically moral. For a resourceful person can be a moral scoundrel, but most of us, nonetheless, think of resourcefulness as generally a virtue, an admirable and praiseworthy quality of character. And similar things can be said about strength of purpose. I mention the non-moral goods and evils of human life and the fact that some virtues aren't specifically moral ones because I think the best arguments for Berlin's thesis of the impossibility of perfection concern these non-moral but ethical values; and I also believe that some of the most important lessons that feminism has to teach us, lessons that tend in the direction of Berlin's views, concern just these sorts of non-moral, but highly important, human values.[3] And let me now mention one aspect of patriarchy that can constitute the basis, or at least the starting-point, for what I have to say about the Berlin thesis.

Under patriarchy certain traits of character are regarded as virtues in men, but not in women: for example, assertiveness and adventurousness. And other traits are considered virtues in women, but not in men: for example, self-effacement. Still other traits, even under patriarchal or sexist assumptions, are assumed to be virtues in both men and women: e. g., prudence, kindness, and patience. And we find similar phenomena in respect of human goods. If adventurousness is a virtue only for men, that is in part because adventure, having adventures, is considered appropriate and a good thing only for men. On the other hand, really intimate personal relationships are regarded as much more important for women, much more necessary to their well-being, than they are thought to be for men; and of course, and by the same token, careers have been seen as much more important to a male's (having a good) life than to a female's. But even under patriarchal assumptions, some things can be considered good—to make for a better life—for both men and women: for example, aesthetic pleasure(s) and, arguably, knowledge and wisdom.

Feminism, of course, tells us to suspect and reject the assumption that certain goods and virtues can be relative to gender or sex in the above-mentioned ways (or any others). But once we free ourselves from what I take to be invidious sexist or patriarchal assumptions, I think we end up with other ethical difficulties—but *they are difficulties that confront men and women equally.* And it is the exploration of these difficulties that I believe leads in the direction of Berlin's views. If, for example, we are willing to grant that adventure is as relevant to women's lives as it is to men's, there is a very direct argument to the conclusion that perfect happiness—and also perfect virtue—is impossible for *any life,* so let me now tell you what I think that argument is.

Adventure means substantial risk and insecurity—something just doesn't count as an adventure or adventurous if real risk and actual insecurity aren't involved. But in that case, adventure involves an evil: not a moral evil, but the personal evil or personal ill of being at risk and lacking security. To that extent, adventure and security are incompatible or clashing personal goods. But that isn't the whole ethical story. You can't have a great complete French meal and a great complete Japanese meal on the same evening (without risking indigestion or worse), and so to some extent these are incompatible personal or human goods. But I don't think anyone thinks or has to think that a French meal is less than perfect, less than ideal, because it isn't a Japanese one, and the same vice versa; whereas a life of security is, arguably, less than ideal precisely because it will be lacking in adventure (some will say that it is for that reason somewhat boring). And by the same token, a life of adventure has the disadvantage of involving insecurity, and that means that such a life will be less than perfect, less than perfectly happy or good.

So adventure and security not only clash as goods, but also each entails that a life is less than absolutely and perfectly happy; and that means that it makes sense to characterize them as *paired* but merely *partial* goods. By contrast, the good of wisdom or of aesthetic pleasure doesn't seem to undercut other goods in a way that makes it inevitable that one's life be less than perfect, so such goods shouldn't, I think, be characterized as merely partial—they are just plain good things (in life). But just above I mentioned the connection between the putative good of adventure/adventuring and the character trait, the supposed virtue, of adventurousness. Many of us, at least in the West, think of adventurousness as a kind of virtue, but notice that that virtue is opposed to (but also paired with) another trait that we also tend to regard as a virtue: namely, prudence.

Now philosophers in the West sometimes use the word "prudence" as a technical term connoting what Aristotle and others have called practical wisdom. But in ordinary English, "prudence" has a less philosophical meaning and refers (at least in part) to a (realized or exemplified) practical concern for one's own (or possibly other people's) long-term security. That it what we are thinking of when we say that it is prudent to take out life insurance and to avoid smoking cigarettes, and imprudent to act otherwise. Prudence in this ordinary sense is a valued character trait that opposes or conflicts with adventurousness, but also is naturally paired with it. One can't be (being) prudent, if one is (taking the sorts of major risks that are involved in being) adventurous; and if one is prudent, one can't really be adventurous. But, as with adventure and security, more is involved. These character traits not only clash, but also entail a lack of perfect (moral and non-moral) virtue. If one is really adventurous, one is *lacking* in prudence: that is, there is something about one that is less than fully or perfectly admirable. And by the same token, if someone is prudent, really prudent, then that person is lacking in adventurousness and people who know that won't be able to totally admire the person in question. So prudence and adventurousness can be considered opposed and partial virtues, in the same way or sense that security and adventure are opposed and partial human or personal goods; and if this is so, then Berlin was right about the impossibility of perfect virtue and of perfect happiness.

But now come the objections. Didn't Flaubert, for example, say that one should be settled and regular in one's life in order to be adventurous in one's work? (I am paraphrasing.) Doesn't this show that adventure and security need not clash and are therefore not partial goods in the sense just mentioned?

I don't think so. As Flaubert indicated, being adventurous just in one's work isn't being adventurous or having adventure in one's life, and if one doesn't have adventure in one's life, then one can't really be said to be having adventures. So there is nothing in Flaubert's dictum that runs counter to what I have said about partial goods and virtues and the impossibility of perfection.

But haven't I been assuming that adventure is as relevant to women as it is to men? And do I have any right to make such feminist assumptions? Some people hold—and perhaps this is truer of today's Chinese than it is of today's Americans—that adventure should be reserved to men and that adventurousness shouldn't be considered a valuable trait in women. Of course, even if we make these assumptions, adventures can occur to people who in no way want(ed) to have those adventures, but the point is that a *desire for* or *tendency to seek* adventure wouldn't be admirable in a woman and that the having of (non-crippling, non-fatal) adventures would represent something desirable in a man's life, but not in a woman's.

However, even if we treat adventure and adventurousness as having positive value only in relation to men's lives, we still face, still can't avoid, a certain impossibility of ethical perfection. Even if women aren't supposed to be adventurous, men *are* supposed to be prudent, but male prudence is incompatible with male adventurousness for all the reasons given above, and in that case, even if we have no argument to show that women's lives or virtues can't be perfect, we do have an argument that purports to show this about men. And the idea that perfect happiness and virtue are impossible (even just) for men certainly clashes with Aristotelian and, more generally, with traditional assumptions about virtue and "the good life."

However, our whole argument here and earlier assumes or presupposes that adventure and adventurousness (often) are positive values, and that might be questioned. When I read an ancestor of the present paper at East China Normal University last year, two of the senior philosophers in the audience questioned the value of adventurousness and told me that the traditions of Confucianism have no place for such a value or virtue. So one might wonder and I have wondered whether adventure and adventurousness are just Western values, and thus whether one can in any objective sense or way claim that adventure is really a (partial) good or that adventurousness is really a (partial) virtue. I am and have been assuming here that all or most of us—whether Chinese or Westerners—would like to gain a better understanding of what *really* are the virtues or goods of human life, so if the value of adventure is culturally relative, the whole argument for the impossibility of perfection collapses. Similar issues, however, arise with regard to all the examples that I shall be using (or that Berlin used) to argue for the impossibility of perfection, so I would like to mention the examples and, at least for the moment, prescind from the issue of cultural relativity, in order to make the best case (otherwise) for the impossibility of perfection. We can then later return to the issue of relativity and consider in detail how it affects and whether it really undercuts the Berlinian thesis.

As a matter of personal history, I first recognized the ethical conflict between security and adventure and between prudence and adventurousness at the same time that I first realized the gendered and blinkered way in which patriarchy views the values of adventure and adventurousness. And a feminist, at least a Western feminist, will want to say that adventure and adventurousness are positive values as much for women as they are for men. But in the light of what I have been assuming and saying, this then leads us to the conclusion that perfect happiness and virtue are as impossible for women as they are for men: for no one can combine prudence and security with adventurousness and adventure, and yet there will seem to be something missing or lacking in any life that fails to contain one or another of these elements.

So the example I have used, if only tentatively, to argue that perfection is impossible relates to and, I believe, is illuminated by issues that have been raised by feminists. And there is another kind of example—one that I think is even more significant and interesting than the one we have just spoken of—that also grows out of and illustrates some important issues and ideas in feminist ethics. As I mentioned earlier, it used to be thought—and by many people still is thought—that a career and career fulfillment are important to or for men in a way that they aren't important to or for women. But feminists believe that these things are just as important for women as they are for men, and I am strongly inclined to think that they are right. However, and as is well known, the choice between career and family is (at the very least) a difficult one, and in feminist terms it is or should be as difficult for men as it is for women. Men should care about their families as much as women do, and if they do, they will at least in principle have as difficult a time balancing career and family as (so many) women do. But what if this choice is not just contingently difficult? What if, suitably refined, it illustrates the impossibility of perfection just as strongly as the choice between prudence and adventurousness does?

These are issues that I want to discuss a bit later, but before we do so, I'd like to show you how the issue of the impossibility of perfection can be illustrated independently of any issues involving feminism. Berlin's favorite illustration of his thesis was the choice between liberty and social equality, but Ronald Dworkin (2006, ch. 4) has, I believe, shown that these two values could in principle be jointly (and fully) realized. However, Berlin also invoked the clash between tact(fulness) and frankness as illustrating his thesis about necessary imperfection, and I in fact think that such an example, if described in fuller detail than Berlin and others have ever done, can move us toward accepting that thesis.

Everyone recognizes that the (putative) virtues of frankness and tact stand in some kind of opposition. They are naturally seen as paired and opposed because there are so many situations in which a choice has to be made between being tactful and being frank, situations in which one cannot exemplify both of these qualities of character. But an Aristotelian take on such issues would want to hold that whenever there is a choice between tact and frankness, there is a *right* choice in the matter, a choice not open to ethical or moral criticism. (This can derive from an acceptance of the doctrine of the unity of the virtues, but it needn't.) However, I don't believe that what we think of as virtues are as well-behaved as this typically Aristotelian assumption about right and wrong would entail, and the issue of frankness vs. tact can help to explain why.

In the Aristotelian view (and speaking rather roughly), frankness and tact never clash *as virtues*. In any case where tactfulness is called for, frankness (being frank) wouldn't count as virtuous or praiseworthy—and would in fact be out of place. And in that case, when one acts tactfully in response to situational ethical requirements, one's lack of frankness will simply not be open to ethical criticism. Now recent discussions of moral dilemmas should make us somewhat suspicious of these Aristotelian ideas, but I would like to articulate my suspicions by mentioning a case where it seems to me the previous Aristotelian take on frankness vs. tact doesn't hold water.

Imagine that you have a friend who is always getting himself into abusive relationships that eventually turn sour and become intolerable for him. You have previously pointed this out to your friend, but he says he has no idea what you are talking about and enters into new and abusive relationships without seeming to have benefited in any way from what you or other friends have told him. (He is also totally unwilling to talk to a therapist about his problems.) So imagine further that your friend comes to you after his latest relationship has broken up and deplores the awful bad luck (as he puts it) that has led him once again into an unhappy and unsuccessful relationship. But he has no idea how abusively he has been treated (in this relationship or the others) and simply asks you, implores you, to tell him why you think this sort of thing is always happening to him. "What am I doing wrong?" he asks. However, you have told him in the past that he has a tendency to accept abuse, and you don't believe there is any chance that he is going to change his ways or his thinking (assume he is no longer young). So what do you say to him?

Well, since he is imploring you to tell him what you think, you might (once again) be frank and truthful with him and explain the role that he himself seems to play in bringing about these disasters (e.g., by accepting abuse, from the start, in the intimate relationships he enters into). But you have every reason (let us assume) to believe that if you say this to him, it won't really register (positively) with him or make any difference to his future behavior, whereas, *if you just commiserate with him and say that you don't understand how he can be so unlucky*, he will feel much relieved or consoled by what he takes or will take to be your understandingness and what is clearly your sympathy vis-à-vis his situation. So what do you do?

I don't think that there is a right (and entirely satisfactory) answer to this question. In other cases, there is reason to choose tact over frankness or frankness over tact, but in the present case I think ethical considerations are finely balanced, and one's eventual choice of either the tactful or the frank thing to say may show more about oneself than about the ethical issues operating in the particular situation I have described. Moreover, and this is the main point, whatever choice one makes will be less than ethically ideal. If one is tactful, one will have compromised one's frankness with a friend who is imploring one to be frank, and to that extent one is open to the (mildish) criticisms that what one has done is less than ideal and that, more particularly, one has shown oneself to be somewhat lacking in the virtue of frankness. By the same token, if one is frank, one will have acted in a way that isn't entirely kind (or tactful), and, once again, what one has done will seem less than ethically ideal. Or so, at least, it seems to me. So I believe that this example illustrates the Berlin thesis and cuts deeply against an Aristotelian understanding of (the) virtue(s).[4]

But let us now return to the question of career vs. family. We have discussed two very different examples that can move us toward belief in the impossibility of perfection, but I think that the issue of career vs. family—suitably tweaked or refined—offers us the most interesting and important illustration of Berlin's thesis precisely because of its relevance to central tenets of feminist thought. I say that the issue needs to be tweaked because the contrast or opposition between career and family is not stark and pervasive enough to show a genuine ethical impossibility. Some people don't have families, and some careers are ethically rather insignificant or compromised, but there is a deeper issue of opposing ethical choices that is relevant to every intelligent human life, and I shall now try to say what that is.

Some of our deepest relationships occur within a family context: as between parents and children or between spouses/partners. But of course some people who don't get married or have long-term partners do have emotionally deep relationships with other people: friendships being just one example of this possibility (but what about the relationship between a teacher and a student?). And deep relationships of love or friendship are commonly regarded as among the best things in human life.

Similarly, some people don't in the strictest sociological sense have careers (did Beethoven or Emily Dickinson have a *career*?), and some careers are rather devoid of ethical value(s)—like a career in the Mafia or some careers in advertising. But what may be said about some of the best careers is that they involve creative self-fulfillment and accomplishment, and most Aristotelians and others who think that there can be objective answers to questions about whether something (really) is good for us have regarded self-fulfillment or accomplishment as among the most important personal goods of human life.

Now the difficulty of choosing between career and family is a well-known one, but I think a deeper and more daunting ethical choice can be specified in the terms that I have just been describing. If one is involved in certain personal creative aspirations, if one is seeking to accomplish certain important things in one's life, that can come into tension with one's desire and need for close personal relationships, the goods of creative achievement and deep personal relationships are at the very least difficult to combine in a single life, and this arguably deeper variation on the theme of career vs. family is also familiar to us nowadays.

I call it deeper because it seems to me, for reasons given just above, more pervasive of the human condition (or the condition of any other intelligent beings there may be) and because it can be said to provide a better illustration of and argument for the Berlin thesis than we can obtain by focusing just on the narrower issue of career vs. family. But this claim needs to be justified, and that is what I shall attempt to do now.

First, if we assume feminist values, then the ethical choice between creative accomplishment and deep relationship(s) will be equally relevant and difficult for men and women. Women will lose out if they lack an outlet for creative self-fulfillment/accomplishment, and men will lose out if their focus on the latter, or on their *careers*, leaves them without the resources for the most rewarding kinds of intimate or deep personal relationship. And I think we nowadays should want to assume that both deep relationships and personal accomplishment are good for both men and women. What I shall begin to argue now, however, is that these values in the strictest sense necessarily clash and that a life lacking deep personal relationships and a life lacking a high level of creative self-fulfillment are each less than ideal from the standpoint of happiness.

Consider what typically happens and has to happen when someone finds creative fulfillment in their career or life's work. They not only have to work very hard at what they do, but they have to be very devoted to what they are doing: they have to want it or its results very badly. And let us say that they accomplish what it is in them to creatively accomplish—so that we can say that they have attained or created something very good in their personal lives. But what about their family of origin, their friends, or the family they may have created through marriage or otherwise? If they are so fixed or bent on what they are doing or trying to accomplish in their career's or life's work, will there be psychological energy left over for the fullest sort of devotion to others, the kind of devotion that the fullest good of intimate or close personal relationships depends upon? If one cares so much about one's creative project, then one really can't care as intensely and fully about one's spouse, parents, children, or friends as someone lacking such an intense project could care about them.[5] But since we think (very roughly) that the good of relationships is enhanced by greater (mutual) caring and devotion, the person with the personal creative goals will miss out on the fullest good or goods that personal intimacy and relationship can offer.

However, there is a very obvious objection to this line of argument that now needs to be considered. Why couldn't someone with enormous talent or genius accomplish great things fairly easily and without being particularly devoted to what they were doing or accomplishing—and wouldn't this then in principle leave them psychologically free to be as devoted and caring with intimates as the fullest and most-fulfilling personal relationship(s) could require or entail? But whom do we have in mind here? Even Mozart doesn't fit this bill because he had to work hard to take the melodies that were always coming into his head and organize or orchestrate them into actual pieces of music, and also because he was apparently very devoted to what he was doing. But consider a super-Mozart who creates whole musical works without much effort and even without much interest in what he or she is doing. Wouldn't such a person be quite capable of all the potential good of personal relationships plus the full personal good of creative accomplishment?

I am inclined to think not. We think that accomplishment is more meaningful, and more of an accomplishment, if it doesn't come easily, if it involves struggle along the way, and so what this super-Mozart achieves strikes me as less of a personal good than what we imagine to characterize the creative accomplishment(s) of a Beethoven who (we know) did have to struggle and sweat in order to compose his great music. This may be a Romantic view of things, but I think that many of us do see the personal good of creative accomplishment(s) as at least partly a function of the difficulty of, or the struggle involved in, such accomplishment(s), and if that makes sense, then even the super-Mozart who is totally devoted to friends or family will miss out (at least to some extent) on something that we think of as a good, even a great thing in human life (when it occurs).

But let me consider one more possibility. It might be held that a perfectly happy life might be possible if one focused on personal creativity and intimate relationships in a serial order: devoting oneself to a certain career early on in life (and let us assume that it is a career, like mathematics, where one can do one's best work while young) and then shifting gears into a greater or a great devotion to friends, a spouse, a family. But such a person will have missed out to some degree on intimate relationships early on in her life—and will perhaps poignantly appreciate that fact from the perspective of her later devotion to friends, family, etc. And from the later perspective they will also have reason to regret the fact that they are no longer engaged in creative work—if they are at all objective, such creativity will be sensed or felt as missing from their later life. So I don't in fact see any way in which the goods of personal intimacy/relationship and creative self-fulfillment can be combined in any ideal or ideally happy way.

This illustrates Berlin's impossibility of perfection thesis very starkly—and in a manner that is (perhaps uniquely) relevant to (and poignant for) our time—at least as things have been developing in the West and as it looks as if they have been developing here in China. Western women often deplore the difficulties of choosing between career and family, but they often see those difficulties as due to their own personal inadequacies or, alternatively, as due to lingering patriarchal or other unjust features of the societies they live in. But, if what I have been suggesting is correct, then women should stop beating themselves up (and men shouldn't blame them) for the difficulties in question. They may be inevitable for any conceivable society of intelligent beings that is a relevant target of ethical thought. And that fact, if it is one, may illustrate the truth of the Berlin thesis in a more important and contemporaneously relevant way than any of the other arguments that I have been giving you.

But let me now return to an issue that we set to one side earlier, the question of cultural relativism. If one thinks that careers are not appropriate for women and that personal intimacy is not important, and even somewhat undignified and unfitting, for a man, then the just-mentioned putative illustration of the Berlin thesis will not be at all convincing. And this might then—as a kind of sop to those in the West who think differently about these matters—lead one to espouse a kind of social or cultural relativism about human goods, virtues, and (more generally) values. But I want to resist this. I want to say that when today's or yesterday's men were emotionally unengaged with their families (or less engaged than their wives), they were missing out on something. And we owe this insight, as I take it to be, to some extent to the women's movement. And by the same token women who are so devoted to their families (and friends) that they never experience the satisfaction of great personal creative accomplishment (and I assume one can't really, fully have this just by raising children imaginatively and well) are also lacking something (good) in their lives and in such a way that we can't really say that their lives are totally and *perfectly* wonderful.

Let us, then, turn next to our previous examples. I mentioned earlier that some professors here in China had questioned my assumption that adventure is among life's goods (even for men) and that they had told me that Confucianism has had no room for such a category of good. This might lead one toward some sort of relativism, but even if it didn't, it could make one question the adventure/security example that I earlier used to illustrate and argue toward the Berlin thesis. But one thing that I *didn't* mention earlier is the reaction of (at least) one of the students who heard my lecture at East China Normal University. After my talk and after I had heard the professors' reactions, I asked this student what he thought about the matter, and he said that he and the younger generation of Chinese students did recognize a certain value to adventure and adventurousness—however differently their professors and the traditions of Confucianism regarded these questions. That makes me think that Chinese thinkers might eventually want to accommodate and acknowledge the at least partial value of adventure and adventurousness, and in that case we would *all* have to acknowledge that the "choices" between adventure and security and between adventurousness and prudence do move us in the direction of Berlin's thesis.

What also leads me in this direction is the fact that Chinese (fictional) literature actually contains some rather striking examples of adventure and adventurousness. P. J. Ivanhoe has recently acquainted me with the sixteenth-century Ming dynasty author Shi Nai'an, whose well-known work *Shuihuzhuan* (a title variously translated as *All Men Are Brothers, Outlaws of the Marsh,* or *The Water Margin*) presents adventure and adventurousness in a favorable light. So I am at this point convinced that the issue of adventure/adventurousness vs. security/prudence can move both Western *and* Chinese thinkers in the direction of Berlin's views.

But let me now and finally return to my earlier illustrative example of frankness vs. tact. After the very same lecture at East China Normal, one of the professors also told me that tact is no sort of Confucian virtue—after all, he said, it involves shading or hiding the truth, a lack of truthfulness. However, I remember that at the time I was very surprised by this remark because it has always struck me that the Chinese on the whole are very refined in their manners and, as far as I can tell, that refinement often consists in being tactful where less-refined or less-sensitive people would be blunt. And the Chinese I have seen be tactful don't seem to be at all ashamed of or guilty about their tactfulness, so I really wonder why Chinese people or philosophers would want to say that tactfulness isn't a virtue. Of course, it may not be a moral virtue; but neither is resourcefulness a moral virtue in the strictest sense, and that doesn't prevent us from calling it a virtue. Presumably the term *de* and/or some other Chinese word can be used to indicate a positive attitude toward resourcefulness. And if the same can be said and done about tactfulness, that is all that one needs to get oneself into hot water with the example of the choice between tact and frankness. And one more point.

Xiao Yang has pointed out to me a passage in the *Analects* (7.31) where Confucius deliberately speaks and acts tactfully and later appears to be satisfied with what he has done. And there is also *Analects* 8.2, where Confucius seems to be saying that truthfulness or frankness has to be tempered sometimes by politeness or tact.[6] So I really wonder whether the Chinese or Confucianism can treat tactfulness as entirely lacking in ethical value, and if they can't, and as I just said, the choice between frankness and tact will illustrate and move us toward the thesis of the impossibility of perfection.

However, you may think that I am too happy about what I have been saying. If Berlin is right, our ethical understanding and capacities are, in important ways, more qualified and less coherent than what we have assumed and hoped for, so I *agree* that we have reason to resist Berlin's conclusions and even prefer Aristotle or Confucianism, if we can in good intellectual and moral conscience do that. But there is another way of seeing things. There are complexities in the modern world and of modern life that Aristotle and the Confucian tradition never anticipated, and perhaps a view that entails the clash of ethical values and the impossibility of attaining perfection better reflects our world than the more harmonious but also simpler picture that the earlier traditions variously paint for us. We live in times where the (idea of a) conflict between individual rights and the good of society as a whole is more palpable than it was in earlier times, before the idea of human rights had really come to the fore. And, similarly, the clash or choice between career and family didn't and couldn't occur in more patriarchal times, when careers were reserved for men and women were supposed to do most or all of the "emotional work" in any relationship and in any family.

Such complexities can lead one to wonder whether any harmonious philosophical picture of harmoniously related virtues and goods can be adequate to *our* circumstances,[7] and so, even if we have some intellectual reason to resist a move away from traditional Confucian or Aristotelian thinking, there are also reasons to try on some new thinking for size. Berlin's views and my own illustrative examples and arguments may help us to move toward better ways of coping with and understanding the ethical complexities of our time,[8] and it is also worth noting that nothing in Berlin's picture or my own involves a refusal to acknowledge objective ethical goods or virtues. Some goods or virtues may have to be qualified or conditionalized in certain ways, but none of this means that we can't try to find a true or truer picture of valid human values. So I think that we should explore the brave new ethical world that Isaiah Berlin has so prophetically adumbrated and see how well it helps us to cope—both in our philosophical understanding and in our actual activities and practices—with present-day realities.

9 Structured Inclusivism about Human Flourishing

A Mengzian Formulation

Matthew D. Walker

During the last few decades, the issue of whether Aristotle subscribes to an exclusive or inclusive conception of *eudaimonia*—"happiness" or "human flourishing"—has been the subject of ongoing scholarly debate. According to exclusivist interpreters, Aristotelian *eudaimonia* consists of just one intrinsic good, usually identified with the exercise of the contemplative intellect in accord with its proper virtue of *sophia* (theoretical wisdom). On the inclusivist reading, by contrast, *eudaimonia* consists of more than one such intrinsic good. Indeed, according to inclusivists, *eudaimonia* is a complete and self-sufficient end because it is a composite end lacking in none of the intrinsic goods that make for a good life. Thus, inclusivists maintain that virtuous actions and other intrinsic goods are valuable for the sake of *eudaimonia* by somehow *composing eudaimonia*.

According to one interpreter, Richard Kraut, it is not only incorrect to attribute inclusivism about *eudaimonia* to Aristotle, but doing so generates further difficulties. For instance, Kraut thinks that if one proposes a *simple inclusivism*, i.e., a view according to which *eudaimonia* is a simple second-order aggregation of first-order intrinsic goods, then one endorses a philosophical non-starter. "[I]f there need be no connection between any one component of happiness and any other," Kraut writes, "then there is no explanatory value in the statement that some single good is desirable for the sake of the larger whole" (Kraut 1989, 212). In other words, if *eudaimonia* is a mere aggregate of goods, then the alleged parts of *eudaimonia* are not really valuable for the sake of *eudaimonia* after all, for there is no proper *whole* to which they belong.

Kraut, however, recognizes that one might attempt to avoid the problems of simple inclusivism by arguing that *eudaimonia* is not a simple aggregate but, rather, an organized whole containing parts. To motivate such a *structured inclusivism*, Kraut allows, the inclusivist might point out that parts can be valuable for the sake of the wholes that they compose in all sorts of cases. For instance, a heart can be valuable for the sake of the whole of which it is a part, viz., the whole living body. But if one tries to avoid the problems of simple inclusivism by adopting structured inclusivism, then Kraut thinks that one faces a central problem, viz., that it is very hard to see how the relation obtaining between a body and its parts could possibly obtain between *eudaimonia* and its putative parts:

The body is not a mere aggregate of parts, and this allows us to understand how each of them operates for the sake of the unified whole. … But no one would hold that the many intrinsic goods alleged to be components of happiness (friends, honor, virtues, pleasure, and so on) are related to the larger whole as are parts of the body.

(Kraut 1989, 212n10)

If one combines Kraut's two charges, one ends up with the conclusion that inclusivism about *eudaimonia* fails. Either the inclusivist is committed to viewing *eudaimonia* as a mere aggregate (in which case one cannot identify *eudaimonia* as a whole for the sake of which various goods are constitutively valuable) or else the inclusivist is committed to the allegedly unpromising view that the components of *eudaimonia* are related to *eudaimonia* in the way that body parts are related to a body.

In this paper, I do not address the interpretive question concerning whether Aristotle is really an inclusivist or exclusivist about *eudaimonia*.[1] Rather, I briefly defend the independent philosophical cogency of inclusivism about human flourishing against Kraut's worries. As a test case, I examine the conception of human flourishing offered by the early Confucian philosopher Mengzi (Mencius). I do so for three reasons. First, as a thinker, Mengzi (371–281 BCE) was roughly contemporaneous with Aristotle (384–322 BCE), and he occupies a position in Chinese culture roughly analogous to Aristotle. Second, although determining Mengzi's exact views is difficult (since the *Mengzi*, like a Platonic dialogue, is not a systematic treatise), and although it is important not to read into Mengzi terms and concerns popular from contemporary debates in Aristotle scholarship, Mengzi nevertheless proposes an account of the human good that can be plausibly described as an account of human *flourishing*. Moreover, the *Mengzi*'s account of human flourishing can be described as an inclusive one at that, i.e., an account that construes flourishing, at least to some extent, as a composite. Third, and most importantly, in developing his views, Mengzi explicitly makes the move that Kraut insists that "no one" would make. That is, Mengzi develops a view according to which flourishing *is* related to its components as a body is related to its parts. In fact, Mengzi often seems to *localize* the parts of one's flourishing to the parts of one's body. Hence, although certain forms of structured inclusivism may be open to Kraut's worries, I argue that by appealing to Mengzi's account, one can respond to Kraut's puzzlement about how structured inclusivism could possibly make sense.

Flourishing and Nature in Mengzi: Preliminaries

I begin with some preliminary remarks about Mengzi's views. First, as I have suggested, Mengzi's conception of the human good can be reasonably described as a conception of human flourishing. Although Mengzi does not use any particular term that one can readily translate as "flourishing," Bryan W. Van Norden (2007, 22) argues that the lack of a particular Classical Chinese term for this notion does not preclude Mengzi from having a conception of flourishing. Indeed, as Van Norden points out (2007, 38), the pervasiveness of agricultural, plant, and sprouting metaphors in Mengzi (e.g., at 2A2.16, 2A6.5–7, 6A1, 6A7–9) makes it entirely natural to attribute a conception of "flourishing" to him. Given these metaphors, one can reasonably say that Mengzi identifies flourishing with the fulfillment and blossoming forth of human nature (*xìng*), where this nature consists in those dispositions that human beings realize when they are nurtured without harm and attain full maturity.[2]

This general point about "human flourishing" in Mengzi raises a question about what dispositions Mengzi thinks that human nature includes. In reply, Mengzi seems to waffle between more and less restrictive answers. For instance, at one point, Mengzi seems to identify human nature solely with the cognitive-affective dispositions of the heart (*xīn*). According to Mengzi, these dispositions include reflection (*sī*: 6A15.2), i.e., the disposition to fix one's attention on what is appropriate and to develop one's virtuous inclinations. They also include the dispositions for the four cardinal Mengzian virtues themselves. Thus, in his more restrictive-sounding moments, Mengzi writes, "A gentleman (*jūnzǐ*) regards the benevolence (*rén*), righteousness (*yì*), propriety (*lǐ*), and wisdom (*zhì*) that are based in his heart as his nature" (7A21.4).[3] Likewise, Mengzi elsewhere insists that without the heart's guidance, one is "not far from" a beast (6A8.2; cf. 2A6.1, 2A6.4, 4B19.1). Hence, one might think that Mengzi identifies only the dispositions of one's heart as one's *human* nature.[4]

The above passages, however, do not necessarily commit Mengzi to a restrictive conception of human nature. Although Mengzi thinks that human beings approximate a bestial condition if the heart's dispositions are destroyed, it does not follow that human nature necessarily excludes the dispositions that we share with animals. For instance, the above passages are consistent with the less restrictive view that shared dispositions constitute parts of human nature (only) insofar as the heart guides them appropriately. These passages are also consistent with the even less restrictive view that although these shared dispositions are perhaps less *distinctively* human than the dispositions of the heart, they nevertheless remain components of human nature without qualification.

I take Mengzi ultimately to be committed to the expansive view that human nature includes *all* of our innate dispositions.[5] At 7B24.1, for instance, Mengzi suggests that not only will the dispositions of one's heart constitute human nature, but so will the dispositions that one shares with animals: "The mouth in relation to flavors, the eyes in relation to sights, the ears in relation to notes, the nose in relation to odors, the four limbs in relation to comfort—these are matters of human nature." To be sure, Mengzi goes on in this passage to add that a gentleman will not *refer* to these latter dispositions as human nature, but instead will view them as "fated" (*mìng*), i.e., brute conditions of our existence to be accepted as the "decree" of Heaven. Yet the general tenor of 7B24.1 is to undermine any strong dichotomy between the elements of human nature and the characteristics that we possess by fate. For after asserting that a gentleman will not refer to his sensual dispositions as human nature (but instead as fated), Mengzi immediately goes on to insist that the cognitive-affective dispositions of the heart, including the dispositions for virtue, are *also* fated (though he adds that the gentleman will call them nature). If the gentleman will not *refer* to the dispositions of one's sense organs as (constitutive of) human nature, this could be—as A. C. Graham (1990,

38–39) plausibly suggests—because Mengzi thinks that it is good habit to identify one's nature only with one's best dispositions, viz., those of the heart.[6] (I shall soon say more about Mengzi's grounds for rank-ordering dispositions.)

So Mengzi offers an *expansive* conception of human nature. And I take it that this expansive conception provides the basis for what I identify as Mengzi's correspondingly *inclusive* conception of human flourishing. Put concisely, flourishing, for Mengzi, consists in the complete blossoming forth and fulfillment of human nature; but human nature consists in our full range of innate dispositions; hence, our flourishing will consist in the complete blossoming forth and fulfillment of the full range of our innate dispositions.

Thus, to turn to 6A14—a crucial passage in the *Mengzi*, and one on which I focus in what follows—Mengzi says: "People care for each part of themselves. They care for each part, so they nurture each part. There is not an inch of flesh they do not care for, so there is not an inch of flesh that they do not nurture" (6A14.1). To be sure, one might read Mengzi's claim here as a purely factual report on what human beings tend to care about. As a matter of psychological fact, Mengzi might seem to be saying, human beings *do* tend to care for each part of themselves. Yet if our nature consists of all our dispositions, then all the parts of one's nature will count as *appropriate* objects of one's concern. While Mengzi will have more to say about these matters, each part is nevertheless *such as to be* nurtured because each is (ultimately) constitutive of our flourishing.

At this point, even if Mengzi's view differs from other inclusivist accounts of the human good, it is still fair to identify Mengzi's view as a form of inclusivism, at least insofar as Mengzi does not identify human flourishing with one narrow "monistic" good or disposition (e.g., the dispositions of the heart alone, or one of the heart's dispositions in particular).[7] Yet, to show that his conception of flourishing can escape Kraut's objections against inclusivism, Mengzi must show that the parts of human nature (and so, the parts of flourishing) form an ordered whole, not merely a simple, second-order aggregate of dispositions. I now examine how Mengzi addresses this issue.

Organizing Principles in Mengzian Flourishing

For Mengzi, human nature—and thus, flourishing—is an organized composite, and it is organized partly on account of its *hierarchical structure*.[8] To understand this structure, I turn to a passage in which Mengzi ranks the parts of the body:

> [I]f we want to examine whether someone is good or not, there is no other way than considering what they choose to nurture. The body has esteemed and lowly parts; it has great and petty parts. One does not harm the great parts for the sake of the petty parts. One does not harm the esteemed parts for the sake of the lowly parts.
>
> (6A14.2)

Just as some parts of the body are greater and more esteemed than others, Mengzi suggests, so too are some parts of one's nature (and flourishing). In particular, as one might expect from our earlier discussion, Mengzi thinks that *the heart* (with its dispositions) is one of the greater and more esteemed parts, and that it is dominant in our nature (and flourishing). Hence, to be a good person, Mengzi thinks, one will choose to nurture—one will grant a certain priority to—the heart and its dispositions. At first blush, of course, one might think that a good person need not have a good life. But if flourishing consists in the development of those dispositions constitutive of human nature in a fashion proportionate to their value—i.e., in a fashion that grants due priority to the best dispositions—then one can see how Mengzi can say that the good person will flourish. For the good person, of all people, grants this due priority to developing his best parts.

The thought that certain parts of one's nature are superior to other parts requires spelling out. After all, one might worry that there is no plausible way to rank the value of one's parts: one simply has such-and-such parts and that is all there is to say.[9] To account for this hierarchy of parts, Mengzi appeals in 6A14 to what I call a *principle of sacrifice*: where *X* and *Y* are both goods, if one would sacrifice *X* instead of *Y* in case of conflict, then *X* is subordinate to *Y*. And if *X* is subordinate to *Y*, then, Mengzi thinks, one has reason to grant priority to *Y* over *X*.[10]

Mengzi's acceptance of this principle of sacrifice need not commit Mengzi to the claim that if some *X* is subordinate to some *Y*, one should (ordinarily) cultivate that *Y at the expense of* that *X*. First, although he speaks in a different context (concerning practical choice, not the structure of human nature), Mengzi suggests that while cases of *conflict* might require one to pick some good *Y* at the expense of some good *X*, one should ordinarily (when possible) pick *both* that *X* and that *Y*: "Fish is something I desire; bear's paw [a delicacy] is also something I desire. *If* I cannot have both, I will forsake fish and select bear's paw" (6A10.1; my emphasis). Second, Mengzi's reference to body parts in 6A14 is revealing, for one typically does *not* face the need to sacrifice (i.e., to "harm") one body part for the sake of another. Deciding whether to sacrifice one's hands for one's kidneys is not a conflict that we usually face. Hence, I take it that Mengzi appeals to our intuitions— or, perhaps, to our inclinations—about which parts we would choose to preserve and to sacrifice in cases of conflict only to support his claims for the existence of a natural hierarchy of parts, not to restrict our flourishing to one of them.

So although Mengzi does think that human nature is hierarchically organized, and although this hierarchy establishes a set of priorities for us—i.e., it suggests that we should focus more on developing some parts of our nature instead of others—it nevertheless is consistent with an inclusive view of flourishing, one according to which one should develop all of one's parts constitutively for the sake of flourishing. Since all are components of our flourishing as a whole, when Mengzi says that the one who nurtures the petty parts becomes a petty person, but the person who nurtures the great parts becomes a great person (6A14.2, 6A15.1), Mengzi is saying only that the better person puts a priority on cultivating the great parts. He is not committed to the stronger view that one should cultivate only the great parts (because these are the sole components of one's flourishing). Thus, Mengzi does not say that people who eat and drink are to be despised, but, rather, only those who are "always" eating and drinking (6A14.5). If such people are to be despised, that is because the excessive effort that they spend on eating and drinking requires them generally to neglect the cultivation of their higher parts. Their *excessive* attendance to the lowly and petty parts of their nature requires them to "lose what is great" (6A14.6).

Beyond appealing to our intuitions about which parts of our nature we would not sacrifice for the sake of other parts in cases of conflict, Mengzi can explain why certain parts are such as not to be sacrificed, and so why certain parts are superior in the hierarchy. Mengzi's insight, I take it, is that some parts are better (and so, more worthy of being preserved in cases of conflict) because those parts are *more directive*. So, according to what I call Mengzi's *principle of directiveness*, some part Y of a whole is better than (or superior to) another part X if Y plays a more directive role in the functioning and flourishing of the whole than X does. For Mengzi, the heart and its dispositions are dominant in human nature (and flourishing) because they provide a certain guidance over one's other parts (and dispositions). Without this guidance, the lower parts are apt to disrupt one's excellence (or greatness), prevent the full development of one's nature, and so, preclude one's full flourishing.[11]

Responding to Gongduzi, for example, Mengzi says, "It is not the function of the ears and eyes to reflect, and they are misled by things. Things interact with other things and simply lead them along. But the function of the heart is to reflect" (6A15.2). Here, Mengzi indicates that the heart has a certain directive role over such parts as the ears and eyes. Without guidance by the reflecting heart and the heart's virtuous inclinations, the sensual dispositions associated with one's ears and eyes will be exercised in a haphazard way. More specifically, they will be exercised in the pursuit of whatever chance pleasures attract one's attention. Without the heart's reflection, then, one will fulfill the parts of one's nature in a disordered fashion inconsistent with the fullest cultivation of one's human nature. Hence, the heart, in virtue of its directive disposition for reflection, has priority over other parts. Mengzi suggests that the heart's directiveness over the other parts of human nature is visible in the vital harmony of the sage's body. The virtuous dispositions of the heart, Mengzi says, are "clearly manifest in his life and demeanor. They fill his torso and extend through his four limbs. Though he says nothing, his four limbs express them" (7A21.4).

One might worry that our intuitions about which parts of an organized whole should be sacrificed in cases of conflict need not match our assessments of which parts are apt to be most directive. For example, consider the case of an athletic team traveling to compete in a game in another city. If (i) there is an insufficient number of seats on the team bus, but (ii) the members of the team otherwise form a sufficiently unified whole, then one can well imagine a case in which the team might willingly "sacrifice" the most directive member, viz., the coach, and travel to (and compete in) the game without the coach's guidance. If so, do we have a case in which Mengzi's principle of sacrifice conflicts with his principle of directiveness? I do not see that it does. Given that sacrificed body parts are non-replaceable (or generally non-available), Mengzi's principle of sacrifice is best understood as a principle concerning *permanent* (or general), rather than temporary, sacrifice. If one accepts this strong formulation of the principle, it is less clear that the team would sacrifice the coach: for without the coach's *general* direction, the team as a whole is apt to suffer.[12]

Now, on the basis of Mengzi's remarks on the directive role of the heart, one can conjecture that Mengzi thinks that human nature (and flourishing) has another principle of structure beyond simple hierarchical organization (according to the principles of sacrifice and directiveness). It is reasonable to think that Mengzi believes that the components of human nature (and flourishing) constitute a mutually supporting system and are *reciprocally related* as well. Although Mengzi is not explicit about this precise point, the lower parts of human nature—i.e., those having to do with sensual dispositions—apparently subserve the higher parts to the extent that the lower parts are hierarchically subordinate to the higher parts. Yet, as 6A15.2 (on the heart's function for reflection) indicates, the heart's virtuous inclinations in turn regulate and order one's sensual inclinations. Thus, given such reciprocity between higher and lower elements of human nature, Mengzi has additional grounds for thinking that human nature is an ordered whole, and that its parts, in their complete fruition, are constitutively valuable for the sake of flourishing.[13]

Structured Inclusivism and External Goods

In this chapter, I have argued that Mengzi provides us with an account of human flourishing that is capable of meeting Kraut's worries about inclusivism. Mengzi can avoid Kraut's objections because, although Mengzi identifies flourishing with a composite end, viz., with the complete sprouting forth of the full range of dispositions that constitute human nature, Mengzi gives us reason to think that human nature is an ordered whole structured both hierarchically and reciprocally.[14] The picture that I take Mengzi to offer, then, looks like this: the dispositions of the lower parts (i.e., those of the mouth and stomach (6A14.6), ears and eyes (6A15.2)) are subordinate to those of the heart. But the dispositions of the heart, although dominant in flourishing, are not sufficient for flourishing, for these dispositions are subordinate to flourishing as a whole, i.e., to the *complete* development and sprouting forth of one's human nature, which (per 6A14.1) requires one to care for and nurture all of one's parts. So although we go wrong if we grant priority to our petty parts, our flourishing requires that we nevertheless make an essential place in flourishing for the nurture of these parts as well.

In this chapter, I have focused on presenting a *Mengzian* formulation of structured inclusivism about human flourishing. Nevertheless, Mengzi's view, I believe, invites comparison with the view of *eudaimonia* that Henry Richardson (1992) attributes to Aristotle, a view according to which (i) some intrinsic goods are choiceworthy for their own sakes and for the sake of higher ends (e.g., contemplation), and (ii) the higher ends are choiceworthy in turn for the sake of *eudaimonia* as a whole. As Richardson argues, this structure ensures that a hierarchy of ends is maintained, while also ensuring that less final intrinsic goods are included in *eudaimonia* as well. Of course, if Mengzi and Aristotle share similar views about the basic *structure* of flourishing, they have different views about its specific *content*. Whereas Aristotle believes that the intellect plays the dominant—and guiding—role in one's flourishing, Mengzi is willing to grant to sentiment a higher place than Aristotle does. And for those who find Aristotle's intellectualism to be off-putting, yet find structured inclusivism about human flourishing appealing, Mengzi offers resources for a different, less intellectualist, structured inclusivist picture of the human good.

What is especially interesting in Mengzi's own account is its explicitness in mapping the hierarchy of parts of flourishing directly onto the hierarchy of parts of human nature. In this way, I have suggested, Mengzi is capable of responding directly to Kraut's worries. A contemporary appropriation of Mengzi's views on human flourishing might depart from Mengzi's particular view that *the heart* (as opposed to, say, the brain, or certain of its processing centers) is the seat of our virtuous dispositions. Yet it might still attempt to link various kinds of goods (e.g., sensual pleasure) to dispositions associated with various parts of the human body (e.g., of the ears, the eyes, the mouth, etc.).

But this (close) mapping raises questions about Mengzi's views on the place of so-called "external goods" in flourishing, e.g., items such as wealth, honor, and social position. For Mengzi *does* make a distinction between those things that are "in oneself" (e.g., benevolence, righteousness, etc.) and those that are "external" (e.g., wealth, honor, etc.) (7A3; cf. 6A6.7). Similarly, he distinguishes between "Heavenly honors" (which he identifies with virtues) and "human honors" (which he identifies with lofty political offices, such as duke, High Minister, etc.) (6A16). As it stands, Mengzi observes that we all do desire externals (2B10.6; 5A1.4). But such external goods are not *parts* of one's human nature in the way that, e.g., one's benevolent dispositions are. Mengzi insists that it neither adds to, nor subtracts from, the gentleman's nature if he gains (or loses) great holdings of land or wealth. "This is because what belongs to him is already settled"—viz., his virtuous dispositions (7A21).

For these reasons, one might suspect that Mengzi views externals as what Stoics call "preferred indifferents." On this view, externals are *preferred*, since we in fact desire them; but they are ultimately *indifferent*, since they are external to our virtuous nature, which, by itself, suffices for our flourishing. To be sure, Mengzi suggests that externals can fail to conduce to our flourishing (5A1.4). Indeed, externals can be actual *impediments* to our flourishing (to the extent that they can blind us to our own inadequacies and need for self-improvement) (7A11). Moreover, we often pursue externals in ways that bring shame upon us (4B33.2).

While the status of external goods according to Mengzi requires fuller discussion, I suggest that we should resist the "preferred indifferent" reading. On the contrary, I propose that Mengzi identifies externals as, potentially, *derivative* components of flourishing.[15] First, although externals may not be constituents of our virtuous natural dispositions, externals can still be indispensible constituents of activity that *fully displays or expresses* such dispositions. Thus, externals can be constituent features of virtuous deeds, such as benevolent giving or filial assistance. Second, if Mengzi identified externals as actually preferred, but ultimately flourishing-neutral, it is unclear why he thinks that wise rulers should expend so much energy ensuring that the population possesses them (see, e.g., 1A7.21–22; 7A23). Mengzi indicates that part of the benefit that externals confer consists in their conduciveness to the background security and stability required for the unimpeded performance of virtuous deeds. Hence, only when a father has a stable livelihood and sufficient means to serve his parents, or to nurture his wife and children, will he "rush toward the good" (1A7.21). If he lacks such means, starvation will put his life and agency at risk, and he will lack "leisure for cultivating ritual and righteousness" (1A7.22). In and by themselves, externals do not constitute flourishing, and they may well be either neutral or even harmful on their own. But when enjoyed within a life of virtuous agency, Mengzi suggests, they do play a secondary part in flourishing.[16]

10   The Target of Life in Aristotle and Wang Yangming

Benjamin I. Huff

The eudaimonist approach to ethics proposes to guide our lives by organizing them around the pursuit of one goal: the chief, highest, or ultimate good. Having a clear sense of what makes one's life as a whole good, we can organize our pursuit of other goals so as to promote this, and not to interfere with it. In Aristotle's words, "If, like archers, we have a target, are we not more likely to hit the right mark?" (*Nicomachean Ethics* 1094a22).[1] The Greek term *eudaimonia*, from which *eudaimonist* derives, is often translated *happiness*, but in a eudaimonist context, the content of *eudaimonia* is left to be determined by the theory. Hence, for the purposes of this paper, I will treat *eudaimonia* simply as another word for the highest good.

The eudaimonist approach is especially associated with Aristotle, who systematized it. Yet it was present in Plato's work and served as a standard for Greek, Hellenistic, and Christian philosophical ethics for centuries afterward. It was also a major influence on Enlightenment thinkers such as Hobbes, Kant, and Mill, even when they resisted some features of it. In this paper, then, I will treat eudaimonism as an approach that is as viable today as it has been through history. Aristotle's work serves as a useful guide but does not answer every question that we may have. In reconstructing a contemporary eudaimonism, Confucian thought also has much to offer.

In formulating our conception of the chief good, we face two fundamental pressures. On the one hand, we want to identify the best possible way for a human being to live. On the other hand, we want to identify the good as something achievable. Aristotle is mindful of these two pressures, but it is not clear how he means to respond to them. In this paper I consider a range of responses available to eudaimonists and argue that the Confucian thinker Wang Yangming offers an appealing strategy. I then argue that a similar strategy is available in an Aristotelian context. Despite working in a different time, place, culture, and philosophical context, Wang raises very similar questions about how to understand the goal of life, or highest good, and he answers them in a theoretically sophisticated way that complements the work of Western eudaimonists.

Measuring the Highest Good

Early in the *Nicomachean Ethics*, Aristotle raises the question of how the highest good is achieved. He concludes that whatever its cause, it is reasonable that it should be "widely shared," and attainable "through some kind of learning and personal effort" (1099b18–20). Yet elsewhere Aristotle often speaks of the chief good as something lofty enough that one wonders how many would in fact be able to achieve it. Thus he seems to feel and respond to both of the pressures that I have described, but not to resolve them.

Ambiguity on this point, however, rests in part on a more basic ambiguity as to how the highest good is to be measured or quantified. We may make progress on this question by examining Aristotle's claim that the highest good is self-sufficient. To be the goal around which we organize our lives, the highest good must be a *governing* end: we must be able to meaningfully organize our other pursuits toward achieving it. Similarly, we must not pursue it for the sake of anything else, or else it would in turn be governed by those other things. In other words, the highest good must be good in itself, *complete* or *perfect* (*teleion*). Finally, the goodness of a life must be entirely captured in the highest good, or its guidance would be incomplete. There must not be anything else needed to make a life "worthy of choice and lacking in nothing" (1097b15–16); in other words, the highest good must be *self-sufficient*. Since the highest good is lacking in nothing, it cannot be improved by adding anything else to it.

Another way to put this is that the chief good "is not counted as just one thing among others" (1097b17)—it is good in a way that outshines other goods. What Aristotle means by this is clear, as he deploys this pattern in X.2. Eudoxus argued that pleasure is the good because "pleasure, when it is added to any other good … makes the other good more worthy of choice" (1172b24–5). However, Aristotle notes that this argument actually counts against pleasure: if combining other goods makes it greater, then pleasure is merely one good among many, and hence not the chief good. The chief good, then, is something incomparable, which cannot be improved by the addition of other goods.[2]

Thus we are seeking a good which cannot be improved. However, there are at least three ways of understanding this idea. One might suppose that (a) the highest good is itself a sort of maximum, the pinnacle of goodness for a life, (b) it is not a matter of degree, but something unitary that one simply achieves or does not achieve, or (c) it is a matter of degree and can be improved, but only by more of itself, not by adding other, different goods.

One might suppose that the way to establish the structure of the highest good is to simply look at Aristotle's specific account of happiness, and examine its structure. However, the precise contours of Aristotle's account are heavily disputed. Is happiness virtuous activity in general, or the activity of a specific virtue, such as theoretical wisdom? Is it virtuous activity alone, or combined with other goods, such as honor, pleasure, material wealth, good birth, and so on? Moreover, my goal is not simply to ask how Aristotle describes happiness, but how we should describe it, given a eudaimonist starting-point. Hence I propose to first identify what structure we should want in a eudaimonist account, and then look for accounts with this structure, including a preferred interpretation of Aristotle's ambiguous text.

The Good as a Maximum

Our first hypothesis is that the highest good is a kind of maximum. This is an appealing idea for the simple reason that it makes sense to aim at the best possible outcome in planning one's life. In this view, a life can exhibit varying degrees of goodness, but the highest good is the greatest possible goodness. Aristotle seems to have a maximum in mind when he says things like, "Whatever is worthy of choice for him he [the person with *eudaimonia*] ought to have, or else he will be lacking in that respect" (1170b17–18).

In this approach, however, one worries that the highest good will not be achievable enough. Surely most lives do not achieve maximum goodness, but some imperfect lives are still better than others. Hence we will need some other way of distinguishing lives that are more and less successful. Moreover, it would seem even more important to know what the goodness of a life is more generally—the goodness of which the highest good is a maximum. Without knowing this, it is not clear that we could understand the maximum. Thus, either the highest good is not a matter of degree (as per option b), or, if it is, we will need an account of the goodness of a life that admits of degrees (as per option c) in addition to an account of the maximum. Hence I now turn to our other options.

The Good as Unitary

A conception of the highest good as something one simply achieves or does not achieve, and not a matter of degree, has the advantages that I mention above, without the disadvantages. One might imagine that the best life differs from others by a kind of quantum leap, a qualitative shift, or a unique achievement. In this approach the highest good is the best possible outcome for a life, but there is no reason to expect that most people will fall short of it, nor any need to separately specify what the maximum is a maximum *of*. This approach also, arguably, fits well with the *content* of the highest good. The Stoics, for instance, argued that the highest good is virtuous action, and virtue is a matter of striking the mean, so the highest good is like ripeness: as a piece of fruit is not good to eat either before or after the point of ripeness, virtue is not a matter of a lot or a little, but of getting things right, of appropriateness and proportion for each particular occasion.[3]

It is true that virtue is a matter of getting things right, analogous to ripeness. However, there are still degrees of virtue: one can be more or less generous or temperate, just as a fruit can be more or less ripe. When one considers what the Stoics take virtue to be, they are clearly describing something that admits of degrees, namely, one's readiness to place right action above all other considerations. For most of us, our priorities shift slowly, and disproportionate appetites take time to subside through habit and experience.[4] If the Stoic view of the goal of life corresponds to the endpoint of a process of increasing moral refinement, then it is not unitary after all, and has the disadvantages discussed above for a conception of the chief good as a maximum. Understanding the highest good as something unitary is appealing from the standpoint of building a theory, but it is difficult to imagine an actual, unitary achievement that could be the self-sufficient aim of life if the Stoic attempt fails.

The Good in Degrees—Composite

I conclude, then, that the most reasonable path is to follow option (c): the chief good can be realized to a greater or lesser degree, but it is self-sufficient in the sense that nothing else is better, and no other good can increase it. As Aristotle reports Eudoxus' view, "the good is [only] increased by the addition of itself" (1172b26).

One version of this response is W.F.R. Hardie's (1965) notion of an inclusive end. In the inclusive view, the highest good is self-sufficient because it already includes everything that is choiceworthy in a life, in the best amount, including along with virtuous activity other things that are worth choosing for their own sake, such as pleasure, honor, friends and material goods.

A difficulty arises for this response, however, when we note that we seem to have described another sort of maximum. Even though happiness may not refer to a maximum of any of the goods that it includes, it is a kind of maximum in its own right, insofar as it is the best possible combination of other goods. Like virtue, the complete package of goods for a human being would be a mean "in respect of … the definition of its substance," but "with regard to what is best and good it is an extreme" (Aristotle 1107a7–9). There will be few people who have exactly the optimum combination and proportion of these components, but those who are close are still presumably better off than those who are far away. Thus we encounter the same problem as before, of accounting for people who fall short of the maximum, by either excess or deficiency in the various components.

The Good in Degrees—Single

Accordingly, we must consider whether there may be some single good that is not better when combined with other goods, but that can nonetheless be realized to greater or lesser degrees.[5] Richard Kraut takes this view, maintaining that "happiness consists in just one type of good," (1989, 298). This approach also fits best with Eudoxus' assumption that "the good is [only] increased by the addition of itself" (Aristotle 1172b26). One candidate for this good is theoretical contemplation. Clearly, one can engage in contemplation to a greater or lesser extent, and in *Nicomachean Ethics* Book X Aristotle ties it directly to a varying degree of *eudaimonia*: "Happiness, then, extends as far as contemplation, and the more contemplation there is in one's life, the happier one is …" (1178b29–32).

Contemplation thus seems to meet the formal criteria that we need for the highest good: it is a single, complete, governing end, and it gives a meaningful measure for varying degrees of goodness. The problem with this candidate is that as a matter of content it is so implausible. To say that other goods such as health, friends, and the activities of the virtues of character are needed for one to be able to contemplate is plausible, but to say that they do not add to a life's goodness in their own right is not. Also, as Aristotle acknowledges, extensive contemplation requires a degree of leisure that few people enjoy.

Wang Yangming offers us an account of the highest good that fits the pattern that we are looking for, in *Instructions for Practical Living*. Further, he offers it in response to essentially the question we are concerned with here: it is clear that not everyone can personally achieve the ultimate in what makes a life good, and yet among those that fall short of this we need to be able to distinguish between lives that realize the good to some degree and lives that do not.

Wang Yangming and the Achievements of the Sages

In *Instructions for Practical Living* I.99, a student asks, "Sagehood can be achieved through learning. But the abilities and efforts (*cái lì*) of sages Bo Yi and Yi Yin are after all different from those of Confucius. Why are they all called sages?"[6] Wang answers with an analogy:

> The reason the sage has become a sage is that his mind has become completely identified with the Principle of Nature and is no longer mixed with any impurity of selfish human desires. It is comparable to pure gold, which attains its purity because its golden quality is perfect and is no longer mixed with copper or lead.

Sageness, then, is like the purity of gold, and gold is one incomparable good. Yet one can possess this good in varying quantities. Wang continues:

> However, the abilities (*cái lì*) of sages differ in degree, just as the several pieces of gold quantitatively differ in weight. The sage-emperors Yao and Shun may be compared to 10,000 pounds; King Wen and Confucius to 9,000 pounds; Kings Yu, Tang, Wen, and Wu, to 8,000 pounds; and Bo Yi or Yi Yin, 4 or 5,000 pounds.

How exactly should we understand this notion of varying "abilities"? In brief, the single good that Wang attributes in differing quantities is sagely accomplishment or achievement. To show clearly that this is what he means, however, requires some analysis.

In English, the word *ability* is ambiguous; it can refer to (1) a trait that makes one able to do something, or (2) the thing that one is able to do. For example, it can refer to the coordination and skill to be able to juggle, or to the action, juggling, that this skill enables. For clarity, hereafter I will use "ability" only in the second sense, and will refer to the trait in the first sense as an *ability-trait*. As I will explain, based on the way that he uses the word, we can see that Wang here is using *cái lì* to refer to an action one is able to perform, corresponding to *ability* in the second sense.

It is quite straightforward to identify differences between the sages, in a manner that reflects Wang's proportions, if we focus on the actions for which they are known. Yao and Shun were emperors who brought harmony to all their domain. Others were rulers of lesser domains, or ministers acting on a correspondingly lesser scale. Insofar as they reflect the outstanding character of these sages, we could also refer to these actions as *feats* or *achievements*.

That Wang has in mind these actions or achievements is confirmed later as well. After distinguishing the qualitative and quantitative features of the sages, Wang emphasizes that we should focus first on the qualitative, purity, and let the quantitative follow: "to be pure gold depends not on quantity but on perfection in quality, and to be a sage depends not on ability or effort (*cái lì*) but on being completely identified with the Principle of Nature" (I.99). He then describes those who follow the wrong priority as "undertak[ing] the task (*shìyè*) of the sage-emperors Yao and Shun" when "they have the evil [impure] mind of … Jie and Zhou" (I.107). Evidently, then, the quantitative features of the sages are their tasks—their characteristic actions or accomplishments.

Similarly, in I.100, Wang describes Zhu Xi as having made this mistake of approaching things backwards or "upside down," by writing "many books" without having first directed sufficient "effort toward self-cultivation." He is like

> a person who, seeing someone else with a piece of pure gold of 10,000 pounds, does not take steps to refine his own … but foolishly hopes to match the 10,000 pound piece in quantity. He throws in mixed elements of pewter, lead, brass, and iron … In the end it is no longer gold at all.
>
> (I.99)

Though he eventually recognized his error, by then Zhu had written so much that he did not live "long enough to correct the many mistakes" (I.100). Again, the quantitative feature here is the magnitude of Zhu Xi's (in this case flawed) accomplishments.

If we take *cái lì* as a reference to an ability-trait, we might suppose that the sages' differing achievements are simply *expressions* or manifestations of proportionally differing traits. Philip Ivanhoe, for example, takes *cái lì* as a reference to differing inborn traits (2002, 50–52). This reading is problematic, however, for two reasons. First, while Wang refers to inborn differences in I.99, these are not quantitative, like the difference between 5,000 and 8,000 pounds of gold. Rather, they are qualitative, differences in purity, as between gold, copper, and lead: "In the matter of purity and impurity of physical nature, some men are above average and some are below." Second, although differences in purity affect how difficult it is for one to become a sage, by the time that one becomes a sage these differences have been overcome: "the success of all of them is the same." Thus, the differences in purity are not the differences that Wang describes between the abilities of sages such as Bo Yi, King Wen, and Confucius.

Similarly, in several other passages Wang uses *cái* and certain cognates to refer to the differing, limited talents of various people. Hence one might suppose that these differing talents are traits that explain the different achievements of the sages. However, in most of these passages Wang also describes another kind of talent, the talent of the perfected sage, which transcends these limitations. For example, "Zeng Dian's indication was that he was not such a [limited] utensil" (I.29), or, "Confucius, on the other hand, was expert in all three" (III.286). Rather, the ability-traits or talents of these sages are the same trait or talent, which is equally unlimited for each of them.

In I.67 Wang further explains this unlimited talent, and also explains where it comes from:

> Ability is what one can do, like Kui's music and Ji's agriculture. Their accomplishment was due to the fact that the substance of their minds became completely identified with the Principle of Nature ...
>
> (Wang 1963 trans., modified)

Here again, the examples of ability that Wang gives are not traits but the achievements in music and agriculture for which Kui and Ji are admired. We might ordinarily be tempted to explain Kui's and Ji's differing achievements as results of quite different and independent talents or ability-traits. However, Wang assures us that the differences in what sages accomplish do not turn on differences in their personal traits, whether moral or intellectual. Rather, the trait that explains their achievements is the same for both—the sageness of I.99—and this trait fits them for the one task as well as the other:

> When ... the mind becomes completely identified with the Principle of Nature, one's ability is not restricted to any particular thing. If Kui and Ji had exchanged places, they would have been able to accomplish each other's tasks also.[7]

Since the explanatory trait is the same, differences in the scale or character of their actions are, rather, due to differences in opportunities and circumstances:

> In a position of wealth and in noble station [the superior person] does what is proper to a position of wealth and to noble station, and in a position of difficulty and danger he does what is proper to a position of difficulty and danger.

The differences between the sages' actions thus reflect their sagely judgment as to what their differing circumstances call for. Though the actions that are appropriate may vary widely from one situation to another, the true sage will be equal to any occasion.

This is a dramatic claim, but natural in the context of Wang's thought. For Wang, the Principle of Nature is the organizing principle of every thing and process in the universe. Hence, if one aligns one's mind with the Principle of Nature, one can know and understand everything, and hence accomplish anything. This knowledge is implicit in all of us as *innate* or *original knowledge*, and while it is obscured to some degree in most of us by the turbidity of our psychophysical constitution or *qì*, it can be fully realized through mental and moral discipline, primarily the exercise or *extension* of innate knowledge. Wang describes this plenipotence: "The innate knowledge of my mind is the same as the Principle of Nature" (II.135), and therefore, "Although there is an infinite amount of change and variety in the world ... if one responds to them by merely extending ... innate knowledge ... nothing will be left out of its operation" (II.190); "This is why the wonderful functioning of innate knowledge has neither spatial restriction nor physical form and is unlimited" (II.189).

With this background, we can appreciate the precise philosophical sense that Wang gives to *ability* in I.67:

> the substance of their minds became completely identified with the Principle of Nature, so that whatever its function might be it issued from the Principle of Nature. Only this can be called ability.

Ability (*cái*), then, is the functioning or operation of one's mind in action. Most people's knowledge is obscured by impure *qì*, and so the functioning of their mind is limited. By contrast, the mind of the sage is no longer obscured but "completely identified with the Principle of Nature," and hence its function or ability is "not restricted to any particular thing," but is potentially unlimited.

The sage's ability is potentially unlimited, but this does not mean that a sage in fact does everything. Wang reaffirms this point in I.21 regarding Yao, Shun, Duke Zhou and Confucius: their achievements, monumental as they were, are things that "any sage can do." Still, Yao and Shun did not edit the Six Classics (as Confucius did) or establish the ceremonies of the Duke of Zhou. This is because "a sage does a thing when the time comes," according to what suits the occasion and circumstances.

Wang thus offers two dimensions of comparison between lives, qualitative and quantitative, which are valuable in distinct ways. Purity, or qualitative excellence, is attainable by anyone and worth pursuing, even if one's circumstances are highly constraining, as they were for Yan Hui. Great achievement without purity is worth little, as a large quantity of lead is worth little even in comparison with a small quantity of gold. Indeed, action on a grand scale can easily make one a deplorable Jie or Zhou if pursued without regard to purity, as though amassing 10,000 pounds of lead and other worthless substances. However, great achievement is something to be celebrated in the sage, and multiplies the value of the sage's purity.[8]

Sageness corresponds to the purity of gold, and the scale of accomplishment corresponds to the amount, but we may wonder what in the moral realm corresponds to the gold itself. Another passage of the *Instructions* helps to establish what is already implicit in the analysis above: "The highest good is the original substance of the mind. It is no other than manifesting one's clear character to the point of refinement and singleness of mind. And yet it is not separated from events and things" (I.2). Purity and quantity are inseparable in gold, though each may vary. In a similar way, one's character and its manifestation or operation in action are inseparable for Wang, as a lamp is inseparable from its light, and this manifestation is the highest good.

As in much of *Instructions for Practical Living*, Wang here is commenting on a classical Confucian text, the *Great Learning*, whose first line reads, "The Way of learning to be great consists in manifesting the clear character, loving the people, and abiding in the highest good" (Chan 1963, 86–7). The *Great Learning* underscores the importance of knowing "what to abide in," to enable "deliberation" so that "the end [can] be attained." It thus offers an intriguing parallel to

Aristotle's interest in knowing the goal or target of life so that, "like archers," we are more likely to achieve it. What we are to abide in, of course, is the "highest good (*zhì shàn*)." The word that Chan translates "highest" (*zhì*) could also be translated "final" or "ultimate." The *Great Learning* thus is naturally read as a eudaimonist text, identifying the highest good and then recommending the steps to achieve it.

The text specifies a number of steps along the way, including "investigation of things" and "extension of knowledge." However, in Wang's view these are all to be understood as phases or aspects of one process: "The various steps from the investigation of things and the extension of knowledge to the bringing of peace to the world are nothing but manifesting the clear character" (*Instructions* I.89; cf. Ivanhoe 2009c, note 127). Evidently, then, the manifestation (*míng*) of clear character, or luminous virtue (*míng dé*), begins in the rectification of one's heart, extends through loving the people, and concludes in the realization of the ultimate good (*zhì shàn*). One expresses one's character in one's actions, whether inward or outward, small or great. Thus the manifestation of clear character, or in other words the actions and accomplishments of a person whose mind is identified with the Principle of Nature, are the highest good, comparable to a quantity of pure gold.

In a Kantian mood, we may be reluctant to accept that the concrete achievements of a Yao or Ji are relevant when evaluating their lives from an ethical standpoint, and rather insist that purity of heart or will is all that matters. For instance, Stephen Angle states that "all that matters, to be a sage, is one's moral purity" and that "sagehood is centrally about virtue," de-emphasizing the idea that the "sage can do all" (2009a, 19–20). Indeed, one might read Wang himself as making this point as he criticizes those who "cripple their spirit ... investigating the names and varieties of [external] things" (I.99), along with those who "confin[e] their comparison to quantity" or who "hope single-mindedly only for exalted position and who admire greatness" (I.107). These people are misled by focusing on the sages' external accomplishments.

However, Wang's criticism of those who "cripple their spirit" is not that they pursue extensive knowledge, but that while doing this "they do not direct their efforts toward the Principle of Nature ..." Neglecting this foundation, they "seek sagehood *only* in knowledge and ability" (I.99, my emphasis), and hence are "putting the cart before the horse" (III.299). As Wang explains in *Instructions* I.3, all the other personal capacities of the sages, when properly acquired, are "offshoots of the mind that is sincere ... Nevertheless, there must first be such a mind before there can be these offshoots." Again, Wang's criticism of those who admire greatness is not merely that they are interested in positions of influence, but that they hope "only" for these, and because they neglect their own purity of mind they are attempting "the task of the sage-emperors Yao and Shun" with "the evil mind of the wicked kings Jie and Zhou" (I.107).

It is accurate to say that sagehood is a matter of one's character, the state of one's heart or *qì*. However, it is clear that for Wang and other Confucians, much of the point of becoming a sage is to be able to make a difference in the world, for the better. In the *Great Learning*, the sage-kings' goal in setting out to "rectify their minds" is to establish peace not only in their own hearts, or in their families or even states, but "throughout the world" (Chan 1963, 87). To separate character from its operation and accomplishments, as Kant does, is to reject the unity of knowledge and action, a perennial theme of Wang's work (*Instructions* I.5, 8; Cua 1982). If one's character is pure, then the more fully it is expressed and realized, the better, and in fact one will be earnestly concerned to manifest one's character in concrete action and accomplishment.

The manifestation of clear character, as Wang describes it, is the appropriate focus of lifelong, daily effort, and the desire to achieve it should shape "[a]ll the thousands and thousands of [our] thoughts" (I.92). One who achieves it is "self-sufficient without depending on the pursuit of external things" (I.107). Evidently, then, it is not improved by the addition of other goods, but it can be achieved to a greater or lesser degree, and in two ways. On the one hand, there are degrees of purity of mind, distinguishing between the sages, those still striving for sagehood, and those whose lives are misguided and can only be failures. On the other hand, there are degrees of greatness in the accomplishments that manifest this purity, reflecting the differences in achievement of Yao and Shun, Confucius, Bo Yi, and the ordinary person of good character. Wang thus offers us a goal with the formal properties required for the highest good in a robust eudaimonist account.

Extending Wang's Model

An interesting question at this point is to what extent a similar account is available outside the distinctive context of Wang's thought. For example, in Wang's view, we all have the mind of a sage within us already, and this mind is identical with the ordering principle of the cosmos. If we leave aside questions of how we attain the character of a sage, however, and focus on the role of clear character in constituting the highest good, Wang's model has a ready analogy in Western virtue ethics: the manifestation of clear character is closely analogous, if not equivalent, to action in accordance with virtue, and Aristotle may be read as claiming that virtuous activity itself is the highest good. Aristotle may mean activity of intellect, of character, or both, but, having earlier set aside the purely intellectual activity of contemplation, I will now emphasize virtue of character.[9] Aristotle does not clearly indicate how virtuous activity is to be quantified, but what he says can readily be interpreted in keeping with Wang Yangming's model.

Aristotle speaks of virtue of character as an extreme, the best, "more precise and superior to any skill" (1106b15). Thus it is appropriate to compare Aristotelian virtue to the purity of gold. Similarly, while the virtuous person will express his character in whatever circumstances he encounters, some circumstances allow for a more complete expression than others:

> For the generous person will need money for doing generous actions; and the just person will need it for repaying debts … And the courageous person will need power, and the temperate person opportunity, if they are to accomplish any of the actions that accord with their virtue. For how else will he, or any of the others, make manifest what he is?
>
> (1178a29–34; cf. 1099a34–1099b1)

Aristotle emphasizes here that happiness is not merely the possession of virtue, but its expression or manifestation. A virtuous person with greater resources and opportunities can put her virtue into action in greater ways, and hence achieve a better life. We may identify this greater scale of goodness with what Aristotle calls *blessedness*. As in the case of Wang Yangming's ordinary person, however, the person of modest means can still realize *eudaimonia*, if to a lesser degree: "we can act in accordance with virtue even from modest resources. ... And it is enough to have moderate resources, since the life of a person whose activity conforms with virtue will be happy" (1179a4–9).

At times Aristotle seems to indicate that only those few who can afford a life of leisure can achieve happiness, whether through the political life or through contemplation. However, Aristotle's text is also amenable to the view that the highest good is virtuous activity, whatever its scale:

> the truly good and wise person ... bears all the fortunes of life with dignity and always does the noblest thing in the circumstances, as a good general does the most strategically appropriate thing with the army at his disposal, and a shoemaker makes the noblest shoe out of the leather he is given ...
>
> (1101a1–6)

As Wang Yangming's superior person manifests clear character, whether in wealth and station or difficulty and danger, so for Aristotle, arguably, one's activities in almost any context will realize the highest good so long as they express virtue.[10] Identifying the target of life as a single, incomparable goal which can nonetheless be realized to widely varying degrees, I suggest that Wang's model and its Aristotelian analog are appealing models for contemporary eudaimonism.[11]

11 Varieties of Moral Luck in Ethical and Political Philosophy for Confucius and Aristotle

Sean Drysdale Walsh

Introduction

One is beholden to moral luck if, due to forces and situations outside of one's control, one *might* have lacked *ren* (true goodness), or *might* have been a *junzi* (superior person), or even *might* have been a murderer. For example, a kind person with a kind family might have had a very different ethical character had the person been bought up in a cruel family that advocated for a hateful ideology. One has moral luck if one is the last person to get into an inspiring ethics course that helps to change one's character for the better. One's moral fortitude may wax and wane on a daily or even hourly basis, and it is a matter of luck whether one is morally tested during the waxing or waning periods (e.g., one might be more morally sensitive *after* that daily first cup of coffee). Moral luck is also, I believe, a central concept in the moral and political philosophies of Confucius and Aristotle, philosophies which are golden means between the extremes of (i) the deficiency of moral luck required by Kant and (ii) the excessive moral luck required by classical utilitarianism.[1]

For Kant, no moral luck is required for full moral virtue, since any agent has the knowledge, freedom, and strength simply to *will* the right maxim at any time.[2] For classical utilitarians, an agent's actions and character can be fully moral by accident, since the long-term consequences of either might by luck have maximal utility. I will argue that, for Confucius and Aristotle, the virtues are required for full moral worth (*contra* classical utilitarianism), and moral luck is required for knowing what is virtuous, as well as for gaining, developing, maintaining, and exercising the virtues (*contra* Kant). For Confucius and Aristotle, the most important moral luck is not in the long-term consequences that are often outside of one's control (*contra* classical utilitarianism), and the virtues give a powerful, internal stability that is necessary to morality (similar to Kant but *contra* utilitarianism).

Also, some contemporary philosophers argue that Aristotle requires *significant* luxury and moral luck in the ethical life, and argue that Confucius rejects moral luck as a core part of the ethical life.[3] Contrary to such contemporary philosophers, I argue that the following four forms of moral luck obtain in similar forms for both Confucius and Aristotle:

1. Luck in acting well without virtue, which can lead to ...
2. Luck in the development and maintenance of virtue, which can lead to ...

3.   Luck in the expression of virtue in action, which can lead to …
4.   Outcome luck in hitting the external targets of virtuous action.

I argue that both Confucius and Aristotle require a very similar, *modest* form of moral luck in one's situation and one's nature. I will frame Aristotle on moral luck in terms of his discussion of torture on the rack, and I will frame Confucius on moral luck in terms of his discussion of his favorite disciple, Yan Hui.

I also discuss the role of moral luck in the political philosophies of Aristotle and Confucius. For both, political institutions and governments can contribute significantly to moral luck; bad political institutions can make people worse, and good political institutions can make people better. For both, a core function of government and political institutions is to help human flourishing in part by ameliorating moral luck by providing moral exemplars, education, security, and food for the people.

Luck in Acting Well Despite Lacking Virtue

Even though Aristotle's *hoi polloi* (the many) and Confucius's *xiao ren* (small, petty people) lack virtue and thus cannot exercise virtue (the exercise of which is *eudaimonia* for Aristotle), there is moral luck for those who lack virtue. First, consider Aristotle, who gives three criteria that demarcate "merely doing the right act" from "doing the right act *from* virtue"—to do the right act from virtue one must (a) know that it is right, (b) do it for the right reasons, and (c) do it from a firm, stable character (1105a29–35). Thus, one can do the right act *without* virtue. In the *Eudemian Ethics*, Aristotle compares luck (*tuche*) with throwing dice (1247b15–18) when he says that those who lack good reasoning can have the luck to live and act well despite lacking reason (and thus also lacking virtue) (1247b18–28). Aristotle says that these unvirtuous people act well despite lacking wisdom (*sophia*) and reason (*logos*), just as people can sing well despite lacking practice, lacking an understanding of musical theory, or even lacking an understanding of what they sing (1247b21–28). So Aristotle believes that some succeed in doing the right thing by luck while lacking reason, virtue, and even a clear understanding of what they are doing.[4] To me, this phenomenon is common enough—e.g., children often do the right thing without understanding what they are doing. Aristotle says that it is better to have good luck (*eutuches*) and to sing and act well than to sing and act badly (1247b27–28). Aristotle says that good luck or fortune (*eutuches*) produces well-doing (*eupragia*) (1246b37–1247a3). Aristotle goes on to say that some irrational people are most fortunate to have *good desires* by luck, especially when compared to those who have bad desires by luck (1247b34–1248a11).

Aristotle also says that a core function of government is to ameliorate moral luck for the people (including for the *hoi polloi* and young who lack virtue). In the *Nicomachean Ethics* (*NE*), Aristotle says that a core function of good political institutions is to train and educate the young (who lack virtue) in virtue (1180b29). This training allows the young to *practice* the correct, virtuous action, despite lacking virtue. This practice is essential to developing the virtues (1105b4–12). In the *Politics I*, Aristotle says that the function (*telos*) of good government (*polis*) is to help all people in the city *to live* (and thus act) *well* (even those who *lack* virtue, such as the *hoi polloi*) (1252b27). If a government could not get unvirtuous people to act well, that government would be a failure. For Aristotle, good government and good political institutions mediate against bad luck by helping people live and act better than they would otherwise.[5] As I mentioned previously, for Aristotle it is better for one to act well and desire well by luck, even if one lacks the virtues.

Confucius's *Analects* often also says that there is moral luck for the small people (*xiao ren*) who often lack virtue; it is an important role of government to produce this good luck. According to Confucius, a good government makes the small people more virtuous. Confucius says that when the ruler and government ministers are virtuous, the people will act well as wind blows down grass, as the straight straightens the crooked and the inferiors follow their superiors.[6] Confucius says,

> If you [the ruler] want what is good/adept (*shan*), the people will at once be good/adept (*shan*). The virtue (*de*) of the superior person (*junzi*) is that of wind; the virtue (*de*) of the small, petty person (*xiao ren*) is that of grass. When a wind passes over the grass, it cannot choose but bend.
>
> (12.19)[7]

In *Analects* 9.14, Confucius says that the moral goodness of a superior person (*junzi*) even spreads to the crude (*lou*) barbarians, and in 2.1 Confucius says that people will follow the virtuous man as if he were the North Star. In *Analects* 13.6, Confucius suggests that if rulers are virtuous, the government will run effectively. Effective government contributes to the well-being and good actions of the "small people," who lack virtue. Confucius compares the word for "governing" to the word for "correcting" and says, "To govern (*zheng*) means to rectify/correct (*zheng*). If you lead the people with correctness, who will dare not be correct?" (12.17). For Confucius, there is luck in acting well for those who are not fully virtuous, since even the lowest people will not dare to act incorrectly under good governing.[8] Moreover, for both Aristotle and Confucius, a core function of good government is to help unvirtuous people to act ethically better. Whether or not one has such a good government is a matter of luck; Aristotle and Confucius recognize that people generally have little control over their government and rulers.

Luck in Developing and Maintaining Virtue

In the previous section I discussed the moral luck of acting rightly when one lacks virtue.[9] This kind of luck is connected to the next kind of luck: the luck in *developing* the virtues. This is because acting well without virtue can aid in the development of virtue. In *NE* II, Aristotle says that it is essential to develop virtue by habituation, which requires that one regularly *practice* acting well before one has the virtues (1105b4–12). In *Analects* 17.2, Confucius says, "By nature (*xing*), men are *nearly* alike; by practice (*xi*), they get to be wide apart" (my italics).[10] Confucius says that such practice (*xi*) is crucial to the development of virtue, and suggests that there is luck in being able to effectively practice with a good teacher.[11] Confucius's word for "practice," *xi*, also can mean "habit," which is reminiscent of Aristotle's idea of practicing virtuous actions as the means to habituating character.

Not only do good governments, good rulers, and good teachers make us morally lucky, but also we can be morally lucky at birth. Recall that in *Analects* 17.2 Confucius says that people are born *nearly* alike by nature (*xing*). Confucius does *not* say that people are born *exactly* alike by nature in the ability to develop and practice virtue effectively. After all, Confucius says that the sage (*shengren*) is *born* morally better than the rest of us and does not require the same "lesser learning" that the *junzi* requires (19.12), and those who are born with better knowledge are more apt to be virtuous (16.9).[12] For example, Confucius says that some are born morally lucky:

> Those who are born with the possession of knowledge are the highest class of men. Those who learn, and so *readily* get possession of knowledge, are the next. Those who are dull and stupid, and yet compass the learning are another class next to these. As to those who are dull and stupid and yet do not learn— they are the lowest of the people.
>
> (16.9)[13]

Here Confucius is suggesting that there is luck not only in being born with knowledge, but also in being apt to develop virtue despite not being born with knowledge.

In *NE* I.4, Aristotle expresses a similar idea when, after discussing those who have good starting-points in life, he quotes Hesiod and says:

> He who grasps everything himself is best of all; he is noble also who listens to another who has spoken well; but he who neither grasps it himself nor takes to heart what he hears from another is a useless man.
>
> (1095b10–13)

Those who are lucky enough to know and understand the good by themselves have the best starting-point. Those who are lucky enough to learn the good from others have the second-best starting-point. But those who neither grasp the truth for themselves nor learn it from others are useless and most unlucky. For both Aristotle and Confucius, some people are lucky to be born with better abilities to grasp the truth, and some are lucky to have better teachers and better upbringings. In the *Rhetoric*, Aristotle says, "Let us consider good birth ... it is the way of all men who have something to start with to add to the pile ..." (1390b16–17). Aristotle goes on to say that such well-born men can become exceptionally virtuous, but often such men become decadent. Aristotle cites Alcibiades and the descendants of Socrates as people who are born with good luck (*eutuches*) but squander the luck through decadence (1390b26–33).

Also, consider Aristotle's natural slave. Aristotle thinks that to become a natural slave (by birth or by an accident) is bad luck for the slave. Aristotle's natural slave (*physei doulos*) is one who by nature lacks the ability to reason for oneself, and it is clearly better to reason for oneself (1254b16–21). A natural slave is not able to grasp important ethical truths for oneself. However, in the *Politics* I.6, Aristotle says that a natural slave who listens to a good master who gives good guidance is more fortunate than a natural slave with a bad master. According to Aristotle, a good master is good for the natural slave, and a master who hurts his natural slave also hurts himself (255b7–15). It is not only a matter of luck whether or not one is born a natural slave, but also it is a matter of luck whether the natural slave gets a good master.

Aristotle says that the development of virtue not only depends on having a fortunately good nature (e.g., not the unlucky bad nature of a "natural slave"), but also depends on having good habituation and practice (1103a14–17) through good teaching and upbringing (1095b3–9).[14] In the *Nicomachean Ethics*, Aristotle says:

> Some people believe that it is nature that makes men good, others that it is habit, and others again that it is teaching. Now, whatever goodness comes from nature is obviously not in our power, but is present in truly fortunate men as the result of some divine cause.
>
> (1179b20–30)[15]

Similarly, in Plato's *Republic*, Socrates says that to develop the virtues one must be like wool that is prepared to take on the dye (428d-430b). The wool must by *nature* be the kind of thing that can absorb the right dye, and, even further, the wool must be properly prepared by human beings so as to be apt to take in the dye permanently. For Plato, Aristotle, and Confucius, human beings can be more or less apt by nature to absorb the virtues by habituation, and these apt human beings need to be properly prepared by good teachers, good family, and good government to best develop and maintain virtue.

So not only are some people born better for developing virtue, but also some people by luck have better opportunities for effective practice for developing and maintaining virtue. Confucius says that some are lucky to be able to develop and practice the virtues in a community with good teachers, rituals, and government.[16] Consider also that Confucius occasionally insists that he is neither *ren* nor a *junzi*, despite his hard work. It takes Confucius *years* of practicing virtue to get the right heart and mind (*xin*) at the age of 70 (*Analects* 2.4). *Ren* comes and goes sporadically, even for a *junzi* such as Yan Hui, and Yan Hui himself says that Confucius helps his self-cultivation. Self-cultivation is required for developing *and* maintaining *ren*, even for Yan Hui (6.3, 6.7, 9.11). The opportunities for the most effective self-cultivation and practice of virtue can often come by luck. Good government, rituals, and teachers play an important role in helping such people to cultivate and maintain virtue.

For example, the *junzi* may lack both ability (15.18) and righteousness (*yi*) (17.23). The *junzi* even occasionally makes moral mistakes, relapses, and becomes non-*ren* (4.5, 14.6, 19.21). Good practice prevents such relapses. The *Analects* suggest that the *junzi* must continue to make *progress* so as to maintain *ren* (12.8, 14.24, 15.10). The *junzi* needs this progress so as to prevent more frequent relapses, since the *junzi* needs regular refinement in order to maintain virtue (12.8, 15.10). The *junzi* also finds three kinds of friends to be a great source of personal improvement

(16.4, 15.10), and must withdraw from a sufficiently bad community. It is a matter of luck if such friends are available for the *junzi*'s self-cultivation. It is also a matter of luck whether the *junzi* is required to withdraw from a bad community, and this unfortunate situation may make the cultivation of virtue more difficult. Confucius suggests that a *junzi* does best with the right community, teachers, rituals, and friends in which self-cultivation, moral progress, and thus moral maintenance are strongest. Even Yan Hui made mistakes (6.3) and lacked *ren* every few months (6.7), and insisted that he could cultivate and develop virtue better with the help of Confucius's regular instruction (9.11).

Aristotle also agrees with Confucius that luck in friendship and community is required in the *maintenance* of virtue, and thus luck is required to prevent loss or abatement of virtue. In Aristotle's view, only gods are entirely self-sufficient (*autarkes*) in everything, and only gods are immune from luck (*tuche*) (1047b34). Aristotle says that humans, lacking in self-sufficiency, need good friends in order to do or learn anything well (1155a4–32). Even the virtues of the most virtuous are not entirely self-sustaining. Aristotle believes that a virtuous person can lose virtue by bad luck. Aristotle says that, although virtue friendships tend to endure (1158b10, 1159b4–8), a virtue friendship can end because one virtuous friend loses virtue (1165b13–23; cf. 1256b12–13).[17] Such loss of virtue can be due to external circumstances similar to those discussed in the *Analects*. Martha Nussbaum argues that, for Aristotle, one needs luck in order to maintain virtue, since one needs good friends and a "supporting political context" for the "development *and maintenance* of adult good character" (Nussbaum 1986, 337; cf. Curzer 2005) (my italics). For example, the magnanimous man loses the *virtue* of magnanimity (and does not merely lose the ability to *exercise* the virtue) when he loses the ability to help others, and having these abilities depends on luck (1124a20–25). The ability to help others is part of the virtue itself, and we may lose the ability by accident or age or disease.

In the *Rhetoric*, Aristotle suggests that anyone loses the ability to trust others if one's trust has been seriously and repeatedly violated, and this wears away the virtues of friendship even in the best of us (1388b33–1389b13). We humans cannot have the virtues of friendship if we are surrounded by bad people with whom true friendship is impossible. Virtue can fade by lack of opportunity to practice and exercise the virtue. Moreover, in the *Nicomachean Ethics*, Aristotle says that one cannot engage in virtuous activity if one has lost good friends through death, since friends are instrumental to virtue (1098b32–1099a8). Since virtuous activity is needed in order to maintain virtue, losing friends can eventually lead not only to losing the *activities* of friendship but also the *virtues* of friendship.

Also, Aristotle says that people in the prime of life tend to have certain virtues (1390a29–b10), but later often lose those virtues, due to the constant disappointments that come with advancing age (1389b13–23). Aristotle (depressingly) suggests that, while the body is in its prime from the age of 30–35, the mind ceases to be in its prime at the age of 49 (1390b9–10). When the mind is not in its prime, virtue fades (full virtue requires a good, strong mind, after all). Nussbaum argues that, for Aristotle, when *eudaimonia* is seriously "marred and spoilt" by bad luck (1100a7–9, 1101a1–14), the long time that it takes to recover *eudaimonia* (which just is *virtuousactivity*) is not only due to the time required to recover the *activity*, but also due to the time required to fully recover *virtue* itself (Nussbaum 1986, 337). Both activity and virtue in the life of the virtuous can be marred by bad luck.

Luck in Exercising the Virtues: Aristotle's Torture Victim

Aristotle famously says that one needs luck in order to *exercise* the virtues that one has. Aristotle says that even if one is able to run the fastest, one might by bad luck not have the opportunity to run (e.g., one might be unlucky in a coma, or imprisoned). Aristotle says that a person who is chronically asleep cannot have *eudaimonia* if that person cannot exercise the virtues in virtuous *activity*, and the person with the best ability lacks *eudaimonia* if she cannot participate in the Olympics (1098b35–1099a5).[18] Aristotle says that the perfectly virtuous person would act well *if* she was in circumstances in which the virtues can be properly exercised, but being in such circumstances is a matter of luck that is not entirely up to the virtuous agent herself.[19] As discussed earlier, Aristotle also thinks that the exercise of virtue is required in order to develop and maintain virtue. Thus, the luck in exercising virtue also translates into luck in developing and keeping virtue.

Some philosophers believe that the lucky circumstances required by Aristotle for full exercise of virtue include being generally rich and powerful.[20] I disagree. Aristotle says that the virtuous person "bears all the misfortunes of life with dignity," and says that only "*modest means,*" including those of community, friends, and food, are required for the exercise of virtue and *eudaimonia* (1179a4–9; cf. *Analects* 15.7). In *NE* X.8, Aristotle reinforces the idea that *eudaimonia* requires only modest means when he says:

> Being a man, one will need external prosperity; for our nature is not self-sufficient… as our *body must be healthy and have food* and other attention. We must not think that the man who is to have *eudiamonia* needs many things or great things. Moreover, we can do fine (*kalon*) actions even if we do not rule earth and sea; for even from *moderate resources* we can do the actions that accord with virtue. This is evident to see, since many private citizens seem to do decent actions no less than people in power do—even more, in fact. It is enough if *moderate resources* are provided; for the life of someone whose activity accords with virtue will be happy (*eudaimon*). Solon surely described happy people well when he said they had been moderately supplied with external goods, had done what he regarded as the finest actions, and had lived their lives temperately. For it is possible to have moderate possessions and still do the right actions. And Anaxagoras would seem to have supposed that the happy person was neither rich nor powerful, since he said he would not be surprised if the happy person appeared an absurd sort of person to the many (*hoi polloi*). The many (*hoi polloi*) judge by externals [such as wealth], since these are all they perceive.
>
> (1179a4–17)(my italics)

Consider this example, in which someone develops, maintains, and exercises the virtues under circumstances of extremely modest means. There was a successful Jewish businessman who, by his own lights, had led a selfish life and lacked virtue (thus lacking *eudaimonia*).[21] Later, however, this man was forced into a Nazi concentration camp, where he was abused, used for hard labor, fed little, and housed in deplorable conditions. However, he became an important member of the Jewish community in the camp, and was the center of a network that saved many lives. From Aristotle's point of view, this man had *eudaimonia* for the first time; indeed, the man said that in the camp his life was good for the first time. The man was exercising the virtues and contributing to the well-being of a community, which is the expression of the highest good in accord with the highest human science, political science (1094a28–1094b13).

However, it is a matter of luck that this man had enough food so that he could exercise his reason properly, since at some point of nutritional deprivation one's brain does not function well. It is also a matter of luck that he lived in the right kind of community in which he could properly exercise the virtues. If he had been placed in chains in solitary confinement, he would have lacked the right kind of community and opportunity to develop and exercise the virtues. One needs the luck to have the friendship, community, and health necessary for the proper development and exercise of the virtues.

Now compare this example to Aristotle's example of torture on the rack. Aristotle's discussion of happiness on the rack occurs in the context of his discussion of *pleasure*. Aristotle is arguing that pleasure is *unimpeded* activity (and pain is impeded activity) (1153a30, 1153b13) when he says:

> This is why all think the happy life is pleasant and weave pleasure [as unimpeded activity of the soul] into happiness, quite reasonably, since no activity is complete if it is impeded, and happiness is something complete. Hence the happy person needs to have goods of the body and external goods added, and needs fortune (*eutuches*) also, *so that he will not be impeded* in these ways. Some maintain, on the contrary, that we are happy when we are broken/tortured on the rack *and* fall into terrible misfortunes, provided that we are good (*agathon*). Willingly or unwillingly, these people talk nonsense.
>
> (1153b17–21)

The point that Aristotle is making here is that some things external to one's soul can go so badly, due to bad luck, that the activity of the most virtuous soul is impeded. Aristotle is not saying, however, that severe torture automatically impedes the proper activity of the soul by preventing the exercise of the relevant virtues.[22] The courageous person who is fighting off pain is in some sense impeded in body but can be unimpeded in the exercise of his virtuous activities.

Take the famous example of Themistocles' reliable servant, Sicinnus. In 480 BCE, Sicinnus allows himself to be captured by the Persian army to feed King Xerxes false information that the Greek navy is hiding at the Straits of Salamis and can be crushed if Xerxes hurries there with his fleet.[23] Imagine that in order to achieve a Greek victory, Sicinnus must purposefully allow himself to be captured, submit to torture, and give false information about the location of the ships of Themistocles. Certainly, as in the case of the supremely courageous man who is suffering as a result of pursuing courageous activities, Sicinnus' activities are impeded in some ways (e.g., his body is impeded, and he suffers bodily pain). However, Sicinnus' suffering on the rack is part of a shared activity or game plan that is necessary in order to secure victory and the well-being of the *polis*. In this case, Sicinnus has fortune on his side and completes his activities *through* being tortured on the rack, and the torture does not impede the relevant virtuous activities. Similarly, the severe suffering of the Jewish businessman in the concentration camp does not impede his virtuous activity. Indeed, even during great bodily suffering, one can take pleasure in one's activities going well (such as those of helping one's community).[24]

Luck in Exercising the Virtues: Confucius's Yan Hui

Now compare Sicinnus' and the Jewish man's "modest means" (with the pains and pleasures) to those of the virtuous Yan Hui in the *Analects*. Confucius says that (despite his hunger) Yan Hui has sufficient rice, water, and shelter to take pleasure (*le*) in both learning and contributing in his Confucian community (*Analects* 6.11, 7.16, 7.19). Yan Hui is hungry but takes pleasure in exercising his virtue. While some[25] refer to the following *Analects* passage to show that luck is not important to Confucius's ethics, I believe that the passage shows just the opposite:

> The Master said, "A person of character (*xian*) is this Yan Hui! He has a bamboo bowl of rice to eat, a gourde of water to drink, and a dirty little hovel in which to live. Other people would not be able to endure his hardships, yet for Yan Hui it has no effect on his joy (*le*)."

> (6.11)

Confucius echoes this sentiment when he says in *Analects* 7.15 that he himself needs the same things in order to have proper joy:

> The Master said, "With coarse rice to eat, with water to drink, and my bended arm for a pillow; I still have joy in the midst of these things. Riches and honors acquired by inhumanity are to me as a floating cloud."

Rather than showing the lack of need for good luck, such quotes show that a certain kind of modest luck is important for the joy of virtuous people, and the greatest joys for virtuous people are in the exercise of the virtues, such as putting the learning of virtue into practice (*Analects* 1.1, 7.16).

The moral luck of Yan Hui is much the same as the kind of luck in the case of the Jewish man and Sicinnus. Like Sicinnus, Yan Hui had the right conditions and the right modest means, including the right community, sufficient food, and sufficient shelter. Yan Hui's modest amount of luck is all that is needed in order to develop, maintain, and exercise the virtues, but the modest luck is indeed necessary. Yan Hui's exercise and development of virtue is augmented, due to his lucky situation of being able to learn in the community of Confucius and the disciples. According to his own lights, if Yan Hui had not had the luck of having a great teacher like Confucius, he would not have learned as much, developed so much virtue, and thus would not have been able to put such learning and virtue into practice (and thus would not have exercised the virtues) (6.3, 6.7, 9.11).

In *Analects* 1.1, Confucius says that it is a great pleasure to put such learning into active practice. To take pleasure in putting such learning into practice is to take pleasure in virtuous activity, and it may be a matter of luck to be able to exercise the virtues in such actual practice.[26] In *Analects* 9.13, Confucius says "If you have a jade, sell it! I myself await an offer," meaning that we should put our virtue (the jade) into active practice. Famously, Confucius often lamented that he lacked the luck to put his virtue (the jade) into practice in government, where one often has a great impact on the well-being of a community. However, Confucius (like Aristotle) had significant outcome luck, since his philosophy was taken up by many after his death.

Conclusion: Luck and Moral Stability

For both Aristotle and Confucius, good governments, like the virtues themselves, stabilize our moral lives and mitigate against bad moral luck, but cannot overcome it entirely. Good government can secure the basic necessities that help us to act better early in our pre-virtue lives, which can also help us to develop the full virtues. Confucius says that good government can help one to develop the love of learning and virtues through good ritual and rulers. Confucius's *Analects* says that an important role of government is to secure the conditions for making people ethically better. When the ruler is virtuous, the people will act well as wind blows down grass, as the straight straightens the crooked and the inferiors follow their superiors (*Analects* 12.19). In the *Nicomachean Ethics*, Aristotle says that the function of good political institutions is to train and educate the unformed young, and that this training allows the young to *practice* and develop virtue (1105b4–12). In the *Politics*, Aristotle says that the goal of government is to help all people in the city to live and act well (1252b27). Thus, good government mediates against bad luck by helping people to live and act better than they would otherwise.[27]

Also, Confucius and Aristotle can both account for the moral importance of (a) Kantian inner moral strength, which is very stable, as well as (b) the moral importance of hitting the consequentialist, external targets of virtue. The virtues for Confucius and Aristotle make (a) and (b) very reliable, but not necessarily so, since they are still subject to some moral luck. Confucius and Aristotle (*contra* Kant) require some moral luck in the moral life, but only require the "modest means" that Yan Hui had. For Confucius and Aristotle, once we *have* the virtues (by such modest luck), our moral lives are extremely (but fallibly) stable, due to our *inner* goodness (*contra* utilitarianism). Confucius says that the *junzi*'s life has a stable (albeit fallible) moral goodness even when there is lack of food or good rulers. In *NE* I.10, Aristotle says that King Priam's virtuous life can be shaken only by "serious misfortune," and while Priam's life cannot be wretched, since he has the virtues, Priam cannot be permanently blessed (*makarios*) due to his bad luck (1100a7–9, 1101a1–14).[28]

Confucius, when reflecting on virtue, stability, and permanence, says, "Only the wisest and the stupidest do not change" (*Analects* 17.3; cf. 19.12). For Confucius, only the virtue of the wisest person, the *sage*, is permanent and stable enough to withstand anything. The rest of us need moral luck in order to change and develop in the right way; even Confucius and Emperor Shun were not sages, according to the *Analects* (6.30, 14.42).[29] Even the *junzi* makes mistakes and acts badly on occasion, and needs the luck of receiving proper lower learning, since he is not virtuous from the beginning to end of life like the sage.[30] For Aristotle, only the dead can be permanently *eudaimon*, and even these fortunate dead are subject to the fortune that later befalls family and friends (1101b5–9).[31]

Analects 1.2 says, "Once the roots are firmly established, the way (*dao*) will grow." However, it may be a matter of luck whether or not our filial roots originally are of the right nature and get firmly established by the right family and community. It is a matter of outcome luck whether the strong filial roots extend long into the future. However, because of the stability of virtue, "The *junzi* is self-possessed and relaxed, while the small person (*xiao ren*) is full of worry" (7.37).[32] The *junzi* is less anxious about the vicissitudes of the world, since the *junzi*'s goodness is made stable by the virtue that comes from within (2.4). The *junzi* is anxious about the way (*dao*) and not poverty (15.32), whereas the small person is anxious about material things, which are particularly sensitive to luck.[33] There are various things that make our moral goodness more stable, including good governments, good habits (virtues), good friends, good teachers, good parents, good upbringings, good age, and even adequate food and sleep. Confucius and Aristotle both recognize that the things that bring stability to our moral goodness come in part from moral luck.[34]

Part III

Practicality, Justification, and Action Guidance

12 The Practicality of Ancient Virtue Ethics

Greece and China

Yu Jiyuan

Introduction

One charge against virtue ethics is that it is unable to provide solutions to practical moral issues, and hence can hardly be a normative rival to utilitarianism and deontology. As one critic remarks, "People have always expected ethical theory to tell them something about what they ought to do, and it seems to me that virtue ethics is structurally unable to say much of anything about this issue" (Louden 1997: 205). This charge is hardly new, for even long before the contemporary revival of virtue ethics, H. A. Prichard claimed that an appropriate moral philosophy should address the issue of what one ought to do, yet Aristotle's ethics is not up to that task and is therefore disappointing.[1] In response to this charge, the defenders of virtue ethics insist that normative virtue ethics exists and can guide actions by telling us what one should do. Virtue ethics can come up with a large number of rules, "not only does each virtue generate a prescription—act honestly, charitably, unjustly, but each vice is a prohibition—do not act dishonestly, uncharitably, unjustly" (Hursthouse 1996: 25). It should also be noted that one reason for the revival of virtue revive is precisely because of the limits, conflicts, and application of the action-guiding rules.

The debate is significant by itself, yet it occurs and develops within the framework of contemporary normative ethics, as both sides of the controversy approach the issue from the assumption that moral philosophy has to tell us what we should do. It is not my purpose in this paper to enter the debate directly. Rather, what I would like to do is to put aside this contemporary perspective and ask instead a different question regarding the practicality of virtue ethics. Virtue ethics is an ancient approach. Indeed, it is in ancient Greece that ethics is called "practical science." How, then, do the ancients themselves view the issue of practicality? Do they think that their ethics is practical? If so, how? This essay is an effort to understand the practicality of ancient virtue ethics in the light of their own vision rather than according to our own conception. Since virtue ethics is an approach shared by both ancient Greek philosophers and classical Chinese Confucians, I would like to draw from both of these traditions in order to achieve a better understanding of this notion of practicality and of the difference between ancient and contemporary virtue ethics. The next section shows that there is a notion of practicality which is prominent in both ancient Greek and ancient Chinese virtue ethics but which differs from contemporary ethics. According to this notion, ethics is to transform people's lives. The next following section examines several representative ancient figures in order to give a glimpse of how they could claim that their respective ethics can actually transform people's lives. The final section offers some explanation as to why this notion of practicality is neglected in today's ethics, and raises the prospect of its revival.

Practicality in Ancient Greek and Chinese Virtue Ethics

It is immediately clear that the issue of practicality is at the core of ancient virtue ethics. When Socrates changes the course of philosophy by conceiving philosophy as a practical enterprise rather than a theoretical inquiry, he does not simply mean that philosophy is in search of practical knowledge; rather, it is to take care of people's souls (*Apology* 29e, 38a).[2] He declares that he has a mission from the Delphic oracle and that the purpose of philosophy is to act as a gadfly to stir up the Athenians (*Apology*, 30e; cf. also, 30a, 33c, 40b–c.). The remark "unexamined life is not worth living" clearly shows that what is examined is "life" rather than "knowledge" or "proposition." If Greek philosophy undergoes a shift of course in Socrates, Chinese philosophy focuses on ethics from the very beginning. Philosophical discourse is to find and justify the Heaven-based human *dao* (way), which is the correct way to live and the correct way to organize a community. Just as Socrates has a sense of divine mission, Confucius is said to be used by Heaven "as the wooden tongue for a bell" (*Analects* 3.24).[3] His mission is to restore the *dao* that has been lost and to bring people back from the wrong path or way.

Aristotle divides knowledge into three types: theoretical, practical, and productive, and he puts ethics under the category of practical science. While theoretical sciences (including mathematics, physics, and first philosophy) are concerned with eternal truth and are for the sake of understanding, a practical science (1) is concerned with human affairs and for the sake of living well and acting well, and (2) aims at practical impact rather than a purely intellectual exercise to fulfill the desire to know. For Aristotle, the second aspect is even more important. He claims that "Our present discussion does not aim, as our others do, at study; for the purpose of our examination is not to know what virtue is, but to become good, since otherwise the inquiry would be of no benefit to us" (*Nicomachean Ethics*[*EN*] 1103b27–9; cf. also, 1095a5; 1099b29–32; *Eudemian Ethics* [*EE*] 1216b1–25).[4] The goal of ethical investigation is not to obtain theoretical knowledge, but to turn a student into a better person. Aristotle even goes so far as to hold that ethics is not worth pursuing if it does not result in making us better human beings.

The belief that ethics has a direct bearing on our way of living is a dominant characteristic of philosophy in the Hellenistic and Roman eras. In that period, philosophy was mainly considered as an art of living, with an emphasis on the need to involve oneself practically. Inner tranquility (or freedom from disturbance, *ataraxia*) was the common goal of Stoicism, Epicureanism, and skepticism, although each school provided its own recipes for how to reach this practical goal.[5] Similarly, in Chinese philosophy, the followers of Confucius continue to emphasize the practical bearing of its philosophy. The goal of Confucianism is "inner sagehood and outer kingship." For Xunzi, "The utmost attainment of learning lies in moral performance" (Xunzi 1988–94: 8/33/114). This feature is also shared by other schools. For the Daoist Laozi, bad students would laugh at his teaching; yet, "when the best student hears about the *Dao*, he practices it assiduously" (*Laozi* 41, in Chan 1963). Mohism extends its utilitarian project to the nature of philosophy itself, to the effect that only those doctrines that can be translated into conduct can be taught.

Apparently, to make ethics efficacious is at the center of each ancient ethicist's perspective. The notion of practicality, however, is different. In contemporary normative ethics, being practical means telling us what to do. To this effect, ethics must provide one or one set of rules for the agents to apply in order to solve particular problems. In contrast, ancient virtue ethicists in Greece and China do not share this position, not because they do not recognize the value of the action-guiding rule, but because they believe that the cultivation of character from which an action is issued is far more fundamental. As Aristotle states clearly, ethics cannot establish universal principles in order to provide clear guidance on how to act in all possible situations (*EN* 1094b14–22). It can be true only for the most part, and cannot deal with things "in every case" (*EN* 1094b21–5, 1095a4, 1098a29–b3, 1103b14–1104a10, 1112b8). This is not because ethics is incapable of finding the necessity, but because there is simply no necessity in the subjectmatter of ethics. Human situations and actions are infinitely various and indeterminate: "The general account being of this nature, the account of particular cases is yet more lacking in exactness; for they do not fall under any art or set of precepts, but the agents themselves must in each case consider what is appropriate to the occasion" (*EN* 1104a3–10). He therefore emphasizes the role of *phronimos* and the contextuality of practical reasoning. Similarly, the action-guiding rule has an important role to play. One crucial requirement for achieving *ren* (virtue, humanity, or benevolence) is the observance of social rites (*li*) (*Analects* 12.1). He also holds a theory of "rectification of names" (*zhengming*) (*Analects* 12.11), according to which the correct assignment of titles and social roles gives clear guidance and ensures a good order. Nevertheless, appropriateness *yi* (what is fitting or what is appropriate) is even said to be the most important factor for being an excellent person: "In his dealings with the world the excellent person is not invariably for or against anything. He is on the side of what is appropriate" (*Analects* 4.10; see also 17:23). Just as Aristotle, in coming to particular issues, Confucius trusts the virtuous agent's situation-sensitive practical wisdom rather than the rules and the rule-application procedure.

For ancient ethicists, being practical is in contrast to being theoretical. The ultimate goal of ethics is not the disinterested search for truth or the achievement of abstract knowledge. Ethics as a practical science aims at improving people's lives. It is for one to live and for one to transform oneself. It "transforms" people, rather than just "informs" them. Apparently, the charge that virtue ethics is not practical, so far as ancient virtue ethics is concerned, is anachronistic and misguided. We should understand ancient virtue ethics in its own structure and terms, rather than imposing our interest and framework. If we look at ancient virtue ethics from inside out, it is practical, albeit in a different sense.

Ethics as Transformative of People's Lives

How, then, do ancient philosophers think their virtue ethics can be practical in this way? This is a rich area for study, and here I can examine only briefly some representative figures in both Greek and Chinese tradition. Given the space, I discuss Plato's Socrates and Aristotle on the Greek side and Confucius and Mencius on the Chinese side. Needless to say, each of their positions is sophisticated, and each is open to many controversies. Hence, my discussion is limited to some general points that are germane to the topic of this essay. The objective is not to provide a detailed discussion of each position but to identify a common tendency and highlight some suggestive reasons that are behind the ancient confidence that virtue ethics can to help make better persons.

Socrates: "Say What You Believe"

In the *Apology*, when Socrates hears from the Delphic oracle that no one is wiser than him, he is perplexed and sets out to find a counterexample in order to *elegxein* (refute, cross-examine, or censure) the oracle (*Apology* 21c). This is how he starts his characteristic philosophical activity. The proper name to describe his activity, "elenchus" (examination, refutation) is derived from *elegxein*, although it is a modern scholarly innovation rather than Socrates' own usage. The subject matter of Socrates' elenchus is not limited to moral issues, yet it is the examination of the issues related to the moral question "how ought we to live?" that makes this practice philosophically significant (*Gorgias*, 487e7–488a2; *Republic* 352d). Socrates never examines the rationale of elenchus itself, and does not seem to regard his examination as a systematic method. This has given rise to numerous debates about the nature, guiding principles, scope, and limitation of elenchus, largely inspired by the works of Gregory Vlastos (see Vlastos 1983).

The elenchus exhibits often (although by no means universally) a structure like this. Socrates asks a question X (what is x? e.g., what is piety? what is temperance? etc). The interlocutor confidently affirms some thesis P in answer to the question X. Under Socrates' examination the interlocutor finds P problematic and tries to defend it. In the process, the interlocutor accepts other premises Q and R which Socrates introduces. Then, under further questioning, it appears that Q and R entail not-P. As a result, the interlocutor finds himself in the situation where he believes both p and not-p and is "at a loss" (*aporein*) about what to believe. Elenchus, however, does not just expose inconsistency of beliefs. More importantly, it examines people and their way of living. In the *Apology*, Socrates makes it very clear that his mission is to take care of people's souls. Elenchus leads the interlocutor to see whether his life is in agreement with his endorsed values. The interlocutor who is scrutinized undergoes a self-transformation and often ends in a state of perplexity and with a much humbler attitude. Elenchus, then, is neither eristic nor rhetoric. It is not a logical game; nor is it a matter of pure rational argumentation. Rather, it has a dual function, as a testing of persons as well as of beliefs.[6] Yet, how can Socrates' elenchus combine these two functions? What reasons does he have for believing that elenchus can help people to take care of the soul?

Socrates claims that he examines "any one of you whom I happen to meet," and "anyone I happen to meet, young and old, citizen and stranger" (*Apology*, 29d, 30a2–3). Nevertheless, he has a strict requirement of his interlocutor. That is, the interlocutor must tell what he really believes about the moral question that Socrates raises. Vlastos calls it the "say what you believe" constraint (Vlastos, 1983, 35; see *Euthyphro* 6b, 9d; *Protagoras* 331c–d; *Laches* 193c6–8; *Gorgias* 458a1–b1, 500b; *Crito*, 49c–d; *Republic*, 1. 346.). It is a demand for sincerity. Once an interlocutor says what he actually believes, the beliefs that are examined characterize the values of his life. Hence, the confusion and inconsistency that was brought to light by elenchus is the interlocutor's own. The interlocutor comes to see that many of his most basic value claims are incoherent and problematic. Such a revelation brings the interlocutor to a proper sense that his life might be guided by inadequate moral convictions, and also to a kind of awareness that some change is necessary. The refutation of these beliefs entails that the interlocutor's own life or a part of it is discredited.

Yet even if the interlocutor sincerely says what he believes, why would he be willing to reflect and modify his beliefs once he was led to see the inconsistencies in his own? It turns out that Socrates' ethical discussion assumes the following psychology of eudaimonism: "It's for the sake of what's good that those who do all these things do them" (*Gorgias*, 468b10; cf. 499e; *Meno*, 77c–78b, R. vi. 505d11). All human beings have an unconscious or self-conscious rational desire for the good, that is, *eudaimonia* (happiness or flourishing or well-being). People might hold different and even mistaken conceptions of happiness, yet everyone desires his or her own happiness. Hence, if one is aware that his own beliefs are problematic, the sense of one's own inadequacy frustrates the rational desire for the good and the agent cannot consistently pursue happiness.

Correspondingly, Socrates' elenchus will not work if the interlocutor is not willing to follow the rule of "saying what you believe" and does not tell the beliefs that one stands ready to live by. A typical example is provided in *Republic* 1, in which when Thrasymachus holds that injustice is fine and that justice is not a virtue, Socrates presses him: "I believe that you aren't joking now, Thrasymachus, but are saying what you believe to be the truth." To this Thrasymachus replies: "What difference does it make to you, whether I believe it or not?" (*Republic* 349a–b). When Socrates once again requires: "do not do that, contrary to your opinion," Thrasymachus says: "I'll answer so as to please you" (*Republic* 350e). Toward the end of the discussion, Thrasymachus himself says to Socrates, "Let that be your bequest, Socrates, at the feast of Bendis" (*Republic* 354a). This attitude makes it difficult for him to be an appropriate interlocutor. Beginning with Book 2 of the *Republic*, he is no longer the interlocutor and is replaced by two decent characters, Glaucon and Adeimantus.[7]

Aristotle: A Good Upbringing

Just as Socrates demands that his interlocutors state their own opinions, Aristotle also has a special demand for the audience of his ethics. That is, they must already have had a good upbringing and have a good character. It is this requirement that is behind his claim that his ethics is to turn his audience into better persons. Aristotle states this requirement clearly: "Any one who is to listen intelligently to lectures about what is noble and just and, generally, about the subjects of political science, must have been brought up in good habits" (*EN* 1095b4–5). What, then, is involved in being "brought up in good habits"?

A good upbringing, according to Aristotle, provides good starting-points (*archai*, also first principles): "For the facts (*to hoti*) are the starting-point, and if they are sufficiently plain to him, he will not need the reason (*to dioti*) as well; and the man who has been well brought up has or can easily get starting-points" (*EN* 1095b2–8). Here *to hoti* or starting-point means ethical beliefs and values, such as "do not steal," "be temperate," etc. If one is well brought up, these ethical values should have been instilled. Such a person is aware of what sort of things one should do and should not do, and also realizes that certain things are good in themselves. She does not need to be persuaded to accept the claims of morality, and what she needs is to understand better why the sort of life experience she has had is good.

A good upbringing also includes "delight in and to be pained by the things that we ought" (*EN* 1104b12–3). A qualified student is cultivated to have "noble joy and noble hatred" (*EN* 1179b25). Human beings have a natural tendency to do bad things because they bring about pleasure, and to avoid doing noble things because they cause pain and no pleasure. Pleasure and pain are the kinds of things that can easily corrupt a soul: "It is by reason of pleasure and pains that men become bad" (*EN* 1104b21–22; see also 1179b33–34). Children, like animals, pursue bodily pleasures to the point of excess (*EN* 1153a28–31). The youth also tend to follow sensuous passions and pursue what the passions direct (*EN* 1095a4–9). Whether an upbringing is good or not depends to a large extent on whether it teaches one not only to feel less pain but also to feel joy in performing virtuous acts such as being temperate or being generous. This kind of joy is generated from the belief that he is acting "for the sake of the noble (*to kalon*)" (*EN* 1115b10–3, 1120a23–27). This kind of enjoyment constitutes one's ethical taste. The enjoyment in doing the right thing is a crucial feature of being virtuous (*EN* 1099a16–21).

To summarize, in order to be an appropriate student of Aristotle's ethics, "the character, then, must somehow be there already with a kinship to excellence, loving what is noble and hating what is base" (*EN* 1179b29–31). Such a character, for Aristotle, is "like earth which is to nourish the seed" (*EN* 1179b26). Habituation shapes patterns of motivation and response in her and lays down the ground for her to listen to teaching. Without these instilled values, teaching is futile. For teaching must start from these and proceed to explain why right acts are right. Aristotle's students are well on their way toward virtues but have not reflected on the reasons and the end of a virtuous life. His ethics can help his audience to know and to choose, and help them to improve and to achieve the full virtue. It is in this sense that it can turn them into better persons.

The "good upbringing" requirement excludes several groups of people. The first group is those who are too young (*EN* 1095a2). The youth can be divided into two sub-groups, those who are young because of age, and those who are young because their character is immature and they are still guided by passions. The former sub-group does not have a certain amount of experience of life, and has not grasped the "starting-points" yet. The latter sub-group may have enough life experience but the controlling element in their life is passion rather than reason: "To such persons, as to the incontinent, knowledge gives no benefits" (1095a10). The second group to be excluded is those who are already brought up but are not brought up well and hence do not have good character. A person in this group is instilled with the wrong "starting-points." She does not have the correct ideas of what should and should not be done, and does not realize that things like virtue and justice are good in themselves. She is among those who "have not even a conception of what is noble and truly pleasant, since they have never tasted it"; further, he does not obey the sense of shame, and can be restrained from bad acts only through the fear of punishment; finally, this group lives by passion as well (*EN* 1179b13–14), just as those who are young in character. Since "in general passion seems to yield not to argument but to force" (*EN* 1179b28–29), this group is unreceptive to moral reasoning, and will not even hear argument: "What argument would remold such people?" (*EN* 1179b16).

Although his ethics excludes those who are not brought up yet and those who are not well brought up, his ethics has important things to say about how a child can be well brought up. He takes pains to emphasize the importance of the early environment of growth, because ethical virtue (*ēthekēaretē*), as its name indicates, is grounded in *ethos* (social custom or habit, *EN* 1103b24–6). He also believes that the state plays an important role in habituation through its coercive power of the laws, and that the primary concern for state legislation should be habituation and the citizens' character (*EN* 1180b29). For this reason, he does not separate ethics from politics and treats his studies of *politeria* as a continuing project of his discussion of happiness and character. Hence, although he does not seem to have much patience for converting wicked adults, he still tries to guide his students to provide a better political and social environment in order to generate good character.

Confucius: The Malleability of Human Nature

As mentioned earlier, Confucius has a deep sense of mission to restore the *dao* in the human world (*Analects* 4.12). Human *dao* is the correct way to live. Yet, how does he think that he can motivate people to live and practice his vision of *dao*? Since the heavenly *dao* that embodies in human life is human virtue (*de*), to acquire human *dao* means to cultivate human *de* (*xiu de*). In his approach to what virtue is, Confucius introduces another term, *ren* (usually rendered as benevolence, humanity; I prefer excellence). *Ren* is what Confucius believes human *de* is or should be. In other words, his theory of *ren* is his version of the theory of *de*. So the question becomes, how does Confucius get people to cultivate *de* or *ren*?

There is some relatively general advice. For example, "To return to the observance of the rites through overcoming the self constitutes *ren*" (*Analects* 12.1); and *ren* is "to love your fellow men" (*Analects* 12.22). The latter requires extending filial love. Yet how is it possible to make one return to the social rites, and how is it possible to make one extend his or her filial love? Confucius knows very well that human beings have a natural tendency to be attracted to physical pleasure and to avoid living in a virtuous way (*Analects* 4.6, 9.18, 15.13). He opposes appeal to force or punishment but emphasizes an attitude of reverence (*jing*) and sincerity (*cheng*) in practicing social rites (*Analects* 3.4, 3.17). It is crucial for a virtuous person to be true to his own heart. The truly virtuous act must genuinely come from the heart. A virtuous person is delighted in doing virtuous actions and in being virtuous (*Analects* 4.2, 4.6).

Confucius does not say explicitly how his ethics can actually achieve his goal. However, from his practice and his self-description, I think that the key point lies in his belief that human nature is indeterminate and amenable to reform. He says: "It is only the most intelligent and the most stupid who are not susceptible to change" (*Analects* 17.3). There are few, if any, who fall under these two categories. So far as the majority is concerned, "men are close to one another by nature. They diverge as a result of repeated practice" (*Analects* 17: 2). Confucius seems to think that there are two major ways to effect some modification in the nature of his audience. The first is his faith in the power of teaching, and the second is based on his trust in the influence of the role-model.

Confucius's self-image is that he is a teacher and learner, and he wishes to change people's lives through teaching. His teaching is open for everyone: "The Master said, 'in instruction there is no such thing as social class'" (*Analects* 15:39). As long as one is willing to learn and is able to pay him something as a present, the person can be his student. "The Master said, 'I have never denied instruction to anyone who, of his own accord, has given me so much as a bundle of dried meat as a present'" (*Analects* 7.7). The only requirement is intellectual. "I never enlighten anyone who has not been driven to distraction by trying to understand a difficulty or who has not got into a frenzy trying to put his ideas into words" (*Analects* 7.8).[8]

Although his teaching is open to everyone, Confucius has the students' particular circumstance and personality in mind when he instructs. Although Confucius considers himself to be a transmitter rather than an inventor, he has a theoretical discourse and he himself claims that his discourse is unified (*Analects* 4.15). Nevertheless, in his teaching, he does not present the theory and justify it through argumentation. He does not even offer any universal definition. Rather, for the same question, he gives different answers to different interlocutors, and in many cases these different answers are not even consistent. It is wellknown that he has many different replies to the same question "what is *ren*?" "what is piety," etc. The following case exemplifies Confucius's way of teaching (*Analects* 11.22). Zilu asks: "should one immediately put into practice what one has heard?" Confucius answers that Zilu is hardly in a position to do it because his father and elder brothers are still alive. Yet when Ran Yu asks the same question, the master replies, "yes, one should." In explaining this inconsistency, the Master says: "Qiu (Ran Yu) holds himself back. It is for this reason that I tried to urge him on. Yu (Zilu) has the energy of two men. It is for this reason that I tried to hold him back." Different students should be taught in different ways. The pointed answer is meant to help a student to develop an appropriate character, given where he is at. The Chinese term "to teach" (*jiaoyu*) is composed of two characters: teach and nurture. Confucius does not use this term, but to a great extent it is because of his teaching activity that the term developed.

In addition to his targeted and individualized teaching, Confucius also spent many years travelling with his disciples from state to state, hoping to influence rulers. This was not just to get some rulers to adopt his own political ideals, but also because he believed that rulers have to be rolemodels. We have mentioned that Aristotle combines ethics with politics on the grounds that legislation plays an essential role in habituation. Confucius also combines ethics and politics, but for a different reason. In his belief, to do politics (*zheng*) is to "correct" (*zheng*) (*Analects* 12.17), that is, to set up oneself as example. The effective way of ruling is not to appeal to force, but to "guide them by virtue, keep them in line with the rites, and they will, besides having a sense of shame, reform themselves" (*Analects* 2.3). Yet to guide people by virtue, the ruler must first be virtuous.

De (virtue) in Chinese was originally associated with "moral charisma" that one gets. Once an agent possesses virtue, he has the charismatic power to influence others, just like the wind influences the grass (*Analects* 12.19). The strong moral character of the rulers has great political significance. Having it or not having it directly determines the efficacy of his leadership: "If a man is correct in his own person, then there will be obedience without orders being given; but if he is not correct in his own person, there will not be obedience even though orders are given" (*Analects* 13.6; see also 13.13). If a ruler is virtuous, the people will look up to him and follow him. The good ruler must serve as a model for others to emulate: "The rule of virtue can be compared to the Pole Star which commands the homage of the multitude of stars without leaving its place" (*Analects* 2.1). Moral exemplification leads people to correct or improve themselves: "When the excellent feels profound affection for his parents, the common people will be stirred to *ren*" (*Analects* 8.2). I think it is because of his confidence in the impact of model emulation that Confucius traveled for so many years and took great pains to persuade and convert the rulers.

Mencius: The Good Human Nature

Mencius's project is to defend Confucius's way by providing a psychological basis for the latter. To undermine the challenges from Mozi's utilitarianism and Yang Zhu's egoism, he argues that Confucian values are already in our original human nature. Each human being has four innate roots or sprouts for virtue (*Mencius* 6a6). The sprouts form a tendency toward the good. When the root grows or becomes mature, it becomes a full-blossom virtue. Human beings have all the same potential or heavenly conferred nature, yet they become rather different as moral beings. Why? "This is only because there are people who fail to make the best of their native endowment" (*Mencius* 6a6).

How, then, can this theory actually motivate people to adopt and live the Confucian way? Mencius appears to believe that once a person is aware of such a good nature, she is on the way to becoming a better person. That is, he has confidence in the impact of enlightenment and persuasion. Partly for this reason, a significant part of Mencius's philosophy is devoted to demonstrating and explaining the existence of innate human goodness. He refutes the alternative views of human nature and also provides positive proof that human nature has innate goodness.

He infers from the preferences that our senses share to the conclusion that we possess the same hearts (*Mencius* 6a7). He also seeks to identify spontaneous and morally meaningful natural inclinations in human beings, and then takes these inclinations as real manifestations of good human nature: "What a man is able to do without having to learn it is what he can truly do" (*Mencius* 7a15). In his well-known story of the well and the child (*Mencius* 2a6), the man's reaction in saving the child is without any calculating consideration of consequences or self-interest. It is instantaneous and spontaneous, and hence, for Mencius, it must be a true aspect of man's nature.

The book of *Mencius* provides us with a striking example of how Mencius applies his ethics to transform a king. In *Mencius* 1a7, Mencius visits King Xuan of Qi and tells the king that the virtue of a true king is to care for his people. The king asks: "Can someone like myself tend the people?" The question reveals that the king lacks confidence in himself. He knows well that he has caused his people great pain by over-taxing them and by sending them to war in order to expand his territory. He also realizes that he has personal weaknesses ("I am fond of money. ... I am fond of women" (*Mencius* 1b5)). Given his theory that we are all born to have a good nature, Mencius assures the king that it is still possible for him to become a good king. The king asks again: "How do you know that I can?" To convince him, Mencius brings up a story about the king himself. One day the king happened to see an ox being led to slaughter. He could not bear to see the ox shrinking with fear, so he spared the ox and ordered it to be replaced with a lamb. With Mencius' therapeutic persuasion, the king comes to see his own motivation clearly: "Though the deed was mine, when I looked into myself I failed to understand my own heart. You described it for me and your words struck a chord in me." From this, Mencius proceeds to point out that "the heart behind your action is sufficient to enable you to become a true king." He infers as follows: If one is strong enough to lift a hundred pounds, one must be able to lift a feather; if such a person does not lift a feather, it is only because he fails to make an effort. Now since the king cares about an animal, his lack of caring for people is not because he is not able to do it (*bu neng*), but because he does not make the effort to do it (*bu wei*).

This text has given rise to a significant debate regarding the nature of extension. Is it true that it is due to *bu wei* (making no effort to do it) rather than *bu neng* (not being able to do) that the king lacks compassion for the people? On what grounds can Mencius get the king's compassion in the case of the ox to extend toward his people?[9] I treat *Mencius* 1a7 as a case in which Mencius demonstrates how his philosophy can have a practical effect. He thinks that his philosophy can change people, and he shows us with an example how he attempts to transform people. The story of the ox enables the king to appreciate his own intuitive moral responses and reminds him that he has inborn moral seeds. The king comes to realize that he has a potential to be good and to do good things. This step is apparently effective, for once the king is brought to see and appreciate his true motivation, he is "pleased."

Mencius then proceeds to show the similarity between the suffering of the ox and the suffering of the king's subjects and to try to make the king generate the appropriate response towards the latter. Given that his moral sprout is both rational and emotional, the extension must involve both dimensions. Is Mencius effective at this step? It depends on what the goal is here. If the king is expected to change his behavior right away and immediately become a good king, it does not sound likely that this would happen. Such a projected goal would also contradict Mencius's theory of moral cultivation. The weak and fragile roots could easily be overwhelmed by strong appetites and passions. It is Mencius's belief that the roots can be grown only if the agent constantly exercises great self-effort (*Mencius* 4a19). The agent should not lose self-respect (*zi qi*) and should not cripple oneself by denying one's own potentialities (*zi bao*) (*Mencius* 4a10). The agent should also cultivate the vital energy (*qi*) and develop the "state of unmoved mind" (*bu dong xin*) (*Mencius* 2a2). Furthermore, the agent must also practice social rites (*Mencius* 3a5), and study the paradigmatic examples of history (*Mencius* 2a2 and 2a9). Accordingly, between *bu neng* and *bu wei*, there is a matter of cultivation. The king needs to go through a process of ritualization and emotional training. The root needs to be developed, and the development takes time.

But I think Mencius's purpose is rather to put the king on the way to becoming good by making the king realize his own potential and by showing that the extension is sound both rationally and emotionally. Just as the interlocutors of Socrates feel disturbed once their confusion is exposed, Mencius's "analogical reasoning" seeks to make the king feel disturbed. The king may not immediately proceed to exercise his new appreciation, yet he should pause to think about his previous behaviors. That is, the analogy should be able to make him start the process. As we are told on a different occasion, Mencius makes it clear that the king needs more help to enable his root to grow: "Even a plant that grows most readily will not survive if it is placed in the sun for one day and exposed to the cold for ten. It is very rarely that I have the opportunity of seeing the king, and as soon as I leave, those who expose him to the cold arrive on the scene. What can I do with the few new shoots that come out?" (*Mencius* 6a9). The king has the potential (*neng*) but he needs cultivation in order to actually exercise it (*wei*). If Mencius were given sufficient opportunities, he could provide great assistance. Thus, Mencius's ethics not only shows the human potential for being good, but also can help the agent to develop this potential.

Summary

To sum up, there are significant differences among these philosophers about how to carry out their ethical ideals, just as they are different regarding what their ethical ideals are. The Greek side has specific requirements for its audience. For Socrates, the interlocutor has to tell his own opinion; for Aristotle, a student must have a good upbringing. The Chinese side assumes views on human nature, either because it is amenable (Confucius) or because it innately has a tendency toward the good (Mencius). Furthermore, Confucius's teaching is open for everyone. He does not have the Socratic requirement that the interlocutor say what he truly believes, and he also does not have the Aristotelian requirement of a good character. Aristotle thinks that effective teaching starts from a good character, while Confucius thinks that any character can be changed by teaching. Nevertheless, although Confucius does not take character into consideration in admitting students, his teaching points to the individual. Furthermore, there are striking contrasts between Mencius and Aristotle. In Aristotle's view, argument cannot change a person who does not have a good character. A moral lecture about how to extend natural ethical roots, no matter how logically effective, is not sufficient to make an uncultivated agent actually engage in extension. Yet in Mencius, even if a character is bad, argument or persuasion remains useful and can start the process of transformation. It is never too late to cultivate oneself. Nevertheless, beyond their differences there is a common approach. Each of these ancients has a perspective about how his respective virtue ethics can be practical. This is a central concern for them in developing virtue ethics. All these perspectives are related to the audience, either their character or their human nature.

Practicality and Contemporary Ethics

We have pointed out that ancient Greek and Chinese virtue ethics share a specific notion of practicality, and have also shown some of their main ways of making virtue ethics effective. This approach to ethics is characteristic of Chinese as well as of Greek virtue ethics and is indeed a common feature that unites these traditions. In order to realize that there is such a notion of practicality in ancient ethics it is important for us to understand how the ancients themselves think of the practical nature of virtue ethics, and to make further comparison between these two ancient traditions. More importantly, we have noticed that such a notion of practicality is neglected in the debate about whether virtue ethics could be normative. This reveals a significant difference between ancient virtue ethics and contemporary virtue ethics. Earlier in the essay I quoted Aristotle's remark at *EN* 1103b27–9 that the aim of his inquiry into ethics is not to know what virtue is but to make a better person. It is clear that although we are reviving Aristotelian ethics, what we are interested in is his theoretical approach to ethics, but we have more or less ignored his claim that virtue ethics is "to make a better person." In this sense, the revival of virtue ethics is partial.

We cannot help but wonder how we should treat this notion of practicality. Is it justifiable to ignore this notion in today's discussion of virtue ethics? Is it necessary and possible to revive it as well? This is, of course, an issue too big to be properly dealt with here. I can only raise the question and make some preliminary remarks for further discussion. It is not accidental that the ancient notion of practicality is neglected in current debate regarding the normativity of virtue ethics. To a great extent, this is determined by different ways of doing ethics between the ancients and us. Ancient philosophers are motivated to do ethics because they take it as a way of life. It is deeply personal rather than professional. They are committed to their life-ideal and seek to convince others that their way of life is the only one that is correct. Their ethical discourse is the expression and justification of their specific perspective of how human beings should live. Hence, it is not surprising that it is of central concern to them whether their chosen way of life would be efficacious. Ancient philosophers seek to embody their philosophy in life; to discuss ethics is a process of self-cultivation and self-growth. Socrates explicitly expresses that, in examining other people, he himself is also examined (*Apology* 28e4–6; *Charmides* 166c–d; *Protagoras* 348c; *Gorgias* 500b–c). For Confucius, one of his top worries is the failure to cultivate virtue (*Analects* 7.3).

In contrast, nowadays ethics is an academic discipline and a theoretical inquiry. It is predominantly devoted to conceptual classification, thought experiments, and argument construction. Even "applied" or "practical" ethics is primarily a matter of applying ethical ideas and principles to difficult concrete moral cases such as abortion, euthanasia, animals, war, etc. Ethicists are trained and employed professionals. Most practitioners of ethics are doing it out of intellectual interests and academic training, and few of them relate ethical views to their own lives. There are professional norms to determine what sort of study should be done and how to conduct scholarship. To follow these norms is crucial for one's career. Thus, to be an ethicist is one thing, and to live one's life is another. Ethical discourse is not developed with the purpose of justifying a certain way of living, and indeed the view that there is only one correct choice of living is utterly rejected. It is not an integral part of discussion about whether and how one's theoretical work is related to actual life.

Since ancient philosophers present a way of living that should be practiced, and for each of them his ideal is the only true way to live, their students are taught to adopt and practice that way. Neither teaching nor learning is purely intellectual. Teaching seeks to transform the self and to achieve spiritual progress in the students, and students are supposed to become the followers of the way of life that the teacher advocates and embodies. Students are required to constantly practice what they have learned. Aristotle once criticizes those people who do not practice repeatedly. They "take refuge in theory and think they are being philosophers and will become good in this way, behaving somewhat like patients who listen attentively to their doctors, but do none of the things they are ordered to do. As the latter will not be made well in body by such a course of treatment, the former will not be made well in soul by such a course of philosophy" (*EN* 1105b12–17). The *Analects* begins by emphasizing the inseparability of learning and practice: "Is it not a pleasure, having learned something, to try it out at due intervals?" (*Analects* 1.1). One of the traditional ways to learn Confucianism is to recite the classic text over and over again, and the assumption is that through repeated readings, one can relive the teacher's life.

In contrast, such a manner of teaching would nowadays be called "indoctrination", and would most likely get the professor of ethics into trouble. A course on ethics is to teach students to critically examine various ethical concepts, arguments, and theories. A professor is expected to train students how to think independently and critically, but it is not in his or her job description to take care of the soul of the students or to turn them into morally better persons. That is, he or she trains only intellectual virtues, not moral virtues. Correspondingly, with some exceptions, students take the course mainly for intellectual interest or for credits, and rarely for personal examination or spiritual progress.

Owing to these differences, it is difficult for us to completely copy the ancient ways of making virtue ethics practical, as presented in the preceding section of this paper. In today's college setting, teaching ethics means theoretical instruction. The

Socratic requirement ("the interlocutor has to tell her own opinion") can hardly be applicable in a classroom, with the possible exception of one-to-one teaching. The Aristotelian requirement ("a student must have a good upbringing") cannot be followed in admitting students. Mencius's view of human nature ("human beings innately have a tendency toward the good") is controversial and can hardly be a premise in teaching. Although Confucius's position that human nature is changeable is widely accepted, for the sake of actualizing the changeability, he employs a peculiar way of teaching which points to a student's particular background and circumstances, and gives a specific answer to each. It is a challenge for us to follow the same practice in classroom teaching. Of course, there are far more modes of practice in ancient philosophical schools, and some of them we might still borrow, at least to some extent. Yet the difference should be clear in a general sense.

The important point, however, is that, even though we cannot completely copy ancient ways of making virtue ethics practical, the ancient perception that virtue ethics should effect some transformation in the agent's life remains significant and attractive. As shown in the second section of this essay, between the Greek and Chinese ancients, and even within each tradition, there are many differences, but that does not prevent them from having the same goal of transforming people. Contemporary virtue ethics has revived the ancient theoretical approach to ethics that ethics should be concerned with the character of the agent and with the whole course of the agent's moral life. Yet for the ancients this approach has a practical goal of effecting the cultivation of character, and this goal is an integral part of ethics. Why should contemporary virtue ethics leave out this goal? Ethics not only needs to know what virtue is but also should be able to help to cultivate it. No matter how many differences there are between the ancients and us, human beings today still need to cultivate their characters and improve their ways of living. Hence, in the debate about whether virtue ethics can be normative, in addition to arguing that virtue ethics can also have rules to guide actions, we should also keep alive this ancient perspective of practicality and make efforts to link the study of virtue to the conduct of life in modern society.

13 How Virtues Provide Action Guidance

Confucian Military Virtues at Work

Lo Ping-cheung

The Charge of Lack of Action Guidance

Robert B. Louden in his widely reprinted essay (Louden 1997(1984)) argues that virtue ethics suffers from several shortcomings, the first of which is its inability to provide action guidance in resolving moral dilemmas in applied ethics. He concludes in that section of the essay, "Virtue theory is not a problem-oriented or quandary approach to ethics: it speaks of rules and principles of action only in a derivative manner. And its derivative oughts are frequently too vague and unhelpful for persons who have not yet acquired the requisite moral insight and sensitivity. Consequently, we cannot expect it to be of great use in applied ethics and casuistry. The increasing importance of these two subfields of ethics in contemporary society is thus a strike against the move to revive virtue ethics" (Louden 1997, 206).

As a rebuttal of Louden's argument, P. J. Ivanhoe and Rebecca L. Walker have collected a number of articles that offer clear examples of virtue ethics actually at work in various practical fields (Walker and Ivanhoe 2007).[1] This essay attempts to provide another example from Chinese professional ethics, *viz.*, military ethics. I first briefly explain the "military [strategy] school" of thought in pre-Qin China and its representative writings. I then explicate the pivotal role of virtues in these treatises, and analyze how, according to their authors, virtues offer action guidance in decisions on when to wage wars (*ad bellum* issues) and how to conduct wars (*in bello* issues). On the basis of these analyses I argue for the robust presence of Confucian virtue ethics in these treatises.

The *Seven Military Classics* and the "Military [Strategy] School"

The English-speaking world is familiar with the treatise *The Art of War* by Sunzi (Sun-tzu). But "art of war" (*bing fa*) is in fact a genre of writings on military strategy and tactics that include many other texts. The Seven Military Classics is the best representative of this "art of war" corpus.[2] This set of treatises is the military bible in premodern China since 1078 CE (Johnston 1995, 45–47). It has a long history of interpretation, both for the whole set and for most individual books. These seven treatises are listed in chronological order in Table 13.1.

The first five of the Seven Military Classics are generally considered to be more important. This is not only because they are the earliest writings, but also because

Table 13.1 The Seven Military Classics

	Title in pinyin	Title in Sawyer	Era	Years
1	Master Sun's Art of War	Sun-tzu's Art of War	Spring and Autumn	770–476 BCE
2	Master Wu's Art of War	Wu-tzu	Warring States	475–221 BCE
3	Sima's Art [of War]	The Methods of Ssu-ma	Warring States	475–221 BCE
4	Master Weiliao	Wei Liao-tzu	Warring States	475–221 BCE
5	Taigong's Six Secret Teachings	T'ai Kung's Six Secret Teachings	Warring States	475–221 BCE
6	Three Strategies of Huang Shigong	Three Strategies of Huang Shih-kung	Later Han Dynasty Tang Dynasty	100–220 CE 618–907 CE
7	Questions and Replies between Li Weigong and Li Wei-kung	Questions and Replies between Tang Taizong and Tang Tai-tsung		

they are composed in the most creative period of Chinese civilization, comparable to classical Greece, the time of the "various masters of the hundred schools of thought" (*zhu zi bai jia*). These five treatises to a large extent represent the "military [strategy] school" (*bing jia*) among the many philosophical schools of thought in the pre-Qin era.[3] The masters of this school learn from masters of other schools and debate one another. Hence there are traces of Confucian, Daoist, and Legalist motifs in the writings of the "military [strategy] school." At the same time, by virtue of endemic warfare during that period, nearly every master of other schools of thought was intensely concerned with military affairs. The treatises of the "military [strategy] school" need to be read in this cultural context,[4] and this essay is confined to analyzing only these five treatises.[5]

The Pivotal Role of Virtues in the Military

A conspicuous moral dimension in all five treatises is the pivotal role that virtues play in their discussion of military matters. In this section I offer some examples, by no means exhaustive, from each of the five treatises and provide some analysis.

Master Wu's Art of War

The fourth chapter of this treatise is entitled "On Generalship." It starts off by contending that the cherished virtue of courage is not enough: "In general when people discuss generalship, they usually focus on courage. However, courage is but one of a general's many characteristics" (Sawyer 1993, 217). Generally speaking, an ideal general should possess these four valuable dispositional traits: awesomeness, virtue, benevolence, courage (Sawyer 1993, 218). This moral discussion has military implications in terms of tactics, *viz.*, we should watch out for the weak dispositional traits of the enemy and adjust our tactics accordingly:

In general the essentials of battle are as follows. You must first attempt to divine the enemy's general and evaluate his talent. In accord with the situation exploit the strategic imbalance of power; then you will not labor but will still achieve results. A commanding general who is *stupid and trusting* can be deceived and entrapped. One who is *greedy and unconcerned* about reputation can be given gifts and bribed. One who *easily changes his mind and lacks real plans* can be labored and distressed. If the *upper ranks are wealthy and arrogant* while the lower ranks are poor and resentful, they can be separated and divided. If *their advancing and withdrawing are often marked by doubt* and the troops have no one to rely on, they can be shocked into running off. If the *officers despise the commanding general* and are intent on returning home, by blocking off the easy roads and leaving the treacherous ones open, they can be attacked and captured.

(Sawyer 1993, 218–19; emphasis added)

In short, by watching out for these six character flaws one can conquer the enemy with minimal violence. Hence "the essentials of battle," according to this passage, is not a comparison of weaponry or a comparison of strategy and tactics, but a comparison of the dispositional traits of the commanders. Tactics are then chosen in accordance to the character flaws of the enemy commander.

Most of these military treatises also deal with statecraft, as warfare is part of statecraft. The very first chapter of this treatise is entitled, "Planning for the State," and says,

For this reason the Sage rests the people in the *Way* (*Dao*), orders them with *righteousness*, moves them with the forms of *propriety* (*li*), and consoles them with *benevolence*. Cultivate these four virtues and you will flourish. Neglect them and you will decline.

(Sawyer 1993, 207; emphasis added)

Virtues and vices of leaders are not only the determining factors of the winning and losing of wars, they are also the determining factors of the flourishing and decline of civil governance. Hence, the emphasis on the pivotal role of virtues in military personnel is no accident.

Taigong's Six Secret Teachings

Chapter 19 of this treatise is also entitled "A Discussion of Generals." It sets forth the view that generals have five critical "talents" and ten excesses. The five "talents" or virtues are: courage ("cannot be overwhelmed"); wisdom ("cannot be forced into turmoil"), benevolence ("will love his men"), trustworthiness ("will not be deceitful"), loyalty ("will not be of two minds") (Sawyer 1993, 62). The ten excesses include: "being courageous and treating death lightly; being hasty and impatient; being greedy and loving profits; being benevolent but unable to inflict suffering; being wise but afraid; being trustworthy and liking to trust others; being scrupulous and incorruptible but not loving men; being wise and indecisive; being resolute and self-reliant; and being fearful while liking to entrust responsibility to other men." We should be vigilant of these dispositional weaknesses because the enemy can devise corresponding tactics to exploit them. The author then concludes, "Thus 'warfare is the greatest affair of state, the Dao of survival or extinction.' The fate of the state lies in the hands of the general" (Sawyer 1993, 62–63). In other words, the fate of the war and the fate of the country lie not in the strength of weapons, the size of army, the strategy and the tactics, but in the character strengths and weaknesses of the commanding generals.

The next chapter (Chapter 20), "Selecting Generals," continues this discussion: "There are fifteen cases where a knight's external appearance and internal character do not cohere" (Sawyer 1993, 63). Hence we should administer character tests to find out their virtues and vices.

> First, question them and observe the details of their reply. Second, verbally confound and perplex them and observe how they change. Third, discuss things which you have secretly learned to observe their *sincerity*. Fourth, clearly and explicitly question them to observe their *virtue*. Fifth, appoint them to positions of financial responsibility to observe their *honesty*. Sixth, test them with beautiful women to observe their *uprightness*. Seventh, confront them with difficulties to observe their *courage*. Eighth, get them drunk to observe their *deportment*. When all eight have been fully explored, then the worthy and unworthy can be distinguished.
>
> (Sawyer 1993, 64)

Hence, once again, superior generals are those who have superior dispositional traits rather than those who have only fierce fighting skills. Background checks in recruitment should include a thorough character clearance.[6]

Master Sun's Art of War

In Chapter 1 of this world-famous treatise, the author sets forth five major factors that affect the outcome of a war: Dao, heaven, earth, generals, regulations. The factor of the generals consists of five dispositional traits: wisdom, credibility, benevolence, courage, and strictness (Sun Tzu 1994, 167). One prominent commentator, Tu Mu, elaborates,

> If wise, a commander is able to recognize changing circumstances and to act expediently. If sincere, his men will have no doubt of the certainty of rewards and punishments. If humane, he loves mankind, sympathizes with others, and appreciates their industry and toil. If courageous, he gains victory by seizing opportunity without hesitation. If strict, his troops are disciplined because they are in awe of him and are afraid of punishment.
>
> (Quoted in Sun Tzu 1963, 65)

Roger Ames aptly comments, "The first and foremost defining feature of the consummate military commander is that he must be an exemplary person (*chün tzu/junzi*), and must ply his military skills from a foundation of superior character. In this respect, the military commander is like any other officer in the service of the state. His ability to achieve great things within the parameters of his office – his efficacy – is a function of his cultivated humanity rather than any specific set of skills" (Sun Tzu 1993, 87).

Sima's Art [of War]²

In the third chapter of this treatise the author explains the *dao* of warfare:

> In general, to wage war: Employ spies against the distant; observe the near; act in accord with the seasons; take advantage of [the enemy's] material resources; esteem *good faith*; abhor *the doubtful*. Arouse the soldiers with fervor of *righteousness*. Undertake affairs at the appropriate time. Employ people with *kindness*. When you see the enemy, remain quiet; when you see turbulence, *do not be hasty to respond*. When you see danger and hardship, *do not forget the masses*. Within the state be *generous* and foster good faith. Within the army be *strict in discipline* and martial. When the blades clash, be decisive and adroit. Within the state there should be harmony; within the army there should be standards. When the blades clash, investigate. Within the state display *cooperation*; within the army display *uprightness*; in battle display *good faith*.
>
> (Sawyer 1993, 135; translation modified and emphasis added)

In other words, in addition to strategic and tactical maneuvers, virtuous leadership of the generals is indispensable. The same point is made in Chapter 4.

> In general, with regard to the people: Rescue them with *benevolence*; engage in battle with *righteousness*; make decisions through *wisdom*; fight with *courage*; exercise sole authority through *credibility*; encourage them with profits; and gain victory through achievements. Thus the mind must embody *benevolence* and actions should incorporate *righteousness*. Relying on [the nature of] things is *wisdom*; relying on the great is *courage*; relying on long-standing [relations leads to] *good faith*.
>
> (Sawyer 1993, 141; emphasis added)

Again, as affirmed in other treatises, virtuous character is important not only in warfare in particular, but also in statecraft in general. "In general the Dao for imposing order on chaos consists of first, benevolence; second, credibility; third, straightforwardness; fourth unity; fifth, righteousness; sixth, change; seventh, centralized authority" (Sawyer 1993, 137). In short, in time of peace, rule by virtue; in time of war, fight by virtue.

Master Weiliao

Again, the key to success of a general is the possession and exercise of good, stable character and the absence of character flaws:

As for the commanding general: ... He should be *composed* so that he cannot be stimulated to anger. He should be *pure* so that he cannot be inveigled by wealth. Now if the mind is deranged [by emotion], the eyes are blind, and the ears are deaf – to lead men with these three perversities is difficult!

(Sawyer 1993, 243–44; emphasis added)

And the same is true in statecraft (Sawyer 1993, 248).

Three interim conclusions can be reached regarding the analyses above. First, though the five treatises of the "military [strategy] school" are famous for being manuals of all kinds of military affairs in ancient China, especially in military strategies and tactics, they have a heavy emphasis on the critical role that various virtues and vices play and advocate strongly for the development of strong moral character. In this sense, these treatises are rather Confucian in concern. Their writers probably understand that, even when warfare is comparably primitive, the violence of warfare can turn humans into monsters. Hence the need to cultivate firm, moral dispositions so that soldiers and generals can spontaneously respond in a moral manner.[8] Second, just as an ordinary citizen needs to cultivate a strong moral character which partly constitutes the *telos* of being a good person and leading a good life, a professional needs to cultivate a strong moral character which partly constitutes the *telos* of being a good professional and, in this case, an excellent military general. Third, with hindsight, we can find many legendary military stories, East or West, to substantiate the claim that, in the final analysis, wars are often won by commanders with critical character strengths and lost by commanders with major character flaws. As the old saying goes, "character is destiny." A superior general defeats both the enemy within and the enemy without.[9]

This moral primacy of character is true of other professions as well. Robert B. Louden, a former critic of virtue ethics, admits, "There exists now a growing body of 'applied virtue ethics' literature which seeks to understand better those ideals of character which are relevant to the various professions. Writers in this area of virtue ethics have made a convincing case for the claim that reflection on what kind of persons professionals should be is a needed corrective to the dominant rule orientation in applied and professional ethics" (Louden 1990, 101–102).[10]

Military vs. Civilian Virtues

The virtues lists quoted in the last section have much resemblance to virtues lists in classical Confucianism. Hence the virtues of the public life (statecraft and warfare) are, by and large, continuous with the virtues of the personal life, with one exception. In the subsequent intellectual history of China there have been some vocal Confucian critiques of Master Sun's *Art of War* (*Sunzi Bingfa*), denouncing the text for advocating vice.

One major reason for the negative reaction is Sunzi's programmatic statement in Chapter 1: "[The Military] is the Way (Tao) of deception (*gui*)" (Sun Tzu 1994, 168).[11] An additional statement in Chapter 7 reinforces this view: "Thus the army is established by deceit (*zha*)" (Sun Tzu 1994, 198).[12] His *Art of War* was thus deemed a text that would corrupt morality very much in the way that Machiavelli's *The*

Prince was viewed in Europe during its early reception. In Confucianism, soldiers and generals alike need to cultivate virtues. To suggest that the quintessence of the military is all kinds of immoral tricks would require military men to cultivate vice on a daily basis.[13] It was Xunzi who first set up the antithesis between the Confucian way of *ren* and *yi* (benevolence and righteousness, i.e., morality) and Sunzi's way of *gui* and *zha* (Xunzi 1998–94, II, 218–221).

I submit that this charge is not justified. As mentioned in the last section, in Chapter 1 of the treatise Master Sun articulates five cardinal virtues of a good general: wisdom, credibility, benevolence, courage, and strictness. Wisdom (*zhi*) goes first because of the emphasis on the creative use of deceptive tactics in warfare. Here lies the division of mind between the Military Strategic School and the subsequent Confucian school. On the one hand, this understanding and cherishing of *zhi* has been widely accepted in Chinese society (cf. Raphals 1992). "*Zhi*" includes resourcefulness, as articulated in the expressions "witty and very resourceful" (*zuzhi duomou*) and "clever strategy" (*zhilüe, zhimou*). Down through the ages, as reflected in a number of idioms, Chinese people have accepted that a military leader needs to be both brave and astute (*zhiyong shuangquan*), that in some combat situations "the only way to take the enemy position is by strategy, not by forceful attack" (*zhike zhiqu, buke qianggong*), and that battle on the highest level is a battle of wits (*douzhi*). On the other hand, since Mencius, "*zhi*" in the sense of wisdom, as just explained, was not appreciated by Confucian philosophers. Though "*zhi*" was affirmed by Mencius as the fourth cardinal virtues after *ren* (benevolence), *yi* (righteousness/justice), and *li* (observance of rites), "*zhi*" does not mean wisdom as explained above (*pace* many translators). Rather, "*zhi*" in *Mencius* denotes an innate moral sense of right and wrong (II.A.6, VI.A.6). As neo-Confucianism has been dominated by the Mencian tradition, there has been a lack of appreciation of wisdom as a cardinal virtue. Hence the nervousness about Master Sun's advocacy of deceptiveness.

Some critics of Sunzi worry that the calculative mentality of employing deceptive devices may encourage vices when carried over into ordinary life. When one becomes accustomed to cheating his opponents, one may start to cheat on his family, friends, and employers.[14] A reply to this legitimate doubt is that one needs to be vigilant of the discontinuity between military and civilian life. The configuration of cardinal virtues for a virtuous commander is different from that of a virtuous civilian.[15] Shrewd, astute, resourceful, and tricky wisdom has a prominent place in the former,[16] but not in the latter. Despite our metaphors, life is *not* a battlefield; the mission in life is not to pursue one's enemies and conquer the hostile people around us. As long as Sunzi's *Art of War* is a bible only on the battlefield and not in professional and daily life, we can put the charge of moral corruption to rest.[17]

How Military Virtues Guide Military Actions

It is a standard view among virtue ethicists today that virtues do generate prescriptions or prohibitions to guide actions (Hursthouse 1999, Slote 2001). How this operates in the five treatises of the "military [strategy] school" will be briefly explained in this section.[18]

Ad Bellum *and Conflicting Virtues*

Morally speaking, the decision to wage a war must be based on weighty justification. The treatise *Sima's Art [of War]* is the most Confucian among the five treatises. It starts with Chapter 1, entitled "Benevolence the Foundation," which immediately articulates a moral justification *ad bellum*.

> In antiquity, taking benevolence (*ren*) as the foundation and employing righteousness (*yi*) to govern constituted "uprightness." However, when uprightness failed to attain the desired [moral and political] objectives, [they resorted to] expediency (*quan*). Expediency comes from the need for warfare, not from harmony among men. For this reason if one must kill a man/men to give stability and order to the people, then killing is permissible. If one must attack a state out of love for their people, then attacking it is permissible. If one must stop war with war, although it is war it is permissible. Thus benevolence is loved; righteousness is willingly submitted to; wisdom is relied on; courage is embraced; and credibility is trusted.
>
> (Sawyer 1993, 126; trans. corrected)

In other words, in general, an exemplary virtuous ruler of *ren* and *yi* would not wage wars. However, circumstances sometimes demand flexibility (*quanbian*). In that case, *ren* and *yi* would reluctantly condone warfare as a temporary measure of expediency (*quanyi*). The word "*quan*" is used in other Confucian texts to discuss moral dilemmas. Hence a resort to *quan* is a morally justified, temporary deviation from the standard norm (*jing*) as a result of weighing (*quanheng*) the relative rightness of the options.[19] As some ancient commentators put it, "When ancient kings resort to the military, though it is toxic for the country, the intention is prompted by the benevolence of being unable to bear people's suffering. ... The Ancient Sage Kings conduct all affairs out of benevolence and love. Even when they reluctantly resort to armed force it is still out of benevolence and love. It is not for the sake of acquiring more land and more cities. ... Benevolence is not only the basis of governance; it is also the basis of war" (Zhu 1992, 543–545; trans. mine).

Another passage that deserves our attention is from *Master Wu's Art of War*, also from the first chapter:

> In general the reasons troops are raised are five: to contend for fame; to contend for profit; from accumulated hatreds; from internal disorder; and from famine. The names [of the armies] are also five: "righteous army," "strong army," "hard army," "fierce army," and "contrary army." Suppressing the violently perverse and rescuing the people from chaos is termed "righteousness." Relying on [the strength of] masses to attack is termed "strong." Mobilizing the army out of anger is termed "hard." Abandoning the forms of propriety (*li*) and greedily seeking profit is termed "fierce." While the country is in turmoil and the people are exhausted, embarking on military campaigns and mobilizing the masses is termed "contrary."
>
> (Sawyer 1993, 208)

The term "righteous/just army" (*yi bing*) appears here, which is vastly popular in subsequent times. The author fully knows that most wars at that time are unrighteous or unjust wars, and he enumerates many of them. The only justified cause that he mentions here is "suppressing the violently perverse [or the wicked] and rescuing the people from chaos." This cause of righteousness is frequently mentioned in the other treatises. For example, in *Master Weiliao* it is said, "In general, [when employing] the military do not attack cities that have not committed transgressions or slay men who have not committed offenses. ... For this reason the military provides the means to execute the brutal and chaotic and *to stop the unrighteous*" (Sawyer 1993, 254; emphasis added). The context, especially toward the end of the paragraph, indicates that this terse description means to punish and even kill the "one man," *viz.*, the tyrant. Accordingly, the virtue of justice/righteousness and the vice of injustice/unrighteousness are concretely specified in these passages. They provide action guidance in the decision to wage war or not.

In short, virtuous rulers need to engage with tragic moral dilemmas, and the values deeply entrenched in their character help them to discern the right thing to do in weighing whether to wage a war or not. Virtues do provide action guidance even in such a dark time.[20] To wage a war is not something that an exemplary moral king (Sage King) would like to do. It is contrary to *ren*, one of his cardinal dispositional traits. But as a last resort, when nothing works to rectify the injustice/unrighteousness, his sense of justice/righteousness prompts him to wage the war, however reluctantly he proceeds.

Virtues in Bello

In a righteous expedition one should provide concrete evidence of one's good motivation and character. A virtue ethics of just/righteous war should include this component. In the five treatises of the "military [strategy] school" there is some discussion that in waging wars we should show our moral character and that war is not a matter of *realpolitik* – anything that can win the war is fair and square. In three treatises there are detailed instructions on what soldiers should refrain from doing during warfare. For example, at the end of Chapter 5 of *Master Wu's Art of War* is this instruction:

> Now as to the Way for attacking the enemy and besieging his cities: After his cities and towns have already been shattered, enter each of the palaces, take control of their bureaucrats, and collect their implements [of administration]. However, wherever your army goes do not cut down the trees, destroy houses, take the grain, slaughter the animals, or burn their supplies. *Thus you will show the populace that you do not harbor vicious thoughts.* Accept those who seek to surrender and settle them.
>
> (Sawyer 1993, 223; trans. corrected and emphasis added)

This passage unequivocally explains that the just cause that justifies the war needs to be manifested in conduct during war so that the right intention and motive can be revealed. The business of the "righteous army," according to the first chapter of this treatise, is "suppressing the violently perverse and rescuing the people from chaos." This is how the "righteous army" differs from the four kinds of unrighteous armies. Hence there should be a self-conscious effort, prompted by the sense of righteousness, not to spread the violence and savagery to the common people.

In another treatise, *Taigong's Six Secret Teachings*, there is an instruction on how to besiege large walled cities.

> Be careful not to engage them in battle; just sever their supply routes, surround and guard them, and you will certainly outlast them. Do not set fire to what the people have accumulated; do not destroy their palaces or houses, nor cut down the trees at gravesites or altars. Do not kill those who surrender nor slay your captives. Instead *show them benevolence and righteousness, extend your generous Virtue to them.* Cause their people to say "the guilt lies with one man." In this way the entire realm will then willingly submit.
>
> (Sawyer 1993, 87; trans. modified; emphasis added)

Similar to the earlier quoted passage, this treatise also contains the prohibition against intentionally harming noncombatants and damaging their properties and the instruction to treat prisoners of war humanely. Such efforts are made in order to manifest the Confucian cardinal virtues of benevolence and righteousness (*ren* and *yi*) to them.[21]

In short, a virtuous king and commander wages war out of great reluctance, as it is not part of his disposition. This great reluctance and good character needs to be shown by the discreet discrimination between combatants and noncombatants. In waging wars, one's nonbelligerent moral character and pure motive of combat needs to be shown by not intentionally harming noncombatants, not damaging their properties, and treating prisoners of war humanely.

From Virtues to Virtue Ethics

Roger Ames is correct to point out that these military treatises should be considered "applied philosophy" (Sun Tzu 1993, 41). If there is virtue ethics in these five military treatises, it will be applied virtue ethics. There are three reasons to support the antecedent. First, as explained above, the pivotal role of virtues for military commanders is much stressed. There is an unmistakable emphasis on the primacy of their moral character, rather than on systematic, well-specified moral rules or military instructions for them to follow. Second, as David Solomon explains, "A virtue theory takes judgments of character or of agents as basic in that it regards the fundamental task of normative theory as depicting an ideal of human character. The ethical task of each person, correspondingly, is to become a person who has certain dispositions to respond in a characteristic way to situations in the world" (Solomon, 2004, 814b). In the section on military vs. civilian virtues above I have explained that in making the moral decisions on when and how to wage wars, the decisions are modeled on what the Sage Kings have done. The Sage Kings are the exemplary moral agents. Third, as Michael Slote articulates, "Virtue ethics makes primary use of aretaic terms in its ethical characterizations, and it either treats deontic epithets as derivative from the aretaic or dispenses with them altogether" (Slote 2001, 4). In the same section I have also explained that the aretaic commitments in these treatises are spelled out as deontic action guides. Specifications of the Confucian virtues of righteousness/justice and benevolence, in particular, are provided to guide military conduct *ad bellum* and *in bello.*[22] Needless to say, though, how these prescriptions and proscriptions are to work in a variety of complex military situations is not exhaustively dealt with in these treatises. But the near consensus among virtue ethicists today is that virtue ethics cannot and will not "provide a thoroughly systematic account of moral deliberation to guide us in every detail," as "the deliberation and practical wisdom appropriate to the moral life eludes formulation" (Kotva 1996, 32).

As pointed out above, the term "righteous/just army" (*yi bing*) appears in *Master Wu's Art of War*. This term and its synonym (*yi jun*) have been immensely popular in the course of Chinese history. It is very much more frequently used than a related term "righteous/just war" (*yi zhan*), first used in *Mencius.*[23] The reason for this predilection of language stems from virtue ethics, *viz.*, it is more important to aspire to be a righteous/just person than simply to do righteousness/justice. I do not think that the same predilection of language has existed in the West.

14 Rationality and Virtue in the *Mencius*[1]

Xiao Yang

Introduction

How does Mencius give rational justifications for his normative claim that one ought to practice "virtue politics" (*dezheng*) or "benevolent politics" (*renzheng*)? This is the question that I want to address in this paper.[2] This is part of a larger project on the style and structure of practical philosophy in early China.[3] In this paper I will be able to articulate only one aspect of the complex structure of Mencius's practical philosophy, which has multiple levels and components. I focus on what I call the "level of normative authority." More specifically, I focus on only one of the ways in which Mencius justifies the normative authority of his normative claims. To narrow down my focus even further, I deal with only one (among many) mode of justification in Mencius – namely, his rational justification of certain specific normative claims.[4]

The Idea of Rational Justification and Its Limits

A practical philosophy often contains normative claims about what kind of society is the best regime, what character traits are admirable (what kind of person one ought to become), what one ought to do, what are one's moral obligations, what are the moral constraints on what one can do to promote the good, and so on and so forth.[5] It may also include an account of the normative force (or authority) of morality in general.

Michael Slote has suggested that we should make an analytic distinction between two types of statement regarding the normative force of morality (Slote 2007, 104–6):

(i) There are reasons for being moral.
(ii) Being moral is rational.

It seems that one can reject (ii), and yet still hold (i). Namely, one can deny that being moral is *rational*, but still have other non-rationality-based reasons to be moral. In other words, the normative authority of *morality* might not be the same as the normative authority of *rationality*.[6] For example, as Slote has argued, a care ethicist could claim that it is not irrational to have uncaring motivations and actions, and yet could still have something to say about the (non-rationality-based) reasons why one should be caring:

> If care ethics doesn't say that uncaring motivation and actions are irrational, *does it then have enough to say against (what it takes to be) immorality?* Well, in addition to accusation of uncaringness, the care ethicist can also criticize (actions that display) certain sort of indifference and hostility to others as *heartless*, and that is a very strong thing to be able to say.
>
> (Slote 2007, 106)

Regardless of whether Mencius's ethics as a whole can be characterized as a care ethics,[7] we do find Mencius criticizing one's actions that are indifferent and cruel to the sufferings of others as *heartless*. Mencius believes that the fact that someone is suffering gives a reason for us to do something about it, regardless of whether we have the desire to do so.[8] Mencius further believes that if one does not respond to this reason (if one does not see the fact as a reason) one is *not human (fei ren)*. Mencius says that if one does not practice the "politics that cannot bear the suffering of others" (*bu ren ren zhi zheng*), which is the spontaneous expression of the "heart that cannot bear the suffering of others" (*bu ren zhi xin*), one is "not human" (2A6). Saying that someone is *not human* is as strong as, if not stronger than, saying that someone is *heartless*. And this provides a non-rationality-based reason for being moral. In other words, rational justification has its limits in that it is only one of the ways to display the normative force of morality.

I now focus on rational justification in the *Mencius*. This is partly because most of the scholars acknowledge the existence of non-rationality-based reason for being moral in the *Mencius*, but many of them doubt the existence of rational justification in the *Mencius*. Some even deny that there is rational discursive reasoning in the *Mencius*. I want to show that Mencius does make rational arguments for his normative claims.[9] What is exactly the nature of this mode of argument in the *Mencius*? What is the nature of rationality in the *Mencius*? These are the questions I now turn to.

The Structure of Rational Justification in the *Mencius*

One of the central normative claims in early Confucianism is the claim that a good ruler ought to practice "virtue politics" (*de zheng*), "benevolent politics" (*ren zheng*), or "politics that cannot bear the suffering of others" (*bu ren ren zhi zheng*). By these terms, the Confucians mean an ideal way of governing, which demands that an ideal society ought to have benevolent policies that take care of the weak, the poor, the elderly, and the orphans (*Analects*, 6.4, 16.1; *Mencius*, 1A4, 1A7, 1B5). It also demands that the ruler ought to win the allegiance and trust of the people not through laws, coercion, or physical violence but through virtuous, as well as sincere, and caring actions and policies (*Analects*, 1.9, 2.1, 2.3, 2.19–20, 12.7, 12.17–19, 13.4, 13.6, 12.18, 14.41; *Mencius*, 1A5, 1B14, 2A3, 2B1, 3A2, 4A7, 4A12–13, 4A20, 7A12–14, 7B3–4).

Let me use M to refer to Mencius's virtue politics, and use R to refer to a ruler, What Mencius needs to justify is the following normative claim:

(C) R ought to practice M.

Let us use E to refer to a "desire" in the agent's subjective motivational set in a very broad sense, as Bernard Williams defines it: a desire in the agent's subjective motivational set can be "such things as dispositions of evaluation, patterns of emotional reaction, personal loyalties, and various projects, as they may be abstractly called, embodying commitments of the agent" (Williams 1981, 105). For example, Mencius often mentions a ruler's desire to become the most powerful ruler, to be matchless in the world (*wu di*).

Mencius's strategy of arguing for (C) is to argue for the following two premises:

(1) R already has certain desire (he is already committed to a certain end or project), namely E.
(2) R's practicing of M leads to the realization of E (or R's practicing of M is a means to E).[10]

From these two premises, it follows that R ought to practice M, or that it is (instrumentally) rational for R to practice M.[11]

Now it is clear that the main task of the justification is to argue for these two premises, (1) and (2). I shall refer to them as the "teleology premise" and the "pattern premise," respectively. How does Mencius argue for them?

There are at least three ways to show that the teleology premise – namely (1) – is true. First, in some cases, the teleology premise is obviously true because the conversation starts with the ruler asking Mencius about how to achieve his goal or fulfill his desire. Second, in some cases Mencius makes assumptions about what rulers in general would desire. For example, they all seem to desire the survival of their states or to become the most powerful state (to be matchless in the world), and he further argues that if one does not want the survival of one's state, then one is a "muddled man" or "irrational man" (more of this later). Third, in some cases Mencius helps the ruler to articulate his subjective motivational set, in order to make explicit his commitment to a certain project or goal. I believe that we should include the articulation or specification of one's motivational set as an essential part of practical reasoning.[12]

Now suppose that the teleology premise has been accepted by Mencius's interlocutor, Mencius then needs only to prove that the pattern premise – namely (2) – is true. For instance, for a ruler/interlocutor whose project is to become matchless, Mencius needs only to show to him that the following pattern exists:

A benevolent person is matchless.

(1A5)[13]

A benevolent person is matchless in the world.

(7B3)

If the ruler of a state loves benevolence, he will have no match in the world. When he marched on the south, the northern barbarians complained, and when he marched on the east, the western barbarians complained. They all said, "Why does he not come to conquer us first?"

(7B4; also see 3B5)

In these three passages, Mencius does not explicitly state the conclusion, which is that it is thus (instrumentally) irrational for the ruler not to become a benevolent ruler (or not to love benevolence). However, in other places, Mencius does explicitly state both the premises and the conclusion. Here is an example:

(A) Confucius said, "Against benevolence there can be no superiority in numbers. If the ruler of a state loves benevolence, he will be matchless in the world." (B) If one desires to be matchless in the world by any means but benevolence, then he is *just like someone holding something hot whilst forswearing in order to cool his hand with water.*

(4A7; emphasis added)[14]

Mencius' argument consists of two sentences, (A) and (B). The pattern premise is (A), which is the quotation from Confucius. The teleological premise is the if-part of (B), and the conclusion is the then-part of (B). Mencius here does not waste a word.

One of the most interesting features of Mencius's instrumental-rationality-based mode of justification is that Mencius often tries to start with the existing desires in the subjective motivational set of the ruler whom he happens to be talking to. This is also why, when he is not speaking to a specific ruler, Mencius often would start with desires that rulers in general would have.[15] For example, in the following passage, Mencius implicitly assumes that rulers in general desire the survival of their states, and dislike the demise of their states:

Mencius said: "The Three Dynasties won the Empire through benevolence and lost it through cruelty. This is true of the rise and fall, survival and collapse, of states as well. The son of Heaven cannot keep the Commonwealth (tianxia) within the Four Seas unless he is benevolent; a feudal lord cannot preserve the altars to the gods of earth and grain unless he is benevolent; a minister or a counselor cannot preserve his ancestral temple unless he is benevolent; a scholar or a commoner cannot preserve his four limbs unless he is benevolent. To dislike death yet revel in cruelty is *just like drinking beyond your capacity when you dislike drunkenness.*"

(4A3; emphasis added)

In other cases, Mencius assumes that rulers in general desire honor and dislike disgrace:

Benevolence brings honor; cruelty, disgrace. Now people who dwell in cruelty while disliking disgrace are *just like those who are content to dwell in a low-lying place while disliking dampness.*

(2A4; emphasis added)

At the end of each of the three passages I have just quoted, Mencius draws the conclusion that notpracticing benevolence is irrational. Note that he does not use the general term for "irrational" (*buzhi*), instead each time he uses a vivid concrete example of an irrational behavior. I say more about this below.

Rational Justification in 1A7

In this section, I want to give a close reading of the arguably most disputed passage from the *Mencius*, namely, 1A7. In the passages that I cited in the previous section, Mencius often assumes that the rulers already have certain ends or desires, and he focuses on arguing for what we have called the "pattern premise." What is interesting about 1A7 is that here Mencius seems to be helping the ruler to articulate his subjective motivational set in order to make explicit his commitment to a certain project or end.

This section has three parts. The first is a summary of the structure of 1A7. The second is a discussion of how Mencius helps King Xuan to measure (*du*) his heart-mind so that he can see that he actually has a "big desire" (*da yu*). The third part shows how Mencius argues that it is instrumentally and prudentially rational for King Xuan to practice benevolent politics because it is the effective means to fulfill his big desire.

The Structure of 1A7

Let us divide 1A7 into two parts: the first part is from the beginning of 1A7 to Mencius's following words:

> Why is it that your bounty is sufficient to reach animals yet the benefits of your government fail to reach the people?
>
> (1A7)

This first part will be referred to as 1A7i. And the second part is the rest of 1A7, which I refer to as 1A7ii.

The following is a very brief summary of 1A7i. It starts with King Xuan's practical question of how to become a true King. After Mencius gave his standard "benevolent politics" answer, which is "If he tends the people, he will necessarily become a true King," the King asked a further question about whether he had the capacity to tend the people: "Can someone like myself tend the people?" (1A7i). The rest of 1A7i consists in Mencius's attempt to show to the King that in his heart-mind he had compassion for an ox that was about to be sacrificed, and that he just needed to extend (*tui*) this compassion to the people.

Perhaps no other passage of early Chinese texts has had more ink spilled over it than 1A7. However, scholars tend to focus on only this part of 1A7, and the debate tends to focus on what kind of practical reasoning Mencius's *tui* is, or whether it is discursive rational reasoning at all. There are scholars who consider *tui* analogical reasoning, which is basically "logical extension" that is based on the general rational principle of logical consistency (Lau 2003; Nivison 1980; Reding 1986;

Shun 1989). I shall call these scholars the "first group." There are also scholars who argue that *tui* is not discursive reasoning at all, but rather "emotional extension" (Van Norden 1991; Im 1999; Im 2002), or "analogical resonance" (Ivanhoe 2002b). I shall call them the "second group." There is also a "third group" of scholars who believe that *tui* has two intricately connected aspects: "cognitive extension" and "affective extension" (Wong 2002; Van Norden 2007: 236–46); these scholars reject both the first group's "logical extension" and the second group's "emotional extension" interpretations because, as David Wong puts it, the former reduces Mencian moral reasoning to a top-down logical reasoning in terms of general principles of consistency, overlooking the fact that Mencius's *tui* is based on "comparison between particulars" without the mediation of general principles, whereas the latter draws an "equally mistaken" conclusion that there is no ethical reasoning at all in Mencius (Wong 2002).

In this paper, I will stand neutral regarding the debate about the nature of *tui* in 1A7i because I shall be focusing on 1A7ii, which has been given little attention. As we shall see, Mencius makes use of other types of reasoning, not just *tui*. More specifically, in 1A7ii Mencius gives instrumental-and-prudential-rationality-based argument, which is obviously rational discursive reasoning.

The Specification of Ends in 1A7ii

As we have seen in the passage cited above, 1A7i ends with Mencius's question: "Why is it then that your bounty is sufficient to reach animals yet the benefits of your government fail to reach the people?" This clearly indicates that Mencius's attempt to persuade the King to practice benevolent politics through *tui* has failed, and Mencius is asking why this is the case. One may naturally assume that, in 1A7ii, Mencius might want to try other ways to persuade the King. Indeed, 1A7ii starts with Mencius's following instruction:

> It is by weighing a thing that its weight can be known and by measuring (*du*) it that its length can be ascertained. It is so with all things, but particularly so with the heart-mind. *Your Majesty should measure* (du) *your own heart-mind.*
> (1A7ii; emphasis added)

This is the second time the term "*du*" (measure) appears in 1A7. Its first appearance is in 1A7i. After Mencius tells the King that he spared the ox not because he grudged the expense, but because he could not bear to see it die, the King thinks that Mencius truly understands him:

> The King was pleased, and said, "The *Odes* say, 'The heart-mind is someone else's/But it is I who have taken its true measure (*du*).' This describes you perfectly. For though the deed was mine, when I looked into myself I failed to understand my own heart-mind. You described it for me and your words struck a chord in me. What makes you think that my heart-mind accorded with the way of a true king?"
> (1A7i)

In other words, in 1A7i, Mencius has already helped the King to measure his heart-mind rather successfully. So why is Mencius instructing the King to measure (*du*) his heart-mind, *once again*, in the beginning of 1A7ii?

One way out of this *aporia* is to assume that the goal of measuring the King's heart-mind in 1A7i is to establish only that the King has *compassion* in his heart-mind, whereas there is a different goal in 1A7ii, which is to show that there are otherparts in the King's heart-mind, such as *desire and pleasure*, which, as we shall see, are the concepts Mencius would use in 1A7ii. Mencius would help the King to articulate his desires.

This reading is confirmed by the round of question and answer between Mencius and the King that follows right after the passage we just cited:

> Perhaps your heart-mind *takes pleasure* (*kuai yu xin*) only in starting a war, imperiling your subjects and incurring the enmity of other feudal lords?
> (1A7ii; emphasis added).[16]

This is a very interesting passage, because it is one of very few places in the *Mencius* where we find Mencius entertaining the Augustinian possibility that one does bad things because he takes pleasure in doing bad things for their own sake. However, this possibility is readily dismissed by the King:

> "No. Why should I take pleasure in doing those things? I am only pleased when my big desire (*da yu*) is fulfilled."
> "May I be told what your big desire is?"
> The King smiled, offering no reply.
> "Is it because your food is not good enough to gratify your palate, and your clothes not good enough to gratify your body? Or perhaps the sights and sounds are not good enough to gratify your eyes and ears and your close servants not good enough to serve you? Any of your various officials surely could make good these deficiencies. It cannot be these things."
> "No. It is not these things."
>
> (1A7ii)[17]

From this part of the conversation, we learn that the King is actually a good king in the sense that he does not take pleasure in doing evil things for their own sake, and that his "big desire" has nothing to do with his private desire or pleasure for food, clothes, or comfort. In fact, the King eventually expresses his agreement with Mencius's following articulation of his "big desire":

> One can guess what your big desire is. You want to extend your territory, to enjoy the homage of Qin and Chu, to rule over the Central Kingdoms, and to bring peace to the barbarian tribes on the four borders.
>
> (1A7ii)

The Instrumental and Prudential Justification in 1A7

Having established that the King has the desire that a good king usually has, Mencius proceeds to show that the means to fulfill this desire is to practice benevolent politics. Let me now reconstruct Mencius's reasoning as a linear argument, and I shall change the order of his presentation slightly.

First, Mencius shows that the kind of means that the King has been relying on – namely, politics of force that relies on physical strength and violence– cannot be the effective means to fulfill his "big desire" to "extend your territory, to enjoy the homage of Qin and Chu, to rule over the Central Kingdoms and to bring peace to the barbarian tribes on the four borders," simply because Qi is not as big and as strong as the other big states:

> "If the men of Zou and men of Chu were to go to war, who do you think would win?"
>
> "The men of Chu."
>
> "That means that the small is no match for the big, the few no match for the many, and the weak no match for the strong. Within the Seas there are nine areas of ten thousand *li* square, and the territory of Qi makes up one of these. For one to try to overcome the other eight is no different from Zou going to war with Chu."
>
> (1A7ii)

From this, Mencius concludes,

> Now if you should practice benevolent politics of your state, all those in the world who seek office would wish to find a place at your court, all tillers of land to till the land in outlying parts of your realm, all merchants to enjoy the refuge of your market-place, all travelers to go by way of your roads, and all those who hate their rulers to lay their complaints before you. This being the case, who could stop you from becoming a true King?
>
> (1A7ii)

> Seeking the fulfillment of such a desire by the kind of means you have been employing [politics of force] is like looking for fish by climbing a tree.
>
> (1A7ii)

Here Mencius does not use the term "*buzhi*" (not rational, unwise, imprudent, unintelligent), a general term for "irrational," which he uses elsewhere in the *Mencius*.[18] Instead Mencius says that the ruler's actions are just like "looking for fish by climbing a tree," which is a paradigm of (instrumentally) irrational action.[19]

Mencius further argues that, in addition to instrumental reasons, there are also prudential reasons for the King to practice benevolent politics:

> It is likely to be worse. If you look for fish by climbing a tree, though you will not find fish, there is no danger of this bringing disasters in its train. But if you

seek the fulfillment of your desire by the kind of means you've been employing, putting all your heart and might into the pursuit, there will necessarily be
disaster in the end.

(1A7ii)

Here Mencius assumes that anyone who is prudentially rational, by definition,
would not want to bring disasters to himself. He is implying here that the King
would be (prudentially) irrational if he were to practice "politics of force," rather
than "politics of benevolence."

This conception of instrumental and prudential rationality in the *Mencius* seems
similar to the conception of rationality in Philippa Foot's famous essay "Morality
as a System of Hypothetical Imperatives," in which Foot makes a quintessential
Mencian point about irrational actions: "Irrational actions are those in which a
man in some way defeats his own purposes, doing what is calculated to be disad-
vantageous or to frustrate his ends" (Foot 1978, 162).[20]

The Paradigms of Rationality in Mencius

In the passages that we have cited above Mencius does not use general terms for the
concepts of "instrumental rationality" or "prudential rationality," nor does he use
terms for the concepts of "instrumental irrationality" or "prudential irrationality."
However, the lack of general term in these passages does not imply the lack of the
concept. Mencius often uses concrete paradigm cases of instrumental irrationality to do the job. Instead of saying that R's action is "(instrumentally) irrational,"
Mencius would say that R's action is just like "looking for fish by climbing a tree."
Here are some of his paradigms of instrumentally irrational actions:

(I_1) Looking for fish by climbing a tree. (1A7)

(I_2) Being content to dwell in a low-lying place while disliking dampness.
(2A4)

(I_3) Drinking beyond your capacity while you dislike drunkenness. (4A3).

(I_4) Holding something hot whilst forswearing to cool one's hand with water.
(4A7).

(I_5) Desiring someone to enter [the room] while shutting the door against
him. (5B7).

Similarly, when Mencius argues that it is not prudent for someone to practice
politics of force, he often uses concrete paradigm cases of prudential irrationality
to convey the general idea. Here are some of his paradigms of imprudent actions:

(P_1) Harming the parts of one's body of greater importance for the sake of
those of smaller importance, or the more valuable for the sake of the less valuable. (6A14)

(P_2) A gardener tending to common trees, while neglecting the valuable ones.
(6A14)

(P$_3$) Taking care of one's one finger to the detriment of his shoulder and back. (6A14)

(P$_4$) Seeing danger as safety, looks upon one's own disaster as beneficial to him, and delights in what will lead him to perdition. (4A8)

(P$_5$) Trying to put out a cartload of burning firewood with a cupful of water. (6A18)

(P$_6$) A farmer abandoning his own fields and weeding the fields of others. (7B32)

Unlike in the case of instrumental reasoning, Mencius also formulates a statement that can obviously be regarded as a general principle of prudential reasoning:

The parts of the person differ in value and importance. Never harm the parts of greater importance for the sake of those of smaller importance, or the more valuable for the sake of the less valuable.

(6A14)

Later in this passage, Mencius use the phrase "muddled man" (*langji ren*) to label someone who is acting imprudently without realizing his mistake in doing so (6A14). Mencius does not systematically use a technical term for the concept of an "imprudent agency"; the term "muddled man" might be the closest equivalent term that we can find in the *Mencius*.

Conclusion

To summarize, Mencius seems to believe that instrumental and prudential rationality is constitutive of rational agency. One important implication of this conclusion is that, for Mencius, if one fails to practice virtue politics, it could be because he is not a rational agent (namely, he is a muddled man). It is important to note that when this is the case, it remains true that it is rational to practice virtue politics. Mencius would insist that when one desires the right end and knows the pattern that virtue politics is the means to the end, and one fails to practice virtue politics, we must conclude that one is irrational. It is also possible that one fails to practice virtue politics because he does not really know what the right end is, and this is why we often find Mencius trying to help people to articulate their end. A third possible scenario is that, even though one is a rational agent and has committed himself to the right end, one fails to practice virtue politics because one does not know the pattern which indicates that virtue politics is the means to achieve the end. In all these possible scenarios, it is always true that it is rational to practice virtue politics, and it is irrational not to do so.

15 Between Generalism and Particularism

The Cheng Brothers' Neo-Confucian Virtue Ethics

Huang Yong

Introduction

One of the important features of virtue ethics is its emphasis on particularity. In virtue ethics, as stated by Rosalind Hursthouse, a contemporary virtue ethicist, "an action is right if it is what a virtuous agent would characteristically (i.e. acting in character) do in the *circumstances*" (Hursthouse 1999: 28; emphasis added). Here I emphasize the last word, "circumstances," as a virtuous person does not simply apply universal moral principles to all circumstances. Instead, as Michael Slote, another contemporary virtue ethicist, states when he comments on Aristotle, a virtuous person is "someone who *sees* or *perceives* what is good or fine or right to do in any given situation" (Slote 2001: 5). Indeed, Aristotle himself also claims that virtue is to feel relevant passions, such as fear, confidence, and anger, "at the right times, with reference to the right objects, towards the right people, with the right motive, and in the right way" (Aristotle 1963: 1106b20–22). So a virtuous thing to do in one circumstance or situation may not be so in a different circumstance or situation. This emphasis on particularity is radicalized in moral particularism or anti-theory, which I regard as an extreme form of virtue ethics, or at least a close ally of the latter in their argument against their common rivals, deontology and utilitarianism, two moral theories of generalism. In this essay, after a brief presentation of moral particularism, I shall argue that, while it reflects the Confucian idea of love with distinction as interpreted by the neo-Confucian Cheng brothers, Cheng Hao (1032–1085) and Cheng Yi (1033–1107), there is a blind spot in the former that is avoided in the latter.

Moral Particularism

One of the most influential representatives of moral particularism is Jonathan Dancy. Dancy argues against the generalist moral theory, a view that "the very possibility of moral thought and judgment depends on the provision of a suitable supply of moral principles" (Dancy 2004: 7). There is an absolute [Kantian] conception of moral principles, which "takes a moral principle to be a universal claim to the effect that all actions of a certain type are overall wrong (or right)" (Dancy 2009/2001: §1). The problem with such a conception, in Dancy's view, is that unless there is only one such moral principle, or, if there is more than one, no conflict exists between different moral principles applicable to one and the same situation, a moral principle in such an absolute conception cannot help us determine whether a given action is morally right or wrong. An action may be prohibited by one moral principle (for example, one should keep one's promise) but called for by another moral principle (for example, one should always help people in need when one can).

So Dancy's main target of attack is what he regards as the [Rossian] "contributory" conception of moral principles. W.D. Ross's contributory conception "allows that more than one principle can apply to the case before us," and each principle contributes to counting for or against a particular action; but since an action has many relevant features, some moral principles count for it, while some others count against it; and so "whether the action is overall right or wrong can only be determined by the overall balance of right and wrong in it" (Dancy 2009/2001: §1). Thus, for example, if there is a moral principle against promisebreaking, there may still be cases in which the action with the feature of promisebreaking is considered as right, not because promisebreaking itself becomes a moral feature, but because the action that has the feature of promisebreaking has some other features consistent with some other moral principles that count for the action. This is an atomist view of moral reasons: "a feature that is a reason in one case must remain a reason, and retain the same polarity, in any other" (Dancy 2004: 74). In other words, moral reason is transportable from one situation to another.

Dancy argues against such an atomist view. In his view, there is no guarantee for such transportability. In a non-moral case, Dancy uses the example of perception of red. In a normal situation, the fact that something seems to me to be red is a reason for me to believe that there is something red before me. However, in a situation where I also believe that I have recently taken a drug that makes blue things look red and red things look blue, the same fact becomes a reason for me to believe that there is a blue instead of a red thing before me (Dancy 2004: 74 and 2009/2001: §3). Dancy claims that the same is true in moral cases. For example, normally the fact that I made a promise is a reason for me to keep it, but in some other situations it may become a reason for me not to keep it (for example, if the promise that I make is to not keep the next three promises I will make) (Dancy 2009/2001: §5); normally the fact that an action is prohibited by law is a reason for me not to do it, but in some other situations it may become a reason for me to do it (if the law governs an aspect of private life with which the law should not interfere in the first place, for example) (Dancy 2004: 62 and 2009/2001: §3); normally the fact that I borrow a book from you is a reason for me to return it to you, but in some situations it may become a reason for me not to do so (if you stole it from the library) (Dancy 2004: 60).

So, in contrast to moral generalism, Dancy argues for moral particularism, a view that "the possibility of moral thought and judgement does not depend on the provision of a suitable supply of moral principles" (Dancy 2004: 7). Just as generalism is based on an atomist conception of reason, Dancy's particularlism is based on a holistic conception of moral reasons, according to which "a reason in one case may be no reason at all, or an opposite reason, in another" (Dancy 2004: 7). In other words, "everything appears to be ... context-dependent. If one wants to know whether some feature is of value here, one cannot get one's answer by looking to see how it behaves elsewhere" (Dancy 2004: 184). Dancy does acknowledge the existence of what he calls default values (such features as promise keeping) or default disvalue (such features as lying). Default values or disvalues refer to the features that bring values or disvalues with them to any particular situations, though once they are brought to a particular situation, such values or disvalues may be wiped out or even reversed by other features of the situation (Dancy 2004: 184–187). The difference between features that carry with them default values or disvalues and features that get their values or disvalues only after they are brought into a particular context is this. In the latter, we always need an explanation why a particular feature has a value or disvalue in a particular context. A feature acquires a value or disvalue in a given situation because of the presence of some other features, which Dancy calls enablers, the features that enable the feature in question to have the value or disvalue. If such enablers are not present in a different situation, the same feature in question will not have the value acquired in the previous situation. In the former, however, such an explanation is needed only if these features do not contribute their default values or disvalues in a particular context. A feature loses its default value or disvalue in a given context only because of the presence of some other features in the context that disable it, the presence of the disablers. A default value or disvalue may also be increased by the presence of intensifiers (features that increase the default value or disvalue) or diminished by the presence of attenuators (features that decrease the default value or disvalue) (Dancy 2004: Ch. 3).

The Cheng Brothers as Moral Particularists

Dancy's moral particularlism reflects an important insight in the Confucian idea of love with distinction, particularly as it is interpreted by the neo-Confucian Cheng brothers.[1] The idea of love with distinction in classical Confucianism has often been interpreted to mean that one should have the most intense love within family, which is to be increasingly diluted when expanded to others. However, it acquires a new meaning in the neo-Confucian Cheng brothers, particularly through Cheng Yi's idea of "one *li* in diverse events" (*li yi fen shu*). Cheng Yi develops this idea in his response to a concern raised by one of his students, Yang Shi, regarding Zhang Zai's *Western Inscription*, which appears to Yang Shi to promote a kind of Mohist universal love without distinction. In response, Cheng Yi states,

> The *Western Inscription* explains one *li* in diverse events, while Mozi insists on two roots without distinction. The problem with emphasizing differences [without the one *li*] is that the private desire would prevail and *ren* would be lost, while the problem with [emphasizing one *li*] without many differences is the universal love without rightness.
>
> (*Wenji* 9, in Cheng and Cheng 1989: 609)

In appearance, there is a conflict between Cheng Yi's idea of one *li* in diverse events and Dancy's moral particularism, particularly if we adopt the conventional translation of *li* as principle, for then this idea would mean that there is one principle with many different applications, while the moral particularists' main target of attack is precisely the conception of moral principle, and the title of Dancy's main work in moral particularism is indeed *Ethics without Principle*.

However, this cannot be the case if we keep in mind that Cheng Yi develops this idea precisely in order to show to one of his students, who worries that Zhang Zai is advocating the Mohist doctrine of universal love without distinction, that Zhang Zai's view is consistent with Mencius's love with distinction. For Cheng, while Zhang Zai, just like any other Confucians, does advocate universal love, love for everyone and everything, one's love for different people and different things should be different. For example, the various types of love mentioned by Zhang Zai in the *West Inscription*, respecting the aged, deep love for the orphaned and the weak, care of the son, and filial piety for parents, are not different degrees of the same love, but different kinds of love, each appropriate to the particular object of love. This is the reason why Cheng Yi emphasizes the diversity of love, *fenshu*. When Cheng Yi says that there is one *li* in diverse events, he does not mean that there is an abstract principle, ontological or moral, to be participated in by or applied to diverse situations of love. Any love is particular and concrete: love for one's parents and children, for one's wife or husband, for one's family members and one's neighbors, for one's friends and enemies, for people one knows and people one does not know, for virtuous persons and vicious persons, etc. There is no one true, genuine, abstract, and universal love in addition to all these particular forms of love. They are all called love, as they have family resemblances with each other. Cheng Yi's one *li* serves a different purpose. Our moral intuition tells us that love is good, but why is it good? *Li* is intended to provide an ontological articulation (in the sense that Charles Taylor uses the term) of this sentimental love as good. As I have argued elsewhere (see Huang 2007), as such an ontological articulation, *li* in the Cheng brothers should be understood as *sheng* 生, the life-generating activity, an idea that they borrowed from the *Book of Change*. Thus, after citing from this classic that "the unceasing life-giving activity is called change," Cheng Hao claims that "it is right in this life-giving activity that *li* is complete" (Cheng and Cheng 1989: 33). Cheng Yi concurs: "*li* as life-giving activity is natural and ceaseless" (Cheng and Cheng 1989: 167). This life-generating activity in human beings is *ren*. *Ren*, often translated as humanity or humanness, is regarded as the most essential human nature and the most fundamental human virtue at the same time in the Confucian tradition, which provides an ontological articulation of love as a human feeling.[2] After he said that "the atmosphere of life-giving activity (*sheng yi*) is most spectacular," Cheng Hao continues that "'what is great and originating becomes (in humans) the first and chief (quality of goodness).' This quality is known as *ren*" (Cheng and Cheng 1989: 120). In other words, *ren* is good not only because it is a human value; it is actually no different from the ultimate reality, *li*, the life-giving activity. For Cheng Hao, to be alive is *ren*, while to be dead is the lack thereof. It is in this sense that the two Chengs play different puns on the meaning of *ren*. Cheng Yi understands *ren* from its meaning of the power of a seed to grow into a tree (Cheng and Cheng 1989: 184), while Cheng Hao understands it from its meaning as ability to feel life (as lack of *ren* means "numb") (Cheng and Cheng 1989: 15). In other words, the ultimate reality itself is moral. Thus, having said that "'the ongoing life-giving activity is called change.' This is how *tian* can be *dao*. Tian is *dao* only because it is the life-giving activity," Cheng Hao claims that "to follow this life-giving activity is good. Goodness has a meaning of origin (*yuan*) and so it was said that '*yuan*' is the growth of the goodness. Ten thousand things all have the atmosphere of spring [life], and this is what is meant by 'what continues it [life-giving activity] is good'" (Cheng and Cheng 1989: 29). Here Cheng makes an explicit connection between *li* as the life-giving activity and moral goodness.

Thus understood, *li*, whether in its metaphysical or moral sense, is not the universal principle to be participated in by or applied to particular things. It refers to the life-giving activities present in human beings in particular, and in the universe in general. While different things in the universe, including human beings, manifest different and unique life-giving activities and there is not a universal or abstract life-giving activity in addition to these particular life-generating activities, in the sense that they are all life-giving activities, the Cheng brothers can claim that there is only one *li*. In this respect, it is illuminating to point out an important historical fact. It is true that Cheng Yi's idea of one *li* in diverse events has its Buddhist origin. For example, Huayan Buddhism has a conception of one *li* and many *shi* (events) and claims that the one *li* is complete (instead of partially) in each of the many *shi*. Zen Buddhism holds a similar view, and Chan Master Xuanjue's (665–713) famous analogy of one moon reflected in ten thousand rivers (*yue yin wan chuan*) is used later by Zhu Xi to explain Cheng Yi's idea of one *li* in diverse events. Yet, it is interesting that Cheng Yi himself, obviously aware of this well-known analogy, does not use it to explain his idea. In the analogy of "one moon reflected in ten thousand rivers," there is one real moon that exists in the sky independently of its reflections in ten thousand rivers, which cannot exist without the real moon in the sky. However, as we have seen, for Cheng Yi, there is not a "real" love, like the moon in the sky, that is manifested in different kinds of concrete love. Different kinds of concrete love are all that exist. It is in this sense that I claim that Cheng Yi's one *li* in diverse events, as an explanation of the Confucian idea of love with distinction, is consistent with moral particularism in rejecting any universal moral principles applicable to all different situations and in insisting on the particularity of each life situation.

Problem with Moral Particularism in its Radical Form

However, there is a significant difference between Dancy's moral particularism and the Cheng brothers' interpretation of the Confucian idea of love with distinction in terms of their views of their different assessments of the significance of moral experiences. Dancy does acknowledge that "experience of similar cases can tell us what sort of things to look out for, and the sort of relevance that a certain feature can have; in this way our judgement in a new case can be informed, though it is not forced or constrained, by our experience of similar cases in the past" (Dancy 2009/2001: §8). However, following another moral particularist, John McDowell, who claims that from moral experience we can get nothing but "the capacity to get things right occasion by occasion" (McDowell 1988: 94), Dancy maintains that "there is nothing that one brings to the new situation other than a *contentless* ability to discern what matters where it matters, an ability whose presence in us is explained by our having undergone a successful moral education" (Dancy 1993: 50; emphasis added).

To say that moral experience will increase our moral perceptivity is of course not controversial. The question is whether it is contentless; or if it is also uncontroversial that our ability to perceive is indeed contentless, this must be an ability to perceive some content, and so the question is what content this contentless ability is supposed to perceive. Dancy's answer would be the moral features of the particular action. The question is what features count as moral features. If Dancy is a Rossian type of contributive generalist, the question is easy to answer: we know, by intuition, that a certain number of general features are morally relevant (some are the right-making features and some are the wrong-making features); since such features tend to conflict with each other, a moral judge's job is to perceive the balance of such features in a particular action and decide whether the action overall, or in balance, is morally right or wrong. Dancy, however, has denied any such general moral features, and claims instead that a feature that has value or disvalue in one particular case is not guaranteed to keep this value or disvalue in a different situation. So, in order to answer our question, Dancy has to ultimately appeal to moral intuitionism, although a different type of intuitionism. In an early article, Dancy makes a distinction between generalist intuitionism and particularist intuitionism. According to the former, we have intuitions of some morally relevant features applicable to all our actions, whether we have such intuitions from inborn moral conscience or from previous moral perceptions and whether such intuitions can clearly tell us a given action is overall moral or not. According to the latter, however, our intuition can tell us whether a feature is morally relevant only in a particular action, and whether this same feature is still morally relevant or is still morally relevant in the same way has to be determined by the contentless ability to perceive or intuit again (see Dancy 1982).

Such a particularist moral intuitionism, while attractive in some respects, is problematical. Regardless of whether it will lead to moral relativism (since none of the moral particularists is or is regarded as a moral relativist), there is still a question of whether such particularist moral intuitions are always reliable. In this respect, I think Michael Slote has made a strong case by revealing that not only in some situations is there a lack of the relevant moral intuitions, but "our intuitive moral thinking is internally incoherent or inconsistent" (Slote 1992: 34). To illustrate this, he uses a number of examples from the recent philosophical discussions of the idea of moral luck. One of them is originally discussed by Thomas Nagel: a person is driving a car along a country road. As a result of his pointing out noteworthy sights to his passengers, the car suddenly swerves into the middle of the road. In one scenario, there is a car coming from the opposite direction and therefore an accident occurs, while in another scenario, there is no car coming from the opposite direction and therefore no accident occurs. One of our common intuitions relevant to this situation is that the driver is blameworthy in the first case, but not so, at least not to the same degree, in the second case. However, we have another equally common intuition that is also relevant to this situation: luck should play no role in determining whether a person is morally blameworthy or not. So here there is an inconsistency between our moral intuitions. With this conflict of our moral intuitions, we will be unable to determine whether the driver is morally blameworthy in either or both of the two scenarios.[3]

How the Cheng Brothers Avoid the Problem of Radical Moral Particularism

The Cheng brothers are not moral intuitionists. Not only do they, as we have already seen, have an ontological articulation of our natural emotion of love to show why it is good, but they also have a theory of human nature to show why we should not only maintain but also expand this natural emotion of love. This is closely related to their idea of *tui*, expanding one's natural love gradually from one's family to all sentient beings in the world, the inborn ability that, for the Chengs, distinguishes human beings from animals. Clearly, if this ability is also contentless to get things right, it must be related to some definite content to be expanded; moreover, this is not a content that one has to perceive anew in every new moral experience, but a content that one has already discerned in past experiences, since the ability of expanding must be related to the thing, one's love in past experiences, that is to be expanded, even though this expansion is not simply to transport one's love in one situation to another.

Contemporary evolutionary biology and evolutionary psychology have shown that animals and human beings form a continuum in terms of the concern for the interest of others. For example, it is found that prairie dogs send out alarm calls to warn other members of their group of perceived dangers; female lions suckle cubs of other lionesses, primates engage in grooming behavior to rid members of their troop of parasites, and soldier aphids forgo their own reproduction for the sake of the cline mates (see Bettram 1976; Ridley and Dawkins 1981: 42–43; and Silk, Samuels, and Rodman 1981). It is based on such a recognition that Mary Midgley even goes so far as to claim that "we are not just like animals; we *are* animals" (Midgley 1995: xiii). This idea, however, is not unknown to the Cheng brothers, as we can see from the following passage:

> Mencius regards the four beginnings [of humanity, rightness, propriety, and wisdom] as the four limbs of one's body. … This is not something humanly arranged. They are also complete in animals such as cows and horses. Only because they have different material constitutions are they obscured by the constitution of vital force (*qi*). For example, in children's love for their mother and mother's love for its children, there is also atmosphere of wood [representing the first beginning, *ren*] in cows and horses. Also, how can the heart of shame and dislike [the second beginning] be absent [in animals]? Things such as avoiding harm and seeking benefit and distinguishing between things to love and things to hate are all complete in them. Monkeys, being the most intelligent among animals, particularly resemble human beings. Children and muddled people who are less intelligent than such animals are not few.
>
> (Cheng and Cheng 1989: 54)[4]

In this and some related passages, the Cheng brothers not only tell us essentially what contemporary evolutionally psychology and biology tell us almost one thousand years later; but they also tell us the reason why such altruistic love exists not only in human beings but also in animals: the four beginnings that are to develop into the four cardinal virtues in human beings are also present in animals. In their view, "all ten thousand things have the same nature, i.e. the five constants (*ren*, rightness, propriety, wisdom, and faithfulness)" (Cheng and Cheng 1989: 105). Cheng Hao makes the famous claim that all ten thousand things, including human beings, form one body, by which he means "that they have the same *li*. … [The difference is that] human beings can expand it, while things, muddled by their *qi*, cannot" (Cheng and Cheng 1989: 33).

What is particularly relevant to our discussion here is the difference between human beings and animals mentioned here: the ability to expand (*tui* 推) the inborn love for those in the small circle to those beyond, which exists in humans but not in animals.[5] This idea of *tui* originates from Mencius and, to some extent, Confucius. According to Mencius, "treat the aged in my own family in a manner befitting their venerable age and then expand (*ji* 及) this treatment to the aged of other families; treat the young in my own family in a manner befitting their tender age and then expand this treatment to the young of other families, and you can roll the whole world on your palm" (*Mencius* 1a7). Here Mencius uses the word *ji*, which means the same as *tui*, and the examples he uses to explain the idea of *ji* are the same as those that the Cheng brothers use in the above passage: to expand one's feeling of love for family members to others. Moreover, continuing from the same place, immediately after citing a poem from the *Book of Poetry*, Mencius uses the word *tui* itself to explain the meaning of the poem: "all you have to do is to take your loving heart/mind here to apply it to what is over there. Hence one who expands (*tui*) one's bounty can bring peace to the whole world, while one who does not cannot bring peace even to one's own family. The reason that ancient people are superior to others is that they are good at expanding what they do [in their families]" (*Mencius* 1a7). Although Confucius does not use the world *tui* itself, expansion of one's natural family love is also essential to his teaching. For example, he says that "a youth, when at home, should be filial and, abroad, respectful to his elders. He should be earnest and truthful. He should overflow in love to all" (*Analects* 1.6).

So the idea of *tui* has been important for Confucianism from the very beginning. To highlight it, the Cheng brothers regard it as the distinguishing mark of being human. In other words, while animals love those that they are naturally disposed to love, they cannot expand this love to those that they are not naturally disposed to love. Human beings, however, have the ability to expand their natural love from those whom they are naturally disposed to love to those whom they are not naturally disposed to love. In other words, anyone who does not exercise this ability of *tui* is defective and dysfunctional and therefore is not a characteristic human being.[6]

Conclusion

I would like to conclude by underscoring the importance of this idea of *tui* in the context of our discussion of moral particularism. To say that one should expand one's family love to those outside one's immediate family is not something controversial at all. An important issue here is how to expand this family love. This is made clear in the following passage: "the way the Duke of Zhou treats his elder brothers and the way Shun treats his younger brother are the same. We need to figure out what is their intention. Nothing is needed but to expand this intention in interaction with other people. Of course, there must be distinctions" (Cheng and Cheng 1989: 298). Here, using the examples of Duke of Zhou and Shun, Cheng Yi continues to show that to become a sage one need only expand one's natural love. However, what I want to emphasize is the last sentence: "there must be distinctions," which shows that, when one expands one's love for one's family members to others, one does not simply transport this love to some other objects of love. As we have emphasized, love, to be appropriate, must take into consideration the uniqueness of each object of love. A kind of love appropriate to one person may be inappropriate to another person, and a kind of love appropriate to one person on one occasion may be inappropriate to the same person on another occasion. So the Cheng brothers' idea of *tui*, in connection with the idea of one *li* in diverse events, stands between moral generalism, for which moral action is nothing but to apply the universal moral principle to each particular situation, and Dancy's radical moral particularism, according to which we have to start entirely from scratch in every new situation. According to this *via media*, what happens in moral practice is to expand one's love learned in previous moral experiences to a new situation, with necessary modifications called for by what is perceived as unique in this new situation.[7] In other words, what we can learn from our past moral experiences is not merely the formal ability to get things right in future practices, but also the "content" of what is to be considered as moral and what is to be considered as immoral. Clearly, the content, love in previous moral experiences, is not something universal but is also particular, and one does not simply transport or switch it to a new situation, as different situations are always different.[8] In this sense, the Cheng brothers agree with Dancy's moral particularism. At the same time, however, our moral experience not only enhances our ability to perceive but also tells us what to perceive and thus helps us to find the appropriate love in a new situation. In this sense, the Cheng brothers part company with Dancy in his radical moral particularism.

Part IV

Moral Psychology and Particular Virtues

16　What Is Confucian Humility?[1]

Sara Rushing

Introduction

One will not find much explicit consideration of humility as a concept or a virtue in the Analects of Confucius.[2] Yet humility is a pivotal theme running through the text.[3] On one rendering of the Confucian tradition, humility has been reduced to a demand for blind obedience to authority. In contrast, I argue here that the Analects articulates a theory of humility as a disposition of strength, which prepares one to better practice other important virtues of social and political engagement. As such, Confucius teaches us something about the concept of humility that is lacking in Western thought addressing this virtue (or vice, as some see it).

Humility is a concept ripe for reconsideration in Western political thought. The classical virtue-ethical tradition, originating most fully with Aristotle, notably lacks a distinct concept of humility as a virtue. The Christian scholastic tradition of Augustine and Aquinas gave philosophical voice to humility and located it alongside the other supreme theological virtues of faith, hope, and charity. Humility as articulated in the Christian tradition remains the dominant Western concept. Yet this version involves having a low opinion of oneself and is directly related to subjugation and obedience, which Augustine called "the mother and guardian of all of the virtues in a rational creature"—a creature created by God, for God's purpose, and thus for whom "submission is advantageous." Such a notion is clearly problematic in a secular modern political context.

Perhaps for this reason, scholars have noted that humility has become something of a forgotten virtue in contemporary Western theory and practice (Button 2005; Konkola 2005). As part of the recent resurgence of virtue ethics in philosophy and the "turn to ethics" in political theory, interesting work has been done either to rebrand humility within Christianity by severing that conception from negative connotations of self-abnegation or rote obedience (Exline and Geyer 2004; Herdt 2009; Keys 2008; Richards 1988), or to refigure it beyond Christianity by drawing on other native Western traditions (Button 2005). Bringing the Confucian conception of humility into the mix serves two purposes. First, it highlights certain ways in which so-called Eastern and Western thinking on this virtue may overlap, for example in their recognition that humility is inextricably linked to concepts of relationality and historicity. Second, the Confucian conception may problematize or supplement Western notions, by bringing to bear a certain *kind* of thinking about history, relationality and self-cultivation within specific familial and social orders.

My focus here will be on clarifying the Confucian conception of humility so that it *can* be put into constructive engagement with the Christian conception and its classic and contemporary critiques. In doing so, I explore how humility so understood can be a source of political resistance of sorts. I conclude this chapter, however, by broaching the question of Confucian humility's limits as a tool for social change. Does the *Analects* expose certain shortcomings of humility, though perhaps differently from those suggested in critiques by, say, Aristotle, Machiavelli, Hume, and Nietzsche? If so, are these limitations innate—present not only when humility is contorted for oppressive political purposes, but also in the more politically empowering sense that I examine here? Or, can humility ground a virtue like righteous indignation, and even be the source of that indignation's righteousness, or virtue?

First, what does Confucian humility look like? There are many passages in the *Analects* explicitly criticizing arrogance[4] or expressing Confucius's preference for humble, hardworking students over cultural elites.[5] Furthermore, there are many passages in which Confucius discusses himself along these same lines.[6] Finally, there are many passages on deference.[7] However, I want to distinguish the theory of Confucian humility articulated here from references to humble origins, to a self-effacing tendency closer to "modesty," and to deference, which has certain problematic connotations and, moreover, is an outward demeanor more than an inner virtue.

My interpretation of deference here differs notably from David Hall and Roger Ames's interpretation. In *Thinking Through Confucius*, Hall and Ames translate *shu*—the "unifying thread" binding all of Confucius's thought together (4.15, 15.3)—as "deference." They describe *shu* as Confucius's "methodology" (284), but in a significantly different sense than Fingarette's classic conception of a "negative golden rule" ("Do not do to others what you do not want done to you"), which they find lacking because it is framed purely as a negative and is unidirectional (that is, the movement of coming to some determination about how to act is from a preexisting, already understood "I" to a seemingly symmetrically positioned other, instead of originating with a better or worse other as a way of reflecting on oneself).

For Hall and Ames, deference is more of a relational yielding among differently situated members of an ideally harmonious whole. They explain that, "in any given situation one [should] either display excellence in oneself (and thus anticipate deference from others) or defer to excellence in another" (287). Put differently, they write "Patterns of deference require that 'humility' characterize social interactions, where humility is understood as the appropriate sense of one's relevance in a given context of experiencing. This is a sense of one's intrinsic excellence and its pertinence within an intersubjective context. A primary condition for this quality of humility is a sense of one's excellence and the differential excellence of others" (180–181).

Presumably, humility is in quotes here to indicate that the word itself is not used in the *Analects*. Yet the *notion* of humility that Hall and Ames articulate is precisely the one that I argue is foundational in the text. Does this mean that humility is the "unifying thread" binding all of Confucius's thought together? Perhaps! More modestly, I would suggest that, to borrow Hall and Ames's words, humility is what "brings coherence and meaning to [Confucius's] philosophical reflections" (284). What thus takes shape in the following analysis is a picture of humility that *emerges from* an understanding of the three key sub-themes that I examine, and is reciprocally related to those sub-themes, in as much as humility is also what *enables* one properly to cultivate these essential Confucian orientations. Nonetheless, while humility clearly does crucial work in the *Analects*, I do not argue for interpreting *shu* in terms of humility because I believe that the notion of humility articulated here exceeds the meanings of *shu*.

One final point: though humility as articulated in the Western Christian tradition brings its own negative baggage of lowliness and subjection, which persists in the modern colloquial use of the term, deference has been so inflected by the "Asian values" debate that attempting, as Hall and Ames do, to refigure it for a contemporary engagement with Confucian philosophy, *from within that tradition*, seems fraught. The modern Asian political leaders who mobilized the "Asian values" vision (Bell 2000, 7) posited deference as a virtue of submission to authority in a way that cannily parallels the move made by Han dynasty politicians eager to find in Confucianism a moral imperative of obedience, and thus, as one scholar aptly put it, "to yammer or hammer the population into docility" (Moody 1996, 192). Thus, while I agree with the spirit of what Hall and Ames say about relational yielding within appropriate merit hierarchies, I want to move away from their attempt to ground the *Analects* in "deference."

In what follows, then, I outline the theme of Confucian humility by analyzing relevant passages in terms of three key sub-themes: *learning and reflection* (that is, the importance of listening and learning as a first move always); *realistic self-assessment* (that is, the importance of reflecting properly on one's own abilities first, and not on the failures of others or the failure of others to recognize one's abilities); and *human limitations* (that is, the importance of fate, or one's historicity, and thus of focusing on what is within one's control). These sub-themes are deeply intertwined, and considered together they yield a theory of humility as the disposition, or emotional attitude, that I argue is *foundational* for other important Confucian virtues.

Learning and Reflection

The *Analects* teaches that excessive fastidiousness is no virtue, as in 5.20 when Ji Wenzi reflected three times before acting and Confucius remarked, "Twice would have been enough." But it also teaches that *extensive* attention to others, to one's surroundings, to any lessons being offered or rituals being practiced, and to how one may fit into any situation one encounters, is always the proper point of departure.[8] Consider the following passages: "Zizhang asked about obtaining an official position. Confucius said, 'If you first learn as much as you can, then guard against that which is dubious and speak carefully about the rest, you will seldom speak in error. If you first observe as much as you can, then guard against that which is perilous and carefully put the rest into action, you will seldom have cause for regret. If in your speech you seldom err, and in your behavior you seldom have cause for regret, an official position will naturally follow"(2.18). "Whenever the Master was singing in a group or heard something that he liked, he inevitably asked to have it sung again, and only then would harmonize with it" (7.32). And, of course, 17.8: Loving goodness, wisdom, trustworthiness, and so on without balancing these virtues with a love of learning can only result in vice.

What these passages convey is a kind of ethico-epistemic humility. Each passage suggests a deferral of judgment or action until appropriate learning and reflection has occurred. Importantly, what these and many others do *not* suggest, however, is, as a default position, the tacit assent or implicit respect for authority that the idea of deference typically connotes. This kind of humility, as listening, learning and reflecting first and foremost, involves recognition of one's givenness within situations or, more broadly, within tradition and history. But humility, even in the face of our always-emergent understanding, does not entail the so-called blind obedience that certain caricatures or cooptations of Confucianism have posited. This is because the process of learning and reflection, as Confucius conceives it, never entails merely accepting lessons or tradition as determinative. Part of what makes this conception of humility a foundational and not a "lesser" Confucian virtue (as deference is sometimes characterized (Confucius 2003, 6, 148, 202)), is precisely the critical position, or strength, maintained when one is always open to listening and learning without thereby being committed to consenting or affirming.

Though in 7.29 Confucius is talking about his role as teacher, the spirit of the passage is relevant here. Confucius's disciples resist letting a boy from the Hu village interview with Confucius, as the Hu people were "difficult to talk with [about the Way]." Confucius responds, "In allowing him to enter, I am not endorsing what he does after he retires. Why are you being so extreme?" In the face-to-face engagement with the other, sincere openness to that engagement does not thereby necessitate specific commitments. In fact, if that were the case, the deep commitment to learning would be severely undermined by concern with appearances of moral purity. But the "reflection" part of learning and reflection entails turning that learning on oneself, and it is in this interpretive turn that one maintains critical command of the process of understanding. This power can only come from having opened oneself humbly to true listening *first*, for if one refused to meet with any proverbial "boy from Hu," it would suggest the inability to judge wisely how a lesson encountered should or should *not* be internalized as part of one's own ethical development.

Realistic Self-Assessment

As a link between the categories of learning and self-assessment, consider 1.16, "Do not be concerned about whether or not others know you; be concerned about whether or not you know others"; and 7.22, "When walking with two other people, I will always find a teacher among them. I focus on those who are good and seek to emulate them, and focus on those who are bad in order to be reminded of what needs to be changed in myself." The point of departure for self-cultivation in Confucianism is learning and reflection, which requires being attuned to exactly how the lessons presented to one from external sources are instructive. As Ames and Rosemont (1999) suggest, this is "not solely a cognitive process, but an affective one as well" (60). Proper Confucian learning and reflection begins not from the quest for "true knowledge" of facts or universal moral ideas but, rather, from a feeling of humility in the face of the challenge of ethical understanding and refinement, paired with a trust in and *love* of that process as a project. In this sense, humility is the very condition that enables one to persevere steadfastly in their self-cultivation.

But again, Confucian humility is different from its Christian analog, which seems to embrace a general disposition of self-abnegation. While Confucius is most clearly critical of faux humility (11.26), he also opposes *uncritical* humility, even if it were sincere. The point of learning and reflection is not to internalize the truth that we are by nature fallen, unworthy or incapable. The point is, rather, to determine what a situation demands of us, and how our limitations *and* strengths can be realistically grasped such that we improve our ethical weaknesses and best harmonize the person that we are with the situation at hand. Edward Slingerland's commentary on this point is useful. In 5.6, "The Master gave Qidiao Kai permission to take office. Qidiao Kai replied, 'I cannot yet be trusted with such a responsibility.' The Master was pleased." Slingerland notes that what pleases Confucius is Qidiao Kai's "humility and realistic assessment of himself" (2003, 41). It is not that Qidiao Kai is *by nature* unworthy of such a responsibility, but merely that he recognizes that he is not *yet* ready—there is more learning to be done first.

In a similar vein, take 5.9: "The Master said to Zigong, 'Who is better, you or Yan Hui?' Zigong answered, 'How dare I even think of comparing myself to Hui? Hui learns one thing and thereby understands ten. I learn one thing and thereby understand two.' The Master said, 'No, you are not as good as Hui. Neither of us is as good as Hui.'" Slingerland's commentary supports my sense that Confucius is not merely comforting Zigong by showing solidarity, but is quite sincere here. In other words, if Confucius actually thinks he is as good as Yan Hui, then this passage implies mock modesty. If, however, Confucius truly believes that Yan Hui has a superior kind of moral intellect, to which even Confucius's way of knowing is inferior,[9] then what he expresses to Zigong is better understood as simply realistic self-assessment.

To point to a sub-theme of self-assessment in the *Analects* is to point everywhere. But to distill it in terms of *realistic* self-assessment is, I believe, an important elaboration for my purpose. This realistic dimension, as suggested above, distinguishes Confucian humility from the Christian version, within which one's relationship to Christ is a permanent one of lowliness and subordination (thus the pious Christian's response to praise: "It's not me, it's the Lord."). Proper self-assessment in the Confucian context—made from an attuned understanding of the larger set of earthly relations and abilities within which one must decide how to conduct oneself—may, entirely consistent with a disposition of humility, reveal to one that she is in fact superior in a particular ethical or merit hierarchy. So, for example, 13.10 reads, "The Master said, 'If someone would simply employ me, within a single year I could put things into some kind of order, and within three years the transformation would be complete.'" This is Slingerland's translation, which is somewhat at odds with others.[10] However one translates it, though, Confucius clearly believes that he possesses important qualities that could lead him to be successful in politics, if only someone would give him a job. Unlike the Christian response, then, Confucius seems to be saying, "Hey, it's me!"

From the standpoint of Christian humility, Confucius's confidence in his potential to bring about political change may seem boastful. As one scholar explains, however, this passage actually expresses modesty, because Confucius acknowledges that it would take a year for him to make any difference (Tan, 2008). I want to argue, somewhere between this and Slingerland's reading, that Confucius is expressing an ambitious aspiration, but one grounded in a realistic assessment of his moral capabilities. In this vein take 14.25, where Qu Boyu conveys via messenger that he "wishes to reduce his faults, but has not yet been able to so." Upon the messenger's departure, Confucius declares, "Now that is a messenger! That is a messenger!" Slingerland suggests that Confucius is pleased by what the messenger has told him, for he "approves of Qu Boyu's noble intentions and realistic evaluation of himself" (2003, 165). Unfortunately, from Confucius's perspective, people generally do not hold themselves to such a standard. Most examples in the *Analects* of people confident in their abilities or ambitious in their aspirations are offered as lessons about arrogance. From this perspective, unrealistic confidence is a distinct moral weakness, where realistic humility is a strength because it empowers one to discern more judiciously what they can best contribute.

The fact that most people do not see things this way leads Confucius to proclaim, "I should just give up! I have yet to meet someone who is able to perceive his own faults and then take himself to task inwardly" (5.27). What is significant here is that Confucius did *not* give up. He persisted as a teacher after the loss of his favorite student, Yan Hui, and he persisted as a reformer though repeatedly being denied meaningful employment in government. This point about perseverance provides the link between the theme of realistic self-assessment and fated human limitations. As with self-assessment, to point to a theme of fate (*ming*) in the *Analects* is not novel. But interpreting this theme through the lens of historicity, importantly, focuses what the theme is about.

Human Limitations

In the context of the present discussion I wish to emphasize Confucius's strong sense of how one's historicity comes to bear on one's ethical engagement.[11] The *Analects* makes clear that Confucius believed himself to be out of step with his times. The Way did not prevail such that he had the ethical and political opportunities that he would have preferred. Given how historicity imposes limitations on our control of external factors, truly grasping *ming* matters for the gentleman because he learns to focus on what is within human control, which is often only his own self-cultivation and the very limited realm within which his virtue exerts any gravitational force.[12] The failure to recognize the human limitations imposed by *ming* impedes one's moral progress; "One who does not understand fate lacks the means to become a gentleman" (20.3) because he will focus on matters like profit, power, and position, which he cannot necessarily affect. Furthermore, the desire to effect change beyond what is within one's control puts one at risk of becoming demoralized, and thus giving up. Though the precise tone of 5.27 is difficult to discern for sure, I read Confucius as being momentarily exasperated, but not demoralized. Similarly, I understand 2.21 ("in being a filial son and a good brother one is already taking part in government. What need is there, then, to speak of 'participating in government'?") as a reorienting of Confucius's energies, given his *ming*, rather than an expression of resignation or bitterness at not having secured an important political position.[13]

Exactly how one understands *ming*, though, is crucial here. A brief survey of English-language accounts shows Hall and Ames claiming one end of the spectrum, where *ming* is read liberally as "sponsoring circumstances," and D. C. Lau at the other end, where *ming* as "destiny" seemingly renders Confucius a soft determinist (Hall and Ames 1987, 212; Confucius 2002). In between—though tending toward a conception of *ming* as constructively engageable versus fatalistic—are Raphals (2003) and Chen (2003), among others. Exactly where Slingerland (1996) fits on this spectrum is unclear, though he draws on Hall and Ames's perspective throughout his commentary.

Hall and Ames argue that, "In principle there are no limits to the ability of the authoritative person … to meaningfully influence his conditions. … One's ability to respond meaningfully to even the most 'fated' of circumstances renders them significantly alterable" (215). Similarly, Slingerland argues that, "The Confucian response to an apparently capricious and often inexplicable fate" involves a "realistic and mature redirection of human energy toward the sole area of life in which one does have control—the cultivation and moral improvement of one's own self coupled with a faith in the ability of self-cultivation to produce in one an attitude of joyful acceptance of all that life may bring" (1996, 568). Address the inner realm, and "concerns of the outer realm … will take care of themselves" (1996, 571). Both accounts beg a question: can one meaningfully influence actual "conditions" by understanding *ming*, or is it only one's attitude and response to fate that one can control? If the former, these readings seem anti-fatalistic, but if the latter, they may be as susceptible to the "soft determinist" charge as Lau. Slingerland attempts to confront this concern directly, claiming that his interpretation of *ming* does not amount to a "fatalistic excuse for retiring to a life of ritual," or to some kind of "thinly veiled political cop-out" (1996, 576–77). But he is ultimately vague about how the "joyful acceptance of all that life brings" avoids becoming depoliticizing and conservative. How does optimistically reorienting towards one's fate through man's meaning-making capacity ultimately override the limits on one's ability to influence conditions?

On my reading of the *Analects*, there *is* a limit to how much one can constructively engage fate so as to influence conditions. And while Confucius does not become demoralized or embittered by his historically determined limitations, neither does he suggest that meaning making, joyful attitude, or *only* focusing on internal matters within one's control are the answer. Slingerland and Hall and Ames's treatments of *ming* would go further in showing how humility before our historicity resists politically copping out if they were to link their analysis with other explicitly political passages—passages about *how* to engage critically with others in an attempt to transform the political landscape, and *why*.

Without imposing a Western liberal notion of politics on the *Analects* here (I take seriously that politics and ethics are inextricable for Confucians), it seems that politics cannot be reduced to only ethical self-cultivation. Take, for example, passages addressing when to exit a ruler's court (11.24), decline to engage someone face to face (17.20), resist political compromise (9.13), or leave a state (15.1); or passages on how to truly love *and* despise others (4.3, 17.24), how to deliver an insult in rebuke to ritual impropriety (17.20), or when to attack one who has ruled by personal whim (11.17). If humility is a foundational Confucian disposition, it is partly because it orients us toward our fate in a certain way. This is not by teaching us to turn entirely inward or to cultivate a joyful attitude in the acceptance of subjection to external forces. Rather, humility before our historicity enables us to understand that our actions can often have only a limited impact—that we will be foiled by circumstances—and thus the purpose of acting cannot be determined by the likelihood of success. If actual impact were the gauge, we'd become demoralized and give up. But Confucius won't allow it! There *is* a crucial commitment in the *Analects* to critically engaging others and our circumstances, even though the outcome is never guaranteed; for doing so fosters another important Confucian ethical and political virtue, namely, righteous indignation.

The *Analects* suggests that, far from demanding passivity and therefore posing an obstacle to political reform, humility is actually what enables proper protest and remonstration. This is because humility facilitates critical engagement with others and with our conditions that is neither passive nor arrogant and self-righteous. In a sense, the righteous indignation that humility grounds can be understood as something of a mean between the defect of doing or saying nothing and the excess of acting out of a hubristic desire to be radically transformative, or "historic" in our deeds. Often, all that mere humans in dark times can do is steadfastly express indignation about the corrupted powers that be. Humility is what allows such expressive acts to be ethically *authoritative*—righteous, virtuous—even if they are ultimately not politically transformative.

Moreover, not only does Confucian humility enable one righteously to express indignation, we might even go so far as to say that humility *demands* the proper expression of indignation. Encountering the limitations posed by our fate—recognizing our smallness before the river of history and culture in which we find ourselves swept up—does not function to absolve us from agency or justify our turning toward the merely personal. For while such an encounter reveals the ways in which we are historically given, finite beings, limited in our capacity to simply *will* change, it also allows us to appreciate the ways in which we are *not* thereby limited, and calls us ethically to do what we can in that regard.

Conclusion

Humility refracted through the prism of learning and reflection, realistic self-assessment, and human limitations suggests a particular kind of political engagement that is principled but also pragmatic. Unlike Socrates, for example, who was out of step with his times and willing (even anxious!) to pay the ultimate price for that, the *Analects* has a pragmatic dimension that encourages one to grasp (or grasp differently) the limits of our control over the course of social change: "If the Way is being realized in the world then show yourself; if it is not, then go into reclusion" (8.13). Taken to an extreme, such an attitude *would* be atomizing and depoliticizing. But Confucius clearly critiques excessive fastidiousness here, saying, "Worthy people go into reclusion because the age itself is disordered; those next in worth withdraw because their state is disordered; next still are those who withdraw because of a discourteous expression on their ruler's face; and finally there are those who will withdraw at a single discourteous word" (14.37).[14] A disposition of humility retains its critical force—its dimension of strength, not "meekness"—precisely when it enables one to bear witness against impropriety and corruption, and to the ways in which one can and cannot struggle for ethical and political transformation within the given conditions of existence. Even in a disordered age, Confucius did not simply go into reclusion.

While "bearing witness" may seem trivial as political critique, the *Analects* suggests the punch that Confucius thinks such conduct packs. Furthermore, we see how the authoritativeness of such actions can be understood only as flowing from a prior, fundamental disposition of humility. Humility prevents us from becoming demoralized when our actions fail to produce dramatic change, and it keeps righteous indignation from lapsing into self-righteousness. Humility is thus pivotal within the *Analects*, because it functions as the psychological root of a range of important virtues of social and political engagement. These include, more intuitively, patience, perseverance in one's own self-cultivation, proper shame, and generosity toward others in their process of self-cultivation. Less intuitively, humility functions as the psychological root of righteous indignation.

In a climate of partisan posturing and rampant self-righteousness, like that characterizing contemporary American politics, revisiting the virtues of humility and righteous indignation as they emerge from within Confucianism could be politically productive. Thus one key lesson to be learned in "the West" from engaging with Confucian humility is that humility is a crucial critical, *political* virtue worth being given another chance, unburdened from the notions of meekness and obedience that it has traditionally been associated with.

17   Is Conscientiousness a Virtue? Confucian Answers[1]

Stephen C. Angle

Introduction

Among contemporary philosophers sympathetic to the theoretical centrality of virtue, there is little agreement on the status of conscientiousness. Indeed, there is little agreement even on what the word "conscientiousness" means; for the time being, let us take it to mean consciously ensuring that one does one's duty. Adams and Wallace both take conscientiousness to be a virtue, whereas Roberts calls it a "quasi-virtue" and Slote argues that it is both different from and inferior to virtue.[2] The landscape becomes still more complicated when we add in the vexed concept of "continence," which we can initially gloss as forcing oneself to act rightly, against contrary inclination. McDowell sees continence as fundamentally distinct from virtue, while others like Stohr and Eylon argue that, in important ways, virtue itself is a kind of continence.[3] The dense views on these matters of historical figures such as Aristotle and Kant further muddy the picture.[4]

My goal here is to offer some clarity by drawing on what for some will seem a surprising source: early Confucianism. In one way, this should not be so surprising, because Confucianism is increasingly being recognized as home to one or more type of virtue ethic. No shock, then, that it speaks to issues like conscientiousness and continence. On the other hand, the strategy of seeking clarity by looking to the views of multiple Confucian philosophers, themselves sometimes differing from one another and whose texts are subject to certain interpretive disputes, may seem quixotic. In fact, stepping outside the Western tradition provides a valuable way for Western philosophers to check our bearings. We will see a way of thinking about psychological phenomena and ethical concerns that is clearly related to many of the insights driving the Western debates to which I have alluded, but which parses matters somewhat differently. Briefly, the Confucians hold that conscientiousness is certainly not virtue. It lacks the reliability, flexibility, and (in many cases) style that come with virtue. Conscientiousness has important value, especially for ethical learners, but it is also dangerous.

The *Analects*

Let us begin with the *Analects*, which is much more worried about hypocrisy than interested in encouraging conscientious but not heartfelt behavior.[5] For example, in one early passage Confucius is said to consider all of the following shameful: "clever words, an ingratiating countenance, and perfunctory gestures of respect, ... [as well as] concealing one's resentment and feigning friendship" (5:25; Confucius 2003, 50). In a somewhat later passage, we hear Confucius wonder: "If someone seems sincere and serious in his conversation, does this mean he is a gentleman? Or has he merely adopted the appearance of a gentleman?" (11:21; 2003, 119). Confucius does not trust popular opinions of people; even if everyone in a village likes someone, it is better to know what the *good* people in the village think, or else to judge for oneself (13:24; 15:28). Most famously, in a late passage the *Analects* tells us that Confucius condemned the "village worthy (*xiangyuan*)" as "the thief of virtue" (17:13; 2003, 205). An adjacent passage makes a similar point when it draws an analogy between "assuming a severe expression while being weak inside" and breaking into a home and committing burglary (17:12; 2003, 205). In both cases, a seemingly good exterior is stolen, or at any rate unearned.

The hypocrite and the conscientious person resemble one another very closely in both external behavior and much of their inner psychology. After all, does not the hypocrite consciously ensure that he or she does his or her duty? The difference seems to lie in the consistency with which a conscientious person both tries, and succeeds, in getting him or herself to follow duty. Indeed, the *Analects* does at times commend what looks like conscientiousness. Confucius is asked about "accumulating and exalting virtue (*chong de*)," and he replies: "Emphasize devotion and trustworthiness, and always move in the direction of what is right" (12.10).[6] It is a bit unclear exactly how one is supposed to "emphasize devotion and trustworthiness," which are character traits that one might be expected to take on over time, but as a first approximation, we should presumably strive to follow our superiors' orders and match our deeds to our words. Insofar as one has a grasp on what counts as "right (*yi*)," "moving in the direction of what is right" is more directly accessible. Confucians understood their world to be governed by a code of propriety, and in many places we can see the close relationship between "ritually proper (*li*)" and "right."[7] Although the exact relationship between the externalized rules (the right, the proper) and internal virtues (righteousness, propriety) was debated by various Confucians, it seems plausible to think that here, in the *Analects*, students are being told that a way to "accumulate and exalt virtue" is to follow the rules. Such a reading is supported by another discussion of "accumulating and exalting virtue" from the same chapter. Here, Confucius says more simply that one should "put service first and reward last" (12.21; 2003, 135). In both passages, we see the suggestion that one should do one's duty as a route toward developing one's virtue. One is not yet virtuous enough to do these things more spontaneously; the conscientiousness that is here advocated is clearly the activity of a learner. Still, ethical learning is critical to the project of the *Analects*, so insofar as conscientious behavior can contribute to such learning, it is valued. A problem with such learners is that they may know their duty and yet fail to follow it; in an earlier passage, Confucius explicitly worries that he may "hear what is right yet be unable to move in its direction" (7.3). As I will elaborate below, this is one of the dimensions of conscientiousness's unreliability, and thus one of the reasons why Confucians push for more robust virtue.

A nice way to sum up the ambiguous place of conscientiousness in the *Analects* is offered in an article by Amy Olberding (Olberding 2009). Her topic is the relation between style and moral improvement, and part of her account is based on an extended study of Zigong, one of Confucius's students.[8] She writes that Zigong is "a keen student of Confucius's manner, explaining Confucius's behavior to others and loyally defending Confucius to those skeptical of the Master's authority."[9] Nonetheless, "while Zigong cultivates a learned and refined mien, there is some worry that he is too facile with surface appearance and inattentive to the substantive qualities of character that ought to underlie them."[10] Olberding diagnoses Zigong as weak in "sympathy (*shu*)" but strong in "studied attention to ritual"; she calls him a "technician" and "rule bound" (Ibid., 511). Olberding argues that Zigong's excessive formalism will result in his failure to "offer others tailored responses that acknowledge their particular identities and circumstances," and this has negative effects both on others and on himself:

> His failure registers in the effects of his style on others, [in] their sense of passing unrecognized or being submerged in a uniform otherness that elides the delicate variations of their more particular claims upon Zigong's energies. More subtle is the effect of Zigong's failure on himself. If we assume that Zigong aims, albeit clumsily, to foster fruitful relations with others, his efforts are inept in a particularly pernicious way. In his exercise of technical skill, he grants little access to himself. That is, in Zigong, others may well feel they have encountered a *form*, not a *man*. He not only elides others, he conceals himself. In consequence, he erects a barrier that impedes the ability of others to achieve sympathy with him. … Put simply, technical perfection can generate distrust.
>
> (Ibid., 511–512)

The sentiments in this passage mesh well with the *Analects'* worries about conscientiousness that we discussed above, with the addition of Olberding's recognition that, in an important sense, it does not matter whether a rule-bound "technician" is in fact aiming at moral improvement and fruitful relationships, or is cynically attempting to manipulate people in pursuit of status and material gain. In either case, there is a tendency for the conscientious style to generate distrust. His mild corrections of Zigong notwithstanding, Confucius does not take Zigong to be a "thief of virtue," but the similarity between the two types is still troubling. Again, we cannot discount the value of conscientiousness for learners, but even here we see problems. Olberding thus concludes that the more natural and idiosyncratic model of Zilu, whom she terms a "clown," offers a better route forward than Zigong's "technician" (Ibid., 515).

The *Mencius*

Like the *Analects*, the *Mencius* also expresses worries about conscientiousness. One of Mencius's students asks him to explain who are the "village worthies" excoriated by Confucius. Mencius replies that such people have no aspiration to improve themselves; they say, "Born in this era, we should be for this era. To be good is enough." Mencius remarks that:

> If you try to condemn them, there is nothing you can point to. … They are in agreement with current customs; they are in harmony with the sordid era in which they live. They seem to dwell in devotion and faithfulness; their actions seem to be blameless and pure. The multitude delight in them; they regard themselves as right. But you cannot enter into the Way of Yao and Shun with them.
>
> (7B:37; 2008, 195)

Mencius's use of the word "seem" suggests that his concern may be that village worthies exhibit mere "semblances" of virtue.[11] This reading of the passage also fits well with the context in which the village worthy was discussed in the *Analects*: recall from above that Confucius condemns those who "assume a severe expression while being weak inside": a seemingly good exterior is unearned because it masks inner weakness. And yet Mencius's worry here seems subtly different from that in the *Analects*. It is not so much that village worthies (as he understands them) hide their inner weakness, as that they are celebrated for doing their quite minimal duties and no more. Mencius regarded the moral standards of his age as woefully inadequate; resting content with such customs condemned one to a life of moral mediocrity. The problem with village worthies, therefore, was that they thrived in and actively encouraged[12] a culture of doing no more than one's duty—and they did this at a time when the collectively understood duties were too minimal to lead to genuine moral progress for individuals or for the society. In short, rather than calling Mencius's "village worthies" hypocritical, we should simply see them as conscientious, and Mencius found such conscientiousness deeply troubling.[13]

The closest that Mencius comes to making explicit the distinction between conscientious and virtuous activity comes in the following passage:

> Mencius said, "That by which humans differ from animals is slight. The masses abandon it. The gentleman preserves it. Shun had insight into things. He had scrutinized human roles. He acted out of benevolence and righteousness; he did not act out benevolence and righteousness."
>
> (4B19; cf. 2008, 107)

Mencius believes that humans (unlike animals) have innate promptings toward virtue which need to be preserved and extended; if they are abandoned, one is no different from an animal. Based on his successful extension of these rudimentary feelings (via scrutinizing human roles, among other things), the ancient sage Shun was able to act out of virtuous dispositions, rather than merely doing his best to act in a virtuous way. The English phrase "act out benevolence" is somewhat ambiguous; in light of our discussion in the previous paragraph, it is important to clarify that by "act out benevolence," Mencius does not mean *pretending* to be benevolent—that is, merely "acting." He means to put into practice actions that are benevolent, but not to do so in a way that springs naturally from a benevolent character. Distinctions like this are common in Western virtue-ethical literature, both ancient and contemporary. We can also look to a famous twelfth-century commentary on the text for clarification: "Benevolence and righteousness were already based in Shun's heartmind, and all that he did came from them. It is not that he regarded benevolence and righteousness as fine things and only then forced himself to act" (Zhu 1987, 112; Mengzi 2008, 107). Clearly, Mencius is arguing that sagely virtue is distinct from conscientiousness.[14]

So far we have seen that Mencius, like the Confucius of the *Analects*, has a clear conception of conscientiousness and has serious concerns about it, though Mencius's stress is less on hypocrisy than on one's resting content with mediocrity. Still, again like the *Analects*, we do find in the *Mencius* some recognition that conscientious behavior is important for learners. At one point, Mencius says, "If you wear the clothes of [ancient sage] Yao, recite the teachings of Yao, and perform the actions of Yao—this is to be Yao" (6B: 2; 2008, 159). In order to understand Mencius's point here, it is critical to keep in mind that the Confucian masters often tailor their teachings to the current needs of a specific student. Rather than making a blanket claim that is apt for all, therefore, Mencius is here giving one individual (named Cao Jiao) instructions that will help him to move forward.[15] Similarly, even though Shun was lauded for not forcing himself to "act out" benevolence, in a subsequent passage Mencius says, "Nothing will get one closer to benevolence than to force oneself to act out sympathetic understanding" (7A:4; 2008, 172).[16] The two kinds of forcing are different from one another: in Cao Jiao's case, one consciously mimics Yao with the hope that good behavior and a deeper transformation will follow; in the latter case, one focuses oneself (consciously, thus "forcing") on one kind of motive rather than another. The latter seems more advanced, though still potentially subject to the problems which conscientiousness engenders, as Mencius has made clear.

The *Xunzi*

Conscientiousness plays a larger role in *Xunzi*—the third of our classical Confucian sources—than it does in either of our previous texts. Notwithstanding certain differences from *Mencius*, we will see that the account in *Xunzi* is basically compatible with what has come before: conscientiousness is apt as a learner's state, but troubling if one becomes stuck at this stage. Xunzi is in fact considerably more explicit about the stages of ethical development.[17] One passage distinguishes three "grades of person (*ren lun*)":

1. The "common mass of humanity (*zhongren*)." The fundamental orientation of their heartminds (or "commitment (*zhi*)"[18]) allows for "crooked and selfish motives (*qusi*)," though they hope that "others will consider them to be public-spirited" (K II, 83; Li 157).
2. "Lesser Confucians (*xiao ru*)." Xunzi writes that they are committed to "repressing the merely private and thus are able to be public-spirited. In their conduct, they repress their emotional dispositions and inborn nature and are thus able to become cultivated" (Ibid.).

3. "Great Confucians (*da ru*)." The commitment of these individuals is "at ease with what is public-spirited, [and] their conduct is at ease with cultivation" (Ibid.).

In the hope of the masses to appear public spirited, we can detect some resemblance to the "village worthy," especially the *Analects'* version, which sees such people as hypocrites.[19] Of primary interest here, though, is the middle category. Xunzi also says that these people are "knowing, yet fond of inquiring of others, so they are able to develop their talents." This is strong praise from Xunzi, who, as we will see, puts considerable emphasis on learning from teachers and other "models." Xunzi often characterizes the "merely private (*si*)" in terms of one's physical desires, and believes that the disposition to feel such desires is rooted in our nature. "Lesser Confucians" are able to force themselves to act well, despite the fact that such private desires push them in other directions. Clearly, this is a case of conscientiousness and, indeed, of continence, since these people must repress contrary inclinations. Just as clearly, the highest group (the Great Confucians) exemplify full virtue in the way in which they are "at ease" with public-spirited activity.

In other passages Xunzi expands on these ideas. His characterizations of the lowest and highest categories are largely compatible with what we have already seen. The middle group, though, gets considerably more fine-grained analysis. For example: "He who acts from a fondness for the model is a scholar. He who embodies it with firm commitment is a gentleman. ... [If a man] possess the model but has no commitment to its true meaning, then he will act too rigidly."[20] Both the "scholar" and the "gentleman" fall in between the masses and the sage. Without firm commitment, the mere scholar is likely to be overly rigid in his effort to follow the model. Still, Xunzi has here made explicit the motivation of the "scholar": he is fond of "models (*fa*)." Models include the examples posed by exemplary teachers and ancient sages, as well as explicit ritual directives. Models are key to Xunzi's understanding of ethical progress because (as we will discuss below) he does not believe that we have guidance from innate moral feelings.

In another passage, Xunzi further elaborates on the middle ground between masses and sage:

When a person's conduct is based on the model with maximal firmness so that merely private desires do not confuse what he has been taught, he may properly be called a "resolute scholar."

When a person's conduct is based on the model with maximal firmness and he is fond of cultivating and rectifying himself in terms of what he has been taught so that his dispositions and inborn nature are reformed and improved; ... [when,] although his conduct is generally appropriate, [but] he is not yet fully at ease; [and] when, although his thought and awareness are for the most part suitable, he is not yet completely thorough, ... then [he] may properly be called a "staunch and substantial gentleman."

(Li 140; altered from K II, 75–76)

Once again we see a distinction between "scholar" and "gentleman." The scholar is able to stick firmly to the model, but with such conscientious resolution may come, as noted above, some rigidity. The gentleman's motivation is more internal, more "embodied" because his commitment is now at least partly reflected in transformed dispositions and in the ways that he perceives the world, but he still falls short. Insofar as he is not fully "at ease," he must still monitor himself and ensure that he acts properly. Perhaps he has moved beyond continence, since there are no suggestions here of significant contrary inclinations, but some conscious intervention—some conscientiousness—is still necessary to see that he acts as needed.

In a fascinating passage from the "Undoing Fixation" chapter, Xunzi is even more specific about the different mechanisms that can enable conscientious people to motivate themselves to act properly. Xunzi relates three stories. A man named Ji lived in a cave in order to ponder by himself, but was easily distracted by mosquitoes and gnats. His answer was to carefully keep himself as far away from the distractions as possible; Xunzi calls this "anxiously keeping oneself on guard (*wei*)." The second incident concerns Mencius, who is said to have expelled his wife because he hated the impropriety that she showed in breaking convention.[21] Xunzi calls this "rigidly forcing oneself (*zi qiang*)." Finally, a man named Youzi "hated dozing off so he burned his palm to stay awake." Xunzi classifies this as "endurance (*zi ren*)."[22] All three of these men at least partly achieve their ends, but Xunzi emphasizes the distance between them and a sage. One way of characterizing the difference is that they are focused only on external results; Xunzi says, "Those who are murky understand only external manifestations, while those who are clear understand internal manifestations."[23] Sages "follow their desires and embrace their emotional dispositions" and things simply turn out well ordered, without any need for keeping on guard, rigid forcing, or endurance. Xunzi is not interested here in whether the results achieved by the three men are actually correct, nor does he explicitly draw attention to ways in which their external goals may be undermined by the means taken to achieve them. His point is, rather, that we should not rest content with a murky interior psychology, but work to achieve the state of the sage wherein results come "without striving (*wu wei*)."

So far, we have seen a picture that accords quite well with the previous Confucians. It is possible to conscientiously get oneself to act properly, through a combination of external models (so that one knows what is "proper") and motivational techniques (keeping on guard, rigidity, and so on), but such results are at best a stage on the way toward more full-blown virtue. Each of the passages from *Xunzi* that we have examined emphasizes the need for an inner transformation of dispositions—a coming to be "at ease" with the proper feelings and response. In a famous passage that has drawn much scholarly attention, though, Xunzi might seem to be asserting that a different kind of conscientiousness is possible. We read:

> Life is what people most desire, and death is what people most despise. However, when people let go of life and accomplish their own death, this is not because they do not desire life and instead desire death. Rather, it is because they do not approve (*ke*) of living in these circumstances, but do approve of dying in these circumstances. Thus, when the desire is excessive but the action

does not match it, this is because the heartmind prevents it. … Thus, order and disorder reside in what the heartmind approves of; they are not present in the desires from one's dispositions (*qing*).[24]

At issue is how to understand "approval." It is distinct from and indeed seems to override desiring. Desires are automatic responses of one's dispositions to things, as when one encounters and desires a delicious food. Approval, on the other hand, stems from understanding (*zhi*): Xunzi tells us that it is only the understanding that enables us to take a given object or goal as approval-worthy, and let it guide us (Li 529). In an important article on Xunzi's view of human agency, Bryan Van Norden adds two other remarks about "approval." First, he says that it does not seem to be associated with joy or delight in one's action. Second, Van Norden suggests that the phenomenology of "approving" of something seems to be like "feeling morally compelled to perform … some action" (Van Norden 2000, 124). If we take all these characteristics of approval together, it might be tempting to imagine that Xunzi is talking about something like Kant's pure practical judgment, with the heartmind playing the role of one's morally good "will." Furthermore, since approval seems clearly to be a kind of conscientiousness, we might also think that Xunzi has discovered an important new species: not the compromised motivation of the learner, but a pure sort of motive that, perhaps, should be our ultimate goal.

In fact, no scholars today argue that Xunzi is here anticipating Kant, though there is considerable disagreement about how we ought to understand Xunzi's view.[25] I believe that, with a few additional observations, we can come to see how "approval" is the same kind of conscientious state—or rather, covers the same range of conscientious states—as we saw above. The key is seeing how one comes to approve of something. In a passage just before the lengthy discussion of "approval," Xunzi writes: "Our desires are independent of our approval of them, but we actually seek only what we approve of. It is our nature that our desires are independent from our approval. It is the result of our heartmind that we seek only what we approve of. When a single natural desire is controlled by our heartmind's many aspects, it becomes difficult to classify it as the original, natural desire."[26] T. C. Kline explains that the original desire has been transformed into a more complex motive, in something like the transformation that Aristotle says takes place during practical reasoning. Approval, then, may not be a desire, but "another kind of motive, perhaps something that we could call a practical judgment, that combines both cognitive and conative elements" (Kline 2000, 161). Approval is not a simple mental state, wholly distinct from desire, which can serve as a *sui generis* source of motivation. It is, rather, the result of a process, a filtering and transforming of our desires by our heartmind. In the simplest case of the completely uncultivated person who approves whatever he or she desires, this "process" is empty and automatic.[27] Xunzi says that anyone can approve of things, as distinct from simply desiring them, and so there is no guarantee that approval will always be correct. "If what the heartmind approves of misses the proper patterns, then even if the desires are few, how would it stop short of chaos?" (Li 527). However, in many cases, this will be a result of a lengthy process of conscious cultivation. Especially when we take this into account, we begin to see that approving is closely related to the process of "commitment (*zhi*)" that was at the core of some of Xunzi's earlier discussions of conscientiousness. Recall that the three "grades of person" each had a different commitment.[28] The middle category are committed to "repressing the merely private and thus are able to be public-spirited." We could also say that these people approve of public-spiritedness, and are thereby able to repress the merely private. We also have seen that Xunzi talks about the degree of "firmness" with which one's conduct is based on a proper model. One's understanding and fondness for the model both figure into this firmness; approval, we can infer, is another way of talking about the role of understanding in enabling one to stand firm. Xunzi's stories about Ji, Mengzi, and Youzi, finally, can be seen as further illustrating what different kinds of approval may look like. In particular, it is consistent with everything that Xunzi has said to suspect that approval will often be rigid, just as many of his other discussions of conscientiousness claim. Conscientiousness is an important capacity that we have, but it is no substitute for becoming more virtuous.[29]

One final issue that we should consider is Xunzi's insistence that morality in general, and righteousness (*yi*) in particular, are "external" rather than being—as Mencius thought—"internal" to one's nature. Much ink has been spilled over this topic; very roughly, the dispute is over whether virtuous dispositions emerge through the properly nurtured growth of specific proto-moral capacities that we have innately. Xunzi does not think so. He does hold that our natures are amenable to being shaped, but the means and goal of the shaping are human discoveries. For our purposes, the question is whether this disagreement between Xunzi and Mencius has consequences for their respective views of conscientiousness. It will help us to formulate an answer if we take on board something like Hume's distinction between natural and artificial virtues. For Hume, natural virtues are those "that are rooted directly in the weak sentiment of benevolence"; to fully develop such virtues, one has only to "recognize as a norm what is already latent within our human nature."[30] On the other hand, Hume also wants to be able to account for virtues like honesty or justice which not only do not seem to emerge directly from benevolence, but can even conflict with it. His answer is that the mediation of a convention or compact (with or without conscious agreement) can enable us to redirect feelings of benevolence. Our approbation for the practices associated with convention-governed social life (like promising, laws, and property) can redirect our sentiments, which then come to take on a life of their own within our hearts and minds. These new dispositions are artificial virtues (Wiggins 1996, 137).

Hume's categories do not map perfectly onto either Mencius or Xunzi, but what they do help us to see is this: both natural and artificial virtues are *virtues*. Whatever their origins, they are robust dispositions that spontaneously can guide the style and substance of our reactions to our environment. The virtue of truthfulness, no matter whether understood as natural or artificial, is importantly different from rule-bound truth telling. Admittedly, being shaped by an external model plays a much bigger role for Xunzi than for Mencius, and so we might expect that Xunzi will have more to say about those who are consciously striving to conform to such models. This is indeed what we have seen: Xunzi offers a more subtle—and perhaps somewhat more favorable—treatment of conscientiousness than does either Mencius or Confucius. Nonetheless, the general shape of conscientiousness is quite consistent across all three texts. In all three texts, the goal is the reliability, flexibility, and style that come with virtue.

Conclusion

The main project of this essay has been to show, often via detailed interpretation of passages, that early Confucian philosophers exhibit a concerted and consistent interest in conscientiousness. As I have emphasized, they understand conscientiousness to be both distinct from (and inferior to) virtue, and to have both positive and negative sides. These results have two kinds of immediate payoff. First, by thematizing the idea of conscientiousness (for which there is no single term in these texts) we can better understand the role that rules and models play in early Confucian ethics. Claims made in each of these texts concerning the importance of ritual and other sorts of rules must be read in the context of their views of conscientious rule following, as opposed to fully fledged virtuous responsiveness. Second, the arguments of this essay should help us to better grasp the kind(s) of virtue ethics that these three texts are putting forward. Especially in the *Xunzi*, we see a spectrum of positions that one can occupy as one's degree of ethical cultivation progresses, with increasingly less reliance on conscientiousness. Because actually achieving sagehood is nigh on impossible, these semi-conscientious middle-ground positions are extremely important to our ethical lives, but this does not change the fact that the development of, and reliance upon, a virtuous character remains Xunzi's ultimate goal. In other words, by properly understanding the place of conscientiousness within early Confucian ethics, we are helped to see that the *Analects*, *Mencius*, and *Xunzi* present forms of virtue ethics, rather than a deontological ethics or a unique synthesis of rule- and virtue-based ethics.[31]

In addition to these two immediate rewards, I must grant that I have only scratched the surface of the rich range of comparative questions that one could pursue on the basis of the material here discussed. For example, can we bring together and then generalize upon the various ways in which the texts urge readers to avoid the problematic aspects of conscientiousness, and then on this basis offer advice to ethical learners today (that is, to all of us)? What should we make of the fact that "reason" and "reasons" play a much larger role in most Western discussions of conscientiousness and continence than these notions played in the texts that we have examined here? Speaking of continence, what more might we tease out of early Confucianism concerning this idea—especially in light of the Confucian view that a sage will respond to all relevant values (Angle 2009a, ch. 6)? This seems not to allow for McDowell's notion that "moral" considerations will "silence" others, and yet sagely activity is surely not to be understood as taking place against a background of "contrary inclinations," as the idea of continence suggests.[32] I hope that others and perhaps I myself will be able to pursue these kinds of comparative opportunities in the future. As this essay and, indeed, all the essays in this volume show, the juxtaposition of virtue ethics and Confucianism opens up many exciting prospects for future research and, we can hope, for concrete ethical learning.

18   The Virtues of Justice in Zhu Xi

Kai Marchal

Introduction[1]

To think of the Neo-Confucian thinker Zhu Xi (1130–1200) as a virtue ethicist—or even an exponent of the virtue of justice—must seem novel to readers in the Chinese world. Premodern commentaries on his writings have focused on his use of concepts like "coherence"/"principle" (*li*) or "heart-mind" (*xin*), not "virtue" (*de*). During the twentieth century, when Chinese thinkers attempted to interpret Zhu Xi in the language of modern (Western) philosophy, they most often perceived him as a kind of "Neo-Confucian Kantian" who made assumptions about the moral worth of the individual, the unconditional obligation to right action, and the absolute value of good will—not about the virtues.[2]

The deontological approach has certainly advanced our understanding of Neo-Confucianism, namely by highlighting its emphasis on a peculiar form of moral inwardness which, at least in principle, transcends any social structure and is unrelated to particular actions and situations. But it also faces, I believe, certain structural difficulties that, even to Kantians in the West, would make it rather difficult to accept Zhu Xi as one of their own. In this chapter, I will argue instead that there are important reasons to regard Zhu Xi as an eminent virtue ethicist *avant la lettre*. I will also suggest that his ideas, though belonging to a very different historical and philosophical context, can enrich contemporary debates about the virtues and virtuous life in the West. In particular, I will be concerned with what I call the sense of justice connected to various virtues in Zhu Xi's writings, i.e. the disposition of moral actors to care for the good of others and be concerned about the equal distribution of goods in the community.[3] By carefully re-contextualizing our questions and highlighting potential analogies between the language of modern virtue ethics and Zhu Xi's peculiar discourse, we ultimately realize, I will claim, that the Neo-Confucian moral vision linked to the issue of justice is one of the salient issues that we, as citizens in modern societies (both in the West and in the East), would do well to explore: it will help us not only to broaden our horizons of self-understanding, but also to engage with one of the most critical issues of global philosophy.

In order to clarify these complex matters, I will proceed in four steps: First, I will summarize the general understanding of virtue in Zhu Xi's thought and discuss one important objection to the virtue-ethicist approach; Second, I will explain why I think that, although Zhu Xi's thought lacks one single concept of justice, it still makes sense to speak of various "virtues of justice" in his thought; Third, I will explain the situational nature of Zhu's understanding of these "virtues of justice" and describe one important challenge to this view; Fourth, I will argue that Zhu Xi can solve this challenge and demonstrate that he indeed provides us with a plausible account of the "virtues of justice," an account based on a bold vision of the moral agent's spiritual independence and a deep appreciation of the sphere of non-commensurability.

Was Zhu Xi a Virtue Ethicist *avant la lettre*?

Aristotle has offered not the first but, by many accounts, the most thorough view on human life as based on the virtues. In the second book of the *Nicomachean Ethics*, he famously defines moral virtues as mean dispositions with respect to actions and feelings, and vices as failures to find the mean with respect to them. Contemporary virtue ethicists like G.E.M. Anscombe, Iris Murdoch, Rosalind Hursthouse, or Michael Slote, although not always endorsing the Aristotelian model entirely, agree with him that moral questions should be tackled through the virtues and that issues of character are more fundamental to ethical reflection than rules or principles.

In his conversations with disciples, Zhu Xi constantly refers to the "four virtues" (*si de*) that the Confucian thinker Mencius identified many centuries earlier (in the fourth century BC): "humaneness" (*ren*), "appropriateness" (*yi*), "propriety" (*li*), and "wisdom" (*zhi*).[4] Obviously, there are some slight semantic differences between the Greek term *aretē* (goodness, excellence, nobility, virtue) and the Chinese term *de* (moral charisma, kindness, virtue); but it still seems convincing to relate these terms, with due caution, to each other.[5] For although Zhu Xi nowhere attempts to provide us with a *systematic theory* of the virtues as modern virtue ethicists do, he certainly articulates a coherent vision of moral character and ethical life grounded in the Confucian virtues. In other words, he is concerned with a range of questions that belong to the sphere of "moral psychology": how to achieve a fine character, how the virtues interact, how fine internal states make us respond naturally to various situations, etc.[6] It makes sense to understand these "four virtues" as dispositions constituting human agency and as having both a moral and an epistemic dimension. In other words, moral self-cultivation, according to Zhu Xi, "entails" indeed, as Stephen Angle writes about another Neo-Confucian thinker, "the establishment of a disposition to view the world in a certain fashion, and that the maturation of this disposition is *de* or virtue"(Angle 2010, 317).

However, the virtue-ethicist approach to Zhu Xi faces one important objection, which I want to call the "Kantian inwardness challenge". It is well known by now that Zhu Xi, unlike Mencius (who wanted us to *develop* our "four virtues"), emphasizes the need for their mere *recovery*, since he believes that our "original heart-mind" (*benxin* 本心) already encompasses them (Ivanhoe 2000, 46–47). In the same vein, Zhu often points out that the virtues are merely manifestations of the "heart-mind,"[7] and, commenting on a famous passage in the *Great Learning* (*Daxue*)—"to let one's inborn luminous virtue shine forth" (*ming ming de*)—he claims that "inborn luminous virtue" is identical with either the "heart-mind" or "nature."[8] These and many other passages could easily give us the impression that the four virtues are derived from "heart-mind" and "nature."[9] If we accept the modern scholar Mou Zongsan's claim that the true ground of the Neo-Confucian understanding of human agency lies in the two (closely related) concepts of "heart-mind" and "nature" (*xin xing*), which he interprets as something akin to Kantian free will (supposedly giving access to the noumenal reality of the self (Mou 1968–69, 1: 169)), we might indeed end up with an account centered on a supreme principle of morality (identified by Mou with "coherence" or *li*). This, indeed, would suggest a very different approach from that typically associated with virtue ethics.

Two immediate qualifications are required, however. First, even if we understand the concepts "heart-mind" and "nature" as, in a broader sense, equivalents for "Kantian inwardness", Zhu Xi's thought still lacks a principle similar to the categorical imperative in virtue of which moral requirements are unconditionally binding.[10] Mou, of course, would point to the higher universality of Neo-Confucian principles; but it is still difficult to see how these principles would not depend upon characteristic traits embodied in moral actors. Second, although it is true that, in Zhu Xi's system, the notions of "heart-mind" and "nature" occupy a much more important place than the "four virtues," Mou Zongsan himself admits that Zhu Xi fails to realize the full nature of the correspondence between "heart-mind"/"nature" and "coherence."[11] In other words, the virtues *are*, to some extent, independent from the center of moral inwardness (with its rather metaphysical flavor). We could therefore turn Mou Zongsan's argument back on itself. What Mou perceives as a fundamental weakness of Zhu's thought could in fact be viewed as its strength: Zhu provides us with a more realistic and less unified picture of moral agency and the virtues, which are pervasive in the sense that our daily reactions and modes of moral response are constituted by these virtues.

In sum, I believe that there are enough reasons to believe that Zhu Xi conceives of the sphere of the virtues, namely the "emanation and function" (*fa yong*) of the "heart-mind," as more or less primordial.[12] His understanding of the virtues may even be called "agent-based" (Michael Slote) insofar as the moral evaluations that characterize our ordinary life are not based in an instance prior to virtue, but are derivative from aretaic character evaluations.[13] Thus, Zhu can rightly be considered a representative of the virtue-ethicist approach.

The "Virtues of Justice"

The question "What is justice?" has been at the core of Western moral and political philosophy ever since Plato's *Republic*. Justice has been described as the "master virtue" or a virtue of supreme importance to which Aristotle, in his *Nicomachean Ethics*, gives much more space than any other. Pondering over Zhu Xi's works, we discover that there is not one term which directly corresponds to the Greek notion of justice (*dikaiosunē*). Strictly speaking, Zhu's writings, like those of classical Confucian scholars, are characterized by "[their] conspicuous lack of one word that we can readily translate as 'justice'."[14] Neither do we find huge tracts devoted to the discussion of justice in Zhu Xi. Nevertheless, the claim can be made with some plausibility that ideas of being "just" are tied to a network of concepts and discussions in his commentaries and other writings: *yi* ("righteousness," "appropriateness"), *gong* ("impartiality"), *ren* ("humaneness," "benevolence," "excellence"), *shu* ("reciprocity," "empathy"), *li* ("principle," "pattern," "coherence"), but also apparently less conceptual terms like *xieju* ("measuring by the carpenter's square") or *ping* ("even," "fair"). All these concepts describe certain internal states or aspects of behavior which the Western tradition would connect with the virtue of justice.

That Zhu Xi was in fact concerned with the proper treatment of other people is also demonstrated by a salient feature of his political career (Zhu was as much a political activist as a thinker): over more than forty years, he constantly urged the court to reduce taxes on the population and, at least during one period of his life, actively promoted land redistribution on a large scale as well as the revival of ancient institutions like the well-field system, which, according to most accounts, would have served the interests of the broader population (Tillman 1994, 47–52). In other words, we have reason to expect that justice (in the sense both of reciprocal and of distributive justice) is of primary concern for Zhu.

In fact, it can be argued that Zhu Xi's notion of "humaneness" (*ren*) is, in some important aspects, analogous to the "master virtue" of justice in Plato and Aristotle. For Zhu Xi, "humaneness" not only pertains to the good of other people, but also sets the parameters both for individual moral worth and the goodness of the community. It is also the most important virtue of the ruler.

The most important definition of "humaneness" is the following (from Zhu's commentary to the *Four Books*, published in 1190): "Humaneness is both the coherence of caring and the virtue of the heart-mind (*renzhe, ai zhi li, xin zhi de ye*)."[15] As Zhu writes in his earlier "Treatise on Humaneness" (*Renshuo*, 1169), the virtue of "humaneness" implies "caring for people and fostering the well-being of sentient beings" (*ai ren li wu*).[16] Thus, "humaneness" can be understood as a settled disposition of caring for other beings, a "warm and compassionate concern that extends, in an organic fashion, to all related and relevant aspects of one's context" (Angle 2009a, 78). As *Analects* 4.5 demonstrates, "humaneness" directly concerns questions of acquisition and even distribution of property: the person who possesses true "humaneness" does not accept external goods, unless they are acquired "in the proper way." Zhu emphasizes this point by claiming, in his commentarial gloss, that craving for wealth and despising poverty is not fitting for the morally superior person (Zhu 2001, 70). In addition, as Zhu posits in other passages, "humaneness" encompasses the three other Confucian virtues of "appropriateness," "propriety," and "wisdom," so that we can indeed regard "humaneness" as the Neo-Confucian "master virtue."[17]

Many passages and stories in the Confucian classics flesh out the various dimensions of this virtue: thus the famous story in *Mencius* 1A/7 about King Xuan of Qi and the ox highlights the political dimension of "humaneness," being a warm attitude of care for subordinates, which obviously includes taking care of their material needs.[18]

The Situational Character of Justice and the Challenge of Indeterminacy

As I have already pointed out, Zhu Xi discusses many other virtues which we (in the West) would relate to the virtue of justice. The most important one, it seems, is the virtue of "appropriateness" (*yi*), which is described as essential in Confucian classics like the *Analects* and the *Mencius* and which primarily means having a sense of what is appropriate in a given context (Yu 2007, 144–146). Since Zhu Xi (like most other Confucians) also constantly highlights the difference between "profit" and "appropriateness" (Zhu 2001, 73; 109; passim), "appropriateness" may appear similar to the two Aristotelian ideas that "justice is a sort of proportion" and that particular injustice is associated with the desire to take more than others (*pleonexia*);[19] and there is certainly some truth in this comparison. However, I believe that we will grasp the essential features of Zhu Xi's understanding of the "virtues of justice" more easily by following the lead of "humaneness."[20]

But before doing so, let me stay for another moment with Aristotle. We owe the Greek thinker an extremely rich and complex discussion of the issue of justice. Not only does Aristotle distinguish between a general and a particular sense of justice (the just as the lawful and the just as the equal), but also between corrective, distributive and reciprocal justice; and his views have justly proved to be extremely influential in later times. Ignoring some considerable interpretative controversies, we can summarize his view of justice as primarily concerned with character evaluation and merit, in the sense that all issues of justice (laws, customs, institutions) are thought to be derivative from admirably just character traits.[21] Another distinctive feature of the Aristotelian account which has been repeatedly emphasized by contemporary virtue ethicists is the extremely situational and contextual nature of justice: just behavior is not regarded as merely inner harmony of the soul (like in Plato), but depends on situational factors to which the moral agent reacts in a just or unjust way.

It is rather obvious that Zhu Xi's understanding of the "virtues of justice" shares this situational and contextual character with Aristotle. The paradigmatic case may be the following passage from the *Analects*: when Confucius' disciple Zi Hua goes on a mission to the state of Qi, Ran Qiu (another disciple) asks for a stipend of millet for Zi Hua's mother. Confucius suggests a certain, relatively small amount. However, Ran Qiu is not satisfied and asks Confucius another time. Confucius suggests an even smaller amount. Since Ran Qiu still does not understand the veiled criticism of his teacher, Confucius expresses his discontent more directly. In his commentary, Zhu Xi explains that if Zi Hua was indeed poor, Confucius would certainly have taken care of the welfare of Zi Hua's mother during the absence of her son; there actually was no need to ask for the stipend.[22] In other words, this passage shows that a morally cultivated person does not apply a blanket standard, or refers to some kind of geometrical proportion (like in Aristotle) in order to provide her inferiors with external goods. Instead, if she is a morally cultivated person (as Confucius is said to have been one), she should be extremely perceptive of the details of the situation and make the appropriate decision *naturally*. In other words, all depends on character and intuitive insight into the moral features of the particular situation, and it is not the outcome, but character that is decisive for moral judgment. Neo-Confucians like Zhu Xi indeed "hold that no explicit rules can fully capture what we are supposed to do in a given situation; instead, their focus is on the qualities of the agent that lead to the right responses" (Angle 2009a, 55).

In the *Analects* and the *Mencius*, to possess "humaneness" is characterized in many other ways: to care for others (*Analects* 12.22), to subdue one's selfishness and return to propriety (*Analects* 12.1), to be courageous (*Analects* 14.4, *Mencius* 2A/7), to be free from worry (*Analects* 9.29), to be resolute and firm (*Analects* 13.27), to act as a benevolent ruler (*Mencius* 4A/1–4), to have the feeling of compassion (*Mencius* 6A/6). Now, as I have mentioned before, the virtue of "appropriateness" is also one of the "virtues of justice" in Zhu Xi, and while "humaneness" tends to be somehow elusive, due to its extremely contextual nature, "appropriateness" seems easier to grasp, designating a virtuous disposition regarding taking, gaining, and accepting things (Yang Xiao 1997, 536). But it is not the highest virtue, and, since, at least according to Zhu Xi, the morally cultivated person should strive to become an official at the court and serve the emperor, the practice of "humaneness" (the "master virtue") alone should be the highest goal. "To bestow benefit widely is indeed what a sage desires," writes Zhu Xi in his commentary to *Analects* 6.30—and this goal can be achieved only if we aim at realizing "humaneness" in our daily life, among friends and family, by gradually extending our care to every human being.[23]

Now, it is clear that Zhu Xi's account indeed contains certain features that can easily be construed as weaknesses. Unlike Aristotle, Zhu Xi did not experience the free and equal interaction between citizens in a democratic regime; instead, the background of his view is traditional Chinese political culture where Confucian officials, authorized by the emperor, serve the people. Neither has Zhu ever conceived of the model of the social contract or reflected upon the commercial exchange of material goods and services (it might even be argued that the separateness of persons does not come into full view in his writings). Although Zhu seems to consider some sense of equality among actors as a necessary condition for right action,[24] his commentary on the *Four Books* and other writings do not mention, as far as I see, a single case involving multiple actors, bringing forward equal claims (based on performance, merit, contribution, etc.), and one person (a judge or a ruler) who decides about the legitimacy of their competing claims. Instead, the general paradigm of distribution is the case where one person (normally Confucius, Mencius, or a ruler) allocates external goods to subordinate persons (disciples, the people), who rarely, if ever, bring forward direct claims.[25] In addition, it is rather doubtful whether, for Zhu Xi, the idea of a claim right does make sense: strictly speaking, it is impossible, using Zhu Xi's moral language, to lay claim on external goods directly, since any such claim, for example by directly pointing to them, could easily be interpreted as based on selfishness and, thus, as morally wrong.[26] Zhu Xi might never have fully articulated a clear, systematic and therefore defensible account of the "virtues of justice." His various writings might just contain certain more or less intuitive views about treating others justly.

This said, I still believe that Zhu Xi offers a deep and rather powerful vision of what it means to achieve social justice. In the final section I will explain another crucial dimension of this vision.

Justice and the Sphere of Non-Commensurability

There is one question that we have not yet fully addressed: why does Zhu Xi never bring forward the idea of an external standard like Aristotle's "geometrical method" (associated with distributive justice)? In other words, why is the issue of just distribution and just institutions, for him, necessarily tied to character traits and moral inwardness?

Undoubtedly, Zhu Xi feels the need for a more easily measurable understanding of the "virtues of justice." To come back, once more, to his famous definition of "humaneness": it is crucial to understand that this definition represents a somehow more public and, therefore, verifiable account of this virtue than the one that his predecessors have advanced. Why is this so? Because Zhu Xi rejects two other famous definitions of "humaneness" that were popular among the disciples of Cheng Hao (1032–85). These scholars understood "humaneness" either as the unity between self and world (in terms of a cosmic vision) or as a form of empathy (an affective reaction to all beings).[27] For Zhu, however, both of these models are unconvincing, and he tries to resolve the issue by providing us with a definition that encompasses and mediates between the two other definitions of "humaneness" (as cosmic unity and as empathy). "Humaneness" qua "coherence of caring" has an affective side, but at the same time needs to be formed and understood according to the vision of a larger structured whole.[28]

This vision of a larger structured whole is evident in Zhu Xi's interpretation of the Mencian ideal of a "government of humaneness" (*renzheng*). The ruler, Zhu claims at least twice in his commentary, will realize this ideal by extending his or her "heart-mind" and "let each receive his or her allotment" (*ge de qi suo*; alternatively *ge de qi fen*).[29] This formula, a stock phrase in premodern Chinese thought, appears repeatedly in his writings (and may remind us of Plato's idea of "rendering to everyone his due," as described in the *Republic*).[30] Consequently, Zhu refers to this formula to explain the idea of "equal distribution" (*jun*) mentioned in *Analects* 16.1 (Zhu 2001, 170). And the system of the "well-fields" is thought to be one way of realizing the equal distribution of goods in the community.[31]

So the "master virtue" of "humaneness" is grounded in a larger vision of political and even cosmic harmony.[32] We may of course ask at this point whether the Neo-Confucian discourse on the "virtues of justice" is an example of foundational metaphysics and, if yes, whether there are ways to re-articulate this discourse in non-foundational language. But what I want to emphasize here is that Zhu Xi, although being aware (to some extent) of the need for law, public standards, and institutions,[33] presents a firmly character-based account of how we should treat other people appropriately. Which means that the vision of a structured whole can never be transformed into context-neutral rules or principles.[34] Instead, as Zhu Xi writes at the end of his gloss to *Analects* 4.5, the standard for the right decision will become clearer, the further our process of self-cultivation is advanced (Zhu 2001, 70).

And it is not difficult to see why this is so. There are at least two reasons: first, while the comparability of goods plays a crucial role in the Aristotelian view of justice, Zhu Xi lacks any explicit notion of "good" (*agathon*) and never directly measures and compares different goods, options, or values.[35] It is indeed hard to imagine him calculating the relative values of houses and shoes, as Aristotle does in Chapter V of the fifth book of the *Nicomachean Ethics*.[36] In my view, this is mainly due to Zhu's fear that we might lose our spiritual independence by focusing too closely on the relative value of these goods (in other words, all objects of attachment are considered potential sources of disquiet).[37] Second, for Zhu, morality is identical not with the sphere of transactions (between multiple actors), but with the sphere of the inner self. Therefore, when thinking about what it means to be just, he does not particularly emphasize the common ground that we share with other people, but wants us ultimately to *transcend* the transactional sphere and realize our true selfhood. So, while Zhu Xi admits the importance of the (negatively stated) "golden rule" argument ("What I do not wish others to do unto me, I likewise wish not to do unto others"), he does not believe the corresponding virtue, "empathy" (*shu*) to be as perfect as true "humaneness."[38] For unlike the "empathic" person, whoever possesses true "humaneness" will naturally treat others appropriately and does not need to consciously follow rules anymore. "Humaneness" ultimately leads us away from any interaction or comparison or even competition with others, into the realm of spontaneous, natural action.[39]

Conclusion

In sum, Zhu Xi regards the guidelines for just behavior as deeply internalized. The standard of justice is *necessarily embodied in the moral person's self*; he or she will see the just features of a particular situation and act accordingly, by restoring naturally the correct distribution of goods for all. In other words, Zhu Xi does not want to prescribe to the moral actor what a just distribution would be, nor establish formal procedures and codified rules in the public sphere, for, in his view, any external standard would restrict the spiritual independence of the morally superior person.

Admittedly, we (as members of liberal capitalist societies) may have difficulty imagining how a just pattern of distribution shall emerge under circumstances where no direct competition is allowed and neither the value of goods nor the legitimacy of individual claims is specified. Zhu Xi, however, strongly believed that the "virtues of justice" ultimately lead us into a higher sphere where we, while still being immersed in a particular situation, can both actualize a harmonious order for all beings and preserve our moral purity. In this sense, justice is not understood through the metaphor of the balance, but in terms of virtuous dispositions in human beings. And it can be said that, for Zhu Xi, the fundamental shift in our attitude is more important than any external, action-induced change. Or, as Iris Murdoch writes: "Action is the pointer of the balance. One must not touch the pointer, but the weights" (Murdoch 1998, 158).

The uncritical restoration of Neo-Confucian teachings as "civil religion" (in China or elsewhere) may easily lead to a regime of politically enforced ascetism, which is certainly not desirable. However, in the context of global capitalism and deepening economic inequalities worldwide, there is a real need to rethink non-Western theories of justice and social practices of treating others justly.[40] Nothing precludes the possibility that Zhu's concern for justice might not translate into a powerful philosophical argument again.

19 Is Empathy the "One Thread" Running through Confucianism?

Andrew Terjesen

In the *Analects*, the teachings of Confucius are summarized by Zengzi with the following statement: "All that the master teaches amounts to nothing more than dutifulness (*zhong*) tempered by understanding (*shu*)" (4:15).[1] When Zigong asks Confucius for one word to guide his students, Confucius replies "Is it not 'understanding' (*shu*)?" (15:24).[2] In the West, a lot of attention has been devoted to these passages as evidence that Confucius espoused a version of the "Golden Rule" prescribed by Jesus in the Gospels. Under those readings, *shu* is treated as equivalent to the moral duties associated with that rule.[3] But there is another connection that has been made by Western philosophers based upon these two passages.

Some English translations of *shu* are very philosophically provocative. For example, Brooks and Brooks use the word "empathy" (Brooks and Brooks 1998). Gardner also uses "empathy" for *shu* (Gardner 2007). In an earlier translation of these passages, Slingerland uses "sympathetic understanding" instead of simply "understanding."[4] Translating part of the "One Thread" as "empathy" or a kind of sympathy lends credence to the idea that Confucianism is a form of moral sentimentalism or Care Ethics. Slote has noted that several Confucian thinkers (he names Wang Yangming, Cheng Hao, and Mengzi) "were calling attention to the phenomenon of empathy more than 2,000 years before this was done in the West" (Slote 2010b, p. 304). The connection between Mengzi and Hume has been noted several times, most strongly in Liu, where it is argued that *ren* is best understood as a form of stable Humean sympathy (Liu 2003).

Any attempt to decide whether *shu* can be equated with empathy is complicated by the fact that "empathy" has several closely related meanings, each of which has different implications for ethical theory. Throughout this essay "empathy" will be used in the most ecumenical way possible to indicate any instance in which the perceived mental states of another provoke some kind of response in some other party.[5] Thus "empathy" is defined broadly enough so as to include the aforementioned cases where *shu* has been translated as "sympathy." Such a usage may seem to go against conceptual clarity, but it is driven by necessity and a desire to bring attention to some misunderstandings about empathy-based ethics. The necessity comes from the fact that "empathy" is a relatively new word, entering the English lexicon around the beginning of the twentieth century as an attempt to translate the German psychological term *einfühlung*. Prior to the twentieth century, "sympathy" was used very broadly, so David Hume and Adam Smith founded their ethics on "sympathy," but most commentators agree that the modern term "empathy" better captures their intended meaning. To confuse matters further, after many decades of using "empathy" as a neutral term in psychological research to describe an understanding of someone else's mental state, some psychologists have made the choice to go back to using "sympathy," following the general usage of Hume and Smith (notably Wispé 1991).

When confronted with these linguistic challenges there is a strong temptation among philosophers (especially those who identify with the analytic tradition) to fix the meanings of "empathy" and "sympathy" in order to dispel further confusion.[6] Unfortunately, that fuels the tendency to look for some particular axis of distinction, such as the difference between feeling someone's pain as if it was your own and feeling for someone else's pain (e.g., Slote 2010a). But if we make that distinction and then talk about *empathy*-based ethics, we are suggesting that only feeling someone's pain as your own can be fundamentally relevant to moral judgment. Challenges to empathy-based ethics are usually inspired by situations where someone's empathy fails to move that person in a morally appropriate way.[7] These challenges could be addressed if one adopted an ecumenical approach to empathy that recognized there were several phenomena referred to as "empathy" and these distinct mechanisms might work together in a somewhat loose confederation to produce a moral response. No single form of empathy should be expected to produce all of our moral judgments.

Cognitive Empathy versus Affective Empathy

Slote describes "empathy" as follows: "empathy involves having the feelings of another (involuntarily) aroused in ourselves, as when we see another person in pain" (Slote 2010a, p. 15). By Slote's own admission, his notion of empathy is influenced by the work of the psychologist Martin Hoffman, who writes, "empathy is the vicarious affective response to another person" (Hoffman 2000, p. 29). But Hoffman is describing what he (and other psychologists) call "affective empathy." He gives a second definition of empathy as "the cognitive awareness of another person's internal states, that is, his thoughts, feelings, perceptions and intentions" (Ibid.).

One could combine cognitive awareness with vicarious response, but in at least some contexts (notably counseling and other forms of therapy) cognitive empathy is meant to operate independent of affective empathy. In those contexts, empathy is meant to be a non-judgmental (and emotionally detached) form of understanding. Carl Rogers placed great emphasis upon cognitive empathy in his practice (Rogers 1957). Similarly, "historical empathy" was used as a tool to teach children in Britain about the Holocaust (Davis, Yaeger and Foster 2001). Misunderstanding about the meaning of empathy in that context actually led to public outcry over fears that children were being taught to judge Hitler's actions from Hitler's point of view.

Certainly the choice to translate *shu* as "understanding" or "sympathetic understanding" suggests that cognitive empathy is at the heart of the "One Thread." One passage in the *Analects* that might strengthen this reading is the following: "Do not be concerned about whether or not others know you; be concerned about whether or not you know others." (1:16) In their comment on this passage, Brooks and Brooks specifically connect the second half of the sentence with "empathy" (Brooks and Brooks, p. 171). In an earlier work, Ivanhoe favored the word "consideration" as a close approximation of *shu* (Ivanhoe 1990).[8] That particular word choice serves to remind us that it is possible to think thoughts about someone else's pain (including what the pain might feel like for us) without having to experience the pain. Though we should be cautious about laying too much on linguistic practice, we do not speak of someone being wracked with consideration as if it were an affective response.

It is also worth bearing in mind that the cognitive empathy described here does not have to involve imaginative simulation. "Putting oneself in the other's place" (the translation of *shu* used by Ames and Rosemont (1999)) can be achieved by means of non-imaginative models or rules of inference.[9] The best examples of this are found with autistics (as discussed in Kennett 2002) who are able to reach conclusions about how others are feeling and what to do but are incapable of imaginative simulation. In fact, as Kennett argues, autistics are probably the best counter-example for the claim that moral judgment requires imaginative simulation or the ability to replicate vicarious affective responses (as long as one is willing to grant that autistics are moral agents capable of receiving praise and blame for their actions, as most people would). In most moral judgments, cognitive empathy must be at work, since those judgments often depend upon beliefs about the mental states of others (for example, whether the person is in pain or distress). The autistic examples discussed by Kennett also show the limits of cognitive empathy, as the rules of inference that autistics use lack the nuances of many ordinary emotional states and can be very time-consuming to apply.[10]

Affective empathy is also a form of understanding—so the translation of *shu* as understanding could still work with this usage of empathy. If our emotional states contain information that cannot be conveyed through a propositional belief, then real understanding will require underlying emotional states in order to grasp things.[11] In order to truly understand what someone else is feeling, it may be necessary to replicate their emotional state—otherwise there is information that is lost.[12] While cognitive empathy is logically separable from affective empathy, and may be forcibly separated in a case like autism, "fully" developed empathy in most functioning humans occurs through an affective response that conveys understanding.

The possibility that *shu* might refer to an understanding that is mediated by emotional response is suggested by the following passage. After telling Zigong to guide his life by *shu*, Confucius goes on to say "Do not impose upon others what you yourself do not desire" (15:24). This qualification of *shu* suggests that it relies on emotional experience. Assuming that someone else shares the same desires as we do enables us to do the right thing by them because we act on the richest information about them that we could possibly have (though this particular process may not require simulation). Confucius does not explicitly say that we need to match our feelings to the person we are empathizing with, but it does not seem too great a stretch to suggest that this passage presumes that we would have the same feelings as others and so we can rely on them to give us information about others.

Empathy as a Motivator of Action and Conative Empathy

Regardless, though, of whether our empathic understanding comes from cognitive or affective empathy, these empathic states do not guarantee moral judgments and actions that are what we normally associate with a good person (such as saving children who have fallen into a well).[13] Simply having beliefs about the mental states of someone else is not enough to lead us to see our behavior as wrong or to act to change it. In fact, some people need cognitive empathy in order to do wrong. Sadists would not do a very effective job of satisfying their desires without knowledge of when they were causing pain and when they weren't. Understanding alone (in either cognitive or affective form) is not sufficient to produce a moral attitude.

There is a presumption (going back at least as far as Hume) that our emotions are what moves us to action. In order to ensure that we act for the sake of others, it seems necessary to make their emotional states a part of our psychological make-up. This presumption about the motivational power of affective states is undoubtedly another reason why ethicists interested in the promise of empathy may skim over cognitive empathy in favor of affective empathy (in addition to the idea that the informational content of affective states cannot be reduced to propositional beliefs). Empathizing with someone in pain would produce a feeling of pain in the empathizer and that feeling would produce a response to the situation (presumably to alleviate the pain as one would do if one had actually been the one hurt). The idea that our moral actions must be motivated by feelings appears to be very similar to Mengzi's idea of the four "feelings" as the origins of virtue (see 2A6 and 6A6).

While it does seem to be the case that, in our everyday life, we are moved to action by our emotions, we are not moved by just any emotion. For example, a parent can be well aware (through affective empathy) of how much a particular shot will hurt their child, and yet that parent helps the doctor to administer it. Or someone who ends a romantic relationship can be very aware of the pain it will cause and do it anyway. Even *Mengzi* does not tell us that we would be moved to help the child who fell down the well, only that "anyone in such a situation would have a feeling of alarm and compassion" (2A6.4).[14] What is really important in these situations (at least from a moral point of view) is that having the same emotion as someone else produces a concern in us for their well-being. In that case, the concern is really what matters, not the emotion *per se*.[15]

It is not possible in the space allowed to delve into every morally relevant usage of empathy, but it is worth noting that empathy has been used in some contexts to refer to a state of concern or action that is produced by a situation (and not mediated through a cognitive or affective act). An example of this kind of empathy can be found which at least half the population can relate to—the response that many men have to seeing someone else hit in the groin. In a moment of spontaneity, the male audience may cover their own groin, even though they feel no pain and probably haven't even had time to reflect on what they've witnessed. This conative empathy rarely appears by itself, but it serves to remind us that concern and action can be decoupled from emotion and understanding. A feeling of suffering may not produce a motivation to do something about it and a concern for others may not need an affective state to make it effective. Translations of *shu* as "reciprocity" (Chan 1999) or "altruism" (Zhu Xi 1991) carry enough of a sense of action that one might conclude that *shu* represents empathy in a largely conative sense. This is an intriguing proposition, since there do not seem to be many examples of Western philosophers proposing a predominately conative notion of empathy. This might be explained, though, by the fact that the Western concern with moral justification would not be satisfied with a notion of empathy that seems to jump from action to reaction.

The concern with providing an acceptable moral justification has been an issue for any ethic based on cognitive empathy or affective empathy.[16] Most people feel that they are wronged when something bad happens to them, but just because the mass murderer is angry about his imprisonment should not lead us to conclude that it is wrong. What enables us to know which emotions are moral emotions and which are not? The eighteenth-century philosophers David Hume (Hume 1978) and Adam Smith (Smith 2002) both offer a possible solution. They propose methods by which we can correct our sentiments so that they might serve as objective moral judgments. A corrective for a Confucian moral sentimentalism might rely upon *li*. Mou's interpretation of the "One Thread" gives *shu* both a methodological role (being the principles of reversibility and extension) and a substantive role based on our inner feelings (Mou 2004). However, our application of *shu* is governed by *zhong*, which Mou describes as our devotion to *li*. *Li* becomes the standard governing our analogical thinking in terms both of how we refer and of what emotions of our own we should employ in the analogy.

Does the corrective simply select for certain socially approved emotions, or does it enable us to pick out emotions that are inherently correct? The Confucian tradition that begins with Mengzi's *duan* and continues with Zhu Xi's discussion of *li* as well as Wang Yangming's talk of *liangzhi* would seem to fall into line with the latter opinion—that we have special access to self-evident moral truths through our corrected sentiments (or possibly even through certain natural emotions that every human being shares). The fact that there is often moral disagreement is an issue that must be satisfactorily addressed if one is to employ the latter approach. The former approach (relying upon socially approved or evolutionarily selected for emotions) has been more popular with neosentimentalists, but it raises concerns about relativism and moral antirealism. It also does not seem to be in keeping with the attitude towards morality expressed by Hume and Smith or the Confucians.

Simulative Empathy and Forms of Perspective Taking

Assuming that one could show how the mental and/or emotional state of someone suffering produces a justified moral judgment, critics of empathy-based ethics could still object to the practicality of using any form of empathy to make a moral judgment, based on that fact that we do not have direct access to the minds of others. We must always be skeptical when someone claims to "know" what someone else is thinking. That particular issue may be more pronounced in Western contexts, as some have argued that the Confucian tradition acknowledges that our inner mental states might be exhibited by subtler non-verbal cues (Sarkissian 2010). Some psychologists in America (notably Paul Ekman) have expressed a similar view. Human beings exhibit "micro-expressions" that careful, trained observers can pick up on that would enable one to effectively read their minds (see Ekman 2007). This suggests that the transparency of our mental states might be embraced by both traditions and eliminate this particular problem with empathy.

Given the current problem of explaining the reliability of our judgments concerning the mental states of others, it should not be surprising that empathy is often associated with a process that should yield such judgments. For many people, imaginative projection or simulation is interchangeable with the word "empathy" in English. While it is problematic to say that projective empathy is the only true definition of empathy, it is possible that simulation is the most reliable way to gain access to the mental states of others. However, there seem to be at least two processes that could underlie simulative empathy. These two processes seem to be captured by the two words most commonly used to translate "empathy" into Chinese: *yiqing* and *tongqing*.[17] According to one set of social psychology researchers, "There is one English word 'empathy,' but it seems to cover, or at least make ambiguous, two quite distinct processes. In contrast both Chinese and Japanese have at least two words that separate these processes; *Yiqing* versus *Tongqing* … correspond to the processes of projection versus entering into the other's perspective" (Cohen, Hoshino-Browne and Leung 2007, p. 38). By "projection" they mean to refer to the process of using our own mental states to understand the mental states of others.

That perspective taking in the form of "projection" is what the "One Thread" is all about is suggested by the reference to not doing to others what one does not want done to oneself (see 5:12, 12:3 and 15:24 (the last explicitly connecting it to *shu*)). It is even more tempting to connect this notion of empathy to the example of extension that Mengzi discusses with King Xuan. The analogical reasoning present in that passage also seems indicated by Confucius's reference to "Being able to take what is near at hand as an analogy could perhaps be called the method of Goodness." (6:30) It has been argued that we are equipped with so-called "mirror neurons" that enable us to connect our experience of doing something with our perceiving someone else doing it.[18] The mirror neurons are activated both when we experience performing an action ourselves and when we see others performing the same action. Neurologically, perspective taking merely seems to require shifting the indexical of our experiences.[19]

If this is the mechanism by which empathic concern is created, then there is one major issue that must be addressed—what makes us so sure that we can rely on ourselves to be a good standard for the feelings and behavior of others? An especially competitive person might believe that everyone works to his or her own advantage, and use that to justify preemptive actions like deceiving someone before they deceive you. In order to deal with this problem, one might appeal to a universal human nature. That is something that Hume and Smith seem to do and it is something that Mengzi, Zhu Xi and Wang Yangming definitely do. There is another option though, which is to make more modest claims about what empathy can achieve, and acknowledging that our moral judgments may be defeasible in light of their reliance upon the similarity of our nature to some other particular being. Tiwald's interpretation of Dai Zhen is a promising example of this kind of simulative empathy (Tiwald 2010). Tiwald argues that Dai Zhen's approach is a psychologically realistic way of dealing with the ineliminability of our individual perspective when trying to empathize with others.[20] It is also close to the form of mindreading proposed by Stich and Nichols that uses the individual self as the starting-point and then we modify the beliefs and desires of that self based on our knowledge of the other's circumstances (Stich and Nichols 2003).

Empathic Oneness or Empathic Similarity

Like other forms of empathy, simulative empathy runs up against the concern that it is not sufficient to produce a moral judgment. The process of simulative empathy seems to yield a state of cognitive or affective empathy, but, as I've already noted, there are concerns that this is neither necessary nor sufficient for moral judgments or behaviors to arise. If anything, the biggest concern is that such states can't effect a transformation of our behavior into action. One response to this concern is to focus on what simulative empathy does to us over time and not on what it produces in a particular instance. Simulative empathy has the potential to mingle our concerns with the concerns of others (as we shift perspectives) so that we begin to see connections between our own good and the good of others.[21]

Nivison's arguments regarding the early meaning of *shu* present an impediment to the notion that Confucius (or any of the pre-Han Confucians) was interested in a sense of empathic oneness. As Nivison explains, *shu* seems to denote thinking of what we would want as an inferior (Nivison 1996). Although Nivison still seems to think that *shu* could provide a sense of "common humanity," Nussbaum responds, "Where precisely is the sense of common humanity here? We might equally imagine an argument that said, 'Treat your dogs the way you'd like to be treated by the gods'... there is nothing in that that tends to erode hierarchy in the name of a larger moral community" (Nussbaum 2003, p. 7).

In the Neo-Confucian metaphysic of the Song and Ming dynasties, the interconnectedness of all things is a deep metaphysical fact. The *li* which orders the universe is found in every object and enables it to cohere with the moral order of the universe. Thus Zhu Xi interprets *shu* as "extend oneself" (Zhu Xi 1991, p. 195, n. 61). Of course, Dai Zhen criticizes the Neo-Confucian interpretation of *shu* precisely because it imports a metaphysical claim that seems foreign to the early texts (and undeniably a result of Daoist and Buddhist influences). The disagreement between Dai Zhen and the Neo-Confucians points toward an important issue. The Neo-Confucian approach offers a much more fluid way for our concerns to shift to others, but the metaphysical claims that it rests upon do not seem to fit with current psychology. Dai Zhen's approach is more psychologically realistic, but the empathetic process is open to corruption. For example, our self-interest may resist our attempts to find points of similarity with other beings (or lead us to look for reasons why a particular individual or group should be treated as an exception).

Conclusion

Answering the question "Is 'empathy' the 'One Thread' of Confucianism?" is difficult because empathy is not itself composed of a single thread. Although there is a tendency to pave over the different ways in which "empathy" is used, the term refers to several different yet related phenomena. It is a task for future commentators to consider the distinct forms of empathy discussed above (cognitive empathy, affective empathy, conative empathy and simulative empathy) and determine which, if any, are represented in the Confucian tradition. So far, passages have been identified that might be connected to one or more of these notions. Although the focus has been on *shu*, future discussion should not be limited to a lexical definition of *shu*. Confucian discussions of emotions, relationships, social harmony and the interplay between the social world and the natural world might all be implicated in a discussion as to whether Confucianism is an empathy-based ethic. There are also interesting parallels between the empirical psychological research concerning the many forms of empathy and Confucian discussions of how we ought to interact with other human beings that should be explored further.

One persistent problem for empathy-based ethics is the difficulty in tying together the various forms of empathy into a coherent and functioning system. Each form of empathy has its particular strengths and weaknesses. For example, cognitive empathy excels in situations that involve nearly universal human experiences (like falling down and getting hurt), but stumbles in complex cases. The Confucian tradition hints at a way by which these different forms of empathy could cohere in an underlying moral order and act to reinforce one another. As Hourdequin (in this volume) admits, the Confucian ideals of *li* and *dao* could serve as a grounding for an empathy-based ethic that would respond to the most persistent critique of an empathy-based ethic, that empathy lacks a moral direction. These Confucian ideals would function in the same manner as the correctives proposed by other philosophers like Hume and Smith, but they have the potential to be structured in such a way that a form of empathy still serves as the basis of moral judgment.[22] It is unlikely that any single form of empathy is the single thread running through Confucian ethics, but the different forms might be weaved together like a rope that binds all of our moral judgments.

20 The Limits of Empathy

Marion Hourdequin

Introduction

In calling this chapter "The Limits of Empathy," I aim to raise both a normative and a meta-ethical question. The meta-ethical question is this: can an adequate moral theory be grounded in empathy, or care and empathy, alone? Michael Slote (2007) has developed a sentimentalist ethics grounded in care and empathy, and on my reading of his work, Slote provides a positive reply to the meta-ethical question, affirming both the necessity and sufficiency of care and empathy as grounds for moral theory.[1] Against this view, I argue that empathy has an important and legitimate role to play in morality, but that empathy cannot serve as our sole moral guide.

The normative question that I want to raise is distinct, but related to the meta-ethical one. In fact, the normative issues associated with empathy help to illuminate the meta-ethical position that I defend. The normative question is this: what is the appropriate scope and focus for empathic caring? Any care- or empathy-based ethics must face this question: there are innumerable people, places, organisms, institutions, and objects about which we could potentially care. If we are talking about *empathic* caring, this may restrict the field somewhat—for I may care about my job or my bicycle or my books—but empathic caring seems restricted to those things which, unlike my job or my bicycle or my books, can feel emotion. Even so, and even if we very conservatively and implausibly suppose that it is only individual human beings who can feel emotion and with whom we can empathize, there remain innumerable subjects who can engage our empathic caring. Yet we have limited resources: limited time, limited energy, limited capacities to assist. How should those resources be directed?

The critical point here is that one can't simply advise that we "empathically care," and leave it at that, as if the imperative were self-interpreting. For the person attempting to empathically care, many questions arise regarding when to care, about whom to care, how much to care, and how to express one's care. It is not as if Slote—whose moral theory does tell us to empathically care—is unaware of these issues. But his writings do not fully reveal how deep they go, and how answering these questions requires resources beyond those provided by empathy itself.

I begin below by describing Slote's ethics of care and empathy. I then use two widely discussed passages from the *Mencius* to illustrate some not-so-widely discussed points about empathy and how it should be directed. Finally, I explore the significance of the second Mencian case in the broader context of early Confucian philosophy. Read in isolation, the Mencian passage seems to leave a puzzle about how empathy should be directed; but I argue that this puzzle is resolved by understanding the passage in the context of early Confucian philosophy more broadly. In the *Analects* of Confucius, we see that empathy is focused and directed through rituals: a very specific social background determines the appropriate expression of empathy in various contexts. Although this focusing and direction varies culturally and historically, the Mencian case—*pace* some interpretations of the text, which emphasize the natural development of the virtues[2]—illustrates the important general point that empathy is *not* self-directing and must be supplemented through the provision of additional norms, values, and practices that guide it. If this is right, then an ethics of care and empathy cannot be an ethics of *only* care and empathy: it must be supplemented in some way, and the Confucian approach provides one model of how this can be accomplished.

Slote's *Ethics of Care and Empathy*

In *The Ethics of Care and Empathy*, Michael Slote (2007) argues that empathy is not merely important to moral judgment, but central to it:

> I believe that empathy and the notion of empathic caring for or about others offer us a plausible criterion of moral evaluation. Differences in (the strength of) normally or fully developed human empathy correspond pretty well, I think, to differences in intuitive moral evaluation, and that fact … will allow an ethics of caring that brings in empathy—an ethics of empathic caring—to give a fairly general account of both public/political and private/individual morality.
>
> (16)

More specifically, Slote argues that

> actions are morally wrong and contrary to moral obligation if, and only if, they reflect or exhibit or express an absence … of fully developed empathic concern for (or caring about) others on the part of the agent.
>
> (31)

Thus, for Slote, the permissibility or impermissibility of an act is directly tied to the act's connection with empathic concern. Slote's account here builds on that put forth in his earlier *Morals from Motives* (2001), where he argues that actions proceeding from motives of empathic caring are virtuous (and morally right), whereas actions not so proceeding are not virtuous. One of the explicit aims of this latter book is to show the scope of a morality of empathic caring, and to defend the view that such a morality can encompass not only the "private/individual" realm, but the public and political as well.

An account of morality based in empathic caring faces a number of challenges. One of these relates to the extent to which empathic caring can provide a model for public morality, political morality, and distributive justice, and, as I have noted, Slote takes up this challenge directly. Another critical challenge has to do with the scope, limits, and direction of empathic caring. As Slote acknowledges, his initial characterization of acts as right or wrong depending on whether they flow from a caring motive needs qualification: "A single act may show an empathically caring attitude toward some people, and a lack of empathic caring, even malice, toward others. So an ethics of caring needs to be able to say how a caring individual relates to all the different people she knows or (merely) knows about" (21). It is here that Slote places substantial theoretical weight on the notion of "fully developed empathic concern" (31), which, he holds, can enable us to navigate the difficult waters surrounding questions of immediacy and distance, the limits of obligation, and such pressing contemporary issues as abortion.[3] For example, Slote suggests that normal, fully developed human empathy leads us to care more strongly about those close to us (such as friends and relatives) than those more distant, and that this fact not only explains but justifies our greater obligations to the near and dear (28). A similar point applies to perceptual distance and to temporal distance: with respect to the former, contrary to the arguments of Singer and Unger,[4] it *is* worse to walk by a drowning child when one could easily help, than to ignore a letter from Oxfam. The former act shows an acute deficiency of empathic caring, while the latter does not.

The critical question that concerns me here is whether Slote's notion of "fully developed empathic concern," or what he elsewhere describes as "natural human empathy" or "normal, fully developed human empathy," can bear the theoretical weight assigned to it. I want to argue that it cannot. In doing so, I give particular attention to a specific case—the case of the king and the ox from the *Mencius*—which one might initially take to support Slote's view, but which reveals upon closer examination that "natural human empathy" cannot do all the moral work, and that although "fully developed empathic concern" *might* come closer to accomplishing what Slote hopes it can, to do so, "fully developed" will have to be glossed in a way that makes reference to values external to empathy itself.[5]

The Child and the Well, and The King and the Ox

One of the most famous passages from the classical Chinese philosopher Mencius involves the imagined case of a child about to fall into a well (*Mencius* 2A6).[6] Mencius observes that any person, upon seeing the child about to tumble, would be "moved to compassion"—and this feeling of concern and compassion would not be motivated by a desire to impress the child's parents, to win the admiration of others, or to avert the child's disturbing wails. Simply in virtue of being human, Mencius tells us, each of us has a "heart of compassion," and it is this heart that moves us upon seeing the child at risk.

Before turning to the second and central case that I want to discuss, it is worth noting a few things about this one. First, Mencius posits a natural capacity for compassion, which he believes that all human beings (insofar as they can be called "human") share. Furthermore, Mencius insists that this natural capacity is one that can and ought to be developed; in failing to do so, a person "cripples himself [or herself]." In considering the kind of development that Mencius has in mind, much has been made of his reference to the heart of compassion as one of four "sprouts" (*duan*) that can grow to full fruition. This vegetative analogy suggests a course of natural development: given the right enabling conditions, the sprouts will mature. This view of development is further supported by another passage in which Mencius suggests that the sprouts may be better off on their own than in being helped and coaxed along. In 2A2, we find the story of "a man from Sung who pulled at his seedlings because he was worried about their failure to grow." But the man's efforts bear no fruit: when his son runs to the field to see the results of his father's work, he finds the seedlings withered and dead. Yet we should not conclude from this story that the seedlings require no attention at all in order to mature. Mencius suggests that weeding and helping the seedlings to grow is beneficial, though pulling at them is not. So there is a sense in which the seedlings do not develop exclusively under their own power.

Analogously, one might take the Mencian story to suggest that humans' empathic capacities have a natural developmental trajectory, but that some effort and assistance is required along the way to enable these capacities to realize their full potential. This view seems compatible with an ethics of empathy in which empathy is, ultimately, the central moral guide, and the presence or absence of a motive of empathic caring is determinative of the rightness or wrongness (or virtuousness or viciousness) of a particular act.[7] One way to think about the assistance required to develop empathy is as a set of enabling conditions: social interaction, a caring environment, and the basic necessities of life, for example, might be required in order for empathy to reach its full potential, but the necessity of these enabling conditions doesn't in itself compromise the ability of fully developed empathy to be the central basis for morality, and for motives based on fully developed empathy to play the criterial role that Slote assigns to them.

But let me now turn to a second example from Mencius, the case of the king and the ox (*Mencius* 1A7). In this story, Mencius is conversing with King Xuan of Qi and recounts an anecdote in which the king sees an ox passing by on its way to slaughter. Feeling compassion for the ox, the king asks that it be spared and that a lamb be substituted in its place. When the king affirms that the story is true, Mencius comments, "The heart behind your action is sufficient to enable you to become a true King. The people all thought that you grudged the expense, but, for my part, I have no doubt that you were moved by pity for the animal." The king again affirms Mencius's observation, and Mencius notes the irony of the king's substitution (since an animal was sent to death nonetheless) and uses the case to suggest to the king that although he possesses a perfectly adequate capacity for compassion (*duan*), he has failed to extend[8] this concern to his people. Mencius also notes, when the king responds with embarrassment to the point that his action alleviated suffering for an ox, but not for the lamb, that the king's reaction was perfectly reasonable:

> There is no harm in this. It is the way of a benevolent man. You saw the ox but not the lamb. The attitude of a gentleman is this: once having seen them alive, he cannot bear to see them die, and once having heard their cry, he

cannot bear to eat their flesh. That is why the gentleman keeps his distance from the kitchen.

What are we to make of this remark? How is it that the king is *not* at fault for failing to show concern for the lamb when he *is* at fault for failing to show concern for his people? And if the king's failure is to be understood in terms of underdeveloped empathy, then why does Mencius say that "[t]he heart behind [the king's] action is sufficient to enable [him] to become a true King," and why does he tell the king to stay out of the kitchen?

Here is one interpretation which, though non-standard, offers a compelling explanation of the king's moral failing. In this view, what is lacking in the king is not fully developed human empathy. The problem is that he has not *directed* his empathy properly. And, I submit, the question of how to direct one's empathic concern is not answered by empathy itself; it requires additional moral resources. These additional resources should lead the king to stay away from the kitchen, but to attend to the plight of his people.

That *attention* might figure importantly in Mencius's understanding of empathy and the moral guidance that it can provide is a thought provocatively raised by Manuel Im (1999). On Im's account, moral virtue, for Mencius, diverges in important ways from an Aristotelian picture of moral virtue. For Aristotle, a virtuous person's emotional sensibilities are properly tuned, such that they "motivate [that] person to feel and act in the appropriate and best ways" (Im 1999, 10). But for Mencius, this is not the case. A benevolent ruler who sees an ox or a lamb being led to slaughter will not be able "to bear to see them die" nor "eat their flesh." But, Mencius tells us, although these emotional responses are laudable—in that they reflect a fully developed "heart of compassion"—they are responses that rulers should attempt to avoid, precisely by staying out of the kitchen—that is, by intentionally choosing not to see these animals suffer. Now, whether one agrees or disagrees with the normative ethical intuitions at work here, it seems clear—as Im points out—that Mencius is making a distinction between morally admirable character and morally admirable actions (Im 1999, 9). The king's compassion is morally praiseworthy, but the direction of his emotional attention, and hence his actions, are not.[9]

This analysis seems to me to reveal an important insight about empathy and its limits. We must make decisions about with whom to empathize, and to whom (or to what) to attend—and empathy cannot help us here. There are times when a motive of empathic caring pushes us to intervene when we know that we should not, as when we want to save someone—a child, a student, a patient—from suffering the consequences of painful knowledge or of his or her own errors. There are times when less empathy rather than more is needed, times when empathy should be directed more broadly, and times when it should be directed more narrowly. Knowing what to attend to and how to direct empathy seems to involve something like Aristotelian practical wisdom, but practical wisdom understood in a way that is not merely enfolded into "fully developed empathy" itself, but engages additional knowledge and capacities as well.[10]

If all of this is correct, it indicates that although an act may reflect fully developed human empathy, it may not be the right thing to do. An act's expression of empathic caring is not sufficient for its rightness, as illustrated by the fact that even fully developed human empathy may be misdirected. Slote's theory must be wrong.

Slote, of course, is unlikely to accept this conclusion, and in rejecting it, he might dispute the interpretation of 1A7 on offer, arguing that the king *lacks* fully developed human empathy. Were the king to possess it, he would care for his people rather than concern himself with the fate of a sacrificial ox. That an act expresses fully developed empathic care remains sufficient for its rightness, and the argument above goes wrong by mistakenly attributing to the king fully developed empathic care (or fully developed compassion, or *ren*).

To Slote's credit, the view that the king lacks fully developed *ren* is a plausible and widely accepted interpretation of the text. Nevertheless, appeal to an alternative interpretation can't save Slote's view from fundamental objections.

Let us grant that the king lacks fully developed human empathy. This, Slote must hold, is the source of his moral errors. Now, what is the difference between the present king and the king with fully developed human empathy? The most plausible thing to say is that the mature king possesses not only an emotional orientation that enables him to react empathically to the situations that he encounters, but also the wisdom to guide his encounters such that his empathic responses will be activated in the right ways, at the right times, and to the right extent.

Hoewever, it is hard to see how this wisdom could be derived from empathy itself or be the product of empathy's natural developmental trajectory. Rather, the wisdom in question is an overarching ability to assess the relative importance of the particular moral demands that one faces and to adjust one's attention accordingly; it is a distinct moral capacity. What's more, *even if* the wisdom to direct empathy properly can be considered a part of "fully developed human empathy,"[11] I argue below that this wisdom develops not merely through the provision of "enabling conditions" which facilitate some natural human-wide developmental trajectory of empathy, but through the education of empathy in relation to other values.

Let us look further at the view that the wisdom to properly direct one's moral attention is *built into* fully developed human empathy. This view requires a particular diagnosis of the king's situation. If one accepts the Mencian point that the king has not acted rightly, along with the further assessment that this failure is the result of empathy that is not fully or properly developed, one will have to say (following Slote's account) that *any* person in the king's place who possessed fully developed human empathy would attend to his people and not to the ox (insofar as this empathy was being expressed), and that this is the result of the natural development of human empathy. So far, this diagnosis seems consistent with Slote's account. He speaks of natural human empathy as both reflecting and justifying greater attention to those proximal in location and relationship (i.e., the near and dear). Following this line of argument, one might expect species membership to fit this model of proximity: *ceteris paribus*, natural human empathy is and should be greatest for individual members of our own species, attenuating as evolutionary relationships grow more distant.

The trouble is, this understanding of the case seems to turn on a natural attenuation of empathy as one moves from humans to other animals. Yet the Mencian advice to the king is one that involves *manipulating the king's moral attention to alter the degree of his empathic response.* Mencius does not suggest that a morally mature king would be unconcerned with the ox's welfare, *were he to see the ox;* instead, he says that the morally mature king would "stay out of the kitchen." But is it the morally mature king's *empathy* that guides him in staying out of the kitchen? It is hard to see how. One might of course argue that the king's duties imply that he ought to attend primarily to the welfare of his people, and therefore that he should focus on his subjects rather than on the inner workings of the royal kitchen. If he *were* more in touch with his subjects, then presumably the king's emotional proximity to them would naturally make him empathize more strongly with them than with the ox. In this case, the king's greater emotional proximity to his people would modulate his empathic responses, such that these responses could provide legitimate moral guidance. But notice that the appropriate degree of emotional proximity is here driven not by empathy itself, but by an account of the king's role-related duties. This suggests, then, that empathic responses can serve as effective moral guides only if they are properly directed and channeled with the help of other principles or values.

Another example will bring us to the crux of the problem. Imagine a man named Joseph who is a compassionate and caring person. Joseph lives in Chicago, works downtown, and walks to and from work each day. There are two ways to walk, and each takes about the same amount of time, but on one route, Joseph inevitably encounters a number of homeless persons who ask him for money.[12] On the other route, which passes through a wealthier neighborhood, Joseph has never been solicited. Taking the first route makes Joseph uncomfortable: it reminds him of his privileged position in society, and, recognizing that privilege often is a matter of luck as much as talent, Joseph wonders, as he faces his homeless compatriots, whether he really deserves his privilege in any morally defensible way. At the same time, although Joseph is relatively well off, he doesn't feel that he has enough money to give to every homeless person whom he would encounter, were he to take the former route every day—yet he feels guilty about saying "no" and ambivalent about its moral permissibility. If Joseph avoids the route through the poorer neighborhood, he knows that he will not feel as guilty or as uncomfortable, yet he also knows that his sensitivity to the plight of the homeless—both his literal and figurative *proximity* to them—will be attenuated, and he will be less likely to engage in social action on their behalf.

The trouble with a morality that makes a motive of empathic caring criterial for right action is that it doesn't provide sufficient guidance regarding cases like these. The question that Joseph faces is not so much how to respond when faced with a homeless person asking for money, but whether to face such persons at all, and if so, how often. Admittedly, there may be some indeterminacy here—perhaps there is no single, morally correct answer to how often he should take one route rather than another—but the critical point is that there exists a legitimate ethical question about how much distance to create between oneself and various others, and empathy alone—even when fully developed—lacks the resources to answer this question.

To see this point more clearly, note that Slote's account evaluates actions on the basis of whether they reflect fully developed human empathy, and at the same time suggests that the degree of empathy we *ought* to feel is, in significant part, a function of our relationship to the person(s) with whom we are empathizing. That is, the degree of empathy that one ought to feel is the degree of empathy that would be felt by a person with fully developed human empathy, in similar circumstances. Yet the degree of empathy that would be felt by a person with fully developed human empathy depends on this person's relationship to the object of empathy—whether near or far in space, time, or emotional connection—one's proximity to others is not something simply given. In fact, we can exercise significant control over our proximity to others, and decisions regarding proximity are *themselves* moral issues. Slote's account fails to fully address this point. Though he suggests that the education of empathy ought to include some degree of familiarization with the suffering of others who are not physically proximate to oneself, the justification for this familiarization or how much familiarization is appropriate remains unaddressed—and it is not clear how empathy alone can provide a justification.

As a result, the account remains largely mute on whether or how we ought to modulate our proximity to others (thereby modulating empathy and the actions that issue from it). Without some normative guidance on proximity, Slote's view seems to allow that we can reduce our obligations to others simply by distancing ourselves (physically or emotionally) from them. However, this kind of distancing is not itself morally neutral: it is, in fact, frequently a deep source of moral failing in the world. One can imagine, for example, a person with fully developed human empathy who finds herself in an institution that creates great distance between the decisions she makes and the persons affected by those decisions. The distance is so great, in fact, that she is largely insensitive to the significant suffering caused by her actions (imagine, for example, a corporate employee whose job is to find the cheapest labor market for the production of certain goods). Slote's account seems to force us to say that there is nothing wrong with this employee's actions, because *any person with normal human empathy, when distanced as this employee is from those whom they affect, would act similarly.* But surely this is a counterintuitive result, and it seems to bar investigation into the employee's moral obligation to make herself more aware of the plight of those affected by her actions.

I dwell on these examples because they illustrate clearly the difficulties with Slote's empathy-based criterion for right action. The cases adduced above show that empathy is not enough for morality—and this is a point that Martin Hoffman (2000), on whose work Slote extensively draws, takes pains to acknowledge. On Hoffman's view, empathy must be modulated by other moral principles. For example, Hoffman suggests that although certain principles—such as principles of justice—are distinct from empathy, they may nonetheless become linked to empathic responses in ways that motivate moral action. Hoffman sees empathy as a critical prosocial motive, yet he notes:

> [Empathy] is limited … and not enough by itself to satisfy the demands of justice … because of its over-arousal and especially its bias tendencies. These limitations can be minimized when empathy is combined with reciprocity and embedded in moral principles …

(245)

Hoffman further takes care to indicate that this combining and embedding is not a result of a universal developmental trajectory for empathy: "on the contrary," he notes, "to bring such joining will, I am sure, require cultural resolve, invention, and research" (283). Hoffman thus brings out the point that not only does empathy underdetermine what we ought to do (as I discussed in relation to the problem of directing our moral attention, above), but in some cases empathy might *get in the way* of right action: for example, natural human empathy toward one's in-group can lead to empathic anger and sectarian violence, and empathy—with its inherent partiality—can interfere with fairness in criminal justice.

Empathy and Its Role in Morality

Let us return to the case of the king and the ox. If my discussion of this case is compelling—that is, if we take it to illustrate this general point about the limits of empathy and its insufficiency for right action—then we are faced with the pressing question of what values, virtues, or principles can supplement empathy such that it can be appropriately directed and balanced. The short answer is that Mencius himself provides relatively few clues in 1A7 (the ox passage), or in the text more broadly. But we can learn something from the very fact that Mencius tells the king—*with no further principled explanation of why*—that gentlemen stay out of the kitchen, and that a true king extends compassion to his people. Mencius seems to think that although the king needs reminding of these things, they are in some sense *obvious*. But why are they obvious?

To answer this question, it is helpful to consider the background of Confucian philosophy more generally. In the *Analects*, rituals (the *li*) serve an essential structuring role in morality, and from a cultural perspective, the *li* undeniably had a critically important place in social life. Since the rituals prescribe animal sacrifice, animals should be sacrificed: the king's pity for the animals in this case does no good—it only creates a lot of handwringing as the animals go off to their death. On the other hand, a ruler's compassion for his people is paradigmatic of the overarching virtue of *ren*, or humanity.[13] The *li* help to structure the state such that *ren* is realized; thus the king's patterns of behavior should both sensitize him and reflect his sensitivity to the needs of his people. Following the *li* brings out and, at the same time, directs people's emotional sensibilities. So, in Confucian philosophy, it is ritual that plays a substantial role in structuring and directing empathy[14]—and, one might argue, the *junzi* (humane person) or Confucian sage is one whose moral sensibilities are fully developed and properly directed: this person is able to discern to what and to whom to attend at various times. In this sense, the Confucian sage possesses a kind of practical wisdom,[15] and while one could, perhaps, say that fully developed human empathy *encompasses* this wisdom, in saying so, one would have to acknowledge that the processes that facilitate this development involve more than the basic enabling conditions outlined above; they draw on particular values that specify what is morally important and structure the expression of empathy in appropriate ways.[16]

But what about us, today? It seems implausible that Slote's ethics of empathic caring could or should be supplemented by the Confucian *li*, and this is clearly not what

I would recommend. Nevertheless, as a descriptive matter, there are some parallels between the structuring of empathy in Confucian times and that in our own. Processes of moral education and enculturation still shape and guide empathy today: while we may have a natural inclination to favor those near and dear to us, that inclination is often reinforced socially. Similarly, we (or at least many of us) *learn* not to attend too closely to the homeless person on the corner—for doing so would engage our empathy, and we might be inclined to give the person five dollars, and that (we are taught) will ultimately do the homeless person little good. In the background here are values and principles that go beyond our natural empathic responses.

Thus, as a matter of descriptive fact, our moral attention and our empathic responses are guided to a significant degree, although not determined, by cultural values and accepted patterns of behavior. This point does not settle the normative question of how empathy *should* be directed, of course. In early Confucianism, *ren* (in the broad sense) and *li* play central structuring roles, but in the background, and serving as an ultimate moral ideal, is the *Dao*, or the Way, an ideal of harmonious human relations to one another (and, to a greater or lesser extent in various versions of early Confucian philosophy, to the world at large). A person who is *ren* embodies the *Dao*: her actions harmonize human relations with one another and with the world at large.

In my view, a care- or empathy-based ethics like Slote's needs something like the *Dao* to ground the values and practices that direct empathy through the process of moral education. This may sound implausible at first, especially to certain ears, as no obvious analog to the *Dao* seems to appear in Western moral philosophy. Yet there are a number of contemporary, naturalistic accounts of morality that appeal to the function of morality in human life to provide a similar ground. If we know what morality is *for*, perhaps we can see more clearly how empathy is to be directed, what sorts of things demand our greatest attention, and what sorts of things do not. For example, if a central function of morality is to promote social cooperation and to facilitate interpersonal coordination (Wong 2006, ch. 2), or to harmonize the diverse ends that people hold (Hourdequin 2005), then we can see how excessive empathy toward one's own child might disrupt these functions by leading a parent to prioritize alleviation of the child's distress at being reprimanded over a firm emphasis on respecting others.[17]

Even if supplemented in the way that I have suggested, a functionally grounded care ethics won't be completely determinate, and we may even face tragic choices in deciding how empathy should be directed. Moreover, the normative function of morality, while conceptually constrained by the actual role that morality plays in human life, is a matter of contention, and the account that we settle on may be universalistic, pluralistic, or relativistic. So even if the approach that I'm suggesting is plausible and promising, with respect to the normative question—what is the appropriate scope and focus for empathic caring?—many issues remain. But the important point of *this* paper is that as important as empathy is to morality, it is not self-directing, and to say that an act is right if and only if it proceeds from a motive of empathic care not only leaves ethics too indeterminate, it also would misjudge certain acts: sometimes the motive of empathy, albeit admirable, leads us to do the wrong thing.

Notes

1 Introduction

1 Many sides of this debate can be seen in three issues of the journal *Contemporary Chinese Thought*, vol. 37, nos. 1–3 (2005–6).
2 For one recent argument that viewing Confucianism as virtue ethics has interpretive value, see [Van Norden 2007].
3 One *locus classicus* for this view is *Mengzi* 4B:28. For more discussion, see [Angle 2011]. For another perspective on the contemporary relevance of Confucian humility, see Rushing's essay in this volume.
4 One crucial interpretive matter, were one to want to pursue the relation of Mou himself to virtue ethics, is how deeply Kantian Mou really is. Commentators disagree. Lee Ming-huei is a prominent representative of those who stress Mou's Kantianism; see his contribution to this volume. For some suggestive comments that open Mou up to a more virtue-ethical reading, see [Billioud 2011, 61–2].
5 For representative proposals of how to articulate the needed kind of centrality for virtue, see [Slote 2001, 4] or [Swanton 2003, 5]. In his paper in this volume, Bryan Van Norden uses the term "radical virtue ethics" to refer to what we are here calling "virtue ethics."
6 See [Slote 2007, ch. 3]. Gary Watson has also shown that, on at least certain definitions, "an ethics of virtue can acknowledge 'deontological' reasons" [Watson 1997, 65; see also Ibid, 66].
7 On (1), see Xiao's essay in this volume as well as [Slote 2007, ch. 7]. For some gestures in the direction of (2), see [Angle 2009a, 92].
8 For the role of principles (for example, as rules of thumb) in virtue ethics, see [Hursthouse 1999]. Chen Lai's essay in this volume argues that principles are an important part of the central Confucian idea of *ren*. Lee in this volume points out that Kant has a great deal to say about the nature of agency.
9 See [MacIntyre 2004] and [Woodruff 2001].

2 Virtue Ethics and Confucian Ethics

1 After the Warring States Period, occasionally there are literatures that include both virtuous conduct and virtuous character. For example, in the *Great Treatise of the Book of Changes*, it is stated that "[The hexagram] *Qian* represents the strongest under the sky. Through this quality its operations are always manifested with ease, for it knows where there would be peril and embarrassment, as the vital energy of the heaven is the virtuous conduct of everlasting change and the knowing of danger; [the hexagram] *Kun* represents the most docile of all under the sky. Through this quality its operations are always manifested with the promptest decision, for it knows where there would be obstruction, as the compliance of the heaven is the virtuous conduct of everlasting simplicity and the knowing of obstacles" (Legge 1993: 337; SSJZS 1997: 90), and that

"'The advantageous (*li*) and the correctness and firmness (*zhen*)' refer to its nature and feelings (as seen in all the resulting things)" (Legge 1993: 13; SSJZS 1997: 17).

2 "Morality and social structure are in fact one and the same in heroic society" (MacIntyre 1981: 116). As a contrast to Confucian ethics, this essay will use not only the virtue ethics of Aristotle but also that of MacIntyre. Hopefully, within the comparative perspective an analysis of the early Confucian ethics of virtuous conduct can be made. That is not to say that MacIntyre's discussion of the virtue ethics of the heroic society or the Greek City States is without controversy. Our position here is to compare ethical thoughts on a macro level between the East and the West. Based on this approach, MacIntyre is a natural representative for this purpose.

3 Zizhang, Zigong, and Yanyou followed Confucius in a casual discussion about *li*. The Master said, "I will tell you the meaning of *li*, and help you to master it anywhere and anytime." Zigong asked from across the way: "Please, tell us." The Master said, "Respect without *li* leads to indecency, courtesy without *li* leads to hypocrisy, and courage without *li* leads to treason." He said, "Hypocrisy corrupts kindness and benevolence." The Master said, "Speaking about *li*, Shi (a person) has been excessive while Shang (a state) has been inadequate. Zichan is just like a mother of the people who can provide mothering but cannot provide education." Zigong asked, "Then what is the path for moderation?" The Master said, "*Li! Only li* can be used as a form to manifest moderation" (SSJZS 1997: 1613).

4 Ancient Greek *arête* has been translated as "virtue" today. The original meaning was special strength and capacity.

5 It is worth noting here that "unless a man has the spirit of the rites … in having courage he will become unruly, and in being forthright he will become intolerant," and "to love forthrightness without loving learning is liable to lead to intolerance. To love courage without loving learning is liable to lead to insubordination" (Analects 8: 2; 17: 8). Forthrightness and courage, when not accompanied by learning and the rites, will lead to the precisely same flaw of intolerance.

6 When Aristotle discussed intellectual virtue he also pointed out natural virtues and core virtues. Although he did not clearly give specific definitions, the following passage is worth noting: "This is why some say that all the excellences [virtues] are forms of practical wisdom, and why Socrates in one respect was on the right track while in another he went astray; in thinking that all the excellences were forms of practical wisdom he was right. … When they defined excellence, after naming the state and it objects add 'that [state] which is in accordance to the right reason'; now the right reason is that which is in accordance with practical wisdom" (Aristotle 1984: 1144b14–24). Based on this, it can be said that within Confucian Ethics, virtue cannot depart from the love of learning, while *li* is that which is recognized as the correct principle behind behavior.

7 The later text also mentioned "without change there is no happiness, without happiness there is no intimacy, without intimacy there is no endearment, without endearment there is no love" (translator's note).

3 Virtue Ethics and the Chinese Confucian Tradition

1 Thanks to Stephen C. Angle, Erin M. Cline, Eirik L. Harris, Eric L. Hutton, Pauline C. Lee, Michael R. Slater, Michael Slote, David W. Tien, and Justin Tiwald for comments on earlier drafts of this essay. A condensed version of this essay under the same title appears in Russell (2013).

2 The relationship between the virtues and the related conception of the ideal life, like that between the virtues and the good person, are a matter of debate, but this issue does not affect the general point I am making here.

3 These two types by no means exhaust the full range of theories that fall within the family of virtue ethics.

4 This reading depends on how one understands the relationship of Book X of the *Nicomachean Ethics* to the rest of the work. Some insist that the parts which support this reading, for example *NE* X.6–8, do not represent Aristotle's mature view and should be removed from the text.

5 In his contribution to this volume, "The Impossibility of Perfection," Michael Slote explores one apparent implication of this aspect of the VES view by arguing against the idea that "perfect virtue is possible in principle and such virtue occurs through a harmonization and unification of all the virtues within the perfectly virtuous person." Thanks to Stephen C. Angle for drawing my attention to this point.

6 [Merritt 2000] makes this point in a very clear and forceful way and argues that for this reason VES is better equipped than Aristotelian versions of VEF to rebut situationalism. Thanks to Eric L. Hutton for bringing Merritt's work to my attention.

7 For more detailed accounts of Mengzi's view of human nature and self-cultivation see [Ivanhoe 2000, 15–28; 2002a, 37–46 and 88–95] and [Van Norden 2007].

8 I have argued for the central role of such agricultural metaphors, as distinct from vegetative or craft metaphors, in Mengzi's philosophy in numerous publications but most thoroughly in the two books noted above. This is what makes his view a "development model" of self-cultivation. His later rival Xunzi employs a set of craft metaphors that present self-cultivation as a process of reshaping and orienting a recalcitrant original nature, which is prone to error. He offers a "reformation model." Within the development versus reformation scheme, Aristotle is much closer to Xunzi than Mengzi. For an insightful essay comparing Aristotle and Xunzi on the related issue of moral reasoning, see [Hutton 2002].

9 These included, of course, Kongzi ("Confucius") himself. I will illustrate my point by focusing on the sage kings Yao and Shun, but the point can be supported with numerous other examples. It is telling that Mengzi insists that people who fail to preserve and nurture their moral sprouts "are not human" (e.g. *Mengzi* 2A6), showing that it is their humanity and not some other quality that sages such as Yao and Shun perfect and exemplify. Thanks to Justin Tiwald for suggesting this last point.

10 Chinese thinkers also anticipate current debates about the role of literary figures in ethics. Though fiction came in for criticism by some later neo-Confucians, it has also been an immensely important resource for ethics in the Chinese tradition. For a discussion of this relationship, see [Ivanhoe 2007a].

11 Several passages offer poignant examples of sages expressing their co-humanity with the rest of us. For example, *Mengzi* 5A1 tells us that Shun would go out into the fields and weep because his parents did not love him, even though he had everything else in life that one might hope for. Shun felt the same pain that any of us would feel over such a broken relationship with parents. Thanks to Erin M. Cline for suggesting this illustration.

12 A *li* is a little more than half a kilometer.

13 There are a number of fascinating aspects of Mengzi's conception of empathic care that remain controversial or in need of careful analysis. An example of the former is his notion of how we are to "extend" care. This idea has been explored by David S. Nivison, Kwongloi Shun, Bryan W. Van Norden, David B. Wong, and Craig Ihara. I have summarized their accounts and offered my own interpretation in [Ivanhoe 2002b]. There is important work to be done aimed at making clear precisely what we mean by ascribing "empathic care" to Mengzi. His two most famous cases of empathic caring appear to be quite different and distinctive. In *Mengzi* 1A7, King Xuan of Qi spares an ox being led to ritual slaughter, but in what sense does the king empathize with the ox? Does he simply project human concerns onto the ox or does he somehow try to see and feel *as the ox* does? *Mengzi* 2A6 describes the famous story of the baby and the well, but it does not appear that we are being asked to feel *as the baby feels*. The baby is too young to sense the imminent danger it faces, something noted by Zhao Qi, the very first Chinese commentator on this passage. Mengzi appears to be asking us to think and feel as the baby *should feel* or perhaps as *one who cares for children* should feel. Mengzi

never asks us to put *ourselves* in the other's place and this is significant. Recent research [Decety and Lamm 2009] has shown that focusing on imagining how another feels tends to evoke greater empathic concern; putting oneself "in another's shoes" induces not only empathic concern but personal distress as well.

14 For different reasons, [Slote 2009] and [Angle 2009b] object to reading Mengzi as an advocate of VEF. See also [Van Norden 2009].

15 One of the reasons Mengzi is important for contemporary virtue ethicists is that he fits the core features of VEF and yet presents a form of VEF not found in the Western tradition. Studying his philosophy offers us a way to enrich our understanding of VEF and our ethical lives more generally.

16 For a study which explores the ethical implications of neo-Confucian ideals of sagehood, see [Angle 2009a].

17 Mengzi had neither the term nor any concept resembling "sudden enlightenment." For more on this difference, see [Ivanhoe 2000: 60 etc. 2002a: 106 etc.].

18 For an account of these aspects of Wang's view, see the works cited above and [Ivanhoe 2009c, 104–15]. The "Cheng-Zhu School" refers to the teachings of Cheng Yichuan (1033–1107) and Zhu Xi (1130–1200); this became the orthodox school of neo-Confucian philosophy.

19 I translate the Chinese word *xin* as "heart-mind" to indicate that it was thought to contain faculties of cognition and emotion as well as intention or volition.

20 Wang made use of the fact that we feel more or less connected and concerned with different parts of our bodies to support the traditional Confucian view of graded forms of love and care. I say "analogous" because, as will be clear, on Wang's view, the relationship is not part to whole. Wang believed each thing in the world contained within it *all* the *li*, somewhat like the way in which every cell contains within it all of a creature's DNA.

21 Neo-Confucians believed that a number of factors contribute to the presence of what is morally bad. Most scholars focus on the turbidity or impurity of one's *qi*, which surely is one importance source of what is bad. As is clear in the long quote below, the mere fact of being physically embodied contributes to our tendency to misconstrue our true nature and connection with the rest of the world and hence contributes to bad thoughts, feelings, and actions. This idea can be found in many other writers as well. Zhu Xi identified both of the factors described above as sources of moral depravity and also noted that the particular physical constitution of different creatures limited their capacity for moral awareness. See the passage labeled "section 57" from *The Complete Works of Zhu Xi* [Chan 1963, 621].

22 One finds a similar view in early Hinduism, which describes the central religious task as realizing that *atman* is *Brahman*. Because the *atman* misidentifies itself with the ego, humans tend to see themselves as separate individuals instead of as fundamentally connected to all other things. Thanks to Erin M. Cline for suggesting this comparison.

23 This description already makes clear the need to be careful in equating Wang's version of empathic concern with the views of people like Hume or modern advocates of sentimentalism such as Slote who make clear that caring for another does not involve a loss of self or the merging of individuals. As we shall see when we discuss oneness below, this issue is very much in play among psychologists as well as philosophers.

24 Wang here is paraphrasing the example of the child and well from *Mengzi* 2A6.

25 *Mengzi* 1A7 offers the example of King Xuan being "unable to bear" the anguished cries and frightened appearance of an ox being led to slaughter and goes on to infer a general aversion to seeing any animal suffer.

26 This is important for those who want to explore further the respects in which Wang is a proponent of VES. For his claims about pure knowing make clear that he believes in a distinct *faculty* of moral perception. This makes him more like Western sentimentalists such as Butler and Hutcheson and unlike Hume. For a study that offers a comparative exploration of Wang's views about moral perception, see [Ivanhoe 2011]. For Mengzi's original use of *liang zhi*, see *Mengzi* 7A15.

27 For a more detailed account of this teaching, see [Ivanhoe 2002a, 98–100, etc.]. For a study of the history of the relationship between knowledge and action, see [Nivison 1967].

28 As I have noted in other work [Ivanhoe 2011], McDowell's views about how a proper perception of the noble "silences" competing desires and motivates action [McDowell 1988] have a good deal in common with Wang's notion of the *unity of knowing and action*. [Slote 2010, 13–25, 57–81, etc.] argues that moral sentimentalists endorse something like this view. Thanks to Michael Slote for suggesting these comparisons.

29 For this idea, see the first part of the long passage quoted above. In another passage [Ivanhoe 2009c, 114–15], Wang makes clear that pure knowing is not just a *response to* things in the world but the morally conscious aspect or mode of the principles shared by things and the heart-mind.

30 In the conclusion, I will discuss how a version of Wang's idea is much closer to recent developments in psychology that challenge the standard empathy–altruism model of caring for and helping others.

31 In Wang's most representative philosophical work, *A Record of Practice*, he uses the term *junzi* a total of 24 times and *shengren* 196 times. In addition to this comparative frequency of use, the importance of attaining sagehood was central to Wang's philosophy, while not an explicit goal of moral practice for Mengzi. Mengzi did believe that every person was *capable* of becoming a sage (see e.g. *Mengzi* 6B2), but he did not expect even morally committed people to attain this goal. In fact, he thought sages were extremely rare historical phenomena. Thanks to Eric L. Hutton for discussion on this and other topics.

32 Wang was more of a *guru* figure or Chan master to his immediate disciples [Ivanhoe 2002a, 103, 121–34].

33 Wang's sages exhibit an almost frightening level of independence from social norms, and he often makes clear that this is one of the defining characteristics of sages. Wang thought that sages will often appear to be *insane* when looked at from the perspective of the average person. For a discussion of this aspect of his view, see [Ivanhoe 2002a, 121–36]. Wang's sage bears a certain resemblance to Aristotle's *phronimos*; both are characterized by a remarkable level of self-sufficiency in regard to their actions and self-conception.

34 The embedded quote is paraphrase of Mengzi. See *Mengzi* 2A2, 6A7, and 6A15.

35 This first point is also a feature of Wang's philosophy, but, as is true of so many similarities between Mengzi and Wang, it takes a distinctive shape in the latter. For Wang, the scope of the sage's concern is nothing less than universal, which is a common characteristic of neo-Confucian philosophy.

36 For a defense of a modern conception of filial piety as a virtue, see [Ivanhoe 2007b].

37 This general feature of Confucian philosophy will be discussed in greater detail below in my remarks on Wang's conception of oneness.

38 For an interesting study that focuses on the connection between early Confucian ethics and feminism, see [Li 2000].

39 I have in mind Mengzi's strong claims about the degree of consensus that we can expect to find among informed and reflective people on matters of values and tastes. See for example, *Mengzi* 6A7.

40 [Van Norden 2007, 315–59] explores a number of issues concerning how one might fashion a more pluralistic form of Confucianism (which he refers to as Ruism). For "ethical promiscuity," see [Ivanhoe 2009d].

41 Human beings show a regular and pervasive tendency to favor themselves in numerous ways, for example by claiming personal successes as evidence of excellence while attributing failure to situational factors or by interpreting ambiguous evidence in ways that are self-serving. For some representative studies of this phenomenon, see [Eply and Dunning 2000] and [Pronin, Lin, and Ross 2002].

42 Wang does not discuss the feminist idea that some of us need to become more self-assertive and seek our own good when others are trying to make us feel guilty for doing

so. This is not a common theme among neo-Confucians, though Dai Zhen offers a prominent exception and presents a careful analysis of these very concerns. For Dai's views on this issue, see [Tiwald 2011]. Thanks to Michael Slote for raising this issue in comments on an earlier draft of this essay. For his splendid discussion of this set of problems, see chapter 4 of [Slote 2002].

43 For a study comparing Eastern and Western conceptions of self and their implications for issues related to moral perception, response, and action, see [Markus and Kitayama 1991].

44 The claims in this last paragraph and much of my earlier account of Wang's metaphysical views are taken from [Ivanhoe 2011]. Readers interested in a more complete account of Wang's view of moral perception and its potential for contemporary philosophy are encouraged to consult this essay.

45 As a general claim, such a view finds support in important contemporary psychology [Hoffman 2000]. [Angle 2009a] relates Hoffman's views to neo-Confucian philosophers like Wang Yangming.

46 The current literature often describes other-regarding feelings as either empathy or oneness, but I see no reason to draw too sharp a line here or to regard these as mutually exclusive. It seems that all cases of empathic concern involve a sense of oneness and many cases of oneness entail or generate empathic concern.

47 I have defended a version of this claim in [Ivanhoe 2012].

48 Ensuring that human beings do at times act selflessly or altruistically is a central concern of the so-called "empathy–altruism hypothesis" [Batson 1987].

4 Confucianism, Kant, and Virtue Ethics

1 Thereafter, he developed this point in another article [Yu 2008].

2 This book and *Metaphysische Anfangsgründe der Rechtslehre* (Metaphysical First principles of the Doctrine of Right) were later combined into one book *Die Mataphysik der Sitten* (The Metaphysics of Morals).

5 Toward a Synthesis of Confucianism and Aristotelianism

1 My thanks to Stephen Angle, Michael Slote, the International Society for Comparative Studies of Chinese and Western Philosophy, the Institute of Foreign Philosophy of Peking University, the Centre for Applied Ethics at Hong Kong Baptist University, the participants in the International Conference on Confucianism and Virtue Ethics of 2010, and two anonymous referees for their support and edifying influence.

2 Watson 1997 presents a thoughtful critique of the deontology/consequentialism dichotomy, but also raises some concerns about virtue ethics that I hope to address in a future publication.

3 For further discussion, see Jiyuan Yu (this volume, 129), Wong 2002, and Van Norden (2007, 235–45).

4 On these points see Norton 1988 and Kupperman 1999b. Chen Lai correctly states that "what Confucius was concerned with is not just the minimal standards of virtues and ethical duties." Instead, Confucius encourages us to pursue "a higher human ideal than required by basic ethics" (this volume, 24). Ironically, Chen sees this feature of Confucianism as a reason for *denying* that Confucius had a virtue ethics. Our disagreement may be only apparent, though, as Chen acknowledges that he is discussing "a narrowly specified form of virtue ethics," whereas I have a broader sense in mind. Similarly, Wai Wong-ying's critique of applying virtue ethics to Confucianism (this volume) seems to be based on an overly narrow conception of the former.

5 One hopes that the comparative study of virtue ethics may improve not just our *understanding* of the virtue, but also our *practice* of them. As Jiyuan Yu observes, in a deeply insightful essay, "even though we cannot completely copy ancient ways of making virtue ethics practical, the ancient perception that virtue ethics should effect some transformation in the agent's life remains significant and attractive" (this volume, 140).

6 The present essay is largely constructive, rather than exegetical. But see the fine essays by Matthew Walker and Benjamin Huff in the present volume for exegetical essays on the views of Mengzi and Wang Yangming on human flourishing. I further explore the issues raised in this paper in Van Norden (forthcoming).

7 This can be seen as an application of the "principle of sacrifice" (Walker, this volume, 98).

8 For interestingly different approaches to Plato's ethics, see Friedländer 1970 and Irwin 1995. For contrasting views on flourishing in Aristotle, see Cooper 1987 and Kraut 1989.

9 Is there anything that the variety of flourishing lives have in common? Alasdair MacIntyre has suggested that they all involve participation in some kind of "practice," by which he means a "cooperative human activity through which goods internal to that form of activity are realized" (MacIntyre, 1984, p. 187). MacIntyre has written some provocative essays comparing Aristotelianism and Confucianism (MacIntyre 1991, 2004). However, I think he is mistaken in regarding them as incommensurable.

10 The similarities and differences between Confucian virtue ethics and feminist "ethics of care" are explored in Li 2000. See also Slote 2010a.

11 For a very even-handed review of the evidence, see Neufeld 2007, especially pp. 159–163 and 176–179.

12 My approach to this problem is similar to that of Philip Ivanhoe, who notes in his contribution to the present volume that a contemporary Confucian might explore the ethical implications of the fact that "other people, creatures, and things, while clearly not part of our physical bodies, are parts of our lives and our conception of who we are" (44). Challenging the radical (and metaphysically unwarranted) individualism that is too often taken for granted will open us to "an expanded view of the self" (44), that allows us "to *rethink* the meaning of notions like selfishness and selflessness" (45, emphasis in original).

13 For a fascinating examination of this topic, see Taylor 1992.

6 Virtue Ethics and Confucianism: A Methodological Reflection

1 I am greatly indebted to Stephen C. Angle, whose detailed and quite helpful comments on an earlier version of this paper make its rewriting possible. In addition, this paper owes much to Project 2009EZX001, sponsored by the Fund for Philosophy and Social Science in Shanghai, and Key Project 11JJD720012, sponsored by Education Ministry, China.

2 In Chinese-speaking academic circles, there is a dispute about which of "*de*(德)," "*meide* (美德)," "*dexing*(德行)" and "*dexing*(德性)" is the proper term to translate the English term "virtue." An English reader might be disinterested in this dispute: it is nothing but senseless chatter, from which he or she cannot learn anything more about "virtue." However, from the perspective of a glocal philosophy, the dispute revolving around the proper translation of "virtue" in actuality has concentrated the interaction-dialogue of Eastern and Western thought. The determination of the Chinese-translation term involves how to import and transplant the fundamental content of "virtue ethics" into Chinese thought, but it no less involves how Chinese thought, including Confucianism, will retroact upon virtue ethics.

3 See Chen Lai's essay in this volume.

4 Of couse, such a comparison seems to be unfair to Aristotle, since he has to compete with the whole Confucian tradition.

5 See a discussion on a new theory of morality in the Qianlong and Jiaqing regimes in Wu Xiaofan 2010.

6 For metaphors in the pre-Qin period, see Allan 1997. As for those in Neo-Confucianism, see Bao Yongling 2012.

7 In his essay in this volume P. J. Ivanhoe gives a more detailed discussion of Mencius' metaphor of "sprouts."

8 The term "glocal philosophy" might be similar to "rooted global philosophy" coined by Stephen C. Angle (see the "Introduction" to this volume). Huang Yong's recent research on Confucian virtue ethics exemplifies to some extent such a glocal perspective. See his essay in this volume, as well as Huang Yong 2003, Liu 2011b. In 2011, Huang Yong published three books in Chinese discussing, respectively, ethics, religion, and politics in a glocal age.

7 Confucian Ethics and Virtue Ethics Revisited

1 Wong (2001).
2 Here I am not going to repeat the argument and exposition in the "first investigation" but will only briefly summarize its conclusions: first, even though deontic concepts are derived from aretaic concepts, both are derived from the original heart-mind, namely, *ren*, *yi*, *li*, and *zhi*; therefore *ren*, *yi*, *li*, and *zhi*, understood as the original heart-mind, are the basis of morality. For this reason, it is not suitable to consider Confucian ethics as virtue ethics. Second, it is true that Confucianism emphasizes making evaluations of one's ethical character. The evaluation of acts and choices is only important when they contribute to the enhancement (or destruction) of one's ethical character. Third, it is commonly admitted that Confucian ethics emphasizes virtues, and although most of them are moral virtues, non-moral ones do exist. The former (moral virtues) focus on the perfection of moral character, but not on the happiness of oneself and of others; the latter (non-moral virtues) are required for a holistic life. Neither in the realms of moral virtue nor of non-moral virtue could the problem of "self–*other* asymmetry" indicated by Michael Slote (1992) be found. Fourth, the concept of interest embedded in the concept of self-other asymmetry, which distinguishes between the systems of principled ethics and virtue ethics, is not applicable in the morality of Confucianism. Based on the above reasons, even though Confucian ethics fulfills Slote's criteria of virtue ethics in some respects, it is doubtful that essentially it belongs to virtue ethics.
3 Van Norden thinks that Confucianism can be categorized as Aristotelian virtue ethics (2007), whereas Slote thinks that it is more accurate to conceive Confucianism as taking a Humean/sentimentalist approach to virtue ethics (2010, ch. 4).
4 Wong (2011).
5 To follow Bernard Williams' usage, hereafter I will use "ethical" as the broad term to stand for the considerations that bear on answering the question "what should I do, all things considered?" and "moral" as the narrower term to stand for a special system in which duties and obligations are examined. See Williams (1985), p. 6.
6 Van Norden (2007).
7 Ibid.
8 Van Norden (2007), p. 2.
9 Ibid., pp. 33–34.
10 Ibid., p. 37.
11 Ibid., p. 249.
12 Van Norden does not think that this meaning applies to Confucius and I have argued against this view in Wong (2012).
13 Wong (2012).
14 Also see Wong (2005), pp. 201–204.
15 Van Norden (2007), p. 102.
16 Ibid.
17 Slote (1992).
18 See Wong (2011) for detailed discussion.
19 See note 5 and Wong (2011).
20 See also "Moral Dilemma: A Confucian Perspective" (in Chinese), and "The Confucian Resolution of Moral Conflict, Revisited" (in Chinese). These two articles are included in Wong (2005).

8 The Impossibility of Perfection

1 I want to thank Stephen Angle, P. J. Ivanhoe, and Xiao Yang for helpful suggestions.
2 A. D. M Walker (1993, pp. 44–62) thinks the virtues can't all be harmonized within a single person, but doesn't believe that this undercuts the possibility of perfection. Irreconcilable (suitably accompanied) virtues can represent different "styles" of virtue-perfection.
3 Of course, and as is well known, feminism also has important moral lessons to teach about the nature of justice, human rights, and proper moral ideals.
4 The example might also be thought to count as an instance of moral dilemma, and that may be so. But one shouldn't in that case assume that *other* moral dilemmas necessarily move us toward Berlin's conclusions. I have discussed this issue at length in my *The Impossibility of Perfection* (2011, ch. 4).
5 I am not here carefully distinguishing between how much one cares about particular individuals and how much one cares about one's intimates (those to whom one is close) as a group. But I don't think that is important for present purposes.
6 Also see *Analects* 7.15 and the *Xunzi* 19.5, which seems to refer to the relevant passage(s) in the *Analects*.
7 I am not saying that harmony or harmoniousness isn't a positive ethical value, but I am saying that it may not be possible to fully reconcile or harmonize it with other very real ethical values. In other words, even though harmony is valuable, a realistic value system and/or an adequate picture of the ethical universe may (unfortunately) have to be lacking in that value.
8 In speaking in this way, I don't mean to claim that the ethical complexities we have recently unearthed didn't apply to earlier times, only that we face these complexities more squarely and (self-)consciously than it was possible to do hundreds of years ago. For example, the idea that "emotional work" is as relevant to men as to women may be a new one, but that doesn't mean that the men of earlier times who evaded such work didn't lose out by doing so, just as men today do and would. The impossibilities of perfection that I have been speaking of are in some sense perennial ones—and, as I've indicated, they are supposed to apply to all possible intelligent beings, not just to humans.

9 Structured Inclusivism about Human Flourishing: A Mengzian Formulation

1 I defend an inclusivist reading of Aristotle in Walker 2011. Huff's essay in this volume offers further discussion of Aristotle's criteria for flourishing.
2 On *xìng* in Mengzi, see Graham [(1967) 1990, especially 35; 55]; Bloom [1997]; Van Norden [2007, 214].
3 For the *Mengzi*, I use Van Norden's translation [Mengzi 2008].
4 For this restrictive reading of Mengzi on human nature, see, e.g., Yu [2005].
5 For similarly expansive readings of Mengzi on human nature, cf. Graham [(1967) 1980, 38–39]; Bloom [1997, 24; 26; 28–29].
6 Likewise, as Van Norden [2007, 190] suggests, Mengzi wants to reserve nature to refer to that which we must actively cultivate. We do not need to cultivate sensual appetites, while we do need to cultivate the virtues.
7 One might suggest that Mengzi's account is exclusivist in identifying human flourishing with one overarching good, viz., the completion of human nature. This proposal is not unreasonable, but if we accept it, then I think that Mengzi's account becomes trivially exclusivist, for such a proposal overlooks the full range of *different* dispositions that Mengzi thinks compose the human good.
8 On the "specific structure" of human nature in Mengzi, cf. Ivanhoe [1990, 31–34]. Cf. also Irwin's proposal [1991, 389] that Aristotelian *eudaimonia* has an internal structure according to the "relative importance" of its components.
9 This worry, viz., that it would be arbitrary to propose a hierarchical account of the parts

of human nature, seems to motivate Zhuangzi's question: "Of the hundred joints, nine openings, six viscera all present and complete, which should I recognize as more kin to me than another?" [*Zhuangzi* 2001 [1981] trans. Graham, 51)].

10 For a similar insight about how to rank components of flourishing, see Van Norden's essay in this volume.

11 On the directive role of the heart, cf. Graham [(1967) 1990, 41–42]; Ivanhoe [1990, 33]; Bloom [1997, 28–29].

12 I have benefitted from discussing the athletic case with Brad Cokelet. That Mengzi is concerned with permanent, or general, sacrifice is also suggested by his thought that the "lowly gardener" is one who "abandons" his mahogany tree for his date tree [6A14.3], i.e., who permanently, or generally, sacrifices what is higher for what is lower.

13 If the four dispositions of the heart (and the goods and activities to which these dispositions give rise) are not themselves to form a simple second-order aggregation, then one needs to account for their unity as well. (I thank David Wong for raising this issue.) Here, one might appeal to the role that Mengzi believes that benevolence plays in unifying the heart's dispositions: to possess wisdom, one must possess benevolence; and one must possess these dispositions, in turn, to possess propriety and righteousness [2A7.2–3]. Hence, as Van Norden [2008, 47] notes, Zhu Xi ultimately identifies wisdom, propriety, and righteousness as *manifestations* of benevolence.

14 The *structured* character of Mengzi's account of flourishing is noted as well by Graham [(1967) 1990, 28–29].

15 The account of externals that I attribute to Mengzi invites comparison with a view that Cooper [1985] attributes to Aristotle. For simplicity, I do not discuss Confucius's complex views on externals (as presented, e.g., in *Analects* 1.14, 4.5, 4.9, 4.11, 4.14, 4.16, 7.12, and 8.12). I take Walsh's remarks on Yan Hui's need for moderate resources (in Walsh's essay this volume) to suggest that Confucius might also accept something like the view that I here attribute to Mengzi.

16 I have benefited from an NEH Summer Seminar Fellowship to attend "Traditions into Dialogue: Confucianism and Contemporary Virtue Ethics" (directed by Stephen Angle and Michael Slote in 2008), a post-doctoral fellowship in the Ethics of Virtue at the University of Miami, and a New Faculty Fellowship at Rutgers University, sponsored by the American Council of Learned Societies. I have further benefited from helpful feedback on earlier drafts of this paper by the editors of this volume, Eric Hutton, Benjamin Huff, and David Wong (who commented on this paper for a symposium at the 2009 Pacific APA), and from discussion with participants at the International Conference on Confucianism and Virtue Ethics at Peking University, May 2010.

10 The Target of Life in Aristotle and Wang Yangming

1 Aristotle quotations are from Roger Crisp's translation of the *Nicomachean Ethics* [2000].

2 Some readers [e.g. Heinaman 1988, 43–4; White 1991; and Kenny 1992, 26–7] dispute whether Aristotle endorses this notion of self-sufficiency himself, since he remarks that Plato used an argument of this kind. However, before mentioning Plato, Aristotle has already drawn the conclusion: "This last argument, at least, seems to represent [pleasure] as one good among others," and so not *the* good [1172b27–8]. Further, Aristotle treats this argument as decisive through X.2–3.

3 See, e.g. Cicero [2001] III.33, 46–8. Other Stoic analogies suggest a quantum leap.

4 The Stoics acknowledged progress toward virtue, as indicated, e.g., in Cicero [2001] III.48. Compare *Analects* 2.4, 16.7.

5 This single good may have components, so long as it is clear how they are united, rather than merely forming an aggregate. Matthew Walker's essay in this volume offers an interesting example of how multiple components can contribute to an organically united conception of eudaimonia.

6 I use Wang 1963 for translations, substituting Pinyin romanization, and Wang 1983 for Chinese text.

7 Compare *Mencius* 4B29, 4B31.

8 Wang presents another, analogous model for sagely achievement in I.68, based on quality and quantity of water.

9 Bryan Van Norden argues for an expansive conception of excellent or virtuous activity in his essay in this volume.

10 For a related, but somewhat different view, see chapter 11 of Nussbaum 1986.

11 For helpful comments and discussion I am indebted to Deborah Mower, Sara Rushing, participants at the 2010 International Conference on Confucianism and Virtue Ethics, the editors of this volume, and especially P. J. Ivanhoe and Michael Ing. A Walter Williams Craigie Grant supported my work during summer 2009.

11 Varieties of Moral Luck in Ethical and Political Philosophy for Confucius and Aristotle

1 Other versions of Kantian and utilitarian ethics may accept less radical versions of moral luck, but the original versions did not.

2 For a discussion of Kant's strong claims about moral luck—insofar as Kant believes that the possibility of morality itself required that every rational agent has pure practical reason, which has full moral *control* and full moral *understanding* at all times—see [Walsh 2012]. My interpretation of Confucius is not a Kantian one, and is at odds with Mou Zongsan's Kantian "moral mind" interpretation of early Confucianism. Mou Zongsan believes that all humans, regardless of moral luck, have an innate "moral mind," a complete and pure moral consciousness that is akin to Kant's pure practical reason. Mou Zongsan's Kantian interpretation is discussed and defended in this volume in the essays of both Lee Ming-huei and Wong Wai-ying. On my interpretation of Confucius, human moral consciousness is not universally innate (it is only arguably innate for the occasional sage), and one's moral consciousness depends on luck for its purity and completeness.

3 For example, Jiyuan Yu says, "Indeed, although Confucius acknowledges that fortune affects many aspects of human life, he does not think that it affects one's moral life" [Yu 2007, 190–192]. Yu also argues (contrary to my view) that Aristotle's ethics require more significant luxuries, pleasures, and moral luck than Confucius'. Yu says that for Confucius, there may be some luck in acquiring virtue but *not* in maintaining it, and only *having* virtue is ethically significant (as opposed to *exercising* the virtues one has). I believe that both philosophers require similar, modest forms of moral luck, material good, and ethical pleasures. Cf. [Slingerland 1996, 568–71], [Hall and Ames 1987, 212–15], and [Sim 2007, Ch. 7].

4 See [Kenny 1988, 113].

5 Cf. Aristotle's *Politics* I.3–4 and *NE* VII, in which Aristotle argues that a natural slave needs to be told what to do in order to act well and develop his or her human capacities.

6 See [*Analects* 12.19, 12.22 13.4, 13.6, 13.10, 13.12, 13.13, 14.41; cf. 13.9, 15.33].

7 Cf. [13.6, 9.14, 4.13].

8 Mencius also says that good government mediates against bad luck by providing a *constant livelihood* for the small people to act and live well [*Mencius* 1A3, 1A7, 7A4]. Cf. *Analects* 12.7–9.

9 There is evidence that suggests that many would commit atrocities if they lacked a basically good government and situational luck, and many would not have done so if they had a better government. See [Arendt 1963] and [Miller 2009] on the situational variables for moral goodness.

10 Confucius believes that sages are *born* better [19.12]. In contrast, Xunzi and Mencius believe that all are born *equal* in nature, but require luck (good teachers and government) for proper ritual training. See [*Mencius* 6A17, 7A36; *Xunzi* 4.8, 8.11, 4.10, 23.5b].

11 [*Analects* 4.25, 6.3, 6.7, 7.7, 9.11].

12 See [Angle 2009a] on the Confucian sage.

13 Rosemont and Ames note that *Analects* 16.9's "highest class" is born with *both* the right community *and* inner nature [Confucius 1999, 264n284]. Cf. *Analects* 1.15.

14 Cf. 1095b4–9.

15 According to Anthony Kenny, for Aristotle the gods give some humans inborn "grace" required for developing virtue [Kenny 1992, 77].

16 See [*Analects* 4.25]. Cf. 7.8.

17 Cf. Plato's *Republic* VIII on the slow degrading of states and souls from virtue to vice.

18 See [*NE* 1098b30] for Aristotle's discussion of the lack of completeness (*telios*) and self-sufficiency (*autarkes*) of a chronically sleeping person's life.

19 See [1100b23–30]. For Aristotle, it is common sense [1096a1–3] that luck is required in order to exercise virtue [1099b1–7, 1100a6–8, 1100b27].

20 Cf. [Yu 2007, 185–186, 190].

21 This story was originally related to me by Alasdair MacIntyre, and also reflects the story of holocaust survivor Primo Levi [Levi 1959].

22 In a footnote, Richard Kraut gives a similar interpretation of Aristotle on happiness while being tortured: "It should not be thought that pain by itself is incompatible with *eudaimonia*: the courageous soldier being struck by the blows of an enemy does not lose his happiness while the pain lasts, for the suffering does not necessarily impede his virtuous activity … The victim on the rack does lack happiness (VI.13 1153b19–21), but this is not simply because he is in pain. Rather, Aristotle is assuming that pain induced by instruments of torture is causally connected to the deprivation of *other* goods needed for happiness (b17–19)." [Kraut 1989, 259n51] [my italics]

23 See Herodotus' *Histories* VIII, 75. Note that I am embellishing Sicinnus's story when I begin with "*Imagine* that Sicinnus …"

24 It is important to note the distinction between "feeling pleasure and pain" and "taking pleasure" or "being pleased or pained." For example, imagine a man who had his arm severed in a motorcycle accident. He is about to go into surgery to have the arm reattached. The surgeon tells him that if he wakes up and feels pleasure in his arm, the reattachment was not successful, but if he feels great pain in his arm, the reattachment was successful. When he wakes up, he feels incredible pain, and *he takes great pleasure in having that pain.* He is very pleased with the pain. Similarly, Sicinnus may take pleasure in the success of his unimpeded activities, despite feeling pain.

25 See 7.16, where Confucius says that, for the virtuous, a life of bad food, plain water, and a mere bent arm as a pillow is a great *pleasure* (*le*), whereas the life of wealth is not a pleasure (*le*) if gained inappropriately [cf. 1.1, 16.5]. Contrast this with [Yu 2007, 191], which argues that Aristotle requires that the virtuous have significant pleasure in their virtuous life but Confucius does not. See [Shun 2010a] for pleasure (*le*) in Confucianism.

26 Confucius also seems to value activity in *Analects* 9.17: "The stream flows on like this day and night." Of 9.17, Zhu Zi says our *activity* in pursuing the way must be constant and never ending.

27 Similarly, Mencius says that a government that provides food and employment helps to prevent vice, and that people do better when they are brought up in a good environment under a good ruler and good government [*Mencius* 1A3, 1A7, 6A7, 7A4].

28 Priam's virtuous *activity* ended suddenly, due to bad luck, but for Aristotle *virtue* itself cannot end so suddenly.

29 Sages are rare indeed. See [*Analects* 6.30, 7.26, 7.34, 9.6, 11.26, 4.2, 6.21–22] and [Angle 2009a].

30 See [4.5, 6.3, 6.7, 14.6, 14.24, 15.18, 17.23, 19.12, 19.21].

31 In *Analects* 4.4, Confucius says that if one's heart is set to *ren*, one can do no wrong, which expresses the *stability* of virtue and its power to achieve the external targets of right action. But it may be very rare and difficult to have one's heart fully set to *ren* (cf. 4.6). However, *Analects* 7.30 makes it appear that *ren* is easy to achieve, when Confucius

says "Is *ren* distant? When I wish to be *ren*, *ren* arrives." But it may be difficult to fully *wish* to be *ren* for those other than Confucius (Confucius is suggesting that he, in the *first person*, has ease of wishing *ren*, but others might not find it so easy to wish to be *ren*). Moreover, it took Confucius until the age of 70 to set his heart and mind (*xin*) right [2.4]. So having the right mind to "wish to be *ren*" obtains only after a long and difficult process. Only when one can easily wish to be *ren* is *ren* easily achieved.

32 Cf. *Analects* 4.2; *Mencius* 4B14, 4B28.

33 For more on virtue's *stability* in Confucius and Aristotle, see [1100b9–17, 1179a4–17] and [*Analects* 13.22, 15.1].

34 I would like to thank the participants at the International Conference on Confucianism and Virtue Ethics in Beijing, and thank Steve Angle, Roger Ames, Howard Curzer, Heidi Giebel, Ben Huff, P. J. Ivanhoe, Deborah Mower, Sara Rushing, May Sim, Michael Slote, Andrew Terjesen, Bai Tongdong, Matt Walker, Yang Xiao, and Xiaomei Yang. Some of this project was done while I was in residence at the Institute for Advanced Study at the University of Minnesota. I am grateful for the support.

12 The Practicality of Ancient Virtue Ethics: Greece and China

1 "The fact, if it be a fact, that virtue is no basis for morality will explain what otherwise it is difficult to account for, viz. the extreme sense of dissatisfaction produced by a close reading of Aristotle's *Ethics*. Why is the *Ethics* so disappointing? ... It is, rather, because Aristotle does not do what we as moral philosophers want him to do, viz. to convince us that we really ought to do what in our non-reflective consciousness we have hitherto believed we ought to do, or if not, to tell us what, if any, are the other things which we really ought to do, and to prove to us that he is right" (Prichard 1912: 33).

2 Unless otherwise indicated, all translations of Plato in this book are from Plato 1997.

3 Unless otherwise indicated, the translation of the *Analects* is from Confucius 1979.

4 Unless otherwise indicated, all translations of Aristotle are from Aristotle 1984.

5 For an inspirational study of the idea that philosophy is a way of life in ancient Greece, see Hadot 2002.

6 The dual function is explicitly depicted in the following passage: "[W]hoever comes into close contact with Socrates and associations with him in conversation must necessarily, even if he began by conversing about something quite different in the first place, keep on being led about by the man's argument until he submits to answering questions about himself concerning both his present manner of life and the life he has lived hitherto" (*Laches*, 187e7–188a1; see also, *Euthyphro* 7a–8b; *Gorgias*, 475a–d, 482b; *Protagoras*, 333c7).

7 One of the most controversial issues regarding elenchus is that, besides exposing ambiguity or incoherence among the beliefs of the interlocutors, is it possible for it to establish positive moral truth? In other words, is Socrates' elenchus constructive? Commentators debate heavily over this issue. For some (called "anti-constructivists"), elenchus can only reveal the inconsistency of the interlocutor's belief (see Stokes 1986, 1–35 and Benson 1987), but others are in favor of ascribing a constructive role to elenchus. Vlastos observes that once the inconsistency has been pointed out, Socrates often claims that the initial belief P is false, and the interlocutor generally abandons P under scrutiny, rather than the premises Q and R from which not-P is derived. How to explain this? For the truth of these premises is not established in the process of elenchus. Socrates neither questions those beliefs nor argues for them. They have entered the argument on the basis of the agreement between Socrates and the interlocutor. Yet inconsistency with Q and R does not necessarily mean that P ought to be refuted. For Vlastos, it is on the basis of inductive evidence through previous elenctic examinations that Socrates accepts the truth of his own set of moral convictions. The interlocutors always fail because they hold beliefs that are inconsistent with the beliefs that Socrates holds to be true (Vlastos 1983: 44–56). For various versions along this line of interpretation, see Reeve 1989: 52–3 and Brickhouse and Smith 1994: 19–20.

8 B. Schwartz remarks, "The appropriate inner disposition must be there in the disciple before Confucius can hope to help him in his search for the *dao*" (Schwartz 1985: 79), but I do not see textual evidence to support his claim.

9 The question about the nature of extension was first raised by David Nivison (Nivison 1980: 417–32; Nivison 2002: 138). Of those who attempt to make sense of Mencius' extension, some think that motivationally effective compassion is generated through logical argumentation (Shun 1989: 317–43). Others think that it is a matter of making the king focus his attention on his suffering people (Van Norden 1991: 353–70). Still others suggest that reasoning is necessary but not sufficient, and it also involves significant expansion of emotional capacities. It is a matter of drawing appropriate analogies from the similarity between an ox and the people. There are different versions of this line of explanation. P. J. Ivanhoe calls it "analogical resonance" or "emotional resonance" (Ivanhoe 2002b: 221–41). David Wong (2002, 187–220) names it "analogical reasoning." Wong's paper provides an excellent summary of the debate (Wong 2002: 187–220).

13　How Virtues Provide Action Guidance: Confucian Military Virtues at Work

1 To be fair to Louden, six years later he admits that he has overstated the case and is less critical of virtue ethics (Louden 1990, 101–102). His view in his 1984 article, however, is still held by some philosophers and that article is still reprinted.

2 Sawyer translated the whole set with helpful introductions and detailed notes (Sawyer 1993). Though his translation is not always reliable, for convenience' sake in this article I quote from the Sawyer translation and provide occasional corrections. For transliteration of Chinese terms I use the pinyin method, rather than the dated Wade-Giles system which Sawyer uses.

3 Almost all studies on early Chinese philosophy in English do not include the "military [strategy] school," but, the situation is very different in Chinese publications. Fortunately, there is a brief section on this school in de Bary and Bloom 1999, 213–223.

4 Ames aptly observes in his Introduction, "Discussion of military affairs is pervasive in early Chinese philosophical literature. This in itself is a fair indication of the perceived importance of warfare as a topic of philosophical reflection in China, a concern that is not paralleled in Western philosophical literature. It is a seldom-advertised fact that many if not most of the classical Chinese philosophical works contain lengthy treatises on military thought. … In fact, in the imperial catalog included in the *History of the Han Dynasty*, the military writers are listed under the 'philosophers' (*tzu*) classification" (Sun Tzu 1993, 39–40).

5 *Sun Bin's Art of War* is another important treatise of the "military [strategy] school" of the pre-Qin era, but was not collected in the *Seven Military Classics* because it was not extant at that time. It was recovered in China only in 1972 and is available in several English translations. For the sake of space I shall not include this treatise in my discussion here.

6 Again, for this treatise, good statecraft is to govern by virtuous leadership (Sawyer 1993, 41–42). The Department of Defense is no exception.

7 Among the five treatises of the "military [strategy] school," this treatise is the most Confucian in outlook.

8 For an intellectual history of military virtues in China, see Wang 1998.

9 It follows that a good military education includes moral and character education. This is a universal phenomenon and can be seen by the emphasis on character education in the eminent military academies of the USA today, e.g., US Military Academy, and US Naval Academy. In the latter, the moral, mental, and physical development are emphasized in that order. In *Reef Points*, a small booklet that all midshipmen are expected to commit to memory, in the section "Moral Development and Officership" it is said: "An officer's ability to execute responsibilities simply cannot be separated from that officer's moral character. The officer's entire life is open to examination while living, working, and

fighting alongside Sailors and Marines. Because of this, it is impossible for the naval officer to separate private life from public life" (US Naval Academy 2010, 61).

10 It should be noted that in traditional China there has been a rich range of phrases to refer to the virtues of different professions, e.g., *shangde* (virtues for business people), *guande* (virtues for government officials), *yide* (virtues for medical practitioners), *wude* or *junde* (virtues for the military). Hence the education in professional ethics in traditional China takes the form of cultivation of virtues in professional life.

11 The literal meaning of "*gui*" suggests deceit, treachery, or cunning scheme. Hence the whole sentence in Chinese can be understood as "The military is all about deception/deceit."

12 The literal meaning of this related word suggests deceit, fraud, cheating, or feigning.

13 Sawyer's observation is apt, "Although all the military writings exploit deceit and deception, Sun-tzu's statement is the most explicit formulation of the principle" (Sun Tzu 1994, 305).

14 Hence some contemporary scholars oppose the current trend of applying the *Art of War* in business and management.

15 As Du Mu, an eminent exegete among the Eleven Schools, puts it, "The Kingly Way puts more emphasis on *ren* (benevolence) whereas the Military [Strategy] School puts more emphasis on *zhi* (wisdom)" (Yang, 1999, 7).

16 Subsequent interpreters of Sunzi all agree that wisdom is the first virtue among equals for a virtuous commander (cf. Qiu 2004, 159–160).

17 For an elaborate defense of Sunzi's military ethics, see Lo 2012b.

18 For an extensive analysis, see Lo 2012a, 414–428.

19 Sawyer's translation of "*quan*" as "authority" is wrong; my rendering here is made in accordance to the commentaries (Zhu 1992, 543).

20 Cf. the discussion on tragic moral dilemma in Hursthouse 1999, 71–77.

21 In the treatise *Sima's Art [of War]* there is also the military order of not harming noncombatants and not destroying their properties (cf. Sawyer 1993, 127–128). For the sake of space I do not quote and discuss it in this article.

22 In the typology outlined by Van Norden, the virtue ethics in these five military treatises is between the more radical version and the more moderate version of virtue ethics, resembling the version of Thomas Aquinas (Van Norden 2007, 34–35). There is a strong aretaic commitment, and yet there are detailed specifications of deontic precepts.

23 In the *Siku Quanshu* library of books, compiled in the Qing Dynasty, the occurrences of the terms *yi bing*, *yi jun*, and *yi zhan* are 3222, 3084, and 403 times, respectively. The disparity is overwhelming.

14 Rationality and Virtue in the *Mencius*

1 An early version of this paper was presented at the "Confucianism and Virtue Ethics" Conference in Beijing, May 14–16, 2010. I am grateful to Michael Slote and Steve Angle for inviting me to be part of a stimulating conference, and to the participants for their helpful comments. Special thanks go to Michael Slote for his generous encouragement and inspiration. My deep gratitude goes to my first reader, Anna Sun, as always.

2 It must be emphasized that to give *rational justifications* of one's normative claims is only *one* way to show the normative force (or authority) of one's normative claims. I say more about this in the next section.

3 I use "practical philosophy" rather than "virtue ethics" to refer to Mencius's thought partly because "virtue *politics*" is also an essential component of his practical philosophy, and the term "virtue *ethics*," as it is currently used by virtue ethicists, might be too narrow to be a full characterization of what Mencius does in the *Mencius*. In this sense, "practical philosophy," assuming that it includes both ethics and political philosophy, might be a better term. One may still use the term "ethics" if one uses it in Hegel's sense of "*Sittlichkeit*" (ethics, or ethical life). When "ethics" is used in this way, it is not much

different from "practical philosophy" (see Robert Pippin's important book, *Hegel's Practical Philosophy* (2008)).

4 For a brief discussion about the distinction (and tension) between the level of justification and that of motivation in Mencius, see Xiao 2009, 635–639.

5 Note that only one of the questions, the question about what character traits are admirable, is about virtue. It can be shown that Mencius's answers to the other questions are not always based on (or formulated in terms of) his answer to the question about virtue. This is another reason why I am reluctant to use "virtue ethics" to characterize Mencius's practical philosophy. Contemporary virtue ethicists use the term "virtue ethics" to refer to a third type of ethical theory that is an alternative to deontology (duty-based ethics) and consequentialism (good-based ethics). According to this typology, in order to claim that Mencius is a virtue ethicist, it is not enough if we find a concept of virtue in Mencius because this means only that Mencius has a "theory of virtue." For an ethical theory to deserve the label of "virtue ethics," we must also show that its concept of virtue is a *primary* concept, in terms of which other ethical concepts are defined. The notion of "primary concept" is a central notion in this typology. The following is my formulation of the definition of "primary concept": x is a primary concept in an ethical theory T if and only if (i) x is logically prior to all the other concepts in T, and (ii) all the other ethical concepts in T can be defined in terms of x. When this is the case, we call T an "x ethics" ("x-based ethics"). Note that all the ethical theories classified according to this typology share one thing in common, which is that they all have a "hierarchical" structure: at the bottom there is a primary concept and on the upper levels there are other non-primary concepts. Let me give two examples of ethical theory that has a "hierarchical" structure. The first is Kant's duty-based ethics (deontology), in which the concept of moral duty is a primary concept, in terms of which all the other concepts are defined. For example, the concept of virtue is defined by Kant in terms of his primary concept of duty: a virtue is the reliable disposition to fulfill moral duties. This is why it is not a "virtue ethics," even though Kant has a "theory of virtue." The second is Michael Slote's ethics of care (care ethics), in which the concept of care is a primary concept, in terms of which all the other ethical and political concepts (such as justice) are defined (Slote 2001 and 2007). We now can see the limit of this typology: it is not a complete classification of all the possible ethical theories. It has left out those ethical theories that do not have a primary concept (or a hieratical structure). It is possible that Confucius's or Mencius's ethics may fall into this category. However, to show that it is a "virtue ethics," one has to show not only that there is a concept of (as well as an emphasis on) virtue in Confucius or Mencius, but also that it has a hieratical structure, and that virtue is its primary concept. It seems that we have not yet seen such an argument in the secondary literature on Confucianism and virtue ethics (Xiao 2011). When we see the statement that "Confucian ethics is virtue ethics" in the literature, it is often used to mean a weaker statement, which is that "Confucian ethics is a theory of virtue." For example, this is how the term "virtue ethics" is actually used in van Norden 2007.

6 This is also held by the early Foot (1978), but rejected by Warren Quinn (1994) and the later Foot (2001 and 2008).

7 It can be argued that Mencius's ethics is not a "care ethics" in the sense of the term used by Slote. It is obvious that Mencius has a "theory of care (ren)". And it is logically possible that he could have had a "care ethics." That is to say, it is logically possible to define the concepts of justice (yi), ritual propriety (li), and wisdom (zhi) in terms of benevolence or care (ren). However, as a matter of fact, we do not find such a Slotean account of these other concepts in terms of care in the *Mencius*. It seems that most of the scholars who claim that Confucian ethics is "care ethics" use the term in the sense of "theory of care."

8 We may say that in this sense Mencius can be said to believe that there are "external reasons," and that he is an "externalist" regarding practical reason, to put it in Bernard Williams's terms (Williams 1985). Since the core of the definition of externalism is the belief in the existence of external reason (to put it positively) or the belief that it

is false to claim that there are *only* internal reasons (to put it negatively), it is logically possible for an externalist to hold the view that there are *both* external and internal reasons. In other words, an externalist does not have to deny the existence of internal reasons, even though an externalist must affirm the existence of external reasons, which an internalist must deny. One of the practical implications of this logical possibility is that an externalist *can* make arguments by appealing to internal reasons. What is so interesting about Mencius is that he is just such an externalist.

9 It must be pointed out that the style of Mencius's rationality-based arguments is unique. This point obviously needs more elucidation than I can give here.

10 In this paper I am using the term "means" to cover "instrumental" as well as "constitutive" means.

11 Here I use the term "instrumentally rational" (or "instrumental rationality") in its narrow sense, which refers only to means–end rationality. However, I use the term in its broad sense later in this paper, which includes both means–end rationality and prudential rationality.

12 I give an example of this kind of specification of one's end below. It can be argued that we should attribute to Mencius a "specificationist" view of practical reasoning in David Wiggins' sense (Wiggins 1998).

13 All the translations in this paper are from D. C. Lau's translation of the *Mencius*, with my modifications.

14 Here Mencius does not use a general term for "instrumentally irrational"; instead, he makes use of a concrete paradigm case of instrumental irrationality to convey the idea. I say more about this later in this paper.

15 There are many passages in the *Mencius* where Mencius is talking to a specific ruler, but there are also many passages that have the following general format: "Mencius said: P," where there is no indication that he is talking to any specific person. The passage I am about to quote (4A3) is exactly of this type.

16 Mencius here seems to imply that this might be the reason why the King is not practicing benevolent politics.

17 Here we see that Mencius entertains, but eventually rejects, a notion of radical evil, which is that one does bad things because he takes pleasure in doing bad things for their own sake. He seems to assume that one always desires things under the guise of the good. Mencius's notion of evil is much closer to the Greek and Hellenistic notion of evil (see, e.g., Books 1 and 9 of Aristotle's *Nicomachean Ethics*).

18 The fact that Mencius does have a phrase "*bu zhi* 不智" (unwise, unintelligent, imprudent, irrational) for a general concept of irrationality, although he does not use it here in this passage, shows that I was mistaken to have claimed that Mencius does not have a general technical term for "irrational" (Xiao 2009, 635).

19 I say more about Mencius's use of concrete paradigms of rationality in the next section.

20 It is well-known that Foot later changed her view on this (Foot 2001 and 2008).

15 Between Generalism and Particularism: The Cheng Brothers' Neo-Confucian Virtue Ethics

1 We may even claim that Confucian ethics in general is a moral particularism. Kai Marchal, in his contribution to this volume, particularly in the section entitled "The Situational Character of Justice and the Challenge of Indeterminacy," argues that what counts to be just for Zhu Xu, a neo-Confucian upon whom the Cheng brothers exerted a great influence, is also context-dependent. Of course, that is not a claim that is universally accepted. In his contribution to this volume, for example, although Lee Ming-huei's main argument is that Confucian ethics is better aligned to the Kantian deontology than to the Aristotelian or Humean virtue ethics, since the former is a typical example of moral generalism, while the latter is a type of moral particularism, he would most likely disagree that Confucian ethics is a moral particularism.

2 For a more detailed discussion of the Cheng brothers' argument for the identity between virtue and human nature, see Huang 2003.

3 Drawing on the studies done by experimental ethicists such as Joshua Knobe, Kwame Anthony Appiah makes the analogy between our moral intuitions and sense perceptions: while they are normally reliable, both may malfunction in some cases. What causes the difficulty for intuitionist moral philosophers is, however, their disanalogy: while we can examine the particular sense organ, eyes for example, and the relevant environment to see what is the problem when our sense organ malfunctions, there seems to be no particular organ to examine when our moral intuition malfunctions and therefore to know whether our moral intuition is malfunctioning or not [see Appiah 2008: chapter 3].

4 This view, that the beginnings of the four virtues are present not only in humans but also in (some) animals, at least at its face value, is irreconcilable with Mencius's view that they are unique to human beings. P. J. Ivanhoe notices this irreconcilability in his discussion of the Confucian view as expressed by Mencius. Still, Ivanhoe points out, "in terms of the form, flexibility, persistence, and range of what we care about, a good case can be made for Mengzi's claim" [Ivanhoe 2002a: 185 note 6]. One way to understand or even reconcile this difference between Mencius and the Cheng brothers regarding their views of the difference between humans and animals is to see that, while both humans and animals have these qualities, humans are also born with the ability to expand (*tui*) them, and so these inborn qualities can be regarded as beginnings (*dui* 端) in humans, but animals are not born with the ability to expand them, and so these qualities cannot be regarded as merely beginnings in animals. Understood this way, the difference between Mencius and the Cheng brothers on this issue is not that great, particularly if we can see, as I shall argue in the next few paragraphs, that the Cheng brothers' idea of *tui*, key to their understanding of what is uniquely human, is also central to Mencius.

5 While this essay focuses on the Cheng brothers' discussion about how to expand love, the beginning of the virtue of *ren*, the same thing can be said regarding the beginnings of other virtues.

6 I have made more sustained discussions of this neo-Confucian argument on why a person, in order to be a human being, has to be virtuous (see Huang 2008 and 2011).

7 In this sense, it is to some extent similar to what Gilbert Harman describes as direct inductive inference or transductive inference, which "goes from data about previous cases to a classification of a new case. This classification does not involve first making an inductive generalization from data about previous cases and background assumptions … and then deducing a conclusion about the new case from that inductive generalization" (Harman 2005: 48). On the one hand, it is not to classify the new case into the same category of the previous cases but merely as something neighboring to them; on the other hand, "transductive inferences need not set precedents but will leave other possible nearby cases maximally undecided" (Harman 2005: 54).

8 Bernard Williams, in his argument about the thickness of the morally relevant descriptions of actions, claims that such descriptions are non-transportable from context to context (Williams 1985); and Dancy states that his particularism does not allow the switch argument: "an attempt to determine what to say here by appeal to what we say about something else" (Dancy 1993: 64).

16 What Is Confucian Humility?

1 My sincere thanks to members of the 2008 National Endowment for the Humanities Summer Seminar at Wesleyan University and the 2009 Humanities Montana Symposium at Montana State University for help with this essay. In particular, Stephen Angle, Benjamin Huff, and Howard Curzer provided invaluable assistance.

2 Translations of the *Analects* are from (Confucius 2003) unless otherwise noted. Different translations of the *Analects* distinguish the idea of humility to greater or lesser degrees. In Edward Slingerland's translation, for example, the word "humility" appears in certain

passages that Lau and Ames and Rosemont translate, variously, as modesty, deference, respect and reverence. I work primarily with Slingerland's text not because he enables a theory of humility that other translations fail to support – the theme is palpable, regardless of how specific words are translated – but because he provides useful commentary that helps a non-Chinese speaker to engage more deeply with textual issues.

3 My thanks to the anonymous reviewer who offered support for my claim that humility is pivotal in classical Confucianism by pointing out (1) that the humility (*qian*) hexagram in the *Book of Changes* is the only one regarded as good at all six stages, because of its connection to progress and success, or, in my parlance, perseverance; and (2) that the story of the *yiqi* (the sacred vessel discussed in the *Xunzi* and the *Records of the Grand Historian*) offers a good example of humility, in so far as the vessel is upright when half-filled, but when too full will overflow and empty itself out.

4 4.13, 5.26, 7.36, 8.4, 8.11, 9.3, 11.26, 13.26, 20.0.

5 4.9, 6.6, 7.16, 11.1.

6 7.22, 7.33, 7.34, 9.2, 9.6, 9.8.

7 1.13, 3.7, 4.13, 5.16, 10.1, 11.26, 13.19, 16.10, 17.6.

8 For more on the importance of learning see Chen Lai's chapter in this volume, "Virtue Ethics and Confucian Ethics," particularly the third and fourth sections. In my chapter I focus more directly on the process or practice of "learning and reflection" (*xue* and *si*) as a key "sub-theme" of the *Analects*, whereas Chen focuses on "love of learning" (*hao xue*) as itself a distinct virtue, specifically an "intellectual virtue" of the Aristotelian sort. Despite potentially significant differences in our approaches (for example, I am not inclined to characterize love of learning or learning and reflection as intellectual or "educational" virtues, in the Greek sense), we both agree that learning is *foundational* in the text.

9 7.20, 2.9, 6.7, 11.4, 16.9.

10 My thanks to Stephen Angle for help with interpretive questions. The text says "*san nian you cheng*," which Angle explains does not make explicit any idea of "transformation," as Slingerland infers. Angle suggests "there will be some achievements" as a possible reading, or "the process will be complete." Other interpretations read "in a year's time I would have brought things to a satisfactory state, and after three years I should have results to show for it" (Confucius 2003), and "… in the course of one year I could make a difference, and in three years I would really have something to show for it" (Confucius 1999).

11 I draw here on analyses like Lisa Raphals's (2003) and Rui Zhu's (2006), which highlight the crucial temporal dimension of the Confucian cosmology by emphasizing the importance of *shi* (timeliness) alongside *tian* (Heaven) and the earthly community. In contrast, Ning Chen analyzes fate in terms of Confucian thinking on the "supernatural," but not history, situatedness or temporality (Chen 2003). On the relationship between ethics and historicity, as articulated regarding the Confucian tradition by Zhang Xuecheng, see Ivanhoe 2009a, Ivanhoe 2009b, Nivison 1996, Wang 2002.

12 For an elaboration of the point via the language of moral luck (and in comparison with Aristotle), see Sean Walsh's chapter in this volume. My point here about human limitations, or fate, highlights dimensions of the second and third form of moral luck that Walsh examines.

13 See also 14.32, 14.35, 14.38, 14.39. In a less resolute moment, see 9.9.

14 Of course, this claim requires addressing how we should understand passages such as 8.14 ("Do not discuss matters of government policy that do not fall within the scope of your official duties") and 14.26 ("The gentleman's thoughts do not go beyond his office").

17 Is Conscientiousness a Virtue? Confucian Answers

1 My thanks to Bryan Van Norden and Eric Hutton for helpful comments on an early draft, as well as to participants in the Virtue Ethics and Confuciaism Conference for their feedback and encouragement.

2 Adams writes that "conscientiousness may be taken to be the virtue of excellent responsiveness to obligations one really has to other persons" [Adams 2006, 34]; see also [Wallace 1978]. Roberts says that the "sense of duty or obligation" is a quasi-virtue: "If we can't get people to be concerned about one another, maybe we can get them to feel that they have some mutual obligations" [Roberts 1991, 333]. Slote begins an extensive discussion of conscientiousness by saying, "to the extent we make use of moral rules or claims to guide our actions toward others or have an intrinsic conscientious concern with the moral character of our actions, our connection with other people is less immediate, less personal, than if we simply concern ourselves with their welfare" [Slote 2001, 49].

3 [McDowell 1979], and contrast [Stohr 2003] and [Eylon 2009].

4 We should distinguish the above uses from uses of "conscientiousness" according to which it is a kind of special attentiveness or moral seriousness, the opposite of which is to be overly light hearted or blasé [Kupperman 1991, 72], which seems more like what Roberts calls "virtues of will power" [Roberts 1991, 332n12].

5 This is true throughout the text, from consensus early passages like 5:25 to consensus late passages like 17:13.

6 It is striking that in a recent conference presentation, Hagop Sarkissian translated *zhong*, which I have here rendered as "devotion," as "conscientiousness." I take it that this is a similar sense of "conscientiousness" to Kupperman's idea of attentiveness or moral seriousness; see note 4, above.

7 For one helpful perspective on this complex issue, see [Van Norden 2007, 270–272].

8 She builds on her own earlier work [Olberding 2007] and on that of scholars like Joel Kupperman [1999] and Gier [2001].

9 [Olberding 2009, 510]. She cites *Analects* 1:10, 9:6, and 19:24 as evidence.

10 [Ibid.]. Olberding offers *Analects* 5:15 and 14:29, among other passages, as evidence that Zigong needs to get beyond surface evaluations of others (and of himself). There is a degree to which Olberding's portrait of Zigong is based on imaginative reading between the lines, but even if we were to insist that one or another aspect of her characterization fits the "real" Zigong poorly, her character sketch still serves to illustrate what may be worrisome about conscientiousness.

11 On "semblances" of virtue in the context of Confucianism, see [Mengzi, 2008, 196] and [Yearley 1990].

12 From Mencius's statement that they "regard themselves as right (*zi yi wei shi*)," we can tell that they are aware of what they are doing. They are conformists, but not mindless conformists. I thank participants in the Warp, Weft, and Way blog for helping me to clarify this; see < http://warpweftandway.wordpress.com>.

13 I discuss reasons why Confucians resist the idea that we should distinguish going beyond the moral minimum as "supererogation" in [Angle 2009a, 29].

14 We will see below that Xunzi does not believe benevolence and righteousness to be "internal," but still can make the distinction that Mencius draws here between virtue and conscientiousness.

15 Zhu Xi's commentary makes this point explicit: "If we examine Cao Jiao's questions, we see they are shallow and simplistic. He must be at the point where he is only beginning to see things.... Thus, Mencius answers him in this manner" [Mengzi 2008, 160]

16 Van Norden's translation has "act out *of* sympathetic understanding." The language is very similar to 4B:19, but unfortunately 7A:4 is too concise to make clear whether "act out of" or "act out" is more apt. If we follow Van Norden, the idea has to be that one can force oneself to act from one kind of motive rather than another, and that this is an important step toward developing a robust disposition to act virtuously.

17 I have found the chapter on Xunzi in [Slingerland 2003] to be very helpful in thinking through the issues of this section. References to Xunzi are as follows: "K" refers to Knoblock's translation [Xunzi 1990]; volumes are distinguished by Roman numerals. "Li" refers to Li Tisheng's Chinese edition [Xunzi 1979]. I have also benefitted greatly from Eric Hutton's as-yet unpublished translation.

18 *Zhi* is an important technical term for Xunzi that also plays a significant role in earlier Confucianism. Stalnaker's discussion is incisive; he glosses it as "settled intention" or "our ultimate aspiration or standard" [Stalnaker 2006, 255]. Because it is also something that we can consciously take on and something that can deepen over time, I suggest the translation of "commitment." For further discussion, see [Angle 2009a, 114–115].

19 See also [K II, 75; Li 140], wherein Xunzi says that the virtue of the common people "consists in considering goodness to be following common usages"; this resonates more directly with Mencius's concerns about the village worthy.

20 [Li 33]; translation substantially altered from [K I, 156].

21 For a different version of this story, see [Mencius 1970, 217].

22 [Li 493]; my translations draw partly on [K III, 108].

23 [Ibid].

24 [Li 527]; this translation is drawn, with only minor changes, from Hutton's unpublished translation.

25 David Wong explicitly denies the Kantian parallel [Wong 2000, 141].

26 [Li 527]; my translation. Compare [Hsün Tzu 1963, 150–1].

27 Xunzi insists that all people can "approve" at [Li 195]; see [K II, 120]. Eric Hutton helpfully insisted that I take this fact more fully into account.

28 The commitment of the "common mass of humanity," recall, is such that they are crooked and selfish, presumably as a result of simply following their desires. In this case, we have what is referred to in my main text as an "empty" process of approval (and commitment). I thank Eric Hutton for pointing out that Xunzi makes a distinction between synchronic and diachronic senses of "deliberate activity (*wei*)"; see [Li 506], [K III, 127], and [Hsün Tzu 1963, 139–40]. Hutton suggests that one can also see synchronic and diachronic dimensions to approval and commitment. This makes sense, and viewing null cases of "empty" approval and commitment, as I have suggested, helps us to see the continuity between synchronic and diachronic perspectives.

29 In an excellent recent book comparing Xunzi with Augustine, Aaron Stalnaker points out that, for Augustine, continence is in fact a critical kind of virtue, since virtue itself for Augustine is simply the "continuous striving for something higher, not repose in dependable excellences of character" [Stalnaker 2006, 259]. Concerning Xunzi's understanding of continence, Stalnaker writes (replacing "assent" with the "approval" we have been using): "He seems to have a similar concept, but the idea appears to be relatively uninteresting to him theoretically because he thinks the power of [approval] is common to all humans, and so he is much more concerned with how we might learn to what we should [approve]" [Ibid]. Stalnaker adds elsewhere that according to Xunzi, "even the uncultivated have full possession of the innate power to [approve or disapprove of] particular desires" [Ibid, 256], and so Stalnaker emphasizes Xunzi's "deep distinction between, on the one hand, our initially innate system of spontaneous responsiveness to our environment that includes our dispositions and desires and, the other hand, the reflective and deliberative desires that consist in our judgment of [approval]" [Ibid, 259]. In all of this, Stalnaker seems to be pointing us in a slightly wrong direction, on the one hand drawing too sharp a distinction between "approval" and our transformed dispositions, and on the other hand downplaying the other discussions of continence (or conscientiousness) because they do not fit well enough with "approval." But if approval is what I have just argued, then it fits much better into a single picture. (Indeed, my understanding of the role that "commitment" plays for Xunzi—which is an important link between continence and approval—owes much to Stalnaker's discussion [Ibid, 255].

30 [Wiggins 1996, 132]. The following example from Hume cannot but remind one of *Mencius* 2A:6, in which Mencius claims we will all feel alarm and empathy upon seeing a child about to fall into a well: "A parent flies to the relief of his child; transported by the natural sympathy which actuates him and which affords no leisure to reflect on the sentiments or conduct of the rest of mankind in like circumstances" [quoted in Ibid]. For further discussion of similarities between Hume and Mencius, see [Liu 2003] and [Slote 2009].

31 For contrasting views, see Lee Ming-huei's essay in this volume, and [Liu 2004].
32 See [McDowell 1979], [Stohr 2003], and [Eylon 2009].

18 The Virtues of Justice in Zhu Xi

1 This chapter is a revised version of an earlier draft which I presented at the conference "Confucianism and Virtue Ethics" in Beijing (May 2010). I am grateful to Michael Slote and Steve Angle for inviting me to be part of this conference, and the participants for their helpful comments. I also owe thanks to Jonathan Keir and James Friesen for proofreading the final draft. It also needs to be mentioned that work on this chapter has been generously supported by the Taiwanese National Research Council.

2 Here I am thinking of modern Chinese scholars like Mou Zongsan, Lao Sze-kwang, Yu Yingshi, Chen Lai, or Lee Ming-huei.

3 In a similar vein, Erin M. Cline speaks of a "sense of justice" in Early Confucianism [Cline 2007].

4 See [Zhu Xi 1999, 104; 105; 108; 109; 111; passim].

5 On the background see [Nivison 1996, 17–31], [Yu 2007, 28–32], [Angle 2009a, 51–59], and [Huang Yong 2011]. Zhu Xi essentially accepts the particular virtues described in the Confucian classics [Yu 2007, 160], but values the virtue of "reverence" (*jing*) more than earlier Confucians [Angle 2009a, 151–158].

6 Compare [Shun 2010b]. The term "moral psychology" should, however, be used carefully in Zhu Xi's case: Unlike Aristotle, he was not necessarily interested in empirical descriptions of human psychology, but always presupposed a very particular understanding of moral inwardness.

7 See in particular Zhu's interpretation of the "four sprouts" (*si duan*) in the famous passage *Mencius* 2A/6 [Zhu Xi 2001, 237–238]; compare [Menzi 2008, 45–47].

8 See [Zhu 1999, 88; 260–261; 263–264; 271].

9 In this sense, Wing-tsit Chan translates the term *de* in Zhu Xi's "Treatise on Humaneness" as "character" or "moral quality" of the "heart-mind" [Chan 1963, 593–594].

10 Thus, I don't agree with Lee Ming-huei, who claims that, in *Analects* 17.21, "Confucius explicitly expresses his deontological viewpoint" [the present volume, p. 50; compare Lee Ming-huei 1999]. Admittedly, Confucius here is articulating something akin to a general rule of how we should treat our parents. However, Confucian texts nowhere articulate the idea of a universal law with its strictly *formal* requirements on the agent, that is, of course, a constitutive feature of the deontological account of rational willing.

11 This is Mou Zongsan's main criticism of Zhu Xi: that, for Zhu, the "heart-mind" does not "originally contain" (*ben ju*) the *li* ("coherence", "principle"), but needs to be purified in a process of self-cultivation, until it "ultimately contains" (*dang ju*) the latter [Mou 1968/1969, 3: 243; compare Billioud 2011, 36–38; 172–174].

12 See his "Treatise on Humaneness" [Zhu 2000, 3390–3391; compare Chan 1963, 594].

13 See [Slote 2001, 7–8]; compare [Angle 2009a, 84–85].

14 See [Thomas Lee 1995, 125]; compare [Yang Xiao 1997] and [Joseph Chan 2008].

15 [Zhu 2001, 48]; compare [Angle 2009a, 56]; [Qian 1994, 1: 85–86]. Zhu Xi's extensive commentary to the *Four Books* (the *Greater Learning*, the *Doctrine of the Mean*, the *Analects*, and the *Mencius*) contains the essentials of his cosmological, moral, and political thought [compare Gardner 2007].

16 See [Zhu 2000, 3391] and [Mou 1968–69, 3: 244].

17 Compare [Qian 1994, 2: 145–154].

18 See [Zhu 2001, 207–212]; compare [Gardner 2003, 52–76].

19 See NE 1131a29 [Aristotle 2004, 119]; and NE 1129b1 [Aristotle 2004, 113].

20 For a more detailed discussion of *yi* see [Yang Xiao 1997, 535–540].

21 See [MacIntyre 1988, 122]; [Annas 1993, 312–316]; and [Frank 2005, 81–111].

22 See [*Analects* 6.4/6.5]; [Zhu 2001, 85]. The meaning of this passage is controversial; my analysis is based on Zhu Xi's explanatory glosses [compare Confucius 2003, 53–54].

23 [Zhu 2001, 92]; for the translation see [Gardner 2003, 59].

24 See [Yu 2003, 1: 238–251].

25 For a paradigmatic case see [Zhu 1999, 368–369]; compare *Analects* 6.4, 13.9, 16.1, *Mencius* 1A/5, 1A/7, 1B/5, 3A/3, 7A/23, passim.

26 Compare [Shun 2005]. As Justin Tiwald has demonstrated, Mencius does not grant the people a true *right* to rebellion, and I believe the same holds true for Zhu Xi [Tiwald 2008, 281]. The idea of appealing to a claim-right goes against the general Confucian attitude that one should not demand from others what one needs, but instead concentrate on the cultivation of one's moral self (*fan qi ben* or *fan qiu zhu ji*) – it is to be expected that one's moral perfection will lead others to give what one is in need of [Zhu 2001, 165–166, 208; 211, passim].

27 These two models are known in Chinese as *wu wo wei yi* and *yi jue xun ren* [Zhu 2000, 3392]; compare [Chan 1963, 597].

28 It must appear paradoxical to the Western reader that Zhu can encompass these two dimensions, affective and cosmic, in one single definition: however, in the Neo-Confucian worldview, our "nature," the stillness of our most inner self (the state before any emotion has arisen), directly connects us with the totality of the universe, so Zhu Xi's solution represents the middle between a too externalized understanding of "humaneness" (as affective and thus not closely enough tied to our inner self) and a too internalized understanding where we merely concentrate on the stillness of our inner self and the search for cosmic unity in ourselves, but neglect our feelings and our daily interaction with other people.

29 See *Mencius* 1B/1 [Zhu 2001, 214]; compare *Mencius* 7A/45 [Zhu 2001, 363].

30 See [Zhu 2001, 13; 72; 130; 157]; [Zhu 1999, 256; 367; 398; 695; 1462; passim].

31 See *Mencius* 1A/7 [Zhu 2001, 210–212]. It needs to be pointed out that the well-field system represents an idealized and rather vague blueprint for social reform from the Confucian past, not an arithmetic model of distribution. Especially the late Zhu had doubts whether it could be restored in the present.

32 For the cosmic dimension see Zhu's use of this formula in his commentary to *Analects* 11.26 [Zhu 2001, 130].

33 Compare Zhu Xi's comments on *Analects* 4.11 [Zhu 2001, 71–72], *Mencius* 3A/3 [Zhu 2001, 254–257], and *Mencius* 4A/1 [Zhu 2001, 275–276].

34 This becomes especially clear in Zhu's interpretation of two famous cases, *Analects* 13.18 about the father who stole a sheep, and *Mencius* 7A/35 about Shun's father having killed someone [Zhu 2001, 146, 359–360].

35 As far as the Neo-Confucian discourse is concerned, I do not agree with Yu Jiyuan, who seems to believe that Confucians have an explicit notion of external goods [Yu 2007, 185–189].

36 For a rare example where Zhu Xi actually compares the contribution of different virtues and multiple actors, see his gloss on *Analects* 14.34 [Zhu 2001, 157]. Interestingly, Zhu here again refers to the formula "letting each receive his or her allotment."

37 This fear is evident in his gloss on *Analects* 14.29 [Zhu 2001, 156].

38 See *Analects* 5.12 and Zhu's gloss [Zhu 2001, 78–79]; compare [Gardner 2003, 54–56] and [Nivison 1996, 69–70].

39 See [Gardner 2003, 54–56]. I think that Mou Zongsan is right when he posits that Neo-Confucians want us "to turn from quantity to substance" (*you liang gui zhi zhi*; [Mou 1968–69, 3: 250–251]), i.e., from the sphere of measures and transactions to a higher sphere of true individuality.

40 For example, it could be illuminating to investigate possible similarities between the Aristotelian tradition of social justice and Zhu Xi's thought (which, not coincidentally, plays a crucial role in the recent work of the Chinese Neo-Marxist Wang Hui).

19 Is Empathy the "One Thread" Running through Confucianism?

1 All passages of the *Analects* are quoted from Confucius (2003).

2 Admittedly, there is a big difference between a student's summary of Confucius' underlying philosophy and the word Confucius offers as a guide to another student, given Confucius' tendency to tailor the message to the student (e.g., 11:22). The extent to which the "One Thread" can be seen as a doctrine of Confucius has been debated, but both Van Norden (2002) and Brooks and Brooks (1998) have made convincing cases for regarding 4:15 and related *shu* passages as later interpolations. Nevertheless, these passages were of great importance to later Confucians (especially the Neo-Confucians of the Song and Ming periods, and Tiwald has argued that the Qing Confucian thinker Dai Zhen was a strong advocate of *shu* as the core of moral judgment (Tiwald 2010)), and so the question remains as to whether the "One Thread" can be equated with empathy in some parts of the Confucian tradition.

3 It is not my intent to contribute to the ongoing debate concerning the relationship between *zhong* and *shu* and the parallel (or lack thereof) to the Golden Rule. For those interested in that particular debate Chan (1999) provides a good overview of the major players in the debate.

4 As found in Ivanhoe and Van Norden (2001). The 2005 edition retains "sympathetic understanding." It is not clear if Slingerland decided to go back to this usage or it wasn't updated. The fact that the Glossary entry on *shu* in Slingerland's 2003 translation mentions "sympathetic understanding" would suggest he has not abandoned the notion.

5 Coplan (2011) has argued that in spite of the many linguistic uses of "empathy," we should employ "empathy" in a narrow sense. I would argue against such a move because it is not easy in practice to separate out the different processes that are referred to by "empathy."

6 In trying to set a distinction between these two terms, people will sometimes appeal to linguistic intuitions about the ways in which those words are used. Unfortunately, there no longer seem to be consistent intuitions about their usage, due both to the fact that different disciplines choose to cut the distinctions in different ways and to the inherent fuzziness of the term (which I'll later argue exists for a reason). For example, Tiwald describes "imaginative reconstruction" and "simulation of feelings" as things we associate with "sympathy" (and he is not alone in doing so), but for a number of people "sympathy" can refer only to our attitude towards other people's suffering (Tiwald 2010, p. 78).

7 Prinz (2011) is a recent example of this kind of critique that argues that both Hume and Slote fail to appreciate that our empathetic reactions are not always consistent with our considered moral judgments. The problem with Prinz's critique is that it assumes that there is no corrective for empathic responses. Hourdequin (in this volume) also raises issues about Slote's empathy-based ethic, using examples from the *Mengzi* where *shu* does not seem to provide an unambiguous moral judgment. However, Hourdequin does recognize that the later Confucian tradition might provide a corrective in the form of *li* as a metaphysical concept or *li* as ritual.

8 He has since used "sympathetic understanding" (Ivanhoe 2002) and "sympathetic concern" (Ivanhoe 2000a).

9 The analogical thinking interpretation of *shu* that Nivison (1996) and Lau (2003) argue for could be understood as a form of logical inference, largely devoid of simulation, using rules like the principle of reversibility or extension. I'm not claiming that that is how every proponent of *shu* as analogical thinking understands the process, only that there is so far nothing to exclude that interpretation.

10 Ironically, in situations where an inference can happen quickly (for example, a child falls down and cries) we may not notice that it has happened. Thus, cognitive empathy is often ignored because it does not leave much of an impression, when compared to affective empathy.

11 This idea about the role of emotions in cognition has been gaining steam in recent decades, but I am not weighing in on whether it is actually true. However, it would have to be true in order for an affective state to be considered a form of understanding.

12 Affective empathy may have developed as a workaround to deal with the limits of the inference-based approach of cognitive empathy in complex emotional situations.

13 Hourdequin (in this volume) discusses how empathy seems to fall short in the classic child falling down a well example from the *Mengzi*.

14 All quotes from the *Mengzi* are from Menzi (2008).

15 One response to this could be to collapse the divide between emotion and concern by associating empathy with a particular emotional state (an attention to the needs of others that might be called "empathic concern," "compassion," or "benevolence"). Several passages in the *Analects* and later Confucian works suggest that empathic concern is at the heart of Confucian ideals. Confucius recommends that a young person "should display a general care for the masses" (1:6). And when asked about *ren*, Confucius says "Care for others" (12:22). Mengzi continues this way of talking about the virtuous person in his discussion with King Xuan about the ox (1A7). The paper can't explore all permutations of empathy in detail, but empathic concern would face the same metaethical issue as affective empathy (what makes the feeling of empathic concern a moral sentiment).

16 At least any form that wishes to avoid moral relativism.

17 Interestingly, for the International Conference on Confucianism and Virtue Ethics where a draft of this paper was presented, "empathy" was translated as *tongqing* (literally "share/same emotion"), but that actually surprised one of the attendees who thought it should be *yiqing* (literally, "move/transform emotion"). During the Q&A, Ellen Zhang reported that *yiqing* was used to translate "empathy" when it was first introduced through discussions of Chinese aesthetics that drew upon sources in the Continental tradition and that *yiqing* has been the preferred translation in philosophical circles. But the Continental tradition would not define "empathy" as projecting oneself onto another but, rather, as a form of engagement with the other, so it seems that even in Chinese it is not clear which phenomenon is referred to by each term.

18 The connection between mirror neurons and empathy is explored in (among other places) Preston and de Waal (2002). However, it is worth noting that the evidence for mirror neurons in humans (as opposed to monkeys, where they were originally observed) is still deemed controversial.

19 Gordon's presentation of simulation (Gordon 1995) also makes de-centering the ego the essential part of the process.

20 Some support for Dai Zhen's view also being present in the *Analects* can be found in the *Exoteric Commentary* on *Analects* 15:25, which says, "The fact that you hate hunger and cold allows you to understand that everyone in the world desires food and clothing" (quoted in Confucius (2003), p. 183).

21 Ivanhoe's essay in this volume references the psychological case for oneness being more important than affective empathy in moral action.

22 One possibility worth exploring is that the rituals which shape our moral judgments are themselves the products of empathy. Cognitive or affective empathy may have guided early societies to the kinds of practices that produced the greatest satisfaction for each participant. Of course, to be viable as an empathy-based ethic, the account must be structured so that empathy does more than track underlying social values. Almost no one would deny that empathy is a useful heuristic for moral judgment, but an empathy-based ethic goes beyond that to argue that empathy is the source of justification for at least some of those moral judgments.

20 The Limits of Empathy

1 I have been tempted to read Slote's book, *The Ethics of Care and Empathy* [2007], as offering a care- and empathy-based virtue ethics that builds on his proposal in *Morals from Motives* [2001], but Slote wants to remain neutral in his 2007 book about whether the theory should be construed in virtue-ethical terms.

2 A substantial body of literature emphasizes that Mencius holds that human nature

is inherently good, whereas Xunzi thinks that human nature is bad. The associated suggestion is that morality develops naturally, according to Mencius, whereas it must be inculcated through outside influence, according to Xunzi. As Eric Schwitzgebel [2007, 153] describes the question at the center of the debate: "Is morality something imposed on people from outside (Xunzi) or something that arises in the normal process of human development if people are encouraged to reflect (Mencius)?" Philip Ivanhoe's [2000, ch. 2] interpretation of Mencius tends in the direction of the natural development model, although Ivanhoe acknowledges that self-cultivation in the form of reflection (*si*) is required to become fully moral, and he concurs with the (widely accepted and textually well-supported) idea discussed below that, at minimum, certain background conditions are required in order for virtue to develop.

3 These issues are discussed in detail in ch. 2 of Slote [2007].

4 Cf. Singer [1972], Unger [1996].

5 See Terjesen [this volume] for related discussion. Terjesen notes that an ethic based on empathy faces a justificatory challenge because not all empathic sentiments are *moral* sentiments.

6 Quoted text from the *Mencius* follows D.C. Lau's translation.

7 That is, the developmental model at work here seems compatible with an account along the lines of Slote's – though the broader Mencian view of morality does not seem to resemble an account based exclusively on empathic caring (at least not on its face), as Mencius observes in 2A6 that there is not just one sprout (the heart of compassion, which is the source of benevolence), but four, including also the heart of "shame" (which leads to righteousness), of "courtesy and modesty" (which leads to propriety), and "right and wrong" (which leads to wisdom). Nevertheless, there is a possible reading of Mencius that makes the heart of compassion primary and thereby comes closer to a Slote-style view of morality. On this point, see ch. 2, note 15 of P. J. Ivanhoe's *Confucian Moral Self-Cultivation* [2000] and Liu Xiusheng [2003, ch. 2].

8 Whether this failure of extension reflects a lack of fully developed compassion or, alternatively, a failure to properly direct compassion that *is* fully developed is an issue taken up below. Thanks to Bryan Van Norden, Michael Slote, Eric Hutton, and Craig Ihara for pushing me to consider the former (and probably more standard) interpretation.

9 As Im puts it: "the ethically exemplary person has emotional reactions that make it necessary to avoid certain situations that produce them" [Im 1999, 6].

10 In *Burdened Virtues*, Lisa Tessman [2005] questions whether there exists any ideal of excellence with respect to empathic engagement with the suffering of others. In her chapter, "Between Indifference and Anguish," Tessman argues that there is no Aristotelian mean to be found here. As she puts it, "Because every possible intermediate point in the sphere of sensitivity and attention to others' suffering is marked by indifference and anguish, I am reluctant to characterize any point as an excellent one in any unqualified sense. [Although there may be some morally best balance] … simple excellence is not possible in this sphere given the background conditions and … even the best choices fail to enable flourishing and may even fail to preserve virtue itself" [87].

11 I believe that this position, even if it can be saved by folding elements such as the wisdom to balance competing moral demands into "fully developed human empathy," misleadingly suggests a unified, species-wide trajectory for the development of a kind of empathy that is both necessary and sufficient for moral action.

12 Thanks to Rick Furtak for suggesting to me an example along these lines.

13 Here I am referring to the broad meaning of *ren* that figures centrally in the *Analects* of Confucius. *Ren* in this sense is an overarching virtue that encompasses all the others. Mencius, too, uses *ren* in this broad sense, though he more frequently speaks of *ren* in the narrower sense of compassion or empathy.

14 Terjesen [this volume] makes a related suggestion, drawing on the work of Bo Mou.

15 In Mencius, *zhi* (which Van Norden [2008, 207] describes as "a virtue that consists

of understanding the other virtues, being a good judge of the character of others, and skill at means–end deliberation") perhaps gets closest to this idea of practical wisdom; in Confucius, *yi* is, arguably, the relevant concept. Jiyuan Yu [2006] argues for a close analogy between practical wisdom (*phronesis*) in Aristotle and *yi* in Confucius. He suggests that *yi* involves understanding what a particular situation calls for, or what is appropriate to the situation.

16 Jiyuan Yu [2006, 340], for example, argues that *yi* is "conditioned by the social rites" and is "historically and socially rooted." This is consistent with the view that the *li* play an important role in guiding and modulating moral and emotional responses.

17 Conversely, a parent's emotional engagement with his/her child may lead to excessively harsh or overly emotional responses to the child: Im [1999] cites *Mencius* 4A18 on this point. In this passage, Mencius suggests that the *junzi* does not educate his own son because a father is prone to excessive anger when his son fails to follow parental teachings. Im takes this as further support for the Mencian thesis that emotional responses can and should be controlled by selective exposure to certain circumstances: "the ethically exemplary person has emotional reactions that make it necessary to avoid certain situations that produce them" [1999, 6].

References

Adams, Robert Merrihew. 2006. *A Theory of Virtue: Excellence in Being for the Good*. Oxford: Oxford University Press.

Allan, Sarah. 1997. *The Way of Water and Sprouts of Virtue*. New York: State University of New York Press.

Angle, Stephen C. 2009a. *Sagehood: The Contemporary Significance of Neo-Confucian Philosophy*. New York: Oxford University Press.

———. 2009b. "Defining 'Virtue Ethics' and Exploring Virtues in a Comparative Context." In *Dao: A Journal of Comparative Philosophy* 8:3. 297–304.

———.2010. "Wang Yangming as a Virtue Ethicist." In John Makeham, ed., *Dao Companion to Neo-Confucian Philosophy*. Dordrecht: Springer. 315–335.

———. 2011. "Zhu Xi's Virtue Ethics and the Grotian Challenge." In David Jones and He Jinli, eds., *Zhu Xi Now: Contemporary Encounters with the Great Ultimate*. New York: SUNY Press.

Annas, Julia. 1993. *The Morality of Happiness*. New York, Oxford: Oxford University Press.

Anscombe, G. E. M. 1958. "Modern Moral Philosophy." *Philosophy* 33. 1–19. Also in G. E. M. Anscombe, *The Collected Philosophical Papers of G. E .M. Anscombe*. 1981. Oxford: Blackwell. Vol. 3: "Ethics, Religion and Politics." 26–42.

Appiah, Kwame Anthony. 2008. *Experiments in Ethics*. Cambridge: Harvard University Press.

Aquinas, Thomas. 1981. *Summa Theologiæ* 5. Fathers of the English Dominican Province, trans. Notre Dame, IN: Christian Classics.

Arendt, Hannah. 1963. *Eichmann in Jerusalem: A Report on the Banality of Evil*. New York: Viking Press.

Aristotle. 1926. *The Nicomachean Ethics*. H. Cambridge Rackham, trans. Massachusetts: Harvard University Press; London: William Heinemann Ltd.

———. *Ethica Nicomachea*. In *Works of Aristotle*, vol. ix. Oxford: Oxford University Press.

———. 1984. *The Complete Works of Aristotle: The Revised Oxford Translation*. Jonathan Barnes, ed. Princeton, NJ: Princeton University Press.

———. 1999. *Nicomachean Ethics*. Terence Irwin, trans. Indianapolis: Hackett Publishing.

———. 2000. *Nicomachean Ethics*, trans. Roger Crisp. Cambridge: Cambridge University Press

Bao, Yongling 鮑永玲. 2012. *Seed and Light: A General Examination of the Metaphor System in Wang Yangming's Doctrine of Mind-Heart* 種子與靈光: 王陽明心學喻象體系通論. Shanghai 上海: Shanghai Shudian Chubanshe上海书店出版社.

Batson, C. Daniel. 1987. "Prosocial Motivation: Is It Ever Truly Altruistic?" In L. Berkowitzed., *Advances in Experimental Social Psychology*. New York: Academic Press. 65–122.

Bell, Daniel A. 2000. *East Meets West: Human Rights and Democracy in East Asia*. Princeton, NJ: Princeton University Press.

Benson, H. 1987. "The Problem of the Elenchos Reconsidered." *Ancient Philosophy* 7. 67–85.

Berlin, I. 1997. "The Pursuit of the Ideal." In *The Proper Study of Mankind.* NY: Farrar, Straus, and Giroux.

Betzler, Monika. 2008. *Kant's Ethics of Virtue.* Berlin: Walter de Gruyter.

Billioud, Sébastien, 2011. *Thinking Through Confucian Modernity, A Study of Mou Zongsan's Moral Metaphysics.* Leiden: Brill.

Bloom, Irene. 1997. "Human Nature and Biological Nature in Mencius." *Philosophy East and West* 47. 21–32.

Brickhouse, T. and Smith, N. 1994. *Plato's Socrates.* Oxford: Oxford University Press.

Brooks, E. Bruce and Brooks, Taeko. 1998. *The Original Analects: Sayings of Confucius and his Successors.* New York: Columbia University Press, 1998.

Button, Mark. 2005. "'A Monkish Kind of Virtue'? For and Against Humility." *Political Theory* 33:6. 840–868.

Cai, Xin'an 蔡信安. 1987. "Lun Mengzi de daode jueze" 論孟子的德抉擇 [On Mencius' Moral Choice]. *Taiwan Daxue zhexue lunping* 臺灣大學哲學論評[Philosophical Review of National Taiwan University] 10. 135–175.

——. 2002. "Mengzi: dexing yu yuanze" 孟子：德行與原則 [Mencius: Virtue and Principle]. *Taiwan Daxue zhexue lunping* 25. 41–63.

Cao, Xueqin. 1982. *Story of the Stone, also Known as Dream of the Red Chamber.* Vol. 4. John Minford, trans. New York: Penguin Books.

Chan, Joseph. 2008. "Is there a Confucian Perspective on Social Justice?" In Takahashi Shogimen and Cary J. Nederman, eds., *Western Political Thought in Dialogue with Asia.* Lanhan, MD: Rowman & Littlefield. 261–277.

Chan, Sin-yee. 1999. "Disputes on the One Thread of Chung-shu." *Journal of Chinese Philosophy* 26:2. 165–186.

Chan, Wing-Tsit. 1963. *A Source Book in Chinese Philosophy.* Princeton, NJ: Princeton University Press.

Chen, Ning. 1997. "Confucius's View of Fate (*Ming*)." *Journal of Chinese Philosophy* 24. 323–359.

Chen, Yun 陳贇. 2003. "The Good of Human Nature." *Journal of Modern Philosophy:* 現代哲學 1. 82–88.

Cheng, Hao, and Cheng, Yi. 1989. *Collected Works of Cheng Brothers* 二程集. Beijing: Zhonghua Shuju 中華書局.

Ching, Julia. 1976. *To Acquire Wisdom: The Way of Wang Yang-ming.* New York: Columbia University Press.

Cialdini, Robert B., Brown, Stephanie L., Lewis, Brian P., Luce, Carol, and Neuberg, Steven L. 1997. "Reinterpreting the Empathy–Altruism Relationship: When One into One Equals Oneness." *Journal of Personality and Social Psychology* 73:3.

Cicero. 2001. *On Moral Ends.* Julia Annas, trans. Oxford: Oxford University Press.

Cline, Erin M. 2007. "Two Senses of Justice: Confucianism, Rawls, and Comparative Political Philosophy." In *Dao: A Journal of Comparative Philosophy* 6. 361–381

Cohen, Dov, Hoshino-Browne, Etsuko, and Leung, Angela K.Y. 2007. "Culture and the Structure of Personal Experience: Insider and Outsider Phenomenologies of the Self and Social World." *Advances in Experimental Social Psychology* 39.1–67.

Confucius. 1979. *Analects.* D. C. Lau, trans. New York: Penguin.

——. 1999. *The Analects: A Philosophical Translation.* Roger Ames and Henry Rosemont Jr., trans. New York: Ballantine Books.

——. 2002. *Analects.* D. C. Lau, trans. Hong Kong: Chinese University Press.

——. 2003. *Analects, With Selections from Traditional Commentaries.* Edward Slingerland, trans. Indianapolis: Hackett.

Cooper, John M. 1985. "Aristotle on the Goods of Fortune." *The Philosophical Review* 94. 173–196.

——. 1987. "Contemplation and Happiness: A Reconsideration." *Synthèse* 72. 187–216.

Coplan, Amy. 2011. "Will the Real Empathy Please Stand Up? A Case for Narrow Conceptualization." *The Southern Journal of Philosophy, Spindel Supplement* 49. 40–65.

Cua, Antonio S. 1982. *The Unity of Knowledge and Action.* Honolulu: University Press of Hawaii.

Curzer, Howard. 2005. "How Good People Do Bad Things: Aristotle on the Misdeeds of the Virtuous." *Oxford Studies in Ancient Philosophy* 28. 233–256.

Dancy, Jonathan. 1982. "Intuitionism in Meta-epistemology." *Philosophical Studies* 42. 395–408.

——. 1993. *Moral Reason.* Oxford, UK and Cambridge, US: Blackwell.

——. 2004. *Ethics without Principles.* Oxford: Oxford University Press.

——. 2009/2001. "Moral Particularism." In Edward N. Zalta ed., *The Stanford Encyclopedia of Philosophy* (Spring 2009 Edition). URL <http://plato.stanford.edu/archives/spr2009/entries/moral-particularism/>.

Davis, O.L., Yaeger, Elizabeth A., and Foster, Stuart J., eds. 2001. *Historical Empathy and Perspective Taking in the Social Studies.* Lanham, MD: Rowman and Littlefield.

de Bary, William Theodore and Bloom, Irene. 1999. *Sources of Chinese Tradition.* New York: Columbia University Press.

Decety, Jean and Lamm, Claus. 2009. "Empathy versus Personal Distress." In Jean Decety and William Ickes, eds., *The Social Neuroscience of Empathy.* Cambridge, MA: The MIT Press. 199–214.

Duan, Yucai 段玉裁. 1997. *Commentary on Xu Shen's Explanation of Chinese Characters* 說文解字注. Shanghai 上海: Shanghai Guji Chubanshe 上海古籍出版社.

Dworkin, R. 2006. *Justice in Robes.* Cambridge, MA: Harvard University Press.

Ekman, Paul. 2007. *Emotions Revealed: Recognizing Faces and Feelings to Improve Communication and Emotional Life.* 2nd Ed. New York: Holt.

Epley, Nicholas and Dunning, David. 2000. "Feeling 'Holier Than Thou': Are Self-serving Assessments Produced by Errors in Self or Social Prediction?" *Journal of Personality and Social Psychology* 79:6.

Esser, Andrew Marlen. 2004. *Eine Ethik für Endliche. Kants Tugendlehre in der Gegenwart.* Stuttgart-Bad Cannstatt: Frommann-Holzboog.

Exline, Julie Juola and Geyer, Anna L. 2004. "Perceptions of Humility: A Preliminary Study." *Self and Identity* 3. 95–114.

Eylon, Yuval. 2009. "Virtue and Continence." *Ethical Theory and Moral Practice* 12.137–51.

Foot, Philippa. 1978. *Virtues and Vices and Other Essays in Moral Philosophy.* Berkeley: University of California Press.

——. 2001. *Natural Goodness.* Oxford: Clarendon Press.

——. 2008. *Moral Dilemmas and Other Topics in Moral Philosophy.* Oxford: Clarendon Press.

Frank, Jill. 2005. *A Democracy of Distinction: Aristotle and the Work of Politics.* Chicago: The University of Chicago Press.

Frankena, William K. 1973. *Ethics.* Englewood Cliffs, NJ: Prentice-Hall.

Friedländer, Paul. 1970. *Plato: An Introduction.* Princeton, NJ: Princeton University Press.

Fu, Sinian 傅斯年. 2006. *A Critical Examination of the Ancient Meaning of Xing and Ming* 性命古訓辨證. Guilin 桂林: Guangxi Shifan Daxue Chubanshe 廣西師範大學出版社.

Gardner, Daniel K. 2003. *Zhu Xi's Reading of the Analects. Canon, Commentary, and the Classical Tradition.* New York: Columbia University Press.

——. 2007. *The Four Books: The Basic Teachings of the Later Confucian Tradition.* Indianapolis: Hackett Publishing.

Geach, P. 1977. *The Virtues.* Cambridge: Cambridge University Press.

Gier, Nicholas F. 2001. "The Dancing Ru: A Confucian Aesthetics of Virtue." *Philosophy East & West* 51:2. 280–305.

Gilligan, Carol. 1993. *In a Different Voice: Psychological Theory and Women's Development.* Cambridge, MA: Harvard University Press.

Gordon, Robert. 1995. "Sympathy, Simulation and the Impartial Spectator." *Ethics* 105:4. 727–742.

Graham, A.C. 1990 [1967]. "The Background of the Mencian Theory of Human Nature." In *Studies in Chinese Philosophy and Philosophical Literature.* Albany: State University of New York Press. 7–66.

——. 1990. *Studies in Chinese Philosophy and Philosophical Literature.* New York: State University of New York Press.

Guo Qingfan 郭慶藩. 2004. *Collected Commentaries on Zhuangzi* 莊子集釋. Beijing北京: Zhonghua Shuju中華書局.

Hadot, Pierre. 1995. *Philosophy as a Way of Life: Spiritual Exercises from Socrates to Foucault.* Cambridge, MA: Blackwell.

——. 2002. *What is Ancient Philosophy?* Cambridge, MA: The Belknap Press.

Hall, David L. and Ames, Roger T. 1987. *Thinking Through Confucius.* New York: SUNY Press.

Hampshire, Stuart. 1983. "Two Theories of Morality." In *Morality and Conflict.* Cambridge: Harvard University Press. 10–68.

Hardie, W.F.R. 1965. "The Final Good in Aristotle's Ethics." *Philosophy* 40:154. 277–295.

Harman, Gilbert. 2005. "Moral Particularism and Transduction." *Philosophical Issues* 15. 44–55.

Heinaman, Robert. 1988. "Eudaimonia and Self-sufficiency in Aristotle's *Nicomachean Ethics.*" *Phronesis* 33. 31–53.

Held, Virginia. 2006. "The Ethics of Care." In David Copp, ed., *The Oxford Handbook of Ethical Theory.* New York: Oxford University Press. 537–566.

Herdt, Jennifer A. 2009. "Christian Humility, Courtly Civility and the Code of the Streets." *Modern Theology* 25:4. 541–561.

Herodotus. 1996. *Histories.* Aubrey De Selincourt, trans. New York: Penguin Classics.

Hoffman, Martin. 2000. *Empathy and Moral Development: Implications for Caring and Justice.* New York: Cambridge University Press.

Hourdequin, Marion. 2005. *Nature and Normativity: Biology, Culture, and the Evolution of Ethical Norms.* Ph.D. dissertation, Duke University.

Hsün-tzu [Xunzi]. 1963. *Basic Writings.* Burton Watson, trans. New York: Columbia University Press.

Huang, Huo 黃藿. 1996. *Lixing dexing yu xingfu: Yalisiduode lunlixue yanjiu* 理性、德行與幸福－亞里斯多德倫理學研究 [Reason, Virtue, and Happiness: A Study of Aristotle's Ethics]. Taipei: Taiwan xuesheng shuju.

——. 1999. "Dexing lunlixue de fuxing yu dangdai daode jiaoyu" 德行倫理學的復興與當代道德教育 [The Revival of Virtue Ethics and Contemporary Moral Education]. *Shehui wenhua xuebao* 社會文化學報 [Journal of Culture and Society] 9:1–17. Also in *Zhexue yu wenhua* 哲學與文化 [Philosophy and Culture] 27:6 (2000): 522–531.

Huang, Jingxing 黃進興. 1994. *Youru shengyu: Quanli, xinyang yu zhengdangxing* 優入聖域－權力、信仰與正當性 [Ascending the Holy Realm: Power, Belief, and Legitimacy]. Taipei: Yunchen wenhua chuban gongsi.

Huang, Yong. 2003. "Cheng Brothers' Neo-Confucian Virtue Ethics: The Identity of Virtue and Nature." *Journal of Chinese Philosophy* 30. 451–467.

——. 2007. "Heaven, Principle, and Life-giving Activity: Cheng Hao's Neo-Confucian Conception of the Ultimate Reality." *Asian Philosophy* 17:3. 187–211.

——. 2008. "Why Be Moral?: The Cheng Brothers' Neo-Confucian Answer." *Journal of Religious Ethics* 36:2. 321–353.

——. 2011a. "The Self-centeredness Objection to Virtue Ethics: Zhu Xi's Neo-Confucian Response." *American Catholic Philosophical Quarterly* 84:4. 651–692.

——. 2011b. "Two Dilemmas of Virtue Ethics and how Zhu Xi's Neo-Confucianism Avoids Them." *Journal of Philosophical Research* 36. 247–281.

Hume, David. 1978. *A Treatise of Human Nature*. Oxford: Clarendon Press; New York: Oxford University Press.

Hursthouse, Rosalind. 1996. "Normative Virtue Ethics." In Roger Crisp, ed., *How Should One Live? Essays on the Virtues*. Oxford: Oxford University Press.

——. 1999. *On Virtue Ethics*. Oxford: Oxford University Press.

Hutton, Eric L. 2002. "Moral Reasoning in Aristotle and Xunzi." *Journal of Chinese Philosophy*. 29:3.

Im, Manyul. 1999. "Emotional Control and Virtue in the Mencius." *Philosophy East and West* 49:1. 1–27.

——. 2002. "Action, Emotion and Inference in Mencius." *Journal of Chinese Philosophy* 29:2. 227–249.

Irwin, Terence H. 1991. "The Structure of Aristotelian Happiness." *Ethics* 101. 382–391.

——. 1995. *Plato's Ethics*. New York: Oxford University Press.

Ivanhoe, Philip J. 1990a. *Ethics in the Confucian Tradition: The Thought of Mencius and Wang Yang-ming*. Atlanta: Scholars Press.

——. 1990b. "Reweaving the 'One Thread' of the Analects." *Philosophy East and West* 40:1. 17–33.

——. 2000. *Confucian Moral Self Cultivation*. 2nd Ed. Indianapolis: Hackett Publishing.

——. 2002a. *Ethics in the Confucian Tradition: The Thought of Mengzi and Wang Yangming*. 2nd Ed. Indianapolis, IN: Hackett Publishing.

——. 2002b. "Confucian Self-cultivation and Mengzi's Notion of Extension." In Xiusheng Liu and Philip J. Ivanhoe, eds., *Essays on the Moral Philosophy of Mengzi*. Indianapolis, IN: Hackett Publishing. 221–41.

——. 2007a. "Literature and Ethics in the Chinese Confucian Tradition." In Brad Wilburn, ed., *Moral Cultivation*. Lanham, MD: Rowan and Littlefield. 29–48.

——. 2007b. "Filial Piety as a Virtue." In Rebecca Walker and Philip J. Ivanhoe, eds., *Working Virtue: Virtue Ethics and Contemporary Moral Problems*. Oxford University Press. 297–312.

——. 2009a. "Lessons from the Past: Zhang Xuecheng and the Ethical Dimensions of History." *Dao* 8. 189–203.

——. 2009b. *On Ethics and History: Essays and Letters of Zhang Xuecheng*. Stanford: Stanford University Press.

——. 2009c. *Readings from the Lu-Wang School of Neo-Confucianism*. Indianapolis, IN: Hackett Publishing.

——. 2009d. "Pluralism, Toleration, and Ethical Promiscuity." *The Journal of Religious Ethics* 37:2.

——. 2011. "McDowell, Wang Yangming, and Mengzi's Contributions to Understanding Moral Perception." *Journal of Chinese Philosophy*. 10:3. 273–290.

——. 2012. "Freud and the Dao." In Tao Jiang and Philip J. Ivanhoe, eds., *Freud and China*. London: Routledge and Kegan Paul.

Ivanhoe, Philip J. and Van Norden, Bryan W. eds. 2001/2005. *Readings in Classical Chinese Philosophy* 2. Indianapolis: Hackett Publishing.

Johnson, Robert N. 1997. "Kant's Concept of Virtue." *Jahrbuch für Recht und Ethik* 5. 365–387.

Johnston, Alastair Iain. 1995. *Cultural Realism: Strategic Culture and Grand Strategy in Chinese History*. Princeton: Princeton University Press.

Kant, Immanuel. 1994. "Metaphysical Principles of Virtue." *Ethical Philosophy* 2. James W. Ellington, trans. Indianapolis: Hackett Publishing.

——. *Kritik der reinen Vernunft*. Raymund Schmidt, ed. Hamburg: Felix Meiner, 1976. (A = first edition of 1781, B = second edition of 1787.)

——. "Metaphysik der Sitten." In *Kants Gesammelte Schriften* (academy edition, hereinafter referred to as *KGS*), Vol. 6.

——. *Anthropologie in pragmatischer Hinsicht*. In *KGS*, Vol. 7.

Kennett, Jeanette. 2002. "Empathy, Autism and Moral Agency." *Philosophical Quarterly* 52. 340–357.

Kenny, Anthony. 1988. "Aristotle on Moral Luck." In J. O. Urmson, Jonathan Dancy, J. M. E. Moravcsik, and C. C. W. Taylor, eds. *Human Agency: Language, Duty, and Value.* Stanford: Stanford University Press.

——. 1992. *Aristotle on the Perfect Life*. Oxford: Oxford University Press.

Keys, Mary M. 2008. "Humility and Greatness of Soul." *Perspectives on Political Science* 37:4. 217–223.

Kline III, T. C. 2000. "Moral Agency and Motivation in the Xunzi." In T. C. Kline III and Philip J. Ivanhoe, eds., *Virtue, Nature, and Moral Agency in the Xunzi*. Indianapolis: Hackett. 155–175.

Kong, Anguo 孔安國 and Kong Yingda 孔穎達. 1999. *Commentary on The Book of History* 尚書正義. Beijing 北京: Beijing Daxue Chubanshe 北京大學出版社.

Kotva, Joseph J. 1996. *The Christian Case for Virtue Ethics*. Washington, D. C.: Georgetown University Press.

Kraut, Richard. 1989. *Aristotle on the Human Good*. Princeton, NJ: Princeton University Press.

Kupperman, Joel J. 1991. *Character*. Oxford: New York.

——. 1999a. *Learning from Asian Philosophy*. New York: Oxford University Press.

——. 1999b. "Confucius and the Problem of Naturalness." In *Learning from Asian Philosophy*. New York: Oxford University Press. 26–35.

Lau, D. C. 2003. "On Mencius's Use of Analogy in Argument." In D.C. Lau, trans., *Mencius*. Revised edition. New York: Penguin Books.

Lee, Ming-huei 李明輝. 1990. *Rujia yu Kangde* 儒家與康德 [Confucianism and Kant]. Taipei: Lianjing chuban gongsi.

——. 1990a. "Cong Kangde de xingfu gainian lun Rujia de yi li zhi bian" 從康德的「幸福」概念論儒家的義利之辨 [On the Confucian Distinction between Righteousness and Utility According to Kant's Concept of "Happiness"]. In his *Rujia yu Kangde*. 147–194.

——. 1999. "Lunyu 'Zaiwo wen sannian zhi sang' zhang zhong de lunlixue wenti" 《論語》「宰我問三年之喪」章中的倫理學問題 [The Ethical Problem in *Analects* 17: 21]. In Zhong Caijun 鍾彩鈞 ed., *Chuancheng yu chuangxin: Zhongyang Yanjiuyuan Zhongguo Zhexue Yanjiusuo shi zhounian jinian lunwenji* 傳承與創新：中央研究院中國文哲研究所十周年紀念論文集 [*Transmission and Innovation: A Collection of Papers for the 10th Anniversary of the Institute of Chinese Literature and Philosophy, Academia Sinica*], 521–542. Taipei: Institute of Chinese Literature and Philosophy, Academia Sinica. German version: "Das Motiv der dreijährigen Trauerzeit in *Lunyu* 17.21 as ethisches

Problem." In Karl-Heinz Pohl and Dorothea Wippermann eds., *Brücke zwischen Kulturen. Festschrift für Chiao Wei zum 75. Geburtstag,* 291–308. Münster: Lit Verlag, 2003.

——. 2005a. "Cunxin lunlixue, xingshi lunlixue yu zilu lunlixue" 存心倫理學、形式倫理學與自律倫理學 [Gesinnungsethik, Formal Ethics, and Ethics of Autonomy]. In his *Rujia shiye xia de zhengzhi sixiang* 儒家視野下的政治思想 [Political Thought from a Confucian Perspective], 33–162. Taipei: Taiwan Daxue chubanshe, 2005. The simplified Chinese edition: Beijing: Beijing Daxue chubanshe, 2005. 66–108.

——. 2005b. *Siduan yu qiqing: guanyu daode qinggan de bijiao zhexue tantao* 四端與七情：關於道德情感的比較哲學探討 [The Four Buddings and the Seven Feelings: A Comparative Philosophical Investigation of Moral Feelings]. Taipei: Taiwan Daxue chuban zhongxin. The simplified Chinese edition: 2008. Shanghai: Huadong Shifan Daxue chubanshe.

Lee, Thomas H. C. 1995. "The Idea of Social Justice in Ancient China." In K.D. Irani and Morris Silver, eds., *Social Justice in the Ancient World.* Westport, CT/London: Greenwood Press. 125–148.

Legge, James, trans. 1895. *The Chinese Classics.* London: Oxford University Press.

——, trans. 1993. *Book of Changes.* Hu'nan: Hunan Chubanshe.

Levi, Primo. 1959. *If This Is a Man.* Stuart Woolf, trans. New York: Orion Press.

Li, Chenyang. 2000. "*Jen* and the Feminist Ethics of Care." In Chenyang Li, ed., *The Sage and the Second Sex.* Chicago: Open Court. 23–42.

Li, Ling 李零. 2007. *Reading the Guodian Scripts of Chu Tomb* 郭店楚简校读记, expanded edition. Beijing 北京: Zhongguo Renmin Daxue Chubanshe 中国人民大学出版社.

Li, Xiangfeng 黎翔鳳. 2004. *Commentary on Guanzi* 管子校註. Beijing 北京: Zhonghua Shuju 中華書局.

Lin, Yizheng 林義正. 2003. *The Special Features for Ethical Thoughts within the Gongyang Commentary on the Spring and Autumn Annals* 春秋公羊傳倫理思維與特征. Taibei 臺北: Taiwan Daxue Chuban Zhongxin 臺灣大學出版中心.

Liu, Liangjian 劉梁劍. 2007. *Heaven, Human and the Fluctuating Boundary: A Metaphysical Exposition of Wang Chuanshan* 天‧人‧際：對王船山的形而上學闡明. Shanghai 上海: Shanghai Renmin Chubanshe 上海人民出版社.

Liu, Xiusheng. 2002. "Mencius, Hume, and Sensibility Theory." *Philosophy East and West* 52:1. 75–97.

Liu, Xiusheng. 2003. *Mencius, Hume, and the Foundations of Ethics: Humanity in Ethics.* Burlington, VT: Ashgate.

Liu, Yuli. 2004. *The Unity of Rule and Virtue: A Critique of a Supposed Parallel between Confucian Ethics and Virtue Ethics.* Singapore: Eastern Universities Press.

Lo, Ping-cheung. 2012a. "The *Art of War* Corpus and Chinese Just War Ethics Past and Present." *Journal of Religious Ethics* 40:3. 404–446.

——. 2012b. "Warfare Ethics in Sunzi's *Art of War*? – Historical Controversies and Contemporary Perspectives." *Journal of Military Ethics* 11:3. 114–135.

Louden, Robert B. 1986. "Kant's Virtue Ethics." *Philosophy* 61. 473–489.

——. 1990. "Virtue Ethics and Anti-Theory." *Philosophia* 20:1–2. 93–114.

——. 1997 (1984). "On Some Vices of Virtue Ethics." In Roger Crisp and Michael Slote, eds., *Virtue Ethics.* New York and Oxford: Oxford University Press.

MacIntyre, Alasdair. 1981. *After Virtue.* Notre Dame, IN: University of Notre Dame Press.

——. 1984. *After Virtue.* 2nd Ed. Notre Dame, IN: University of Notre Dame Press.

——. 1988. *Whose Justice? Which Rationality?* Notre Dame, IN: University of Notre Dame Press.

——. 1991. "Incommensurability, Truth, and the Conversation between Confucians and

Aristotelians about the Virtues." In Eliot Deutsch, ed., *Culture and Modernity*. Honolulu: University of Hawaii Press.

———. 2004. "Once More on Confucian and Aristotelian Conceptions of the Virtues." In Robin R. Wang, ed., *Chinese Ethics in an Age of Globalization*. Albany: State University of New York Press. 151–162.

Markus, Hazel Rose and Kitayama, Shinobu. 1991. "Culture and the Self: Implications for Cognition, Emotion, and Motivation." *Psychological Review* 98:2.

McDowell, John. 1979. "Virtue and Reason." *The Monist* 62. 331–50.

———. 1998a. "Comments on 'Some Rational Aspects of Incontinence' [by T.H. Irwin]." *Southern Journal of Philosophy* 27.89–102.

———. 1998b. *Mind, Value, and Reality*. Cambridge, MA: Harvard University Press.

Mencius. 1970. *Mencius*. D. C. Lau, trans. London: Penguin.

Mengzi. 2008. *Mengzi: With Selections from Traditional Commentaries*. Bryan Van Norden, trans. Indianapolis: Hackett.

Merritt, Maria. 2000. "Virtue Ethics and Situationist Personality Psychology." *Ethical Theory and Moral Practices* 3:4.

Midgley, Mary. 1995. *Beast and Man*. London: Routledge.

Miller, Christian. 2009. "Social Psychology, Mood, and Helping: Mixed Results for Virtue Ethics." *The Journal of Ethics. Special Issue on Situationism* 13. 145–173.

Moody, Jr., Peter R. 1996. "Asian Values." *Journal of International Affairs* 50:1. 166–192.

Mou, Bo. 2004. "A Rexamination of the Structure and Content of Confucius' Version of the Golden Rule." *Philosophy East and West* 54:2. 218–248.

Mou, Zongsan 牟宗三. 1968/1969. *Xinti yu xingti* 心體與性體 [The Heart-Mind as Reality and Human Nature as Reality]. Vol 3. Taipei: Zhengzhong shuju.

Murdoch, Iris. 1998. *Existentialists and Mystics. Writings on Philosophy and Literature*. Peter Conradi, ed. London: Penguin.

Neufeld, Michael J. 2007. *Von Braun: Dreamer of Space, Engineer of War*. New York: Alfred A. Knopf.

Nivison, David S. 1967. "The Problem of 'Knowledge' and 'Action' in Chinese Thought since Wang Yangming." In Arthur F. Wright, ed., *Studies in Chinese Thought*. Chicago: University of Chicago Press. 112–145.

———. 1980. "Mencius and Motivation." *Journal of the American Academy of Religion* 47. 417–432.

———. 1996. *The Ways of Confucianism. Investigations in Chinese Philosophy*. Bryan W. Van Norden, ed. Chicago and La Salle, IL: Open Court.

———. 2002. "Mengzi: Just Not Doing It." In Liu Xiusheng and P.J. Ivanhoe, eds., *Essays on the Moral Philosophy of Mengzi*. Indianapolis, IN: Hackett.

Noddings, Nel. 2003 (1986). *Caring: A Feminine Approach to Ethics and Moral Education*. Berkeley: University of California Press.

Norton, David L. 1988. "Moral Minimalism and the Development of Moral Character." *Ethical Theory: Character and Virtue. Midwest Studies in Philosophy* 13. Peter A. French, et al., eds. Notre Dame: University of Notre Dame Press. 180–195.

Nussbaum, Martha. 1986. *The Fragility of Goodness*. Cambridge: Cambridge University Press.

———. 2003. "Golden Rule Arguments: A Missing Thought?" In *The Moral Circle and the Self: Chinese and Western Approaches*. Kim-chong Chong, Sor-hoon Tan and C.L. Ten, eds. Chicago: Open Court.

O'Neill, Onora S. 1983. "Kant after Virtue." *Inquiry* 26. 387–405.

———. 1996. "Kant's Virtues." In Roger Crisp ed., *How Should One Live? Essays on the Virtues*. Oxford: Oxford University Press. 77–97.

O'Neill, Onora S. and Williams, Bernard, eds. Xu Xiangdong 徐向東, trans. 2008. *Virtue*

Ethics and Moral Demands 美德倫理與道德要求. Nanjing 南京: Jiangsu Renmin Chu-banshe 江蘇人民出版社.

Olberding, Amy. 2007. "The Educative Function of Personal Style in the *Analects.*" *Philosophy East & West* 57:3. 357–374.

——. 2009. "'Ascending the Hall': Style and Moral Improvement in the *Analects.*" *Philosophy East & West* 59:4. 503–522.

Pan, Xiaohui 潘小慧. 1992. "Dexing yu yuanze: Kong, Meng, Xun Rujia daode zhexue jixing zhi yanjiu" 德行與原則：孔、孟、荀儒家道德哲學基型之研究 [Virtue and Principle: A Study of the Prototype of Confucian Moral Philosophy Represented by Confucius, Mencius, and Xunzi]. *Wenhua de chuancheng yu fanzhan xueshu yantaohui lunwen ji* 文化的傳承與發展學術研討會論文集 [Proceedings of the Academic Conference on Cultural Transition and Development], 75–87. Taipei: Furen Daxue chubanshe. 1992. Also in *Zhexue yu wenhua* [Philosophy and Culture] 19:12 (1992): 1087–1096.

——. 2006. "Dexing lunlixue zhong de renwen zhuyi jingshen: Cong Virtue Ethics de shidang yiming tanqi" 德行倫理學中的人文主義精神－從 Virtue Ethics 的適當譯名談起 [The Humanistic Spirit in Virtue Ethics: A Discussion Starting with the Proper Chinese Translation of the Term "Virtue Ethics"]. *Zhexue yu wenhua* [Philosophy and Culture] 31:1. 17–29.

Pippin, Robert. 2008. *Hegel's Practical Philosophy: Rational Agency as Ethical Life.* Cambridge: Cambridge University Press.

Plato. 1997. *Plato: Complete Works.* John M. Cooper, ed. Indianapolis, IN: Hackett.

Preston, S. D. and de Waal, F.B.M. 2002. "Empathy: Its Ultimate and Proximate Bases." *Brain and Behavioral Sciences* 25. 1–72.

Prichard, H. A. 1912. "Does Moral Philosophy Rest on A Mistake?" *Mind* 21. 21–37.

Prinz, Jesse. 2011. "Against Empathy." *The Southern Journal of Philosophy, Spindel Supplement* 49. 214–233.

Pronin, Emily, Lin, Daniel Y., and Ross, Lee. 2002. "The Bias Blind Spot: Perceptions of Bias in Self Versus Others." *Personality and Social Psychology Bulletin* 28:3.

Qian, Mu 錢穆. 1994. *Zhuzi xin xue'an* 朱子新學案. *New Studies of Master Zhu* Taipei: Lianjing chubanshe.

Qiu, Fuxing 丘復興, ed. 2004. *A Comprehensive Study of Sunzi's Military Thought* 孫子兵學大典, Vol. 5, *Essential Thoughts* 思想精義. Beijing: Peking University Press.

Quinn, Warren. 1994. *Morality and Action.* Cambridge: Cambridge University Press.

Raphals, Lisa. 1992. *Knowing Words: Wisdom and Cunning in the Classical Traditions of China and Greece.* Ithaca: Cornell University Press.

——. 2003. "Fate, Fortune, Chance and Luck in Chinese and Greek: A Comparative Semantic History." *Philosophy East & West* 53:4. 537–574.

Rappe, Guido. 2010. "From Virtue to Virtues: The Development of Virtue Ethics in Ancient Greece and China." In Lee Ming-huei 李明輝 and Chiu Hwang-hai 邱黃海 eds., *Lijie, quanshi yu Rujia chuantong: bijiao guandian* 理解、詮釋與儒家傳統：比較觀點 [Understanding, Interpretation, and the Confucian Tradition: A Comparative Perspective], Taipei: Institute of Chinese Literature and Philosophy, Academia Sinica. 299–348.

Reding, J. 1986. "Analogical Reasoning in Early Chinese Philosophy." *Asiatische Studien (Etudes Asiatiques).* 40–56.

Reeve, C. D. C. 1989. *Socrates in the Apology.* Indianapolis, IN: Hackett.

Richards, Norvin. 1988. "Is Humility a Virtue?" *American Philosophical Quarterly* 25:3. 253–259.

Richardson, Henry S. 1992. "Degrees of Finality and the Highest Good in Aristotle." In Philippe Rushton and Richard M. Sorretino, eds., *Journal of the History of Philosophy* 30. 327–352.

Ridley, Mark and Dawkins, Richard. 1981. "Natural Selection and Altruism." In *Altruism and Helping Behavior: Social, Personality, and Developmental Perspectives*. Hillsdale, NJ: Lawrence Erlbaum Associates.

Riedel, Manfred, ed. 1972/1974. *Rehabilitierung der praktischen Philosophie 2*. Freiburg im Breslau: Rombach.

———. 1988. *Für eine zweite Philosophie*. Vorträge und Abhandlungen. Frankfurt/M.: Suhrkamp.

Ritter, Joachim. 1960. "Zur Grundlegung der praktischen Vernunft bei Aristoteles" [On the Foundation of Practical Philosophy in Aristotle]. *Archiv für Rechts- und Sozialphikosophie* 46. 179–19.

Roberts, Robert C. 1991. "Virtues and Rules". *Philosophy and Phenomenological Research* 51:2. 325–343.

Rogers, Carl. 1957. "The Necessary and Sufficient Conditions of Therapeutic Personality Change." *Journal of Consulting Psychology* 21:2. 95–103.

Russell, Daniel, ed. 2013. *Cambridge Companion to Virtue Ethics*. Cambridge: Cambridge University Press.

Sarkissian, Hagop. 2010. "Confucius and the Effortless Life of Virtue." *History of Philosophy Quarterly* 27:1. 1–16.

Sawyer, Raph D., trans. 1993. *The Seven Military Classics of Ancient China*. Translated with commentary by Ralph D. Sawyer, with Mei-chun Sawyer. New York: Basic Books.

Schneewind, J. B. 1990. "The Misfortunes of Virtue." *Ethics* 101. 42–63.

Schwartz, B. 1985. *The World of Thought in Ancient China*. Cambridge, MA: The Belknap Press.

Schwitzgebel, Eric. 2007. "Human Nature and Moral Education in Mencius, Xunzi, Hobbes, and Rousseau." *History of Philosophy Quarterly* 24:2. 147–168.

Shen, Qingsong (Vincent) 沈清松. 1992. "Yi li zai bian: Rujia jiazhi cengji lun de xiandai quanshi" 義利再辨：儒家價值層級論的現代詮釋 [Another Discussion on the Distinction between Righteousness and Utility: A Modern Interpretation of the Confucian Theory of Value Hierarchy]. In his *Chuantong de zaisheng* 傳統的再生 [The Rebirth of Tradition], 130–150. Taipei: Yeqiang chubanshe.

———. 1995. "Dexing lunlixue yu Rujia lunli sixiang de xiandai yiyi" 德行倫理學與儒家倫理思想的現代意義 [The Modern Significance of Virtue Ethics and Confucian Ethical Thought]. In *Zhexue yu lunli: Furen Daxue di san jie liang'an xueshu yantaohui lunwen ji* 哲學與倫理：輔仁大學第三屆兩岸學術研討會論文集 [Philosophy and Ethics: Proceedings of the Third Cross-Strait Academic Conference at Fu Jen Catholic University]. Taipei: Furen Daxue chubanshe. 265–297. Also in *Zhexue yu wenhua* [Philosophy and Culture] 22:11 (1995): 975–992.

———. 1998. "You mingxue zouxiang Ruxue zhi lu: Chen Daqi dui Taiwan Ruxue de gongxian" 由名學走向儒學之路：陳大齊對臺灣儒學的貢獻 [The Road from Logic to Confucianism: Chen Daqi's Contribution to Confucianism in Taiwan]. *Hanxue yanjiu* 漢學研究 [Chinese Studies] 16:2. 1–27.

Sherman, Nancy. 1997. "Kantian Virtue: Priggish or Passional?" In Andrews Reath et al., eds., *Reclaiming the History of Ethics: Essays for John Rawls*. Cambridge: Cambridge University Press. 270–296.

———. 1997a. *Making a Necessity of Virtue: Aristotle and Kant on Virtue*. Cambridge: Cambridge University Press.

Shun, Kwong-loi. 1989. "Moral Reasons in Confucian Ethics." *Journal of Chinese Philosophy* 16. 317–343.

———. 2005. "Zhu Xi on *Gong* 公 (Impartial) and *Si* 私 (Partial)." *Dao: A Journal of Comparative Philosophy* 5:1. 1–9.

———. 2009. "Studying Confucian and Comparative Ethics: Methodological Reflections." *Journal of Chinese Philosophy* 36:3. 455–478.

———. 2010a. "On Anger – An Experimental Essay in Confucian Moral Psychology." In David Jones and He Jinli, eds., *Zhu Xi Now: Contemporary Encounters with the Great Ultimate*. New York: SUNY Press.

———. 2010b. "Zhu Xi's Moral Psychology." In John Makeham, ed., *Dao Companion to Neo-Confucian Philosophy*. Dordrecht, Heidelberg, London, New York: Springer. 177–195.

Silber, John R. 1967. "The Copernican Revolution in Ethics: The Good Reexamined." In Robert Paul Wolff, ed., *Kant: A Collection of Critical Essays*. Notre Dame, IN: University of Notre Dame Press. 266–290.

Silk, J.B., Samuels, A. and Rodman, P. 1981. "The Influences of Kinship, Rank, and Sex on Affiliation and Aggression between Adult Female and Immature Bonnet Macaques." *Behavior* 78. 111–177.

Sim, May. 2007. *Remastering Morals with Aristotle and Confucius*. Cambridge: Cambridge University Press.

Singer, Peter. 1972. "Famine, Affluence, and Morality." *Philosophy and Public Affairs* 1:3. 229–243.

———. 2010. "Ethics". *Encyclopædia Britannica Online*. Web. 6 Apr. 2010.http://0-search. eb.com.libecnu.lib.ecnu.edu.cn/eb/article-252575

Slingerland, Edward. 1996. "The Conception of Ming in Early Confucian Thought." *Philosophy East & West* 46:4. 567–581.

———. 2003. *Effortless Action: Wu-wei as Conceptual Metaphor and Spiritual Ideal in Early China*. Oxford: Oxford University Press.

Slote, Michael. 1992. *From Morality to Virtue*. Oxford: Oxford University Press.

———. 2001. *Morals from Motives*. Oxford: Oxford University Press.

———. 2007. The *Ethics of Care and Empathy*. New York: Routledge.

———. 2009. "Comments on Bryan Van Norden's *Virtue Ethics and Consequentialism in Early Chinese Philosophy*." *Dao: A Journal of Comparative Philosophy* 8:3. 289–295.

———. 2010a. *Moral Sentimentalism*. New York: Oxford University Press.

———. 2010b. "The Mandate of Empathy." *Dao: A Journal of Comparative Philosophy* 9. 303–307.

———. 2011. *The Impossibility of Perfection*. New York: Oxford University Press.

Smith, Adam. 2002. *The Theory of Moral Sentiments*. Cambridge: Cambridge University Press.

Solomon, David. 2004. "Ethics: Normative Ethical Theories." In Stephen G. Post, ed. *Encyclopedia of Bioethics* 3. New York: Macmillan Reference.

SSJZS (*Shisan Jing Zhushu*). 1997. *Interpretations and Annotations of the Thirteen Classics* 十三經注疏. Shanghai 上海: Shanghai Guji Chubanshe 上海古籍出版社.

Stalnaker, Aaron. 2006. *Overcoming Our Evil: Human Nature and Spiritual Exercises in Xunzi and Augustine*. Washington, D.C.: Georgetown University Press.

Stich, Stephen and Nichols, Shaun. 2003. *Mindreading: An Integrated Account of Pretence, Self-Awareness and Understanding Other Minds*. New York: Oxford.

Stohr, Karen E. 2003. "Moral Cacophony: When Continence is a Virtue." *The Journal of Ethics* 7. 339–363.

Stokes, M. C. 1986. *Plato's Socrates' Conversations*. Baltimore: Johns Hopkins University Press.

Sun Tzu. 1963. *The Art of War*. Trans. with an intro., Samuel B. Griffith. Oxford: Oxford University Press.

———.1993. *Sun-tzu: the Art of War*. Trans. with an intro. and comm., Roger Ames. New York: Ballantine Books.

———.1994. *The Art of War*. Trans. with intros. and comm., Ralph D. Sawyer, with the collaboration of Mei-chun Lee Sawyer. Boulder, CO: Westview Press.

Swanton, Christine. 2003. *Virtue Ethics: A Pluralistic View*. Oxford University Press.

Tan, Sor-hoon. 2008. Review, *A Cloud across the Pacific: Essays on the Clash between Chinese and Western Political Theories Today*, by Thomas A. Metzger. *Philosophy East & West* 58:3. 420–424.

Taylor, Charles. 1992. *The Ethics of Authenticity*. Cambridge, MA: Harvard University Press.

Tessman, Lisa. 2005. *Burdened Virtues: Virtue Ethics for Liberatory Struggles*. New York: Oxford.

Tien, David W. 2004. "Warranted Neo-Confucian Belief: Knowledge and the Affections in the Religious Epistemologies of Wang Yangming (1472–1529) and Alvin Plantinga." *International Journal for Philosophy of Religion* 55:1. 31–55.

———. 2010. "Metaphysics and the Basis of Morality in the Philosophy of Wang Yangming." In John Makeham, ed., *Neo-Confucian Philosophy*. New York: Springer. 295–314.

———. 2012. "Oneness and Self-Centeredness in the Moral Psychology of Wang Yangming." *Journal of Religious Ethics* 40:1.

Tillman, Hoyt C. 1994. "Ch'en Liang on Public Interest and the Law." *Monographs of the Society for Asian and Comparative Philosophy* 12. Honolulu: University of Hawaii Press.

Tiwald, Justin. 2008. "A Right of Rebellion in the *Mengzi*?," *Dao: A Journal of Comparative Philosophy* 7. 269–282.

———. 2010. "Dai Zhen on Sympathetic Concern." *Journal of Chinese Philosophy* 37:1. 76–89.

———. 2011. "Dai Zhen's Defense of Self-Interest." *Journal of Chinese Philosophy* 38 (Supplement). 29–45.

Tu, Wei-ming. 1976. *Neo-Confucian Thought in Action: Wang Yang-ming's Youth (1472–1509)*. Berkeley, CA: University of California Press.

Unger, Peter. 1996. *Living High and Letting Die*. New York: Oxford.

US Naval Academy. 2010. *Reef Points 2010–11: The Annual Handbook of the Brigade of Midshipmen*. Annapolis: Naval Institute Press.

Van Norden, Bryan W. 1991. "Kwong-loi Shun on Moral Reason in Mencius." *Journal of Chinese Philosophy* 18. 353–370.

———. 2000. "Mengzi and Xunzi: Two Views of Human Agency." In T. C. Kline III and Philip J. Ivanhoe, eds., *Virtue, Nature, and Moral Agency in the Xunzi*. Indianapolis: Hackett. 103–134.

———. 2002. "Unweaving the 'One Thread' of *Analects* 4:15." In *Confucius and the Analects: New Essays*. Bryan Van Norden, ed. New York: Oxford. 216–236.

———. 2007. *Virtue Ethics and Consequentialism in Early Chinese Philosophy*. New York: Cambridge University Press.

———. 2009. "Response to Angle and Slote." *Dao: A Journal of Comparative Philosophy* 8:3. 305–9.

———. Forthcoming. "Anthropocentric Realism about Values." In Chenyang Li and Peimin Ni, eds., *Moral Cultivation and Confucian Character: Engaging Joel J. Kupperman* Albany: State University of New York Press.

Vlastos, G. 1983. "The Socratic Elenchus." *Oxford Studies in Ancient Philosophy* 1.27–58.

Walker, A. D. M. 1993. "The Incompatibility of the Virtues." *Ratio* 6. 44–60

Walker, Matthew. 2011. "Aristotle on Activity 'According to the Best and Most Final' Virtue." *Apeiron* 44. 91–109.

Walker, Rebecca and Philip J. Ivanhoe, eds. 2007. *Working Virtue: Virtue Ethics and Contemporary Moral Problems*. Oxford: Clarendon Press.

Wallace, James D. 1978. *Virtues and Vices*. Ithaca, NY: Cornell University Press.

Walsh, Sean. 2012. "Kant's Theory of Right as Aristotelian Phronesis." *International Philosophical Quarterly* 52:2. 227–46

Wan, Junren. 2004. "Contrasting Confucian Virtue Ethics and MacIntyre's Aristotelian Virtue Theory." In Robin R. Wang, ed., *Chinese Ethics in an Age of Globalization*. Albany: State University of New York Press. 123–149.

Wang, Chuanshan 王船山. 1988a. *Elaboration on the Meanings of ShangshuShangshu* 尚書 引義, *Collected Books of Chuanshan* 船山全書. Book 2. Changsha 長沙: Yuelu Shushe 嶽麓書社.

——. 1988b. *Discussions after Reading the Great Collection of Commentaries on the Four Books* 讀四書大全說. *Collected Books of Chuanshan* 船山全書. Book 6. Changsha 長沙: Yuelu Shushe 嶽麓書社.

Wang, Edward Q. 2002. "Time, History, and Dao: Zhang Xuecheng and Martin Heidegger." *Dao* 1:2. 251–276.

Wang, Yangming. 1963. *Instructions for Practical Living and Other Neo-Confucian Writings.* Wing-tsit Chan, trans. New York: Columbia University Press.

——. 王陽明. 1983. 傳習錄詳註集評 [*Record of Practice with Detailed Annotations and Collected Commentary*]. Taipei: Xuesheng Shuju.

Watson, Gary. 1997. "On the Primacy of Character." In Daniel Statman, ed. *Contemporary Virtue Ethics and Aristotle*. Washinton, D.C.: Georgetown University Press, 56–81.

White, Stephen A. 1991. "Is Aristotelian Happiness a Good Life or the Best Life?" In Julia Annas, ed., *Oxford Studies in Ancient Philosophy* 8. Oxford: Oxford University Press. 97–131.

Wiggins, David. 1996. "Natural and Artificial Virtues: A Vindication of Hume's Scheme." In *How Should One Live? Essays on the Virtues.* Oxford: Oxford University Press. 131–140.

——. 1998. "Deliberation and Practical Reason." In *Needs, Values, Truth*. Oxford: Clarendon Press.

Williams, Bernard. 1981. "Internal and External Reasons." In *Moral Luck*. Cambridge: Cambridge University Press.

——. 1985. *Ethics and Limits of Philosophy*. Cambridge, MA: Harvard University Press.

Wispé, Laura. 1991. *The Psychology of Sympathy*. New York: Plenum Press.

Wong, David B. 2000. "Xunzi on Moral Motivation." In T. C. Kline III and Philip J. Ivanhoe, eds., *Virtue, Nature, and Moral Agency in the Xunzi*. Indianapolis: Hackett. 135–154.

——. 2002. "Reasons and Analogical Reasoning in Mengzi." In Xiusheng Liu and Philip J. Ivanhoe eds., *Essays on the Moral Philosophy of Mengzi*. Indianapolis: Hackett Publishing. 187–220.

——. 2006. *Natural Moralities: A Defense of Pluralistic Relativism.* New York: Oxford.

Wong, Wai-ying. 2001. "Confucian Ethics and Virtue Ethics." *The Journal of Chinese Philosophy* 28:3. 285–300.

——. 2005. *Confucian Ethics: Substance and Function* (in Chinese). Shanghai: Shanghai Joint Publishing Co.

——. 2011. "The Moral and Non-Moral Virtues in Confucian Ethics." *Asian Philosophy* 21:1. 71–82.

——. 2012. "Ren, Empathy and the Agent-Related Approach in Confucian Ethics." *Asian Philosophy* 22:2. 133–141.

Woodruff, Paul. 2001. *Reverence: Renewing a Forgotten Virtue*. Oxford: Oxford University Press.

Wu, Xiaofan 吳曉番. 2010."On the Philosophy of Gong Zizhen: A New Perspective" 龔自珍 哲學新論, Ph.D. Dissertation. Shanghai 上海: Huadong Shifan Daxu 華東師範大學.

Xiao, Yang. 1997. "Trying to Do Justice to the Concept of Justice in Confucian Ethics." *Journal of Chinese Philosophy* 24.521–551.

——. 2009. "Agency and Practical Reasoning and in the *Analects* and the *Mencius*." *Journal of Chinese Philosophy*. 36:4. 629–641.

——. 2011. "Holding an Aristotelian Mirror for Confucian Ethics?" *Dao: A Journal of Comparative Philosophy*. 10:3. 359–375.

Xunzi 荀子. 1979. (Li Tisheng 李滌生, ed., Tr.) 荀子集釋 [Xunzi, with Collected Interpretations]. Taipei: Xuesheng Shuju.

Xunzi. 1988–94. *Xunzi: A Translation and Study of The Complete Works*. Vol. 2. John Knoblock, trans. Stanford: Stanford University Press.

Yang, Bingan 楊丙安, ed.1999. *A Critical Edition of the Eleven Schools of Glosses on Sunzi* 十一家注孫子校理. Beijing 北京: Zhonghua Publication House 中華書局.

Yang, Guorong 楊國榮. 2009a. *Ethics and Existence* 倫理與存在. Shanghai 上海: Huadong Shifan Daxu Chubanshe 華東師範大學出版社.

——. 2009b. *Philosophy of Mencius* 孟子的哲學思想. Shanghai 上海: Huadong Shifan Daxu Chubanshe 華東師範大學出版社.

Yearley, Lee H. 1990. *Mencius and Aquinas: Theories of Virtue and Conceptions of Courage*. Albany: State University of New York Press.

Yu, Jiyuan. 2005. "Human Nature and Virtue in Mencius and Xunzi: An Aristotelian Interpretation." *Dao* 5.11–30.

——. 2006. "*Yi*: Practical Wisdom in Confucius' *Analects*." *Journal of Chinese Philosophy* 33:3. 335–348.

——. 2007. *The Ethics of Confucius and Aristotle: Mirrors of Virtue*. New York and London: Routledge.

Yu, Jiyuan 余紀元. 2008. "Xin Ruxue de 'Xuanyan' yu dexing lunlixue de fuxing" 新儒學的「宣言」與德性倫理學的復興 [The "Manifesto" of New Confucianism and the Revival of Virtue Ethics]. In Zhongshan Daxue Xixue Dongjian Wenxue Guan ed., *Xixue dongjian yanjiu* 西學東漸研究 [Studies of the Eastern Advance of the Western Learning] 1. Beijing: Shangwu yinshuguan. 216–233.

Yu, Yingshi 余英時. 2003. *Zhu Xi de lishi shijie* 朱熹的歷史世界. *The Historical Word of Zhu Xi*. Taipei: Yunchen.

Zheng, Xuan 鄭玄 and Kong Yingda 孔穎達. 1999. *Commentary on The Book of Rites* 禮記正義. Beijing 北京: Beijing Daxue Chubanshe 北京大學出版社.

Zhu, Rui. 2006. "*Kairos*: Between Cosmic Order and Human Agency. A Comparative Study of Aurelius and Confucius." *Journal of Religious Ethics* 34:1. 115–138.

Zhu, Xi 朱熹. 1987. *Sishu zhangju jizhu* 四书章句集注 [Collected Commentaries on the Four Books]. Shanghai: Shanghai Shudian.

——. 1991. *Further Reflections on Things at Hand: A Reader*. Allen Wittenborn, trans. Albany, NY: SUNY Press.

——. 1999. *Zhuzi yulei* 朱子語類. Beijing: Zhonghua shuju.

——. 2000. *Zhu Zi wenji* 朱子文集. Chen Junmin 陳俊民, ed. Taipei: Defuwen Jijinhui 德富文基金會.

——. 2001. *Sishu zhangju jizhu* 四書章句集注 [Collected Commentaries on the Four Books]. Beijing: Zhonghua shuju.

Zhu, Yong 朱墉, ed. 1992. *Collected Commentaries on the Seven Books of Military Classics* 武經七書匯解. Volume 42 and 43 of Collected Works of Chinese Military Treatises 中國兵書集成. Beijing 北京and Shenyang 沈陽: Liberation Army Press 解放軍出版社 and Liaoshen Book Press 遼沈書社.

Zhuangzi. 2005. "Zhuangzi." In Philip J. Ivanhoe and Bryan Van Norden, eds., *Readings in Classical Chinese Philosophy*. Paul Kjellberg, trans. 206–53.

Zhuangzi: The Inner Chapters. 2001 [1981]. A. C. Graham, trans. Indianapolis: Hackett Publishing.

Index

accomplishment 89–90
action (*wei* 為) 51, 52, 115–16, 230n26;
and agent 51, 52; and Aristotle 62, 112;
and benevolence 44; and character 72,
115–16, 129, 150, 213; direction and
empathy 203, 207, 212–14, 215, 217;
evaluation of 49; and inability (*bu
neng* 不能) 136; and justice 199; and
Kant 52, 68, 112; and knowledge 39,
70–2, 112; and rules 127; and
understanding 224n5; and
utilitarianism 68; and virtue 229n3;
and virtue ethics 141, 147–50
Adams, Robert Merrihew 182, 238n2
age 119, 230n31
agriculture: metaphors of (*see under*
metaphors); rituals 32
ai ren li wu 愛人利物 (caring for people
and fostering the well-being of sentient
beings) 195
altruism 45
Ames, Roger T. 55, 144, 150, 174, 177, 179,
203, 230n13, 232n4
analogy 137, 156–7, 232n9 (ch. 12),
242n9
"and," relationship of (*ji* 際) 73
Angle, Stephen 56, 111, 193, 237n10
animals 42, 45, 75, 136, 139, 156, 168, 185,
213–15, 222n21, 236n3
Anscombe, G. E. M. 1, 47, 67, 71, 193
anthropology, philosophical 35, 53, 75
appearance 183–7; *see also* external and
internal
Appiah, Kwame Anthony 236n3
appropriateness (*yi* 義) 78, 84, 97, 105,
129, 196–7, 213; *see also* judgment;
righteousness
approval (*ke* 可) 188–9
Aquinas, Thomas 57; and flourishing
(*beatudo*) 75; and goods 58–60; and
humility 173; and relationships 63–4;

and virtue ethics 233n22; and Wang
Yangming 35; *see also* scholasticism
Aristotle 15–27; and action 62, 112; and
age 119; and artistic production 62–3;
and character 68, 112–13, 115, 131–2;
and community 119; and conflict of
values 87; and Confucianism 56–65,
114–24, 235n1; and flourishing
(*eudaimonia*) 29, 100, 103–13; and
good life 128, 131–3; and habit 20,
132–3; and happiness 86; and human
nature 28, 29, 69–70; and justice 196;
and Kant 53–4; and luck 114–24;
mean, doctrine of 83, 244n10;
and Mengzi 28, 213, 235n17; and
particularism 162; and politics 115–16,
123; and pleasure 121; and reason 29,
69–70; and relationships 63–4, 119;
and Singer 69–70; and skill 61, 67;
and virtue ethics 28–30, 51, 193; and
virtues 20, 131–3, 213; and Wang
Yangming 28, 223n33; and wisdom 21;
and Zhu Xi 240n6; *see also titles of
individual works*
army, righteous (*yi bing* 義兵; *yi jun* 義
軍) 149–51, 233n23
arts 60–1, 62–3, 78, 92
"Asian values" 175
attention 211, 214–16
Augustine 21, 173, 239n29
authenticity 66; *see also* freedom
autism 203
autonomy 49, 52

beginnings, four 168–9
ben ju 本具 (originally contain) 240n11
ben xin 本心; *see* heartmind: original
ben xing 本性; *see* nature: original
benevolence (*ren* 仁): and action 44;
definition of 195, 198, 244n13; and
empathy 76, 198, 214, 243n15; and

41380563R10161

Made in the USA
Middletown, DE
05 April 2019